Encyclopedia
of
White-Collar Crime

Encyclopedia

of

White-Collar

Crime

Edited by

JURG GERBER

and

ERIC L. JENSEN

with the collaboration of
Jiletta L. Kubena

GREENWOOD PRESS
Westport, Connecticut • London

Library of Congress Cataloging-in-Publication Data

Encyclopedia of white-collar crime / edited by Jurg Gerber and Eric L. Jensen.
    p. cm.
 Includes bibliographical references and index.
 ISBN 0–313–33524–9 (alk. paper)
 1. White collar crimes—Encyclopedias. 2. Corporations—Corrupt practices—Encyclopedias.
 3. Commercial crimes—Encyclopedias. I. Gerber, Jurg. II. Jensen, Eric L., 1946–
HV6768.E65   2007
364.16'8097303—dc22   2006029479

British Library Cataloguing in Publication Data is available.

Library of Congress Catalog Card Number: 2006029479
ISBN: 0–313–33524–9

First published in 2007

Greenwood Press, 88 Post Road West, Westport, CT 06881
An imprint of Greenwood Publishing Group, Inc.
www.greenwood.com

Printed in the United States of America

The paper used in this book complies with the
Permanent Paper Standard issued by the National
Information Standards Organization (Z39.48–1984).

10 9 8 7 6 5 4 3 2 1

To our families:
Wanda, Nicole, and Eric
Jan, Ian, and Noel

Contents

Acknowledgments

As is always the case, there are numerous individuals who have contributed to the successful completion of this project. At Greenwood, special thanks go to Steven Vetrano for seeing the merits of the encyclopedia and to Vince Burns for following through with it. Without the able assistance of Jiletta Kubena at Sam Houston State University, this project would never have been completed. Finally, at the University of Idaho, Gary Reed and Ian Jensen contributed their efforts, care and devotion to the project. Many thanks to all of you.

Introduction

Writing about 20 years ago, John Braithwaite (1985) reviewed the state of the white collar crime literature. Undoubtedly oversimplifying the issues somewhat, he began his essay with three sections that emphasized the importance of the inventor of the term white collar crime, Edwin Sutherland: "White collar crime research before Sutherland," "Sutherland," and "the Legacy of Sutherland." Whereas other social scientists (e.g., Ross 1907) and the muckrakers wrote about issues similar to Sutherland's focus of concern, it was not until Sutherland's Presidential Address to American Sociological Society in 1939, and the subsequent publication of his major book (Sutherland 1940, 1949) that the field of study had become "officially" defined.

Unfortunately, after Sutherland's death in 1950 there "followed a twenty year hiatus during which a few diehards, notably Gilbert Geis and Herbert Edelhertz, kept the flickering flame of white collar crime research alight" (Braithwaite, 1985: 4). However, by the 1970s, the field came alive again. Watergate took place and so did a series of bribery scandals. In the process, a social movement against white collar crime came into existence (Katz 1980). Subsequently, research was conducted by numerous scholars who sought to understand causes of white collar crime, its extent, and its control. In what is probably still the best review of the research of that period, Braithwaite (1985) analyzed the causal analyses, the "modus operandi studies," and the "control agency studies" of the period, but concluded that much of the social scientific research was "unimpressive."

While the last two decades of the twentieth century produced numerous studies on white collar crime, the publication of text books devoted to this topic, conferences on the topic, and the creation of the National White Collar Crime Center in 1982, the political climate during much of the period was rather conservative. The semi-official mantra of these conservative times, "Greed is good," provided the fertile foundation for the corporate scandals from the eighties through the first decade and one half of the twenty first century; scandals that included the savings and loan industry, Enron, and Halliburton, to name only a few.

DEFINITIONAL ISSUES

There are almost as many definitions of the term white collar crime, as there are researchers that have addressed the topic. Unfortunately, the concept white collar crime is highly ambiguous and confusing. In the words of Shapiro (1980), white collar crime is a problematic term because:

> It is unclear whether the term characterizes acts or actors; types of offenses or types of offenders; whether it refers to the social location of deviant behavior, the social role or social status of the actor, the modus operandi of the behavior, or the social relationship of victim and offender.

There are perhaps two main problems with the concept. In the minds of many criminologists, white collar crime is a residual category. That is, much of what does not fit into "traditional criminology" is subsumed under this category, making the concept at times unnecessarily broad.

Second, the classic definition of white collar crime provided by Sutherland (1940:7) did not clarify matters much: "A crime committed by a person of respectability and high social status in the course of his occupation." While Sutherland intended to use this definition to separate the study of white collar crime from street crime, the traditional focus of criminologists, he unfortunately introduced more ambiguity than clarity. For instance, his major work on the topic, *White Collar Crime* (Sutherland, 1949), dealt almost exclusively with what we now call corporate crime and dealt only marginally with the criminal activities of white collar *individuals*, the apparent focus of his definition. Put somewhat differently, Sutherland ignored his own definition in his studies of white collar crime.

Beyond the definitional issues, there is also the use of the term "crime" as part of the concept white collar crime. Many legal scholars, following the arguments first articulated by Tappan (1947), have maintained that much of what is subsumed under this concept does not violate criminal statutes. Furthermore, only very few individuals who are accused of having engaged in these behaviors are ever *convicted* of having violated a *criminal* statute:

> We consider that the 'white-collar criminal,' the violator of conduct norms, and the antisocial personality are not criminal in any sense meaningful to the social scientist unless he has violated a criminal statutes. We cannot count him as such unless he has been properly convicted. He may be a boor, a sinner, a moral leper, or the devil incarnate, but he does not become a criminal through sociological name calling unless politically constituted authority says he is. (Tappan 1947:101)

Sutherland (1945:132) had anticipated some of these criticisms by providing an alternative definition of crime as the "legal description of an act as socially injurious and legal provision of a penalty of the act." The use of this much broader definition of crime allowed him to continue the use of the term white collar crime.

Researchers following Sutherland, and the Sutherland/Tappan debate, have generally chosen one of two paths. First, some scholars have proposed new concepts in an attempt to recognize the legal issues raised by Tappan and his followers: "white-collar illegality" (Shapiro 1980), "white-collar law breaking" (Reiss and Biderman 1980), and "elite deviance" (Simon 2006) are some of the concepts that have been proposed. Each of these concepts is sufficiently broad to allow for the violations of norms and statutes other than criminal law.

However, most researchers trained in the social sciences have rejected the narrow legal arguments made by Tappan and his followers and continue to use the term white collar crime, in spite of the legal issues. One reason the term white collar crime continues to be widely used may be because it is "catchy" ("white-collar law breaking" is much more cumbersome). A more fundamental reason lies in the relative power of people likely to commit white collar and street crime, respectively. Street criminals generally do not have enough political clout to affect legal definitions or to have their deviant behaviors encoded in civil or administrative statutes. In contrast, potential white collar criminals are more likely to possess political power. As Geis, Meier, and Salinger (1995) remind us, the study of white collar crime tells us much about power in society. What acts are encoded in the criminal law as opposed to civil and administrative law tells about who has power at a certain moment in time. Likewise, power may be exercised when laws are not enforced or violators are not prosecuted. Limiting the study of white collar crime to instances in which a court has convicted an offender of a criminal law violation would unnecessarily restrict the cases of harmful behavior which researchers could examine.

DEFINITIONS EMPLOYED IN THIS ENCYCLOPEDIA

A number of American white collar crime researchers met for an academic workshop in 1996 that was focused on resolving definitional dilemmas surrounding the concept of white collar crime. At the end of the workshop, participants agreed on the following definition:

> Illegal or unethical acts that violate fiduciary responsibility or public trust, committed by an individual or organization, usually during the course of legitimate occupational activity, by persons of high or respectable social status for personal or organizational gain. (Helmkamp, Ball and Townsend, 1996:351)

This definition is sufficiently broad to address some of the concerns raised in the Sutherland/Tappan debate of half a century ago. It allows for violations of any form of legal statutes (i.e., criminal, civil, or administrative), separates it from organized crime (organized crime is not traditionally committed "during the course of legitimate occupational activity"), and distinguishes between individuals and organizations as actors. It is this last distinction that is especially crucial. While Sutherland had defined white collar crime in terms of individuals acting in the course of their occupations, he was much more interested in the activities of corporations and other organizational entities. Clinard and Quinney (1973:188) recognized this fact when they coined their definition of corporate crime: "offenses committed by corporate officials for their corporation and the offenses of the corporation itself."

Although there is some disagreement even today, most white collar crime researchers agree that the term "white collar crime" is a generic term that is to be used in the sense that Helmkamp and associates have proposed. Terms such as corporate crime, state crime, occupational crime, and so on, are subtypes of white collar crime (for a dissenting view, see Green 1990). Coleman (1990:5), for instance, proposed that: "White-collar crime is a violation of the law committed by a person or group of persons in the course of an otherwise respected and legitimate occupation or financial activity." Subtypes of white collar crime, in turn, include:

- *Organizational crime:* white collar crime committed with the support and encouragement of a formal organization and intended at least in part to advance the goals of that organization; and,
- *Occupational crime:* white collar crime committed by an individual or a group of individuals exclusively for personal gain (Coleman 1990:11).

Organizational crime, in turn, can include corporate crime, governmental crime, but also offenses committed on behalf of organizational entities such as labor unions and churches. At the same time, one should not treat this distinction as an absolute dichotomy. Rather, as Coleman points out, it is better to think of the distinction as endpoints of a continuum. Most forms of white collar crime are *mostly* organizational or occupational crimes, but there are some hybrid forms such as *collective embezzlement.* This term was coined by Calavita and Pontell (1997) in their study of the savings and loan industry. In this instance, corrupt thrift officers used the organizational structures to rob the organizations themselves: it is "crime *by* the organization *against* the organization" (see also Black 2005).

RECENT WHITE COLLAR CRIME RESEARCH TRADITIONS

White collar crimes, particularly corporate crimes have attracted considerable interest from journalists in recent years. The savings and loan scandal of the 1980s, and recent corporate malfeasance such as Enron, Wedtech, and Halliburton have been the focus of much journalistic inquiry. The extent to which this focus has been extended into the criminological and academic communities is questionable, however. For instance, in a review of criminal justice curricula at American colleges and universities in 2000, the subject of white collar crime was not even mentioned (Southerland 2002). Similarly, at the most recent meeting of the American Society of Criminology in Toronto in November 2005, there were a total of 599 different sessions during which scholars reported on their research. In each session there were about three researchers, which meant about 1,800 presentations were held. In the topical index, the conference program listed 30 entries under "White Collar or Corporate Crime." While some of these entries referred to entire sessions (with two or three papers on the topic) and other presentations might have been missed entirely in the index, it is clear that academics lag behind journalists in covering these issues.

There are several reasons for the lack of research among scholars. One important reason is lack of funding. Funding for research on white collar crime, and particularly on corporate crime, has been very limited in recent years in the U.S., although there have been some notable exceptions as Snider (2003) pointed out. There were a number of studies that focused on sentencing outcomes that were funded by federal grants, and most notably a series of studies that looked at the so-called savings and loan scandal of the 1980s. Aside from these studies, during much of the last two decades of the twentieth century the scholarship focused on corporate crime was relatively modest:

> . . . . funding plummeted in the 1980s and 1990s. Economics, law and business more than ever became the favored disciplines in politics and policy venues, and in media, law and academe. In its hypotheses, methodologies, and conclusions, empirical work on corporate crime (when the term was still used) became more conservative. (Snider 2003:63)

At the same time, a number of interesting case studies have been done in recent years. Studies have been published on the marketing of infant formula; the fire that killed several workers at the chicken processing plant in Hamlet, North Carolina; the savings and loan scandal; Arthur Andersen; Enron; Exxon Valdez; Three Mile Island; and Halliburton and Union Carbide, to name only a few. All of these topics are included in this volume.

SELECTION CRITERIA FOR INCLUSION IN THIS VOLUME

More than fifty years after his death, Sutherland is still by far the most important figure in the study of white collar crime. Any discussion of the concept has to start with his contributions to the field. By far the most important contribution was focusing the field on some behaviors. Although his own definition was a bit muddled:

> His personal sense of outrage at corporate criminality was clearly a strong motivating factor for his work. Sutherland did not quarrel with the virtues of an openly competitive entrepreneurial form of capitalism as originally envisioned by Adam Smith. Rather, he was deeply angered by those behaviors and actions of "Big Business" that corrupted and threatened the laudable aspects of the American economic system. (Friedrichs 2004:3)

Although he claimed that he was only interested in refining criminological theory (he developed Differential Association theory) and in being a good social scientist, he was a moral crusader with respect to corporate crime. Angered by corporate misconduct during the Great Depression when millions of Americans were suffering greatly and by war profiteering during World War II (see Geis and Goff 1983), Sutherland set out to uncover corporate misconduct. His book *White Collar Crime* was, in essence, an encyclopedia of corporate crime (although his publisher would not allow him to include the names of the corporations in 1949—*White Collar Crime: The Uncut Version* was not published until 1983).

The editors of this volume have been strongly influenced by Sutherland's approach to white collar crime. We selected topics for inclusion that are in line with the tradition established by Sutherland and used the following selection criteria:

1. We focused on corporate/organizational crime and de-emphasized occupational crime.
2. We made a deliberate effort to include organizational crimes that are not corporate crimes or that link corporations with other institutions. Examples include entries on NASA, Heritage Park and state-corporate crime.
3. We selected both contemporary and historical cases for inclusion in this volume. We sought a balance between historical examples such as the Northern Pacific Railroad stock run of 1901 and modern cases such as Enron.
4. We sought to include examples from societies other than the United States. Entries included here focus on white collar crime in Italy, Switzerland, India, Sweden, Canada, Japan and England, to name only a few.
5. We included some examples of white collar crime that are not truly organizational or corporate in nature, but whose successful implementation hinges on the *appearance* of the involvement of a legitimate organization/corporation ("Contrepreneurial crime" according to Friedrichs, 2004). Examples include the Ponzi Scheme, and the South Sea Bubble.

6. We made a deliberate effort to include theoretical explanations of white collar crime. Sutherland had begun this tradition with differential association theory and other scholars have added their theoretical explanations.

REFERENCES

Black, William K. 2005. *The Best Way to Rob a Bank is to Own One*. Austin: University of Texas Press.

Braithwaite, John. 1985. White Collar Crime. *Annual Review of Sociology* 11:1–25.

Calavita, Kitty, Henry N. Pontell, and Robert H. Tillman. 1997. *Big Money Crime: Fraud and Politics in the Savings and Loan Crisis*. Berkeley: University of California Press.

Clinard, Marshall, and Richard Quinney. 1973. *Criminal Behavior Systems: A Typology*. New York: Holt, Rinehart and Winston.

Coleman, James W. 1990. *The Criminal Elite: The Sociology of White-Collar Crime, third edition*. New York: St. Martin's Press.

Geis, Gilbert, and Colin Goff. 1983. "Introduction." Pp. ix–xxxiii in Edwin H. Sutherland, *White Collar Crime: The Uncut Version*. New Haven, CT: Yale University Press.

Geis, Gilbert, Robert F. Meier, and Lawrence M. Salinger. 1995. *White-Collar Crime: Classic and Contemporary Views, third edition*. New York: Free Press.

Green, Gary. 1990. *Occupational Crime*. Chicago: Nelson-Hall.

Friedrichs, David O. 2004. *Trusted Criminals: White Collar Crime in Contemporary Society, second edition*. Belmont, CA: Wadsworth.

Helmkamp, James, Richard Ball, and Kitty Townsend (editors). 1996. *White Collar Crime?* Morgantown, WV: National White Collar Crime Center.

Katz, Jack. 1980. "The Social Movement against White Collar Crime." Pp. 161–184 in E. Bittner and S. Messinger (eds.), *Criminology Review Yearbook, vol. 2*. Beverly Hills, CA: Sage.

Reiss, Albert J., and Albert D. Biderman. 1980. *Data Sources on White-Collar Law Breaking*. Washington, D.C.: National Institute of Justice.

Ross, Edward A. 1907. *Sin and Society: An Analysis of Latter-Day Iniquity*. Boston: Houghton Mifflin.

Shapiro, Susan. 1980. *Thinking about White Collar Crime: Matters of Conceptualization and Research*. Washington, D.C.: U.S. Dept. of Justice, National Institute of Justice.

Simon, David R. 2006. *Elite Deviance, eighth edition*. Boston, Allyn and Bacon.

Snider, Laureen. 2003. Researching Corporate Crime. Pp. 49–68 in *Unmasking the Crimes of the Powerful*, Steven Tombs and Dave Whyte, editors. New York: Peter Lang.

Southerland, Mittie D. 2002. Criminal Justice Curricula in the United States. *Justice Quarterly* 19:589–601.

Sutherland, Edwin H. 1940. The White Collar Criminal. *American Sociological Review* 5:1–12.

Sutherland, Edwin H. 1945. Is "White Collar Crime" Crime? *American Sociological Review* 10:132–139.

Sutherland, Edwin H. 1949. *White Collar Crime*. New York: Dryden.

Tappan, Paul W. 1947. Who Is the Criminal? *American Sociological Review* 12:96–102.

List of Entries

A

ABC HOME HEALTH SERVICES (MEDICARE FRAUD). Medicare is a government-run health care program that provides coverage to people over the age of 65, people with disabilities under the age of 65, and people with permanent kidney failure, also known as end-stage renal disease (ESRD), which requires dialysis or a kidney transplant. This program falls under the auspices of the Social Security Administration (SSA), having been established in 1965 by the Social Security Act. Medicare and Medicaid, another government-run health care program that offers coverage to different groups of citizens, are administered by a federal agency called the Centers for Medicare and Medicaid Services (CMS), with Medicare currently serving somewhere around 40 million people across its two parts. Medicare is divided into Part A, which is hospital insurance provided to people over the age of 65 at no cost if they or their spouses paid Medicare taxes while working, and Part B, which is medical insurance that requires a person to choose to participate in this program and also requires a monthly payment or premium for coverage. For the purposes of this entry, we will focus on Medicare Part B, which covers doctors' services, outpatient care, physical and occupational therapies, and some home health care services (such as oxygen and durable medical equipment) when such services are deemed medically necessary.

The Centers for Medicare and Medicaid Services (CMS) define *fraud* in very vague terms that encompass any case in which there is a deliberate false representation that could garner a potential unauthorized benefit. This definition covers a broad range of behaviors and schemes, false statements or false claims filing, offering and accepting kickbacks, waiving beneficiary co-payments or deductibles, and false diagnoses, to name a few of the methods commonly used to defraud the Medicare system. According to CMS, the most common forms of fraud against Medicare include billing for services not provided; misrepresenting a diagnosis to justify payment; soliciting, offering, or receiving kickbacks; unbundling or "exploding" charges; falsifying certificates of medical necessity, treatment plans, or medical records to justify payment; and billing for a service not furnished as billed a practice also known as *upcoding*. In an industry that easily provides ample opportunity for white-collar crime, fraud has proven to be a persistent problem. The Federal Bureau of Investigation (FBI) estimates that, in 1999, approximately $1.1 trillion were spent in the health care industry, with as much as 10 percent of that figure being attributed to fraud and abuse. These cases have dramatically increased, costing federal and private insurance companies more than $95 billion each year, with Medicare and Medicaid bearing the brunt of almost 44 percent of the burden of health care fraud. Between 1997 and 1998, the United States government collected approximately $1.2 billion from fraud and abuse cases in the health care system and Operation Restore Trust (ORT), an antifraud initiative targeting the fraud-riddled area of durable medical equipment (DME), and found that, for every dollar spent investigating fraud and abuse in the Medicare system, $23 was recovered in overpayments.

In an effort to combat fraud within the Medicare system further, additional legislation and regulations have been approved that restrict and/or clarify what a Medicare provider can and cannot do. The Clinton administration was particularly involved in fighting health care fraud, utilizing legislative packages and budgetary bills to advance this platform. Legislative changes, specifically the creation of fraud statutes specific to the health care industry, have made the detection and prosecution of these cases easier, because, before these changes were enacted, only generic fraud charges, such as mail fraud, were available to law enforcement agencies. Violations of these regulations can lead not only to the revocation of the supplier's ability to bill for Medicare but also to criminal and civil penalties that can include hefty fines and possibly jail time. Also, the federal government has intensified its efforts to detect this type of fraud with an emphasis on successful prosecution of these cases, especially in cases in which false claims or kickbacks have been discovered. In addition to more comprehensive legislation against Medicare fraud, the FBI established the Health Care Fraud Unit, located within the Financial Crimes Section of the Criminal Investigative Division, in 1992. This unit does not conduct investigations but rather oversees any health care fraud investigations being conducted in any field office and acts as support to a multitude of agencies that must work cooperatively to solve this problem.

One specific example of the need for diligence in this area of fraud is found in the case against ABC Home Health Services. In this case, the Office of the Inspector General for the Department of Health and Human Services reviewed the general and administrative (G & A) expenses claimed by this company in its 1992 Medicare Cost Reports. Upon review, it was determined that ABC Home Health Services had claimed $14,253,875 in unallowable expenses. Under Medicare guidelines at that time, providers were to be reimbursed the cost of providing services to Medicare beneficiaries under Title 42 of the *Code of Federal Regulations* Section 413.1, and the general requirements for a cost to be allowable was that it must be reasonable, necessary for the maintenance of the health care entity, and related to patient care. Some of the areas in which unallowable costs were discovered involved computer and software purchases, salary costs, owner's compensation, unnecessary expenses for leadership conferences, marketing and promotional activities, entertainment and gifts, board of directors' fees, decorations, lobbying, and other miscellaneous fees. This particular company was so bold as to attempt to seek payment or reimbursement from Medicare for costs outlaid in patient solicitation activities, *Phantom of the Opera* tickets, gourmet popcorn in custom tins for physicians, Mardi Gras tickets, and board of directors' fees that amounted to $2500 per meeting for each of the six board members, five of whom were immediate relatives of the co-owners. These obvious instances of fraud led the government to conduct a thorough investigation into ABC Home Health's G & A expenses, with a finding that these unallowable costs be removed from the 1992 cost reports. Additionally, it was this case that spurred many of the changes to legislation and regulation surrounding Medicare providers today in an effort to prevent this sort of abuse of the Medicare program from reoccurring, specifically concerning the areas of patient solicitation and of gifts and marketing tactics.

Although this case provides but one extreme example of one of the many avenues available for Medicare fraud, there are numerous cases of both small- and large-scale fraud available for review, thus demonstrating the huge drain these crimes are placing on the budgetary expenses for CMS and further highlighting the need to be diligent in the fight against Medicare fraud.

See also: Health Care Industry; Insurance Industry Fraud

FURTHER READING

Adminastar Federal. "Home page of Medicare Adminstrator for Indiana, Kentucky, and Some Surrounding States." Available at http://www.adminastar.com. Accessed July 28, 2006.

Bourjolly, Lisa, and Moak, Erin. "Health Care Fraud." *The American Criminal Law Review* 41 (2004): 751–808.

Centers for Medicare and Medicaid Services. Home page. Available at http://www.cms.gov. Accessed July 28, 2006.

Cigna Government Services. "Homepage of Medicare Administrator for Region D." Available at http://www.cignamedicare.com. Accessed September 06, 2006.

FBI. "About the Health Care Fraud Unit." Federal Bureau of Investigation Website. Available at http://www.fbi.gov/hq/cid/fc/hcf/about/hcf_about.htm.

FBI. "Common Health Insurance Frauds." Federal Bureau of Investigation Website. Available at http://www.fbi.gov/majcases/fraud/fraudschemes.htm.

Medicare. "Medicare Fraud Overview." The Official U.S. Government Site for People with Medicare. Available at http://www.medicare.gov/FraudAbuse/Overview.asp.

Palmetto GBA. "Homepage of Medicare Administrator for Region C."Available at http://www.palmettogba.com. Accessed September 06, 2006.

TriCenturion. "Region A DME PSC Table of Contents." Available at http://www.tricenturion.com/content/reg_ab_dme_psc_toc.cfm. Accessed September 22, 2006.

AMANDA L. FARRELL

ABSCAM, OPERATION. In 1977 the Federal Bureau of Investigation (FBI) began a sting operation, known as Operation Abscam, that was to become one of the most controversial and depraved scandals in congressional history. Looking for informants involved in white-collar crimes to help it make criminal cases, the bureau conscripted Melvin Weinberg, international con artist and convicted swindler, who was then facing a prison sentence for fraud. In exchange for a sentence of probation, Weinberg helped set up a phony company known as Abdul Enterprises, purportedly owned by a fictitious Arab sheikh. The cover story claimed that "Abdul" was a multimillionaire who wanted to withdraw his money from Islamic banks (which, by religious proscriptions, paid no interest) and invest it in profitable American business ventures.

Among the first notable figures caught in Abscam was Angelo Errichetti, the former mayor of Camden, New Jersey, and one of the most powerful politicians in the state. He accepted payoffs from "Abdul's representative" (Weinberg) in exchange for assisting the sheikh to obtain an Atlantic City casino license. Errichetti later introduced Weinberg to senior U.S. Senator Harrison Arlington Williams, Jr., New Jersey's best-known political figure, who, along with three partners, proposed a lucrative investment for the sheikh's money. His group would borrow $100 million from Abdul and buy the nation's largest titanium mine, located in Virginia. Williams, as one of the highest-ranking Democrats in the Senate, could channel government and defense contracts to his partners. He knew that his participation in the deal had to be hidden, since using his office to help obtain titanium contracts would be an obvious federal crime. He did not know that his meetings with Weinberg were being tape-recorded. In Weinberg's words, Senator Williams "had been left standing bare-assed in Macy's window."

In 1979, Errichetti was told that "Abdul" and an ersatz emir named "Yassir" were concerned about political unrest in their country and wanted to remain in the United States. Errichetti arranged meetings with two congressmen from Philadelphia, Michael Myers and Raymond Lederer, who pledged the use of their offices to help Abdul and Yassir obtain asylum. The price was $100,000 per congressman, which was later "marked down" to $50,000. The FBI set up hidden microphones and cameras in a hotel suite at New York's Kennedy Airport to record the transaction. In a scene that would become familiar to tens of millions of television viewers, Myers boasted of his congressional influence and accepted a briefcase containing the $50,000 payoff. Lederer's performance mirrored that of Myers. He promised to push a bill on behalf of Abdul and Yassir and calmly took a $50,000 bribe.

Representative Frank Thompson of New York was the next to be caught in the Abscam net, accepting the $50,000 bribe and promising to recruit more congressmen. John Murphy of New York followed and, after accepting the usual bribe, made a pitch for a $100 million loan so that he could secretly purchase a Puerto Rican shipping line.

The next congressman to take the bait was John Jenrette, Jr., of South Carolina, who was a member of the important House Appropriations Committee. When asked by an undercover agent whether he would accept the sheikh's bribe, he declared, "I've got larceny in my blood. I'd take it in a goddamn minute."

The final Abscam catch was Rep. Richard Kelly, who was accompanied by three intermediaries: attorney William Rosenberg, who was reportedly looking for a cut of the loot; accountant Stanley Weisz, who claimed he could get Abdul forged gold certificates; and convicted gangster Gino Ciuzio, who claimed that he "owned" Kelly.

The sting operation ended shortly thereafter, to the disappointment of Weinberg. He lamented, "I wish we coulda done more . . . I think we coulda got at least a third of the whole Congress."

When the Abscam tapes were shown publicly, seven members of Congress had disgraced themselves in front of a shocked and disgusted nation. Each would pay a heavy price for their crimes despite the excuses they offered for their behavior. Myers claimed that, although he accepted the money, it was not really a bribe, since he did not intend to do anything for the Arabs. Despite his additional claim that he was drunk at the meeting, he was sentenced to three concurrent 3-year prison terms. Lederer was the only one of the indicted House members to be reelected in 1980. Like Myers, he was convicted of bribery, received three 3-year sentences, and resigned his seat after the House Ethics Committee recommended his expulsion. Harrison Williams, after vociferously fighting the charges against him, became the first incumbent senator to be convicted of a crime since 1905. He received a 3-year prison term and, facing certain expulsion, resigned from the Senate. Thompson and Jenrette received 3-year and 2 year prison terms, respectively. In an odd postscript to Jenrette's case, his estranged wife, who recently had gained her own measure of notoriety by posing nude in *Playboy*, announced that she had found $25,000 stashed in a shoe in her husband's closet. Some of the hundred-dollar bills were traced to Abscam.

Of all the dubious defenses employed, none was more ridiculous than that offered by Richard Kelly, who maintained that he only *pretended* to take the money as part of a one-man undercover investigation of corruption that he was conducting, and self-righteously blamed the FBI for "blowing his cover." One reporter asked Kelly whether he was planning to plead insanity. Kelly received the lightest sentence—6 to 18 months confinement.

Despite its success, Abscam remains one of the most controversial law enforcement operations in recent American history, for at least two reasons. First, the central role of Melvin Weinberg, a career criminal, represented a troubling strategy on the part of the FBI. According to Weinberg, "There's only one difference between me and the Congressmen I met on this case. The public pays them a salary for stealing." In a sworn statement, Weinberg's wife alleged that he had perjured himself and had siphoned some of the Abscam bribe money into his own pocket. In a mysterious turn two weeks later, she committed suicide.

The second, and more fundamental, issue is whether enticed bribery is an appropriate law enforcement technique for apprehending white-collar criminals or whether it constitutes unlawful entrapment. When entrapment is used for those on the social fringe, it generates little critical attention. Abscam suddenly questioned the fairness of undercover tactics and the moral acceptability of enticed bribery to solicit crimes that otherwise would not have been committed. Regardless of whether the Abscam defendants were tricked or beguiled, one thing is certain. The behavior they exhibited is wholly indefensible.

FURTHER READING

Green, Robert W. *The Sting Man: Inside ABSCAM.* New York: E. P. Dutton, 1981.
Marx, Gary T. "Who Really Gets Stung? Some Issues Raised by the New Police Undercover Work." *Crime & Delinquency* 28 (1982): 165–193.
Rosoff, Stephen M., Pontell, Henry N., and Tillman, Robert H. *Profit Without Honor: White-Collar Crime and the Looting of America*, 3rd edition. Upper Saddle River, NJ: Prentice Hall, 2004.
Small, Joseph. "Political Ethics." *American Behavioral Scientist* 19 (1976): 543–566.

STEPHEN M. ROSOFF
HENRY N. PONTELL

A. H. ROBINS. A. H. Robins pharmaceutical company produced the Dalkon Shield, an intrauterine device (IUD) blamed for causing injury to thousands of women, including death, infection, infertility, miscarriages, and birth defects, which eventually led to the bankruptcy of the company. Controversy surrounded both the Shield and Robins, and allegations that Robins ignored and covered up signs of faulty research and design have been numerous. The company was named after Albert Hartley Robins, a pharmacist who owned an apothecary shop in nineteenth-century Richmond, Virginia. His son, Clairborne Robins, came to work with his father in 1896 and later created the A.H. Robins Company, selling drugs only to physicians. His son, E. Clairborne Robins, entered the business in 1933 and, over the following decade turned the failing company around. By the early 1950s, A. H. Robins had added the cough medication Robitussin to its product line, and sales were taking off. In 1963, sales topped $50 million, Robins acquired the makers of Chap-Stick, and its stock became publicly traded. By 1978, E. Clairborne Robins, Jr., had taken over as CEO and remained at that post until the late 1980s, when the company was bought by American Home Products.

The Dalkon Shield was the first venture into contraceptives for A. H. Robins. In the late 1960s and early 1970s, much controversy surrounded the use of the birth control pill, so there was a large market for a safe and effective method of contraception. A. H. Robins responded to this demand by purchasing the rights to the Shield on June 12, 1970, from the Dalkon Corporation, a small company that had shared ownership between the two creators of the Dalkon Shield, Hugh Davis and Irwin Lerner, and a Connecticut attorney, Robert Cohn.

Issues with the research conducted on the Shield by its creators surfaced quickly. Features of the device's design, including pronged edges and a multifilament string that was thought to "wick" bacteria into the uterus, were claimed to be the cause of thousands of injuries and illnesses. Despite these early issues, the Shield was aggressively marketed to physicians and women in the United States and worldwide. From the time the device hit the market in 1971 and was pulled in 1974, an estimated 4.5 to 5 million Shields were distributed around the world. Despite the Shield's success in its first few years on the market, reports of injuries in Shield users were quick to surface, and the first lawsuit against Robins was filed in 1972. The first Dalkon Shield verdict was reached in the case of a Kansas woman, Connie Deemer, who became pregnant, suffered a perforated uterus, and was subjected to emergency surgery to remove the Shield, which had lodged itself in her abdominal cavity. She was awarded $10,000 in actual (compensatory) damages and $75,000 in punitive damages in what was to be the first of many lawsuits to yield awards to Shield users.

By 1985, Robins and its insurer, Aetna Life & Casualty Company, had already paid out $380 million in Shield-related lawsuits, the number of complaints and actions being filed were steadily increasing, and a class-action lawsuit was filed on behalf of nearly two thousand Shield users. Even with Robins reporting its highest-ever operations earnings of $128 million in 1984 (up 21 percent from the previous year) and its stock holding reasonably well, the Shield-related litigations proved to be too costly for the company. In March 1985, Robins announced that it was setting up a reserve fund to pay out Shield claims totaling $615 million, yielding a nearly $1 billion payout level for the company thus far. Creating the fund, however, left Robins with an over $4 million net loss for the year. In addition, records were being set on the amount of damages being awarded to Shield litigants, with a May 1985 decision awarding Loretta Tetuan, a Shield-user who had lost her uterus and ovaries, $7.5 million in punitive damages and $1.1 million in compensatory damages. In an attempt to protect the company and those who had a vested interest from the potentially devastating cost of more multimillion-dollar Shield-related awards, Robins filed to seek reorganization under Chapter 11 of the Bankruptcy Code in August 1985. This froze all monetary claims against the company and caused the company's stock to plummet to a third of its value.

In 1989, The American Home Products Corporation acquired A. H. Robins as part of the reorganization plan from bankruptcy. The consummation of the bankruptcy reorganization made it so that Robins had immunity from any further Shield-related civil litigation. Instead, as part of the deal, American Home agreed to finance a court-ordered trust to fund Shield claimants, putting $2.3 billion into the trust and additional moneys to the company's shareholders. The trust was responsible for paying claimants against the Shield for the following 20 years. Those persons who claimed injury from the Shield submitted the claim to the Trust, who then decided the amount to be settled based on adjusted historic settlement values. The reorganization also meant that Robins's shareholders received American Home Products stock, resulting in large financial gains, since the American Home Products stock was worth four times the price of the Robins stock before bankruptcy was settled.

See also: Dalkon Shield

FURTHER READING

Couric, Emily. "The A.H. Robins Saga." *ABA Journal* 72 (1986): 56–60.
Mintz, Morton. *At Any Cost: Corporate Greed, Women, and the Dalkon Shield.* New York: Pantheon Books, 1985.
Mumford, S. D., and E. Kessel. "Was the Dalkon Shield a Safe and Effective Intrauterine Device? The Conflict Between Case-Control and Clinical Trial Study Findings." *Fertility and Sterility* 57 (1992): 1151–1176.
Sobol, Richard. *Bending the Law: The Story of the Dalkon Shield Bankruptcy.* Chicago: University of Chicago Press, 1991.

STEPHANIE E. CARMICHAEL

ALLIED IRISH BANK SCANDAL. The Allied Irish Bank (AIB), the second largest bank in Ireland, was rocked by one of the largest scandals in banking history in 2002, losing over $691 million when a currency trader in their Baltimore office invested unsuccessfully in Japanese yen and kept the bank's losses a secret for nearly five years. In 2004, ten of the bank's top officers were discovered to have invested over $920,000 in offshore accounts and used the bank to hide the money for tax evasion purposes. The stock of the bank declined severely, causing great losses for personal investors, including many pension funds. The rogue trader went to jail, and the bank officers still employed resigned.

In 1999, the Allied Irish Bank expanded its operations into the United States by merging two of its previous acquisitions, Maryland Bancorp and Dauphin Deposit Corporation, and creating Allfirst Bank. With Maryland Bancorp, AIB inherited one employee of seven years named John Rusnak, a foreign exchange trader who had formerly worked for the Chemical Bank of New York. Rusnak was an unassuming, married, father of two in his thirties, living in the Baltimore suburbs. In 2001, Rusnak was promoted to managing director in charge of foreign exchange trading, in the global trading section of the treasury funds management section. Although the title and responsibility were impressive, in physical terms Rusnak was the senior man of a two-man department in the outer regions Baltimore office; with a great deal of independence and very little direct supervision from the home office or the auditing department in his branch.

Although Rusnak used a great deal of complex technical jargon about formulas and options to impress superiors and underlings alike in describing his actions, basically he used the bank's money to buy Japanese yen and lost a fortune when the value of the currency dropped drastically and continually. He started losing money and lying about it in 1997, gained ground in 1999, and then started losing again. This is when he made the classic mistake of gamblers and investors who are losing frightening amounts of money. He continued gambling on the yen, increasing his bets, vainly hoping that eventual winnings would enable him to break even. His losses—actually the bank's losses—grew to a phenomenal size.

Rusnak hid his losses by logging fraudulent gains into his computer that canceled out his bad investments, then making fake paper receipts and letters from the Asian banks he worked with. He was able to fool the bank's computer because he would enter two options simultaneously for the same amount, one paying and one receiving, but the paying option would expire that day and the receipt would live a long life. No one checked why so many options would have a one-day half-life. Because of the time zone difference, no one in Allfirst Bank phoned the Asian banks in the middle of the night, so Rusnak was able to lie successfully during the day. He convinced the small department of auditors at the Baltimore branch who were supposed to check on his dealings that all was well. On paper, Rusnak appeared to be a brilliant investor, and he was given hefty annual bonuses based on the bogus gains of his currency speculation. The lack of discipline by the local auditors working with Rusnak, who took the numbers from Rusnak's own computer to determine his cost-to-risk ratio, compounded with the distance and lack of communication with the home office in Ireland, worked to Rusnak's advantage. They took him at his word and did not check the paperwork.

Head of treasury funds supervisor Robert Ray grew suspicious in January 2001. New accounting rules that shed more light on individuals' balance sheets showed Rusnak to be much busier than he should have been. In early February 2002, one of the auditors in Rusnak's branch noticed that no one seemed to be exercising the options that Rusnak was recording, and those options had never been confirmed. Also, Rusnak's log showed a $50 million gain in one 24-hour period in January. When phone calls with Asian banks suggested that Rusnak's receipts were questionable, the bank gave him a deadline over the weekend of February 3 to come up with documentation confirming his investments. He failed to show for work on Monday, the 4th, and the bank called the FBI. When the scandal broke, the 2001 profit reports had to be reduced by 60 percent to cover the shortfalls that had been hidden for so long. Allied Irish Bank stock fell by over 20 percent in a day.

In June 2002 Rusnak was charged with seven counts of fraud, threatening him with a possible sentence of thirty years in prison and a one-million-dollar fine. In October he agreed to plead guilty to one count of bank fraud and received seven and a half years in prison, followed by five years probation in exchange for cooperating with officials investigating whether other people were involved in the scandal.

In October 2002, Allied Irish Bank sold its Allfirst division to M & T Bank of Buffalo, New York, for $3.1 billion and 30 percent of the newly formed bank. In 2004, Allied Irish Bank was fined over $29 million for overcharging customers starting in 1994.

FURTHER READING

BBC News. "'Rogue' AIB Trader Pleads Guilty to Fraud." Available at http://news.bbc.co.uk/1/business/ 2358463.stm.

McNee, Alan. "Case Study: Allied Irish Banks." ERisk.com. Available at http://www.erisk.com/Learning/ CaseStudies/AlliedIrishBanks.asp.

JAMES TIMOTHY LINEHAN

AMPHETAMINE. The distribution of amphetamine-based weight loss medications can be considered as white-collar crime because they were sold worldwide by pharmaceutical companies between 1960 and 1990 even though the damaging effects of amphetamines were well known. Amphetamine was scientifically proven to cause severe, incurable heart and lung disorders, and its effectiveness was far from certain at the time of its marketing. That patients got the advice to combine the course of treatment with a hard food diet proves this last fact. In this case the pharmaceutical industry preferred lucrative economic activities above the lives of women and their families.

Since the 1960s the pharmaceutical industry has been producing weight loss medications based on amphetamines such as phentermine, fenfluramine, or the combination of the two (Fen-Phen). The most important producers of these preparations were Servier and Wyeth (the latter bought out the former). Originally the aim of the medications was to treat medically diagnosed cases of obesity, but doctors readily prescribed the products on demand. In addition to the labeled prescription medicines, many self-made amphetamine cocktails and off-label medications were peddled by quacks.

It is known that these weight loss medications increase twentyfold the risk of the rare lung and heart disorder primary pulmonary hypertension (PPH) and other cardiovascular and lung disorders. The symptoms of PPH include permanent breathing problems, fatigue, and dizziness. Apart from heart-lung transplantation, there is no cure. At present, the symptoms can only be controlled by wearing an apparatus that supplies medication directly into the heart. Side effects of those medications include swollen legs, headache, sickness, and diarrhea.

Governmental response was very slow in coming. After long discussion between governments and industry, the products have finally been withdrawn.

The Food and Drug Administration in the United States, as well as the European Medicines Agency (EMEA), first decided in 1996 to add the risks in the package insert and to limit the occasions for prescription. The pharmaceutical industry could avoid having any reference to causation in the insert. In 1998 the industry decided on its own to withdraw the older amphetamine-based weight loss products. Only in 2000 did the European Commission officially remove the license to produce amphetamine-based weight loss drugs.

In the meantime a new generation of weight loss drugs has been marketed. The first such product, sibutramide, marketed as Meridia, is also an amphetamine-based drug working on the brain. In 2002 it was linked to 33 deaths in Europe and the United States, one of the reasons why the Italian government forbade the distribution. The other product, orlistat (marketed as

Xenical), is not amphetamine-based but acts on the digestion mechanism. The results of the clinical tests do not sound very promising. Nevertheless, the EMEA considered the benefit-to-risk assessment positive.

During the 1990s and early 2000s the market for surgical procedures to reduce stomach capacity and food uptake has exploded. The risks are high, while the effectiveness is not proven in all cases. The market for slimming products and methods is insatiable.

The responsibility in this case is not referable to the pharmaceutical industry alone. The *industry* is responsible because it could have been alerted by the dangers shown by studies published in medical journals such as the *New England Journal of Medicine* and the *Lancet*. Instead of being alarmed, they paid scientists to write research reports in favor of their products. *Doctors* are responsible because they were strongly advised to prescribe only for clinical obesity, but many doctors prescribed off-label drugs and self-made cocktails. *Governments* are responsible because authorities did not react firmly when they became aware of the dangers. They took measures in mutual agreement with the concerned companies.

This conflict was resolved differently in different countries. After the refusal of Servier to settle to case, the company was ordered by the French civil court of Nanterre to pay damage to the victims. This ruling was affirmed on appeal by the company, and more victims brought their cases before a court. In the United States and Canada the pharmaceutical industry paid billions of dollars for the settlement of individual cases and class-action suits. The companies refuse to admit causality between the damage and their products. In Belgium, one patient who participated in a clinical test of the medicine and got PPH won her case against the hospital where the medicine was tested.

This relative success in conflict resolution is partially related to the organization of victims in self-help groups and the support they get from doctors and lawyers. Victims who are members of a patients' association are stuck in a difficult position concerning conflict resolution because these organizations get support from the pharmaceutical industry. As a result, victims in patients' associations risk loss of this financial support if they press for conflict resolution with a pharmaceutical company. Companies are not likely to continue supporting associations that take legal actions against them.

See also: Pharmaceutical Companies

FURTHER READING

European Medicines Agency. "Committee for Medicinal Products for Human Use European Public Assessment Report (EPAR): Xenical." Available at http://www.emea.eu.int/humandocs/PDFs/EPAR/Xenical/106698en1.pdf. Accessed August 2, 2006.
Mundy, A. *Dispensing with the Truth: The Victims, the Drug Companies and the Dramatic Story behind the Battle over Fen-Phen.* New York: St. Martin's Press, 2001.

GUDRUN VANDE WALLE

ARCHER-DANIELS-MIDLAND (ADM). In 1902, George A. Archer and John W. Daniels began a linseed crushing business. In 1923, Archer-Daniels Linseed Company acquired Midland Linseed Products Company to form Archer-Daniels-Midland (ADM) Company. Today, ADM bills itself as the "supermarket to the world." ADM is in the business of procuring, transporting, storing, processing, and merchandising agricultural commodities and related products. Some of ADM's major divisions include corn processing, oils, produce, and grains. With processing plants on four continents and in forty-three countries, ADM is one of the largest transnational corporations operating in the agri-food sector.

In 1996, ADM was the subject of the largest price-fixing investigation in history. ADM operated several price-fixing schemes that cost consumers millions through inflated prices for soft drinks, detergents, poultry, and many other products. Senior executives were indicted on criminal charges for engaging in price-fixing in the international lysine market. Lysine is one of the twenty amino acids normally found in proteins. It is an essential amino acid—that is, the human body cannot make it from other substances. A deficiency in lysine can result in a deficiency in niacin (a B vitamin). Therefore, lysine has emerged as one of the most widely used feed supplements worldwide.

ADM and four other companies, two each from Japan (Kyowa Hakko and Ajinomoto) and Korea (Sewon and Cheil Jedang Ltd.), produced lysine for the global market. Instead of competing with each other, two executives at ADM talked competitors into forming an "amino acids association." The five companies agreed among themselves how much to charge their customers for lysine and how much each producer was permitted to sell annually. These agreements are illegal under U.S. antitrust laws as well as similar laws in many other countries. The businessmen within these five companies knew that they were doing was criminal. They did everything possible to keep the price-fixing conversations and meetings secret.

An FBI informant, Mark Whitacre, former president of ADM's bioproducts division, secretly made audio and video tapes of ADM meetings over the course of a two-and-a-half-year period. Michael Andreas, vice-chairman; Terrance Wilson, ADM executive; and Whitacre were each fined $350,000. Ironically, Whitacre, who pleaded guilty in 1997 to money laundering and tax fraud, received a much more severe sentence than those he exposed. He was sentenced to nine years in prison, whereas Andreas was sentenced to three years in prison and Wilson received a 30-month sentence following appeals to the Supreme Court. Whitacre also had to pay $11.4 million in restitution to ADM and was sentenced to serve 30 months for price-fixing on top of his 9-year sentence for fraud. ADM was fined $100 million, the largest antitrust fine ever. ADM also paid $400 million to settle a class-action antitrust suit. Neither the CEO nor the president of ADM was pursued criminally. Judge Blanche Manning ruled that Whitacre was in charge of the price-fixing conspiracy, but the government's investigation identified over forty-nine executives who had participated in the price-fixing conspiracy. The Japanese and Korean corporations were sentenced to pay fines ranging from $1.25 million to $10 million. Three executives from the Japanese and Korean corporations were sentenced to pay fines ranging from $50,000 to $75,000.

FURTHER READING

Bonanno, A., Constance, D. H., and Lorenz, H. "Powers and Limits of Transnational Corporations: The Case of ADM." *Rural Sociology*, 65.3 (2000): 440–460.

Lieber, J. B. *Rats in the Grain: The Dirty Tricks and Trials of Archer Daniels Midland*. New York: Four Walls Eight Windows, 2000.

Simpson, S., and Piquero, N. L. "The Archer Daniels Midland Antitrust Case of 1996: A Case Study." Pp. 175–194 in H. N. Pontell and D. Schicor (eds), *Contemporary Issues in Crime and Criminal Justice.* Upper Saddle River, NJ: Prentice Hall, 2002.

DEBRA E. ROSS

ARTHUR ANDERSEN. In June 2002, the accounting firm Arthur Andersen was convicted of federal charges of obstruction of justice, arising out of claims that members of the firm had shredded documents related to its auditing of the Enron corporation. As a result of the conviction, the old-line accounting firm collapsed amid scandal and recrimination. The shredding had been ordered by an Andersen attorney after the firm learned of a pending government investigation of Enron, whose multibillion-dollar collapse following revelations of major financial misrepresentations and accounting fraud was major news in the fall of 2001. In the Andersen case an originally divided jury was persuaded to convict, in particular on the basis of critical deletions made from an internal Andersen memorandum, again on an attorney's instructions. This verdict was the first time a major accounting firm had been convicted on felony charges.

Arthur Andersen was founded in 1913 in Chicago and eventually became one of the "Big Five" accounting firms, with some 85,000 employees in 84 countries. Through most of its history it focused primarily on auditing, as was true of other major accounting firms. In the final decades of the twentieth century, however, it built up a substantial management consulting business that ultimately became more lucrative than the auditing division.

By 2000, Enron, a high-profile and seemingly highly profitable energy corporation based in Houston, was paying Andersen more for its consulting services ($27 million) than for its audit work ($25 million). The practice of providing both consulting and auditing services, which had become quite common for the major accounting firms, created an inherent conflict of interest. On the one hand, Andersen was auditing financial recording practices and strategies based at least in part upon the advice of its own consultants; on the other hand, the imposition of especially tough auditing standards might have an adverse impact on retaining the company's consulting contracts. Evidence eventually surfaced that some internal conflicts had arisen within Andersen about some of the "aggressive" accounting practices pursued by Enron, but no decisive action was taken in response to these practices. If a fundamental purpose of an audit is to certify the soundness of the financial reports of a corporation, Andersen seems to have compromised itself and failed dismally in this regard.

The criminal prosecution of Andersen as a company, as opposed to simply the prosecution of directly involved Andersen officers and employees, was certainly controversial. The federal prosecutor in charge of the case was beseeched not to pursue an indictment against the company, as this action would destroy the company. The conviction of Andersen of criminal charges did in fact lead to the disintegration of this company, which had been in business for eighty-nine years. Attempts to save the company—by the resignation of its CEO, Joseph F. Berardino, and by bringing in Paul Volcker, a highly respected former Chair of the Federal Reserve Board, to oversee reform of the company—did not succeed. Nor was the company able to persuade another major accounting firm to purchase it. The collapse of Andersen seemed unfair to the vast majority of its employees not directly involved in the Enron case. Groups of such employees protested the pending indictment, attempting to draw attention to their own competent and honest work.

Prior to the surfacing of the Enron case, however, Andersen had served as auditor for a number of other major corporations, including Sunbeam and Waste Management, that were subsequently found to have fraudulently misrepresented their finances on a massive scale. Andersen had to pay a record $7 million fine imposed by the SEC in the Waste Management case, and it paid hundreds of millions to settle civil lawsuits in these and other cases in which it had served as auditor. The Andersen firm had been warned in connection with its faulty auditing in such cases and had promised not to engage in the practices that led to charges and civil settlements. Accordingly, the Justice Department regarded the Andersen firm as a repeat offender, with criminal prosecution of the company warranted. Furthermore, the Andersen firm was the auditor for the WorldCom corporation, where monumental financial misrepresentations surfaced not long after those at Enron came to light. Andersen was facing major civil litigation in the WorldCom case as well. Altogether, investors lost billions of dollars in these cases, and the Andersen company was regarded as having some significant measure of responsibility for these losses.

If the inherent conflict of interest arising when an auditing firm also provides consulting services was one source of Andersen's complicity in large-scale financial misrepresentations, an evolving company culture may also have played a role. Books written by former Andersen employees after its collapse claimed that in its final era the production of high revenue became the overwhelming goal of Andersen. A "culture of greed" supposedly became dominant, where concerns about the quality of audits and about the unacceptable accounting practices of major clients were wholly overshadowed by this focus on revenue production. Of course, such a company culture was hardly exclusive to Andersen, and in a highly competitive environment it might be said to characterize in varying degrees other major accounting firms as well. Furthermore, the collapse of Andersen benefited the surviving major accounting firms and reduced competition in the field. Some commentators suggested that a major overhaul of the accounting industry was needed, and that a criminal prosecution would not be sufficient to address the problems at hand.

In 2005 the U.S. Supreme Court agreed to consider an appeal of the criminal prosecution and conviction of Andersen on charges of obstruction of justice. The focus of the appeal was on whether an allegedly vague federal Witness Protection Act prohibition against "corruptly" persuading others to destroy evidence had been properly applied in the case. Lawyers for Andersen claimed that the government applied the statute in a way that criminalized the ordinary activities of corporate executives and their lawyers. The Supreme Court, in 2005, overturned the conviction of Andersen on the basis of an improper jury charge. The Court did not rule specifically on Andersen's guilt or innocence, but, of course, the company itself no longer existed.

See also: Enron; Waste Management, Inc.

FURTHER READING

Byrne, John A. "Fall from Grace." *Business Week* (August 12, 2002): 51–56.
Squires, Susan E., Smith, Cynthia J., McDougall, Lorna, and Yeack, William R. *Inside Arthur Andersen.* Upper Saddle River, NJ: FT/Prentice Hall, 2003.

Toffler, Barbara L., with Reingold, Jennifer. *Final Accounting: Ambition, Greed, and the Fall of Arthur Andersen*. New York: Broadway Books, 2003.

DAVID O. FRIEDRICHS

ASBESTOS. Asbestos, the fibrous silicate minerals found in mined rock, has long been used in many commercial products. Common usages of asbestos have included insulation, pipe, roofing shingles, wall plaster, and cement. The mineral is attractive for industrial uses because it acts as an insulator, is a fire retardant, strengthens concrete, and resists chemical breakdown.

Despite its usefulness in industrial applications, asbestos has also long been known to be harmful to human health. The first report that indicated the health hazards of asbestos was published in the *British Medical Journal* in 1924. In addition, internal communications of Johns-Manville, the largest producer of asbestos, reported the dangers of the mineral as early as 1930.

The Health Hazards of Asbestos. The fibrous nature of asbestos makes it difficult for the body to rid itself of the mineral. Inhaled asbestos fibers become lodged in the lungs. The most common diseases caused by asbestos are asbestosis and mesothelioma, a kind of lung cancer. These diseases affect the lungs or the abdominal cavity. It may take 10 to 40 years for these diseases to manifest themselves. In hearings before a congressional committee in the late 1970s, it was estimated that 20 to 25 percent of both factory workers exposed to asbestos dust and persons installing asbestos products die of lung cancer (as cited in Calhoun and Hiller 1988).

An estimated 11 million workers in the United States have been exposed to asbestos dust at work. Since asbestos-related diseases have a long latency period, however, the symptoms of these diseases are very slow to be recognized. Ten thousand Americans die of asbestos disease each year (EWG 2006).

The Johns-Manville Corporation. The Johns-Manville Corporation began manufacturing asbestos products in 1901. It became the largest asbestos manufacturing company in the world. As of the early 1980s, asbestos had thousands of commercial applications. As research began to find health hazards related to asbestos early in the twentieth century, Johns-Manville executives had initiated a twofold program to discredit and contain these findings by the 1930s. One element of this program was to limit the distribution of information regarding the potential health problems related to asbestos. The other element was to sponsor the company's own research to counter the unfavorable findings of other researchers.

By the mid-1960s Johns-Manville could no longer cover up the dangers of asbestos. Several factors contributed to the changes in awareness at this time. First, many persons exposed to asbestos in the past began to manifest related diseases. Second, new research published in 1964 clearly established the long-term health hazards of exposure to asbestos. Third, union concern for worker health and safety increased. Finally, unions and medical researchers joined forces to lobby for federal asbestos dust regulations. In 1972, such regulations were enacted under the Occupational Safety and Health Act.

As these developments unfolded, numerous lawsuits were filed on behalf of injured persons. The court's decision in *Borel v. Fibreboard Paper Products* (1973) held that asbestos manufacturers could be held liable for failure to warn of the dangers of their products. This ruling established the legal precedent for the thousands of lawsuits that followed it. As the lawsuits continued, and jury awards were made, the awards became a financial threat to the corporation.

Another important event in this series of civil lawsuits against Johns-Manville resulted from a plaintiff's attorney obtaining correspondence among company executives dating from the 1930s regarding the actions of the corporation to limit information about the health hazards of asbestos products and the asbestos production processes. These communications were used to challenge the company's claims that there was insufficient medical research on the dangers of asbestos until 1964 and that, as a result, Johns-Manville was not liable prior to that time.

In the late 1970s Johns-Manville launched an effort to have the federal government create a victim relief fund. This fund would have protected the corporation's assets by diverting some of the financial responsibility for health problems related to asbestos from Johns-Manville resources to federal resources. This effort failed.

The next damage-control strategy utilized by Johns-Manville was to file for bankruptcy in 1982. This move was highly unusual, since the corporation had $2.3 billion in assets at the time. Although declaring bankruptcy was a drastic move for Johns-Manville, this tactic did result in some financial protection for the corporation.

Civil Lawsuits. The lawsuits concerning the health damages caused by asbestos continue to mount. In 1995 a Texas court found asbestos manufacturers Owens-Corning, Pittsburgh Corning, and Fuller-Austin Insulation liable for causing the disease or death of 11 former workers. The judgment was for $42.6 million. In 1998 a jury in Texas found Carborundum Company liable and awarded $115 million to 21 steelworkers because they had contracted asbestosis while working at a steel mill (see Rosoff et al. 2002: 159).

A Criminal Indictment. Recently asbestos-related health problems in Libby, Montana, have come to national attention. Libby was the site of a vermiculite mine. Vermiculite is a mineral used in insulation and potting soil, but the vermiculite from Libby is contaminated with a virulent form of asbestos, which is released into the air when disturbed. In a criminal indictment filed in 2005 against W. R. Grace, the owner of the mine, it is charged that in the 30 years of the operation of the plant, 200 people have died from asbestos diseases in Libby (population 2600) and that another 1200 are suffering from asbestos-related illnesses; including many persons who did not work in the mine. In addition, the rate of death by cancer is 30 percent higher in Libby than in the general population. A U.S. Senate bill to compensate the victims of the Libby mine failed to pass in February 2006.

Since national attention has been brought to the victims of the Libby mine pollutants, it has come to light that vermiculite ore from this mine was shipped to 236 different sites in 39 states for processing between 1948 and 1993. Thus, thousands of workers and their communities have been exposed to the health hazards from the processing of the contaminated ore from the Libby mine.

President George W. Bush's Position. In early 2005 President George W. Bush called for limiting asbestos lawsuits. He said, "These asbestos suits have bankrupted a lot of companies. . . . those with no major [medical] impairment now make up the vast majority of claims, while those who are truly sick are denied their day in court" (White House 2005).

See also: Black Lung, Johns-Manville Corporation, Occupationally Related Diseases

FURTHER READING

Calhoun, Craig, and Hiller, Henryk. "Coping with Insidious Injuries: The Case of Johns-Manville Corporation and Asbestos Exposure." *Social Problems* 35 (1988): 162–181.
Environmental Working Group. "'Asbestos Litigation Reform' Reconsidered." Environmental Working Group, 2006. Available at http://www.ewg.org/reports/asbestos/facts/. Accessed August 2, 2006.
Rosoff, Stephen N., Pontell, Henry N., and Tillman, Robert H. *Profit without Honor: White-Collar Crime and the Looting of America.* 2nd edition. Upper Saddle River, NJ: Prentice Hall, 2002.
U.S. Department of Labor, Occupational Safety and Health Administration. "Safety and Health Topics: Asbestos." Available at http://www.osha.gov/SLTC/asbestos/. Accessed August 3, 2006.
U.S. Environmental Protection Agency. "Asbestos." 2006. Available at http://www.epa.gov/asbestos/. Accessed August 3, 2006.
White House. "President Participates in Asbestos Litigation Conversation." January 7, 2005. Available at http://www.whitehouse.gov/news/releases/2005/01/20050107-8.html. Accessed August 3, 2006.

ERIC L. JENSEN

B

BAIT AND SWITCH. "Bait and switch" (also known as "bait advertising") is a fraudulent advertising scheme that consists of two parts:

1. *The Bait*: A good or service that is advertised (generally as being available on terms favorable to the consumer), used to entice the consumer into contact with the merchant
2. *The Switch*: The act of a merchant (or the merchant's agent) of offering a substitute good or service, when there was never any honest intent to sell the one that was advertised.

Bait-and-switch techniques are illegal under federal law and are differentiated from legal sales techniques primarily in that the advertisement in a bait-and-switch scam is not an honest, good-faith effort to sell the advertised good or service but a stratagem used to sell other goods or services. In contrast, a salesperson extolling the virtues of more expensive products in the same category as the advertised good is not an example of a bait and switch, so long as the advertised product is available for sale and customers are not unfairly led into purchasing an alternative item.

Although many buyers may not choose to purchase the substitute good or service offered in a bait-and-switch scheme, the goal of the scam is twofold: to develop leads on consumers interested in purchasing goods or services of the type advertised, and to entice some number of the consumers who have taken the bait to purchase the substitute good or service; either to salve their disappointment over not obtaining the desired good or in an attempt to recoup sunk costs associated with their shopping excursion (such as time spent in line or driving to the store). In some extreme cases, a bait and switch may be combined with other deceptive practices to result in the sale of a substitute good, either against the will of the victim or without the victim's knowledge.

Impact of Differences between Advertisement and Offered Product. Even minor differences between the advertised good or service and the good or service available for purchase may constitute a bait-and-switch scheme if the difference is one that might tend to make some customers likely to be switched from the advertised product to another upon disclosure of the true facts. Federal regulations specifically cite the grade, quality, make, value, currency of model, size, color, usability, and origin of the product as relevant factors, but other factors may be relevant in any particular instance, so long as they increase the likelihood that a customer might succumb to the switch attempt. In a recent case involving Dell computers, for example, the main difference alleged between the advertised good and the one available for purchase was not an item characteristic at all, but rather the price.

This does not mean that all representations made in the advertisement must be verifiably substantiated in the good or product available for sale. Potential bait-and-switch cases are evaluated using the same test used for all other deceptive sales practices—that is, a representation is deceptive only if it is likely to mislead a reasonable customer and if the representation is likely to affect the consumer's choice of whether or not to purchase a good or service.

The decision about whether or not a statement is deceptive requires an evaluation of the overall context and impact of the statement. For example, in a 2002 case, email spammers sent emails promising free PlayStation 2's, directing the recipients to follow certain directions to claim their prize. In reality, no PlayStations were available, and following the instructions resulted in a program being downloaded to the victims' computers that connected to a particular pornographic website with a $3.99 per minute connection charge. Although each victim was provided with a disclosure form that revealed the complete and truthful details of what they were actually entering into, the fact that the disclosures were made in a densely written, eight-page form; that the original product advertised primarily appealed to children; and that the false claims were made in large print meant to grab the eye while the retractions were stated as unobtrusively as possible all combined to make the statements deceptive even though a thorough reading of the terms would have revealed exactly what sort of product the victim was actually agreeing to purchase.

Impact of Product Availability. A merchant who does not have a particular good or service available has not necessarily committed a bait-and-switch fraud; the underlying reason behind the discrepancy must be dishonest. Merchants who have sold their supply of the good, for example, have not committed a bait-and-switch fraud if the merchants made an honest, good-faith attempt to secure a supply of the good sufficient to meet anticipated demand or made clear in the advertisement that the supply was limited. Further, a franchisee's lack of participation in a sale or promotion advertised by the franchise does not constitute a bait and switch if the franchise's advertisements clearly and adequately disclose that the offer is good only at designated outlets (a disclaimer one often notices in television advertisements for national chains).

It is possible for a sales technique to be labeled as a bait and switch even when the good or service is available for purchase. This occurs when the underlying plan involved is a bait-and-switch scheme. For example, selling a token amount of the product is not sufficient to legitimize a scheme whose overall intent is to commit bait-and-switch frauds against the majority of the business's clients.

Point-of-Sale and After-Sale Bait-and-Switch Techniques. Discouraging customers from purchasing the advertised items may also constitute a bait-and-switch scheme, when the discouragement reveals an underlying intent not to sell the advertised good or service. Behaviors that have been found to indicate an underlying bait-and-switch motivation include refusing to show or demonstrate the product; disparaging or mocking the product or its associated warranty, availability of service, or credit terms; refusing to take orders for delivery of the product within a reasonable period of time; using a defective or unsuitable example of the product in demonstrations (the Better Business Bureau has issued specific warnings about sellers of bulk beef, some of whom use unappetizing, fat, and moldy examples of the advertised product to switch consumers to more expensive products); and adopting business practices that are designed to discourage salespeople from selling the advertised product.

A transaction may become a bait-and-switch scheme even after the successful sale of the advertised product if the merchant engages in practices meant to void the sale after it is completed. Examples of this include accepting a deposit for the good advertised but then switching the customer to one that is more expensive (a practice often attributed to bait-and-switch tactics involving the credit, mortgage, and lending industries, when one interest rate is advertised but a different one is actually given); not delivering the good in a timely manner; and delivering an advertised good that is defective or otherwise unfit for the advertised purpose.

See also: Funeral Industry Fraud

FURTHER READING

Dingle, John D. "FTC Policy Statement on Deception." May 2005. Federal Trade Commission. Available at http://www.ftc.gov/bcp/policystmt/ad-decept.htm.

Lazear, Edward. "Bait and Switch." *Journal of Political Economy* 103.4 (1995): 813–830.

U.S. Government Printing Office. "Guides Against Bait Advertising, 16 C.F.R. § 238." May 2005. U.S. Government Printing Office. Available at http://www.access.gpo.gov/nara/cfr/waisidx_05/16cfr238_05.html.

CHRISTIAN DESILETS

BAKKER, JIM AND TAMMY FAYE. The televangelist Jim Bakker, born James O. Bakker, met Tammy Faye LaValley in 1960, while he was enrolled in North Central Bible College, and they were married in 1961. Both came from humble beginnings, which PTL Ministry staff members would later cite as an excuse for the Bakkers' excesses and inappropriate expenditures. In their ministry, the Bakkers developed a strong belief in "prosperity theology," in which the basic premise is that God gives to those who give to Him. This belief became a common theme in the Bakkers' ministry and in their personal lives.

In September 1965, the Bakkers joined Pat Robertson's Christian Broadcasting Network (CBN). While at CBN, Bakker was given the opportunity to develop the 700 Club, a program that became the forerunner of PTL. While working on the 700 Club, Jim Bakker suffered a breakdown from his work, and Tammy Faye Bakker experienced psychiatric problems requiring medication. During this time, the Bakkers' relationship with Robertson began to crumble. After seven years, the Bakkers decided to part ways with Robertson's CBN and move to Charlotte, North Carolina.

PTL. One of Bakker's first actions after leaving CBN was to form a nonprofit corporation, Trinity Broadcasting Systems (TBS), in 1973. This organization was the forerunner to the PTL Ministry. The IRS granted tax-exempt status to TBS as a religious organization in May 1973. Bakker, tired of life on the road, desired to create a show in the same format he had used at CBN. The name of the show was called "Praise the Lord," which was shortened to PTL in the hopes that it would appeal to and draw in nonreligious viewers. Bakker was tapped to lead the program, which was eventually named the PTL Club. On the PTL Club, Bakker promoted the philosophy of "seed-faith giving" espoused by Oral Roberts: give to God and you shall receive back many times over, for God wants His people to prosper (in this life) and rewards their generosity. A subsequent disagreement between Bakker and Paul Crouch, reminiscent of the Pat Robertson days, caused the Bakkers and a large part of the staff to resign from TBS in November 1973.

PTL experienced a phenomenal growth after its initial start in a furniture showroom in Charlotte. By September 1975, PTL had outgrown the furniture showroom, causing Bakker to seek out the purchase of a 25-acre tract of land featuring a three-story Georgian mansion. Bakker claimed that God wanted him to build a village, a miniature version of Colonial Williamsburg, and Heritage Village was born. Construction soon began on a $4 million project to turn Heritage Village into an international religious counseling and broadcast center. The center would be used to broadcast Bakker's program, which was known over the years as "The PTL Club," "The Jim Bakker Show," and "The Jim and Tammy Show." Bakker repeatedly referred to the funding of the project as a miracle from God. Bakker would later falsely claim that Heritage Village and the later Heritage USA projects were debt-free.

By 1976, PTL consisted of a network of 70 TV stations and 20 cable TV broadcasts and was welcomed into homes in the United States, Canada, and Mexico. The additional growth brought a donation increase to the ministry from $817,000 to $5.5 million. The net worth of PTL increased from $129,000 to more than $2 million. By 1978 PTL had installed a million-dollar satellite system, which allowed 24-hour religious broadcasting. The addition of the satellite system allowed PTL to sell remaining air time to other organizations at a profit. The expanding growth in the market also caused PTL to outgrow its facilities and its IRS charter. In November 1976, PTL amended the corporate charter to change its name from Trinity Broadcasting Systems, Inc., to Heritage Village Church and Missionary Fellowship, Inc (HVCMF). The purpose of the organization was also expanded: (1) to establish and maintain a church, and (2) to engage in all types of religious activity, including evangelism; religious instruction; publishing and distributing Bibles and other religious publications; missionary work, both domestic and foreign; and establishing and operating Bible schools and Bible training centers. The expansion would give the organization more freedom in its operations. Once the name and charter change were in place, the groundwork was laid for the move to larger facilities. In 1978, PTL broke ground for the move to the Heritage USA facility.

Heritage USA/Heritage Park. Heritage USA, also known as Heritage Park, was located on the border between North and South Carolina and was an abandoned industrial park before its purchase by PTL. The property eventually spanned 2200 acres. Heritage Park was to become, in Bakker's vision, a "Total Living Center for Christians" and serve as the center of the PTL ministry. Bakker also had plans for a Heritage University on the property, but that plan never materialized.

The compound at Heritage USA began with the PTL executive office building, which was named the World Outreach Center. Then Fort Heritage Center was added to the property; it consisted of 1600 campground sites and facilities for swimming and outdoor recreational facilities. It was at Heritage USA that Bakker showed the ostentatious consumerism that was later found to be a violation of PTL's nonprofit status. The purchase of a $17,000 car for the

Bakkers' daughter, who couldn't legally drive yet; a $25,000 houseboat; and several homes only touched the surface of the misappropriation of ministry funds. It was at Heritage USA that the "Big Barn Auditorium" was built, which became Jim Bakker's television studio. This studio was Bakker's platform, from which he begged for donations to fulfill the many lifetime partnerships that he offered to his followers.

It was at Heritage USA that gross mismanagement of PTL by Bakker's hand, massive wire and mail fraud violations, and Bakker's "affair" with Jessica Hahn, who described the contact as rape, eventually led to the fall of Bakker's personal ministry and the collapse of PTL. A massive oversale of lodging partnerships led to revenue of $158 million for PTL, but the fraudulent sales eventually resulted in the imprisonment of Bakker and three of his top officials in 1987. From Heritage USA, Bakker made fraudulent appeals on air and by mail for his various "lifetime partnership programs." There were four major frauds perpetrated by Bakker through the PTL ministry: the Grand Hotel partnership fraud, the Towers Hotel partnership fraud, the Family Heritage Club (Bunkhouse) partnership fraud, and the 1100 Club partnership fraud. In addition, Bakker and PTL misrepresented the value of gift promotionals to donors. An overview of the frauds that constituted white-collar crime follows.

The Grand Hotel Partnership Fraud. The massive oversale of lodging partnerships began with the Grand Hotel partnership fraud. In November 1983, Bakker unveiled his plan to build a 504-room hotel at Heritage USA. Revenue for the project was generated by selling lifetime partnerships for lodging to faithful followers. In exchange for a $1000 contribution, donors and their families were entitled to a three-night stay in first-class accommodations at Heritage USA in the "PTL Partner Center," which would later be known as the Grand Hotel, each year for the rest of their lives. A limit of 25,000 lifetime partnerships was announced. The program would supposedly reserve 50 percent of the hotel capacity for lifetime partners. In order to manage the plan, PTL entered into a contract with the Brock Hotel Corporation to manage the Grand Hotel. Eventually, PTL would request to increase the 50 percent limit in order to accommodate more lifetime partnerships. However, no mention of the increase in availability was ever mentioned to the public. Constant pleas went out over the air and by mail about the need for additional partners. In each instance, Bakker and PTL officials knew that the true numbers of partnerships sold had exceeded the limit. It wasn't until August 23, 1984, that Bakker announced that the lifetime partnership program had reached its goal. In fact, it had far exceeded the limit. The total sales of partnerships had reached 29,949, which amounted to $4,949,000 over the expected income for the appeal. Bakker appealed again to his studio audience on April 11, 1985, and asked for more partners because some pledges had not been fulfilled. This plea resulted in a total of 34, 983 lifetime partnership sales. An additional plea in July increased the number of sold partnerships to 58,748. By May 31, 1987, 66,683 lifetime partnerships had been purchased by unsuspecting donors. This resulted in revenue of $66,938,820, of which only $35,365,201 was spent on facility construction. The remaining funds were supposed to be earmarked for facility maintenance but were instead used to meet the daily operational expenses of PTL, which included the by that time enormous salaries of the Bakkers and several key executives. The financial pressure on the ministry to meet not only its professional obligations but the exorbitant personal expenditures by the Bakkers and other key officials led to the unveiling of a new partnership appeal.

The Towers Hotel Partnership Frauds. On September 17, 1984, Bakker introduced the Towers lifetime partnership. The Heritage Towers were unveiled on the PTL show in order to offer an additional 500 rooms for partner lodging. The partnerships were priced at $1000, and 30,000 partnerships were available to donors. This development was expected to cost $15 million, with $10 million to go towards the completion of the Grand Hotel. Bakker assured viewers that the remaining sum of $5 million would be earmarked for TV stations. The program was promoted in much the same way as the Grand Hotel Partnership program. The studio audience that day was told that the cost of the partnerships would be raised to $1500 after 30 days. Contributors who purchased two partnerships were promised a seven-day, six-night stay per year at Heritage Park. In addition to the on air appeal, a mass mailing was sent out for the Towers appeal. As before, 50 percent of the room capacity was promised to be earmarked for lifetime partners.

Several variations of this appeal were offered. The Penthouse Promotional offered a week's stay in one of the penthouses in the tower for $10,000. Later, the price was raised to $25,000. The cost for the Tower partnerships was subsequently raised to $2000, which was attributed falsely to limited availability. Yet, in contrast to the Grand Hotel lifetime partner appeal, the number of partnerships sold never reached their capacity. Bakker however, continued to create a false sense of urgency in pushing their purchase. It was during the Towers partner appeal that the Grand Hotel opened in January 1985.

Other variations of the Towers partnership were introduced after the Grand Hotel opened. The Silver 7000 club membership for $3000 supposedly entitled partners to six nights of lodging at the Towers and admission to events at Heritage USA plus two self-improvement workshops per year. A $1,000 Victory Warrior partner would receive three nights' stay and admission to nonfood events at Heritage USA as well as admission to two self-improvement workshops each year. The Victory Warrior partnership program was the most successful fundraiser in PTL history and raised $34,908,076. This program alone exceeded the 30,000 limit of Tower partnerships available. While he was promoting the various Tower partnerships, Bakker was repeatedly told by high-ranking staff members to stop selling partnerships. Eventually 68,755 partnerships were sold for the Tower, far exceeding the pre-established 30,000 limit. This appeal raised $74,292,751. More disturbingly, only $11,422,684 had been spent on the Towers Hotel construction, which was never fully completed.

The Bunkhouse (Family Heritage Club) Partnership Fraud. This partnership was first mentioned on the air by Bakker as early as May 1986, but not officially promoted until August 4, 1986. The promotion promised $500 donors lodging for six individuals for two nights plus free admission to nonfood events at Heritage USA. No limits were announced for this program, but Bakker announced plans to build between 10 and 50 Bunkhouses. Again, a cap of 50 percent occupancy was announced. This partnership was heavily promoted by stating that the Grand Hotel and Towers partnerships were sold out. As of Bakker's resignation in March 1987, only one Bunkhouse had been completed. This meant that only eight rooms of the Bunkhouse were available for the 9,682 partners. The total amount raised through this appeal was $6,681,961, of which only $1 million was spent on construction. The remaining $5 million was spent on the exploding PTL operating costs, which included the Bakkers' personal expenses.

Even though Bunkhouse partnerships continued to be sold in spite of the sold-out warnings stated by Bakker, a shortage of funds instigated the 1100 Club partnership program in November 1986. The 1100 Club partners would be given their choice of four locations for lodging at Heritage

USA for six nights a year for life. Partners could choose to stay at the bunkhouses, Country Farm Inn, or the Heritage Grand Mansion for up to three nights and the campground for up to six nights. In addition, partners would receive free admission to Heritage USA nonfood events and could attend one workshop each year. Unfortunately, donors were not told that the Country Inn Farmhouse, the Heritage Grand Mansion, and the 1100 Club campgrounds were not yet constructed. This appeal raised $10,700,267, with no fund diversion to building costs. Again, the funds were used to support the daily operations of PTL and the Bakkers' excesses.

In addition to the fraudulent lifetime partnerships, Bakker promised promotional items to donors that either never materialized or were grossly misrepresented. In one example, a Heller "David and Goliath" statue was promised to partnership donors. The value was implied to be close to $1000. The quality of the statue was misrepresented, and it was later determined that the statues cost PTL a mere $10 apiece.

The various lifetime partner lodging appeals raised in excess of $158 million for PTL. The majority of the partners never received the benefits they paid for, because funds were fraudulently misappropriated by Bakker and key PTL employees. The majority of the buildings for which Bakker asked for donations were never built. Eventually, the fraudulent schemes and exorbitant personal spending caught up with Bakker and PTL. Bakker was forced to announce his resignation from PTL in March 1987, and the Rev. Jerry Falwell was elected chair of the board. During this meeting, the entire PTL board resigned. PTL was forced to declare bankruptcy in June 1987.

Jim Bakker was indicted on eight counts of mail fraud, fifteen counts of wire fraud (three counts from telephone use and twelve counts from use of television), and an additional count of conspiracy to commit wire and mail fraud, for a total of twenty-four counts. Tammy Faye Bakker was never charged with criminal conduct. Bakker's criminal trial was one of four judicial proceedings concerning the PTL ministry. The Bakkers were ordered to reimburse PTL $5,603,639.47 for excessive compensation by a U.S. Bankruptcy Court. A second case concerned charges of criminal tax evasion by two PTL employees, James and David Taggert. Finally, a civil case was brought against PTL auditors, officers of the corporation, and a director. Eventually, Bakker was convicted of all counts.

The lifetime partners filed a class-action lawsuit that sought $758 million in damages from Bakker and other key PTL personnel. The partners were awarded $129,618,000 in actual damages and $129,618 in punitive damages. Because Bakker received a 45-year prison sentence, later reduced to eight years, the partners are unlikely ever to recover their judgment.

Eventually Heritage USA was sold for $45 million in December 1990 to Morris Cerullo. Cerullo later surrendered ownership of Heritage USA to the New Heritage USA shareholders in an undisclosed agreement. New Heritage USA properties opened in June 1992 as a for-profit corporation.

FURTHER READING

Shepard, C. E. *Forgiven: The Rise and Fall of Jim Bakker and the PTL Ministry*. New York: Atlantic Monthly Press, 1989.

Tidwell, G.L. *Anatomy of a Fraud: Inside the Finances of the PTL Ministries*. New York: John Wiley & Sons, Inc, 1993.

KATHERINE M. BROWN

BARINGS BANK. Barings Bank was founded in London in 1763. Where it rose to become a leading Merchant Bank. As such, it provided traditional banking services to the public, but it also included investment activities in stocks, bonds, commodities, and real estate. By being flexible and creative in crafting financial solutions for companies, Barings grew steadily over time, enjoying an active presence across the globe. The bank focused its activities in the investment sector, so its successes in trading determined its future. In February 1995 the bank discovered that a massive fraud scheme, perpetrated by one of its traders in Singapore, had wiped out the bank's capital and destroyed the 220-year-old institution.

By 1989, Barings had established trading operations at most of the world's exchanges, operating primarily in British Commonwealth countries and former British colonies. In that year, Nick Leeson, a young commodities trader, joined the bank. He had graduated from college and spent two years at Morgan Stanley as a settlements clerk, clearing the huge futures and options deals the traders were making. When he joined Barings, it was in this same role, clearing settlements and learning the back office operations of the bank. Bored with the limited opportunities for advancement, Leeson quickly applied for a transfer, taking a position in the Bank's trading operation in Jakarta, Indonesia. He had applied for the position based on the image of an exotic locale and the flashy marketing materials the bank used to promote its Far East experience. But he soon found the reality to be vastly different, with the operations actually just a hotel room with several computers in it. In his autobiographical account of the scheme, Leeson claims to have learned just how lax the bank's controls were and how much tolerance the bank extended to "superstar" traders. He claims that significant losses were essentially ignored, because they were typically not found until subsequent profits were booked to cover them.

With this experience under his belt, Leeson was returned to London, where he spent the next year or so traveling around the Far East, meeting the various people and learning about Barings' various operations in the region. During that time period, Barings acquired a seat on the Singapore International Monetary Exchange (SIMEX) but had not yet begun utilizing it. In 1992 Leeson was selected to open, run, and manage the new operation in Singapore, managing all aspects of trading on SIMEX. He had been with the bank approximately three years and had a total of five years of experience in banking.

In his early stages, Leeson concentrated on arbitraging currency transactions. This is a fast-paced practice in which speed and timing can enable a slow and steady profit. But for its relatively low risk, it is a stressful and high-energy way to make relatively small profit margins. Leeson soon became disenchanted. With his background in settlements, Leeson was quick to catch any slight errors in the trading slips. Typically small errors would be booked against an errors account in London, with the positives and negatives generally netting out over time. In order to take advantage of the time differential, Leeson asked to be allowed to create a local error account, named the 88888 account. This would later prove vital to his orchestration of the scheme.

One of the keys to making money in this type of trading is the fast-paced nature of the transactions. Deals are done and cleared the same day, reducing the risk but also minimizing the opportunity for profits. As Leeson's group grew on the relatively small SIMEX exchange, their percentage of the total number of deals grew dramatically, making clearing all of the settlements on the same day difficult. As such, Barings was occasionally allowed to hold deals overnight and settle the next day. This would also later prove to become a key element of the scheme.

Soon after these two keys were in place, Leeson discovered a major error. One of his traders had improperly sold a position instead of buying the position, creating a £20,000 loss in the process. Leeson took the matter to his boss, who told him to fire the trader and go on. Leeson instead attempted to hide the loss in the error account, holding the closing not only overnight but over a weekend to attempt to "lose" the transaction in the flurry on Monday's work, hoping that a profit then would cover his loss from Friday. But the markets began moving against this hidden transaction, so that, a few days later, the same still unreconciled trade would create a £60,000 loss. Leeson decided that, rather than admit the situation to his superiors, he would actively manipulate the books to conceal the loss. This was his first foray into the fraud that would eventually destroy Barings Bank.

Over the next two years Leeson expanded upon an increasingly risky trading strategy, making larger and larger bets on the movements of the currency markets. He had discarded the safe but low-margin arbitrage approach in favor of a much more risky but potentially much more profitable series of direct currency gambles. He explained to his superiors that his change in strategy would entail holding positions longer, but he began booking significant profits from his trading activities. But these paper profits only concealed the roller coaster of up and down wins and losses on the trading floor. To cover his losses Leeson had to transfer cash at closing, so, despite the large paper profits being booked, he was continually asking for additional cash from London. By July 1994 Leeson had created and concealed losses totaling over £50 million. With his strategy failing, Leeson took ever increasingly wilder risks. He expanded the size of his positions, making and losing in a single day first millions and then tens of millions. When the scheme collapsed, Barings had to transfer over 7.7 billion yen ($600 million) to the exchange to cover Leeson's margin losses.

Leeson's audacious scheme succeeded for two primary reasons: management failed to look beyond the paper profits to understand how he was generating these tremendous returns, and nobody in London questioned his continual and increasing needs for cash. Barings' failure was in not recognizing that Leeson's activities were essentially a Ponzi scheme, albeit one that relied on a single internal investor to continually cover the snowballing losses caused by the scheme. Its controls failed because of an inability of management to see the impact of the ever-increasing demand for cash into an ostensibly profitable trading division.

FURTHER READING

Erisk.com. "Case Study: Barings." Available at http://www.erisk.com/Learning/CaseStudies/Barings.asp. Accessed September 06, 2006.
Gapper, John. *All That Glitters: Fall of Barings*. London: Hamish Hamilton, 1996.

JONATHAN E. TURNER

BEECH-NUT APPLE JUICE SCANDAL. Originally established as a meatpacking company in 1891, the Beech-Nut Corporation family would eventually include Life Savers, Table Talk pies, Tetley tea, Martinson's coffee, chewing gum, and baby food among its products

(Traub 1988). In the late 1960s Beech-Nut was acquired by the Squibb Corporation. Then, approximately four years later, a relic of the old company was spun off and run by a private group led by Frank C. Nicholas (Traub 1988). This new company sold only baby food and found itself in a highly competitive market dominated by the Gerber Corporation. Beech-Nut sought to market its line as the natural baby food, but would ultimately cave to pressures to reduce costs. In an effort to save money the Beech-Nut Corporation switched to a new juice concentrate supplier, who provided a less expensive apple juice concentrate. The new supplier would eventually become known as Universal Juice. The disproportion between Beech-Nut's 1977 manufacturing budget of over $50 million a year and the meager $250,000 saved per year due to the decision to switch suppliers may seem extreme, but the repercussions that followed this executive decision would serve as a major turning point in the world of white-collar crime (Traub 1988).

In the same time period that Beech-Nut was making their cost effective decisions, a series of accusations would arise concerning adulteration processes taking place within the apple juice concentrate business. Consequently, in 1982 an investigation by the Processed Apples Institute revealed that a company called Food Complex had omitted apples from its product altogether. Food Complex served as Universal Juice's manufacturing arm. It was also discovered that Food Complex was primarily supplying the Beech-Nut Corporation. The primary investigator, Andrew Rosenzweig, a former New York City narcotics detective and future chief investigator for the Manhattan District Attorney's office, would eventually follow a truck of sugar water from the Food Complex facility to the Beech-Nut facility in Canajoharie, New York. Rosenzweig confronted executives at Beech-Nut about using suspect concentrate in their apple juice. Rosenzweig's secret tape recordings of this confrontation ultimately proved to be key evidence against Beech-Nut executives. The recordings revealed John F. Lavery, Beech-Nut's vice president of operations and manager of the plant in Canajoharie, and two other Beech-Nut executives making rationalizations as to why they were using the concentrate and ultimately stating that they had made their last purchase from Universal (Traub 1988).

Even if Beech-Nut had received its last shipment from Universal, Niels Hoyvald, Beech-Nut's president, made the decision to continue selling the tainted product. Moreover, Hoyvald intentionally chose to market the product aggressively. Then on July 29, 1982, the U.S. Food and Drug Administration (FDA) notified Beech-Nut that samples taken from supermarket shelves had been found to be adulterated. In August 1982 the New York State Department of Agriculture and Markets came to the same conclusions as the FDA. Fearing that their product was about to be seized by authorities, the executives at the Canajoharie plant moved the entire inventory (26,000 cases) of tainted juice to a warehouse in Secaucus, New Jersey, which fell outside the state of New York's jurisdiction (Traub 1988). In September 1982 Hoyvald orchestrated the shipment to and eventual sale of 26,000 cases in the Caribbean (Rosoff et al. 2004). Approximately 23,000 cases had been trucked from the company's San Jose, California, plant to Galveston, Texas. In Galveston the cases were loaded on ships and shipped to the Dominican Republic and subsequently sold at a 50 percent discount (Traub 1988). The sale of the appleless apple juice product earned the Beech-Nut Corporation approximately $60 million over a ten-year period (Rosoff et al. 2004).

Eventually, Beech-Nut agreed to a state recall of the juice when New York State authorities threatened to seize the juice. After being threatened with the possible confiscation of the juice by the FDA, Beech-Nut began a nationwide recall. Subsequent investigations by both federal and state investigations would not only bring out details of the cover-up but would also reveal that Beech-Nut had continued selling the juice in its mixed-juice product for six months after the recall.

New York State sued Beech-Nut for selling the adulterated product and imposed a fine of $250,000 (Traub 1988). At the time the said fine was issued, it was the largest penalty ever assessed for consumer violations.

The U.S. Attorney obtained indictments in November of 1986 on Hoyvald, Lavery, Beech-Nut, Zeev Kaplansky (former president of Universal Juice), and Kaplansky's colleague Raymond H. Wells, the owner of Food Complex. "Beech-Nut eventually settled by agreeing to pay a $2 million fine. Kaplansky and Wells, who had earlier settled the apple-institute suit with a financial agreement and by ceasing production of their concentrate, also pleaded guilty" (Traub 1988: 52). In 1988, Hoyvald and Lavery were convicted of violating federal food and drug laws and subsequently sentenced to prison terms of a year and a day, plus fines totaling $100,000 (Rosoff et al. 2004: 61). This sentence was significant in that it was one of the first times that top-level corporate executives actually received prison time for violating federal food and drug laws. It appeared that the time of not holding top-level corporate executives responsible for their actions was coming to and end. However, in March 1989, Hoyvald's conviction was overturned by a three-judge panel in the U.S. Court of Appeals for the Second Circuit (Associated Press 1989). Then, on September 27, 1989, a federal jury was unable to reach a verdict in the case of Niels L. Hoyvald.

Further repercussions for Beech-Nut included the Pentagon's decision to implement the harshest sanction it could impose on a contractor. The Beech-Nut Corporation was barred in 1989 from doing any business with the Federal Government through 1991 (*New York Times*, 1989).

FURTHER READING

Rosoff, S. M., Pontell, H. N., and Tillman, R. H. *Profit without Honor: White-Collar Crime and the Looting of America.* Upper Saddle River, NJ: Pearson/Prentice Hall, 2004.
Traub, J. "Into the Mouths of Babes." *New York Times Magazine* (July 24, 1988): 18–20, 37–38, 52–53.
"U.S. Bars Beech-Nut." *New York Times*, April 6, 1989.

FRANKLIN T. WILSON

BID RIGGING CARTELS. In theory, Japanese government construction contracts are awarded through competitive bidding. The catch is that, for at least a half century, the firms have been rigging the bidding through a cartel known as the *dango* ("conference" in Japanese). The *dango* determines which construction firm will win, making Japan's bidding system a façade. Corruption is essential to the *dango*'s success, so the *dango*'s pervasiveness and persistence proves that corruption is endemic and intractable. Although the *dango* was always deeply inefficient, it became pernicious during the fifteen-year stagnation that followed the end of the "twin bubbles" (stock and real estate) in 1990.

In theory, the bidding system has a secret reservation price to limit abuses by putting a ceiling on the acceptable bid price. Two facts stand out about the reservation price. First, it is set very high, allowing excessive charges to the public. Second, the winning bids come in extraordinarily close to the reservation price; one survey found that the average winning bid was 99.2 percent of the cap. One can infer that the *dango* consistently knows the "secret" cap and had no concern about making this obvious through their bids.

How does the *dango* learn what the reservation price is? Senior bureaucrats in Japan generally take early retirement and are provided with a sinecure in private industry or Japan's large quasi-nongovernmental organization (QUANGO) sector. This is known as *amakudari* ("descent from heaven")—a revealing phrase that shows the great respect once felt for the bureaucrats. Their primary responsibility once they "descend" is to maintain close ties with their successors. A bureaucrat who refused to leak the reservation price would put his career in jeopardy. Bureaucrats are, effectively, immune from prosecution for leaking the reservation price. The "systems capacity" limitations are not resources, but the unwillingness to prosecute senior bureaucrats (who are far more powerful than their American counterparts).

The *dango* is a cartel, and although the conventional economic wisdom is that cartels cannot exercise effective discipline, the *dango* has been able to maintain nearly complete discipline for over a half century. Corruption is part of the explanation. Japan's dominant party, the Liberal Democratic Party (LDP), comprises factions are known as *zoku* ("tribes"). The "construction tribe" is composed of LDP leaders who get a percentage kickback from the winning construction bidders. Faction leaders gain followers by providing campaign funds. The *dango* kickback ensures that the government does not interfere with the cartel. The faction leaders provide the "voice of heaven" (*tan no koe*) when necessary to resolve disputes that might threaten the *dango's* discipline.

In addition to entrenching the LDP in power, the *dango* has major indirect effects. It serves as an informal trade barrier. Foreign construction firms cannot join the *dango*—and if they did, they could be prosecuted in their home nations for bribery. The *dango* directly makes construction far more expensive and indirectly creates an inefficient and bloated industry. The kickback creates strong incentives to spend far too much in public works construction. This, in turn, has done great damage to Japan's environment.

While the *dango* raises prices, it does not necessarily produce excessive industry profits. Domestic entry into construction is fairly easy. Easy entry and bid rigging have led to an industry that is at least twice as large as it needs to be. Many construction firms are insolvent because of their imprudent investments during the twin bubbles.

Japan's overall economic development has been harmed by the indirect consequences of the *dango* in three major ways. Productivity fell for many years in the construction industry, which is so large that it, in turn, materially lowered the nation's overall productivity.

Japan's "main" banks are vital to growth because of the dominant role they play in capital allocation. The collapse of the twin bubbles left the main banks crippled, and Japan covered up their condition rather than "bailing them out." This means that the banks generally do not collect loans from financially troubled borrowers, for if they demanded payment and were not repaid, they would have to recognize the losses. But Japanese banks cannot fund growth unless their loans are repaid. Many of their worst loans are to construction firms. The political support that the *dango* enjoys makes it extremely difficult for the banks to demand repayment from troubled construction firms.

Finally, the *dango* encouraged public works that would make no sense even if the bids were not rigged. As this is written, Americans are deriding the "bridge to nowhere" in Alaska that a Senator was able to demand as part of "pork barrel" politics. Japan is the champion of high-speed rail lines to nowhere and many other "white elephants." The public works budget became so extreme that Japan's deficit became a barrier to growth. The *dango* allocates capital to the least productive uses.

See also: State-Corporate Crime

FURTHER READING

Black, William K. "The Dango Tango: Why Corruption Blocks Real Reform in Japan." *Business Ethics Quarterly* 14.4(October, 2004): 602–623.

Cabinet Office, Government of Japan. *Annual Report on the Japanese Economy and Public Finance – 2001-2002 – No Gains Without Reforms II.* Government of Japan, 2003.

Ito, Takatoshi. "Long-Term Stagnation in Japan and Its Policy Implications." Unpublished memorandum, December 31, 2001.

Kerr, Alex. *Dogs and Demons: Tales From the Dark Side of Japan.* New York: Hill and Wang, 2001.

Woodall, Brian. "The Logic of Collusive Action: The Political Roots of Japan's Dango System." *Comparative Politics* (April, 1993): 297–312.

WILLIAM K. BLACK

BLACK LUNG. Black lung is legally defined as the man-made occupational lung disease caused by the prolonged inhalation of silica and carbon found in coal mine dust. The term *black lung* arose from the black coloring of the lungs due to the heavy deposits of coal dust, as opposed to the pink color of a healthy lung. Other names for this disease include miner's asthma, silicosis, and coal workers' pneumoconiosis.

The risk of contracting black lung disease is directly related to the duration and extent of exposure to coal dust. When present, the most common symptoms are shortness of breath, obstruction of airways, and a severe chronic cough. Black lung disease can be diagnosed through a series of tests including checking patients' history for exposure to coal dust and conducting chest x-rays to discover whether dust deposits are present. Pulmonary function tests are also utilized in the diagnosis of black lung disease. In its most severe state, black lung disease can lead to heart related problems, emphysema, and the risk of premature death for patients. At this time, there is no cure for black lung disease. The treatments undertaken are aimed at the symptoms and complications of the disease. Ultimately, black lung disease can be prevented only by avoiding long-term exposure to coal dust.

Historical Background. Beginning in the 1820s and 1830s, doctors, both in the United States and in the United Kingdom, began to treat coal miners for the early symptoms of black lung disease. In the beginning, doctors called this condition "miner's asthma"; In 1831, however, the term *black lung* was introduced to describe the black pigmentation found in coal miner's lungs.

Despite the efforts of British investigators and the United Mine Workers of America (UMWA), black lung was not widely recognized in the United States until the 1950s. In 1952

Alabama became the first state to provide compensation for coal workers' pneumoconiosis. In 1965 Pennsylvania enacted legislation providing for compensation, subsequently, in 1968, Virginia amended its compensation law to include coal workers' pneumoconiosis.

On November 20, 1968, a devastating coal mine explosion at Farmington, West Virginia, killed 78 miners. In late 1968 a number of miners organized the West Virginia Black Lung Association, which successfully led a campaign to introduce a bill in the 1969 session of the West Virginia legislature making coal workers' pneumoconiosis a compensable disease. When their campaign ran into heavy opposition from the West Virginia legislature, which was heavily influenced by the coal industry, 40,000 miners in West Virginia went on strike, and many marched on the state capital demanding passage of the bill. The strike, lasting three weeks, was one of the largest and longest ever on the single issue of occupational health and played a vital role in the enactment of the Federal Coal Mine Health and Safety Act of 1969 (CMA) and the Occupational Safety and Health Act of 1970.

For the first time in history, through the enactment of the CMA, Congress mandated the elimination of an occupational disease occurring in a major industry. As coal workers' pneumoconiosis was the only disease indicated throughout all of the state and federal statutes up to that time, Congress legalized the term *black lung* as a synonym for that disease in Title IV of the CMA. The CMA also stipulated dates on which decreasing levels of respirable dust must become effective and required that working miners must now have periodic chest x-rays to check for symptoms of black lung disease.

In 1972, Congress established the Black Lung Benefits Act, also the first of its kind, to compensate victims of an occupational disease. In 1977 the Black Lung Benefits Reform Act established a Black Lung Disability Trust Fund, financed by taxes paid by all coal operators. The 1977 law also made coal companies directly responsible for compensation and medical costs for black lung victims that had worked for them. Coal companies reacted by finding bureaucratic means to slow down the enforcement of these regulations, but the UMWA has remained active, continuing to advocate legislative and administrative reforms to make it easier for black lung victims to establish eligibility for benefits.

Recent Government Actions. In 1997, the U.S. Department of Labor proposed regulations that would amend the process by which miners apply for black lung benefits, including limiting the amount of medical evidence to be submitted by either side and allowing greater weight to the medical opinion of those physicians treating the patient who are more familiar with the black lung patient's pulmonary condition. These rules were to take effect on January 19, 2001, but on December 22, 2000, the National Mining Association (NMA) filed a lawsuit in District Court challenging the new regulations and seeking an injunction to delay the implementation of the new rules.

On February 9, 2001, the new regulations were suspended by the judge until the new Secretary of Labor, Elaine Chao, could state her position on the matter. This caused the claims of miners and survivors filed after January 19, 2001, to be halted until the lawsuit was resolved, delaying the process for many months. In the end, the Department of Labor officially sided with the black lung victims; however, the government's position was that the NMA's challenges should not be heard in court as such but should instead be raised in individual benefit claims cases. Both the UMWA and the NMA disagreed, arguing that the District Court had the power to and should settle the matter rather than allowing the issues to be resolved in individual claims cases. On August 9, 2001, District Court Judge Emmet Sullivan upheld the regulations and dissolved the injunction so that the rules could take full effect.

The NMA immediately appealed to the Court of Appeals in which the case was expedited and the parties maintained their positions each had taken in the District Court case. The Court of Appeals issued its decision on June 14, 2002, finding that the court did have the power to decide the case and, with a few minor exceptions, upholding the rules as they apply to cases filed after January 19, 2001. As for the cases filed before January 19, 2001, the court found the regulations to be generally lawful except as to a few minor exceptions. The exceptions noted by the Court of Appeals can be found either in the Court's official decision or online at the UMWA's official webpage.

See also: Brown Lung Disease; Occupationally Related Diseases; OSHA

FURTHER READING

Derickson, Alan. *Black Lung: Anatomy of a Public Health Disaster*. Ithaca, NY: Cornell University Press, 1998.
Smith, Barbara. *Digging Our Own Graves: Coal Miners and the Struggle over Black Lung Disease*. Philadelphia: Temple University Press, 1987.

ASHLEY G. BLACKBURN

BOESKY, IVAN (1937–). Ivan Boesky was considered Wall Street's lead speculator during the 1980s. Ivan Boesky was the son of a Russian immigrant who ran a number of seedy bars around Detroit. Boesky graduated from the Detroit College of Law and bounced from one job to another until he landed on Wall Street in 1966 as a stock analyst. His wife Seema was the daughter of Ben Silberstein, whose real estate fortune helped Boesky launch his own arbitrage firm in 1975. In the high-stakes, fast-paced world of Wall Street, Boesky's specialty was trading stock in companies targeted for takeover, a legal enterprise as long as the trade was based on public—not private—knowledge of imminent acquisitions.

By 1986, Ivan Boesky had become an arbitrageur who had amassed a fortune of about $200 million by betting on corporate takeovers. *Arbitrage* is defined as: (1) a transaction that generates a risk-free profit; (2) a leveraged speculative transaction; and (3) the activity of engaging in either of the above two forms of arbitrage transactions (IQPC). He was investigated by the U.S. Securities and Exchange Commission for making investments based on tips received from corporate insiders. These stock acquisitions were sometimes brazen, with massive purchases occurring only a few days before a corporation announced a takeover. Using an arbitrage fund of capital provided by limited partners, Boesky would pay more than the current trading price for a company's shares, with the expectation of selling them at a higher price once the acquisition was publicly announced. For example, Boesky and others bought a large block of shares in Gulf Western before rumors of a takeover bid drove up the price of that stock. Three days before Maxxam Group officially tendered an $800 million offer for Pacific Lumber, Boesky bought 10,000 shares of Pacific Lumber stock. Although insider trading of this kind was illegal, laws prohibiting it were rarely enforced until Boesky was prosecuted.

Boesky became a close associate of Michael Milken, who had recapitalized Boesky following a significant loss. They spoke almost daily via phone and developed a close relationship, exchanging information and favors until government investigators secured Boesky's cooperation. Boesky dealt with Milken as a client because of the latter's financial prowess. Those who worked with Milken have indicated Boesky was considered something of a nuisance, calling Milken a dozen times for each return call he got from Milken. Boesky's source of inside information from Drexel was not Milken but merger-and-acquisition specialist Dennis Levine, managing editor of Drexel Burnham Lambert, an ambitious young man who was no financial genius but who had ready access to enough of Drexel's inside doings to make him a gold mine of information to Boesky.

As head of the bond-trading department at Drexel Burnham Lambert, Milken was able to raise billions by floating new issues of the so-called "junk bonds." He then used the cash to provide financing to entrepreneurs. In essence, Milken used Boesky as a front to trade stocks in companies in which Drexel had a confidential interest, thus earning millions for both men and their respective companies. For example, Victor Posner, one of Milken's clients, wanted to take over a construction company called the Fischbach Corporation, but Posner had signed an agreement barring him from attempting a takeover unless someone else either tried first or filed a form showing ownership of 10 percent of Fischbach's stock. Milken allegedly instructed Boesky to begin buying Fischbach stock and guaranteed him against any losses he might incur. Milken, Posner, and Boesky therefore conspired to achieve the takeover of the construction company through fraudulent and deceptive means.

Milken's pioneering schemes helped Drexel Burnham Lambert become one of the leading financial firms in the United States by the late 1980s. It also made him very rich, as well as those working with and for him, such as Levine and Boesky. Milken earned $1 billion from 1983 to 1987—more than half of that in 1987 alone. On May 18, 1986, Boesky gave the commencement address at Milken's alma mater, the University of California at Berkeley's business school. "I think greed is healthy," he told his enthusiastic audience. "You can be greedy and still feel good about yourself." The sentiment would be echoed in Oliver Stone's film *Wall Street* (inspired by financial crimes such as those of Milken and Boesky), in which the motto of J. Gordon Gekko is "Greed is good."

However, the government's widespread investigation of Wall Street insider trading throughout the late 1980s gained speed when officials finally snared Boesky. It was Dennis Levine who turned Boesky in. Levine was charged with illegal trading in May 1985, and the Securities and Exchange Commission (SEC) found that Boesky had entered into a secret agreement with Drexel Burnham Lambert in 1984 to defraud their clients, trade illegally on insider information, manipulate the price of stocks, and violate a host of other securities regulations. The government proved that Boesky had been a front for a series of securities violations for which Drexel had paid him millions under the guise of consulting fees. Officials also said Boesky had helped Milken and others destroy documents that proved Drexel's involvement in illegal insider trading.

On November 14, 1986, a few months after that commencement address, the SEC charged Boesky with illegal stock manipulation based on insider information. Boesky pleaded *nolo contendere* to civil charges brought against him by the SEC. He also pleaded guilty to one count of insider trading, for which he received a three-year prison sentence in Southern

California's Lompoc Federal Prison, also known as Club Fed West. He was also barred from dealing in securities and ordered to pay $100 million in penalties—the largest amount ever levied by the SEC at the time. Boesky's plea bargain involved allowing the SEC to record his conversations with junk bond dealers and takeover artists to help the government indict other Wall Street insiders. Boesky proceeded to implicate Milken.

In 1988, federal prosecutors charged both Milken and Drexel Burnham Lambert in what was then the largest securities fraud case in history. Later that year, Drexel paid $650 million in fines to settle the charges. A year later, Milken left the firm to prepare his defense. Without Milken's controlling hand, the junk bond market crumbled, forcing Drexel Burnham Lambert to declare bankruptcy in 1990.

The fallout from the Levine, Boesky, Milken, and Drexel cases, among many others, has shaped many changes in the world of business. Many major securities firms and banks now have new rules of conduct for their employees. Several laws have been implemented to tighten securities laws and to curb corporate takeovers. The issue of business ethics, or lack thereof, has sparked much debate and changes in the business environment and curriculum at business schools across the nation.

See also: Drexel Burnham Lambert; Levine, Dennis; Milken, Michael

FURTHER READING

Bruck, C. *The Predators' Ball: The Junk-Bond Raiders and the Man Who Staked Them.* New York: Simon and Schuster, 1988.
IQPC. "Finance IQ: a Division of IQPC Conferences on Finance & Accounting." International Quality and Productivity Center. Available at http://www.iqpc.com/cgi-bin/templates/document.html?topic= 230&document=70361. Accessed September 25, 2006.
Sobel, R. *Dangerous Dreamers: The Financial Innovators from Charles Merrill to Michael Milken.* New York: Wiley, 1993.
Stewart, J. B. *Den of Thieves.* New York: Simon and Schuster, 1991.
Zey, M. *Banking on Fraud: Drexel, Junk Bonds, and Buyouts.* New York: Aldine De Gruyter, 1993.

DEBRA E. ROSS

BRAITHWAITE, JOHN (1951–). John Braithwaite is a professor in the Research School of Social Science at Australian National University and is a member of the university's Centre for Restorative Justice. His interests include business regulation and white-collar crime. Professor Braithwaite's focus for the past twenty years has been on restorative and responsive regulatory ideas. He has published numerous works either as primary author, coauthor, or editor of books and journal articles. In addition to his work with the more "traditional" forms of juvenile and adult crime, Professor Braithwaite has contributed significant research to the application of restorative justice principles to business crime.

Braithwaite's Life and Works. In the later part of the 1980s, Braithwaite wrote one of his more renowned books: *Crime, Shame and Reintegration.* In this work, he offers a theory that the key to crime control is a "cultural commitment to reintegrative shaming." Braithwaite has used several theories in formulating reintegrative shaming, including, but not limited to: labeling, subcultural, control, opportunity, and learning theories. He utilizes this work to demonstrate that current criminal justice practice creates shame that is stigmatizing to the offender and the victim alike. However, Braithwaite argues that restorative justice seeks to reintegrate the offender by acknowledging the shame of wrongdoing but then offering ways to compensate for that shame, as opposed to stigmatizing the offender. Braithwaite examines the Japanese culture (which utilizes shaming and has a low crime rate) to provide an example of reintegrative shaming.

Over the course of nearly a decade (mid-1980s to the early 1990s), he was a key figure in developing and applying restorative approaches to safety regulation in coal mining. Braithwaite worked with his wife, Valerie, and others in developing and applying restorative strategies to nursing home regulation, including the institution of exit conferences after regulatory inspections.

In addition, Braithwaite has been an active member in a wide variety of organizations. He served on the Economic Planning Advisory Council, which was chaired by the Australian Prime Minister Bob Hawke, from 1983 to 1987. Also, he served as a part-time commissioner in Australia's Trade Practices Commission from 1985 to 1995. From 1994 to 1996, Professor Braithwaite served as a member of the Council on Business Regulation, where his responsibilities included reporting directly to the Australian Cabinet on a review of all laws that impose a regulatory impact on business. In 2000, he participated in a conference in Northern Ireland that examined the possibilities for utilizing restorative justice ideas and practices in an effort to promote peace in that country.

Throughout the course of his career, Professor Braithwaite has won several accolades in both the United States and Europe from: the American Society of Criminology, the Law and Society Association, the American Sociological Association, the Society for the Study of Social Problems, the Institute for Financial Crime Prevention, and the British Socio-Legal Studies Association.

Principles of Restorative Justice. According to Braithwaite, restorative justice is primarily concerned with healing victims' wounds; however, it is also concerned with restoring offenders to law-abiding lives, while additionally mending the harm that has been done to interpersonal relationships and the community as a whole. It seeks to involve all stakeholders and provide opportunities for those most affected by the crime to be directly involved in the process of responding to the harm caused. A central premise of restorative justice is that victims, offenders, and the affected communities are all key stakeholders in the restorative process.

Mercy and forgiveness are the values that define restorative justice; however, they may be limited by the retributive quest (otherwise known as just deserts) for proportional punishment. Conversely, Braithwaite stresses that mercy and forgiveness cannot be forced from the victim. Rather, only by taking full advantage of the restorative values of empowerment and respectful communication does this afford an "open space to deal with the harm of the crime, build respect, and allow for healing." Therefore, mercy and forgiveness, through this process, become the victim's contribution. Empirical evidence in criminal justice settings suggests that offenders want to apologize to their victims and that victims desire an apology from the offender. Moreover, by directly dealing with the destructive act, the act of apology may indeed be the link to reduced recidivism for offenders, as well as empowerment for victims.

See also: Corporate Crime

FURTHER READING

Braithwaite, John. "A Study in Positive Control." *Federal Probation* Vol. 54.2 (June, 1990): 76–78.
"John Braithwaite." Prison Fellowship International. Available at http://www.restorativejustice.org/resources/leading/braithwaitej. Accessed August 7, 2006.
"Professor John Braithwaite." Australian National University. Available at http://www.anu.edu.au/fellows/jbraithwaite/index.php. Accessed August 7, 2006.

ROBERT A. SARVER III

BRE-X SCANDAL. The story of Bre-X begins with a small Canadian start up company that burst into the limelight with a claim to have discovered a mother lode of gold in Indonesia. At the time, this discovery was said to represent 8% of the world's total gold reserves. The so-called "discovery" proved to be a sham. The public announcement of the gold discovery catapulted the value of Bre-X stock in a short period of time, only to drop so rapidly, after the truth emerged, that the Toronto Stock Exchange computer system crashed as a result. Shareholders wound up losing over $3 billion, and the case precipitated a realignment of Canadian stock exchanges. Bre-X is the story of the gold discovery that never was.

In 1989, David Walsh, a stockbroker, started Bre-X Minerals Ltd. in his Calgary, Canada, basement as a subsidiary of Bresea Resources Ltd. Walsh had a checkered professional life up to that point, having being sued for $40,000 for retrading stocks that he had already sold. He declared personal bankruptcy in 1992 as a result of acquiring significant credit card debt. The company did not make any profit before 1993. But it was in that year that Walsh followed the advice of prospector John Felderhof and bought land in the headwaters of the Busang River in the steaming jungle of Borneo.

Prior to his involvement with Bre-X, Felderhof had codiscovered the Ok Tedi copper-gold mine in Papua New Guinea. He had, however, also held $19 million in options in an Australian mining company that went bankrupt before he was able to cash in the options. Several other of his projects in Indonesia had failed, leaving him penniless. Walsh and Felderhoff teamed with Filipino geologist Michael de Guzman to assess the site. De Guzman was charged with drilling to map the ore. Busang had undergone prior exploration by other mining companies with pessimistic results. The Bre-X team reported different results: most surprisingly, an early estimate of 17 million ounces of gold. Bre-X estimated that the amount of gold found would yield an annual after-tax cash flow of $10 million.

Bre-X issued over 150 press releases, presenting an ever rosier picture of core drilling results and portraying the Busang property as containing one of the largest gold deposits ever discovered. The per-share price of Bre-X stock rocketed from 50 cents in 1993 to over $200 in 1997. Bre-X developed a "gold-plated" Web site in which the great rise of Bre-X stock could be charted. Several larger mineral companies made takeover offers, as did Indonesia's President Suharto. On February 17, 1997, Bre-X announced a deal in which the company agreed to share ownership with Suharto and other Indonesian interests and hire the U.S. firm Freeport-McMoRan Copper & Gold to operate the mine. Prior to signing the contract, Freeport

35

traveled to Busang to conduct its due-diligence drilling. What they found would uncover one of the most devastating frauds of the 1990s.

The Bre-X Fraud Exposed. The first bad omen came days before the announcement of Freeport's results. On March 19, 1997, de Guzman fell to his death from his helicopter over the jungles of Borneo. He left behind ten pages of suicide notes—as well as four wives (concurrent). Two days later, Freeport revealed that due-diligence cores drilled next to the locations of Bre-X's reported drillings found no significant amounts of gold. More samples were collected and recommended by Freeport, under protest by Bre-X. Bre-X backed away from its position, however, when details of Bre-X's past methods of assaying its samples came to light. Freeport reported that there were visual differences between the gold particles taken from its samples and those in the samples submitted by Bre-X, suggesting that the Bre-X samples were deceptively "salted" with gold. Freeport withdrew from its planned partnership with Bre-X, leaving a second company hired by Bre-X to analyze the site, Strathcona Mineral Services, to report the fraud.

Ultimately, two evidence areas showed "red flags" of massive fraud. The first red flag was that the Bre-X core samples had been pulverized and prepared for assay at a testing laboratory in the jungle. Samples that normally would be sliced lengthwise, with half preserved for reference and verification, were crushed, leaving behind no verification sample. In addition, normal protocol for transport of such samples typically required the samples to be sealed to prevent tampering and, also, to be heavily guarded. Bre-X samples, however, were found to have been bagged and then shipped on a 30-hour barge trip. To assure that "all was well," the bags were subsequently opened and stored in an unguarded courtyard until the laboratory became available. A second red flag was that the Dayak people, the local inhabitants, had persistently panned for gold in the Busang River for an extended period of two years before Bre-X's discovery and had found nothing, despite Bre-X's claim that gold was visible.

Fallout and Aftermath. On May 7, 1997, three days after Strathcona Minerals publicly announced that the Bre-X claims of a great gold discovery were false, 69.3 million shares of Bre-X were traded. This was the last day of trading before Bre-X stock was removed from three stock market exchanges. The value of a share of Bre-X had gone from 30 cents in the early days of the firm, to $285.60 at its peak after the gold discovery announcement, to a mere 9 cents in the aftermath of the Strathcona report. Bre-X was forced into bankruptcy after its gold assay results were exposed as fraudulent, leaving $3 billion in shareholder losses in its wake.

Of the two remaining key players, David Walsh cashed in over $34 million worth of shares a year before Bre-X's collapse, laying the blame for the fraud on Felderhof and de Guzman. He apologized to investors, moved to the Bahamas, and died of a hemorrhage on June 4, 1998, two weeks after his assets were frozen by the Bahamas Supreme Court. Felderhof made over $87 million by selling off his Bre-X shares in 1996 and 1997, with many of the transactions occurring during the time he was also "hyping" the magnitude of the discovery of gold in Busang.

The financial fallout from this fraud was immense. Many lawsuits were filed against Bre-X. Three of the largest losses belonged to Canadian public organizations, including the Ontario Municipal Employees Retirement Board, the Quebec Public Sector Pension fund, and the Ontario Teachers Pension Plan. The Ontario Securities Commission (OSC) charged John

Felderhof with four counts of insider trading and four counts of issuing misleading press conferences. The trial began in October 2000 and experienced many delays, the most noteworthy of which was an effort of the OSC to have the presiding judge removed on the grounds of suspected bias in favor of the defense. After three and a half years of appeals, the judge was retained and the trial resumed in December of 2004. After several additional delays, the trial was resumed again in February 2005. As of the summer of 2006, the trial of John Felderhof continues, as does the story of Canada's biggest gold discovery hoax ever.

FURTHER READING

Canadian Broadcasting Company Website. "Stranger than Fiction: The Bre-X Gold Scandal." Available at http://archives.cbc.ca/IDD-1-73-1211/politics_economy/bre-X/. Accessed September 06, 2006.
Francis, Diane. *Bre-X: The Inside Story*. Toronto: Key Porter, 1997.
Goold, Douglas and Willis, Andrew. *The Bre-X Fraud*. Toronto: McClelland & Stewart, 1997.

DONALD J. REBOVICH

BROWN LUNG DISEASE. Brown lung disease (also known as byssinosis, cotton bract disease, and cotton worker's lung) is defined as an occupational respiratory disease caused by the long-term inhalation of cotton, flax, or hemp dust and characterized by shortness of breath, coughing, and wheezing. The expression *brown lung* comes from the brown dust on the leaves surrounding the cotton balls.

Dusts from hemp, flax, and cotton processing cause byssinosis, which is a chronic condition involving obstruction of the small airways that severely impairs lung function. Textile workers opening bales of raw cotton are at high risk of developing the lung disorder. Byssinosis occurs mainly in people who work with hemp, flax, or cotton dust and therefore is prevalent in the textile industry.

Symptoms. Symptoms of byssinosis include, but are not limited to, wheezing and tightness in the chest. A protracted cough may develop in the individual as well. Symptoms are usually worse at the beginning of the work week and gradually improve when the individual is away from the workplace. People who have worked with unprocessed cotton for more than one year may show symptoms the entire work week. Physicians usually ask that their patients who are suffering from byssinosis control their dust intake and refrain from smoking, which further exacerbates the symptoms. Patients with more serious symptoms may have to seek out new forms of employment. In an attempt to ease their patient's symptoms, physicians may prescribe asthma drugs (rescue inhalers) and bronchodilators, which help open the patient's airway.

In the early stages, byssinosis can lead to shortness of breath and coughing while at work (otherwise known as acute byssinosis). When the worker is removed from the dusty environment, as at home or on vacation, these symptoms improve or disappear. After approximately five years or longer of constant exposure, the worker may develop chronic byssinosis, which may lead to permanent impairment of lung function.

The inhalation of cotton dust was first identified as a source of respiratory disease more than 300 years ago. However, byssinosis has only been recognized as an occupational hazard for textile workers for less than fifty years. More than 800,000 workers in the cotton, flax, and hemp industries are exposed in the workplace to airborne particles that can cause byssinosis. Only workers in mills that manufacture yarn, thread, or fabric have a significant risk of dying of this disease.

In the United States, byssinosis is limited to workers who work with unprocessed cotton. Overall, more than 35,000 textile workers have been disabled by byssinosis and 183 workers died between 1979 and 1992. The majority of those whose deaths were due to byssinosis lived in the textile-producing regions of North Carolina and South Carolina. These deaths directly contributed to the development of the Brown Lung Association.

History of the Brown Lung Association (1974–1986). The Brown Lung Association was formed by Mike Szpak in 1974. The Association organized local divisions (which were originally located in both North Carolina and South Carolina, with other divisions formed later in Georgia and Virginia), conducted breathing clinics on textile workers, conducted media campaigns on the dangers of brown lung, lobbied for government aide for the workers, and filed workers' compensation claims on behalf of the textile employees. The Brown Lung Association's chief accomplishments included the reform of South Carolina's compensation laws, passage for more stringent federal cotton dust standards, attraction of media attention to the dangers of brown lung, and payment of workers' compensation to those employees disabled by the disease.

The Brown Lung Legal Center emerged from the Brown Lung Association's Legal Committee in the late 1970s. It focused on the legal difficulties of receiving compensation for brown lung victims. The activities of the Brown Lung Association declined during the early 1980s, primarily as a result of deteriorating economic conditions in the textile industry as well as reforms in workers' compensation laws and industrial standards. By 1986, the Brown Lung Association was virtually dormant.

With regards to frequency, severity and preventability, occupational lung disease is the primary cause of work-related illness in the United States. It is principally caused by continuing contact with irritants in the workplace (examples include mineral dust, smoke, fumes, gases, sprays, and vapors). It is possible, however, to develop occupational lung disease from several single-incidence exposures. Occupational lung disease includes diseases that are not occupation-specific but rather are aggravated at work. It also includes diseases related to a specific occupation such as asbestosis (see also **asbestos**), coal worker's pneumoconiosis (see also **black lung**), silicosis (respiratory disease caused by inhalation of silica dust, which leads to inflammation and then scarring of the lung tissue), berylliosis (allergic reaction to beryllium), and farmer's lung as well as byssinosis. In addition, lung cancer, COPD (Chronic Obstructive Pulmonary Disease), and adult-onset asthma can also be triggered by workplace exposures.

Byssinosis is different from other occupational dust diseases in that there are no characteristic chest x-ray findings. In addition, a lung biopsy does not reveal any evidence of the brown dust found on the cotton plants. Except for the work history, chronic byssinosis is indistinguishable from chronic obstructive pulmonary disease. Byssinosis is diagnosed by the work history and the presence of breathing impairment. If worsening of symptoms or airflow obstruction is apparent and can be demonstrated after the employee comes to work, the diagnosis is more reliable.

As with all occupational lung diseases, the symptoms attributable to byssinosis are worse and more prevalent in cotton workers who smoke than in nonsmoking workers. In addition, this is the case for those workers who have chronic byssinosis with irreversible airways obstruction.

See also: Asbestos; Black Lung; Occupationally Related Diseases

FURTHER READING

"A Cotton Tale: Disease and Decrees" *Science News* 119.15 (April 11, 1981): 231–232.
"Brown Lung Theory Some Don't Cotton To." *Science News* 120.15 (1981, October 10), 231.
"EPA Extends OSHA Asbestos Protection to Public Employees." *Professional Safety* 46.1 (January, 2001): 11.
"Quanta." *Sciences* 18.6 (July/August, 1978): 4–5.
University of Maryland Medical Center Website. "Lung Cancer." Available at http://www.umm.edu/altmed/ConsConditions/CancerLungcc.html. Accessed September 06, 2006.
University of North Carolina at Chapel Hill Website. Southern Historical Collection. "Brown Lung Association Records Inventory." Available at http://www.lib.unc.edu/mss/inv/b/Brown_Lung_Association. Accessed September 06, 2006.

ROBERT A. SARVER III

BUFFALO CREEK FLOOD. On February 26, 1972, the Buffalo Creek Flood, which has been called one of the worst man made disasters in history, took the lives of 125 people. The flood occurred after a dam holding coal waste broke, taking down two addition dams, releasing 132 million gallons of coal slurry waste.

In 1945 the Lorado Coal Company, in Lorado County, West Virginia, began a new mine near the town of Saunders. During the mining process, coal waste—material that is dug up but is not coal that can be commercially burned—was dumped into one of three streams, Middle Fork, which flow into Buffalo Creek. This formed what was later referred to Dam 1. In 1966, construction of a second dam, Dam 2, began farther upstream.

In 1967, after the Buffalo Mining Company purchased the Lorado Coal Company, a heavy rainfall washed away parts of Dam 2, which was still under construction, and of Dam 1, causing minor flooding. The West Virginia Department of Natural Resources identified a deficiency in Dam 2, which the company corrected. In 1968, a state engineer, following a complaint by a local resident, inspected the dams and questioned the ability of newly installed overflow pipes in Dam 2 to handle excessive runoff. As a result of the citizen's complaint, it was discovered that neither dam had received proper approval; however, the local prosecutor took no action on the two misdemeanor violations. The West Virginia Department of Natural Resources did, however, require the construction of a third dam, Dam 3.

In 1970, the Pittston Coal Company purchased the Buffalo Coal Mining Company and, a year later, completed construction of Dam 3. A year later, Dam 2 failed and was repaired, and a month later Dam 3 failed, but Dam 2 stopped the water, preventing a flood. Even though Pittston was cited for safety violations, there were no follow-up inspections.

On February 26, 1972, after a heavy rainfall, Dam 3 collapsed at 8:05 a.m. The rush of water and coal waste also took down Dams 2 and 1. Nearly three hours later, the flood waters traveled 20 miles and in its path left 125 people dead, $50 million in property damage, and approximately 4,000 people homeless.

The Pittston Coal Company immediately distanced itself from responsibility, calling the flood an "Act of God" because God had put the water behind Dam 3, which wasn't designed to hold it. West Virginia Governor Arch Moore appointed a commission to study the disaster, but the nine members of the commission were either had connections, or were sympathetic, to the coal industry. This, in conjunction with the Governor's reluctance to place blame on Pittston, lead to a request for Governor Moore to expand on the commission and include others, such as survivors and environmentalists, but he refused to do so. This led to the creation of a citizens' commission, which, along with a federal and a state commission, came to these conclusion that the company was to blame for blatantly disregarding standard safety practices.

There were no criminal prosecutions because a grand jury failed to return any indictments, even though Pittston apparently violated state and federal laws; however, there were three civil suits. *Dennis Prince et al.* v. *The Pittston Company*, a $64 million lawsuit against Pittston, involved 625 adult survivors and family members of victims. Pittston eventually settled for $13,500,000, which was half of its 1972 profits. A second civil case, *Justice v. Pittston Company*, was filed on behalf of the 348 juvenile survivors and resulted in a $4,800,000 settlement. The third lawsuit, *The State of West Virginia* v. *The Pittston Company*, asked for $100,000,000 for punitive damages and cleanup costs; however, in 1977, just three days before he left office, Governor Moore negotiated a $1 million settlement.

Today, the general idea is that improper engineering, insufficient inspections, and improper maintenance resulted in the Buffalo Creek Flood. The safety of coal slurry impoundments remains an issue today (see also **Martin County Coal Slurry Spill**), because similar spills still occur; though none have been as deadly as the Buffalo Creek flood.

FURTHER READING

"Buffalo Creek." West Virginia Division of Culture and History. Available at http://www.wvculture.org/history/buffcreek/bctitle.html. Accessed August 7, 2006.

Erikson, Kai T. *Everything in Its Path.* New York: Simon and Schuster, 1976.

Ewen, Lynda Ann, and Lewis, Julia A. "Buffalo Creek Revisited." *Appalachian Journal* 27.1 (1999): 22–45.

PAUL J. BECKER

C

CALVI, ROBERTO (1920–1982). Roberto Calvi was an Italian banker known for his involvement in the financial scandal and collapse of the Banco Ambrosiano, for his enlisting in the secret and illegal Masonic lodge known as Propaganda-2 (P2), and for his mysterious 1982 suicide.

Starting his career at Banco Ambrosiano in 1946, Calvi became its chairman in the late 1970s. In the 1960s, Calvi met Michele Sindona, a banker with strong connections with the Mafia who, in later years, would be convicted in the United States on sixty-five counts of fraud and eventually poisoned in his cell in Italy while serving a life sentence for murder. By the mid-1970s, Calvi became Sindona's protégé, and their business relationship led to creating a network of offshore corporations to launder or avoid taxation in Italy hundreds of millions of dollars. At the same time, the Vatican took advantage of Calvi's banking activities. In fact, following Sindona's advice, the Vatican Bank, whose president was the American bishop Paul Marcinkus, moved its investments offshore. By the early 1980s, the Vatican's participation in this activity allegedly exceeded $1.25 billion.

Calvi's financial network was also enriched by his affiliation with the powerful Masonic lodge known as P2. Enlisting influential businessmen, politicians, journalists, and members of the Army, the Judiciary, and the Secret Service, P2 aimed at running a "shadow government" by influencing political parties and the media. The Parliamentary Commission described it as a "state within a state." Calvi and Sindona found in P2 an ideal business partner that was willing to handle the political problems that would arise in implementing their financial plans. In exchange, Calvi funneled vast amounts of money into P2 pockets.

Calvi's scheme of transferring money offshore through dummy corporations received a setback when Sindona's own financial empire began to crumble. The collapse of the Italian bank presents a pattern consistent with the later Enron and Parmalat scandals. The money was invested in offshore companies and funds, it then disappeared into a global black hole, and when the cash flow stopped, the system broke down.

In 1981, in the midst of the irreversible collapse of Banco Ambrosiano, Calvi was convicted by an Italian court of illegal currency transactions and was afterwards indicted for embezzlement. In an effort to escape criminal prosecution and to find a new business partner willing to pour money into a dilapidated Banco Ambrosiano, Calvi fled Italy. Just a week after, on

June 18, 1982, Calvi's body was found hanging underneath the Blackfriars Bridge in London, England. Nearly a quarter-century later, the circumstances of the suicide were still unclear. Over twenty years after Calvi's death, prosecutors in Rome filed murder charges against five people, among them an Italian businessman and a convicted killer and a leading figure in the Sicilian mafia. These charges arise out a 1992 Mafia defector's testimony that Calvi had been strangled by a London-based drug dealer connected to the Mafia to prevent the banker, who had agreed to launder large quantities of drugs money for the Mafia, from skimming large profits to keep his bank afloat. The trial began in December 2005. Bishop Marcinkus died in Arizona in February 2006.

FURTHER READING

Cornwell, Rupert. *God's Banker: An Account of the Life and Death of Roberto Calvi*. New York: Dodd, Mead, 1983.

Gurwin, Larry. *The Calvi Affair: Death of a Banker*. London: Macmillan London, 1983.

Raw, Charles. *The Moneychangers: How the Vatican Bank Enabled Roberto Calvi to Steal $250 Million for the Heads of the P2 Masonic Lodge*. London: Collins Harvill, 1992.

"Scandal-Hit Vatican Banker Dies." *BBC News Online* (February 21, 2006). Available at http://news.bbc.co.uk/2/hi/europe/4737052.stm. Accessed September 25, 2006.

ANDREA BOGGIO

C-5A TRANSPORT AIRCRAFT. The C-5A transport aircraft is the second largest airplane in the world. It was originally conceptualized in the 1960s, when the U.S. military establishment hoped to create a fleet of aircraft that could move large numbers of troops and equipment to any place in the world within a matter of days. Though critics charged that such a move would upset the world military balance and possibly cause more harm than good, the U.S. Air Force invested money in three companies to develop proposals for a new fleet of aircraft.

Boeing, Lockheed, and Douglas, the three companies involved in the original bidding process, projected program costs of $2.3 billion, $2.0 billion, and $1.9 billion, respectively for the fleet of planes. The design offered by Boeing was originally accepted but later overruled in favor of Lockheed. Several competing hypotheses have been offered to explain why Lockheed was awarded the contract. One prominent argument is that the Department of Defense wanted to retain Lockheed as a defense contractor in current and future projects. In fact, Lockheed was the government's primary producer of Poseidon and Polaris missiles. Had Lockheed not won the contract, thousands of people at Lockheed's Marietta, Georgia, plant would have been forced to find new jobs.

In November 1968, A. Ernest Fitzgerald, a civilian cost analyst for the Air Force, testified before a Congressional subcommittee that the 120 C-5A cargo jets ordered by the Air Force would cost $2 billion more than anticipated and that the increased expense was partially the result of financial mismanagement. By early 1969, Lockheed's original program cost of $16.5 million per aircraft was increased to $40 million. At the height of the Vietnam War, cost overruns and waste were business as usual in the industries that manufactured the arms of war. According to the contract, two production runs would occur; the first would be priced according to the original bid. The second production run would incorporate the costs from the previous run.

During the initial production run, Lockheed sent a year-end financial report to the Air Force showing no serious problems in the cost of the program. However, when the Air Force sent a team to Lockheed's production plant to examine the financial data, it was discovered that the company was facing a potential loss of $316 million. Only months earlier, a report from then Secretary of Defense Robert S. McNamara claimed that Lockheed faced increased program costs totaling $240 million.

The exact figures for the program overrun were difficult to determine. However, the financial collapse of the program was public knowledge inside the office of the Secretary of Defense. This led many to conclude that Lockheed was attempting to conceal the enormous additional costs of the program in hopes of making a profit during the second phase of production.

As further reference to the possibility of a multimillion-dollar cover-up, the March 1968 ceremony for the formal launching of the C-5A included large press kits stating that the larger-than-life plane had met all cost and production expectations. In one sense, Lockheed was correct. Through a series of lengthy cost reviews, budget modifications, and deletion or omission of financial data, it was possible to conceal the fact that production costs had exceeded established ceiling costs by hundreds of millions of dollars.

Despite inaccurate cost figures, the U.S. Air Force finalized commencement of the second production run in January 1969. All that remained was for Congress to allocate the money. At that time, however, stories of the waste and fraud in the C-5A program started to surface. An investigation into defense spending by the General Accounting Office (GAO) reported that the Air Force paid $317.79 for the toilet pan used on the C-5A. The GAO report also revealed that a common Allen wrench, one of the tools kept onboard the aircraft, cost $9,606. The Allen wrench could have been purchased for less than $1.00 at a hardware store.

Other stories of gross financial abuse included payments for $400 hammers and $7,400 coffee makers. Interestingly, the official reason why the coffee maker for the C-5A aircraft cost so much was because it had been designed to withstand 17 Gs. However, the wings of the plane were not able to withstand the same amount of force. The C-5A entered production before the aircraft was fully tested, which led to a 12-year wing modification program and close to $1.3 billion to correct.

See also: Lockheed Bribing Scandal

FURTHER READING

Fitzgerald, A. E. *The Pentagonists: An Insider's View of Waste, Mismanagement and Fraud in Defense Spending.* Boston, MA: Houghton-Mifflin, 1989.

Hadley, A. T. *The Straw Giant.* New York: Avon Books, 1987.

Rice, B. *The C-5A Scandal.* Boston, MA: Houghton Mifflin, 1971.

The Bisplinghoff Report: Report of the Ad Hoc Committee of the Air Force Scientific Advisory Board on the C-5A, June 1970.

The Whitaker Report: USAF Review of the C-5A Program, July 1969.

ADAM DULIN

CHEMICAL CRIMES. Chemical crimes are acts or omissions during the production, distribution, use, storage, or disposal of chemicals that can reasonably be expected to result in harm to people's health or safety or to the environment itself. The term was developed by Critical Criminology theorists as an alternative to the traditional legal standard of crime, which defines offenses according to criminal law. Chemical crimes occur when (1) the chemical in question can be reasonably expected to cause harm through its production, distribution, use, storage, or disposal; (2) the harm caused by the chemical is comparable to that caused by other types of legally defined crimes (i.e., those reported in the Uniform Crime Report); (3) the producers or users of the chemical have knowledge of the risks that it creates, and/or are indifferent to these risks; and (4) the harm in question can be avoided through the use of alternative technologies. Research on chemical crimes takes four forms.

The first line of research examines definitional aspects of chemical crimes and places emphasis on how power relations shape the social construction of crime. Following an argument popularized by Richard Quinney in the *Social Reality of Crime*, this literature argues that the definition of chemical crimes, like that of other crimes, is constructed in a collective process that appears neutral yet is influenced by politically and economically powerful groups. Specifically, chemical manufacturers play an important role in the social construction of chemical crimes by presenting an image to the public that they protect health by working to develop environmentally friendly practices. This may be accomplished through making small environmental concessions (such as McDonald's decision to stop using styrofoam to package its food products) in order to appease the public's concern, and by using media campaigns designed to make the company appear to be concerned with the environment and the public health. This tactic has been described in the environmental literature as "greenwashing."

A second approach focuses on media coverage of chemical crimes. Scholars who examine this issue have found that while street crime is frequently depicted in the media, little media attention is focused on corporate or business crime, including chemical crimes. Media research on crime reporting addresses social construction arguments and illustrates how the news media shape public opinion concerning the "nature" of crime in our society by excluding coverage of chemical crimes. In many instances, chemical crimes are rationalized by corporate representatives (and environmental regulations) as unfortunate "accidents" even though there may have been a conscious corporate decision to select (typically because of cost) a specific production technology that made the accident more likely. When examining media reports of chemical crimes, researchers find that even when these crimes produce serious harm (e.g., death and injury), they are much less likely to be covered by major newspapers than serious street crime (e.g., homicides, rapes, and robberies).

The third line of chemical crime research focuses on identifying chemicals known to cause harm. The goal of this research is to demonstrate ways in which criminologists can employ medical evidence to identify toxic harms where other forms of data (e.g., standardized measures such as the Uniform Crime Reports) do not exist. This line of research also centers on known technologies that are in use and could, if implemented, reduce the risk of chemical harms. Dioxin, for example, is a chemical waste product that results from the production of chlorine, pesticides, polyvinyl chloride, and paper and from waste incineration. Dioxin is a recognized carcinogen and is thought to be an endocrine disrupter that prevents normal development in animals and humans. The paper pulp industry is one of the largest producers of dioxin in the world. Researchers argue that significant reductions in dioxin could be achieved if paper producers would employ existing chlorine-free paper technology. Some segments of the paper industry have responded to the medical research and converted production to incorporate chlorine-free paper production technology. However, researchers studying chemical crimes have noted that much of the paper industry continues to lobby against chlorine-free technologies and actively participates in and provides funding for the dissemination of misinformation concerning the dangers of dioxin.

Finally, researchers have also examined chemical crimes in relation to the notion of environmental justice. Environmental justice focuses on production processes and the ways that community racial, class, and ethnic composition is related to the spatial proximity of communities to toxic chemical production, storage, disposal, and treatment facilities. Environmental justice research has demonstrated that community race, class, and ethnic characteristics are important determinants of proximity to hazardous waste locations, which has important implications for the study of chemical crimes. First, this research indicates that proximity to chemical hazards is influenced by community race and class characteristics, which also reflect the social and economic power communities wield. Second, this research illustrates that community power structures are important determinants of the likelihood that members of a community will be victims of chemical crimes. Third, this research raises the possibility that corporations target less powerful communities as sites for chemical crimes. Fourth, this research demonstrates that race and class membership affect the likelihood that an individual will become the victim of a chemical crime. Finally, because chemical crime exposure is influenced by community race and class characteristics, this raises the need to study associated health and behavioral problems, some of which are thought to be connected to involvement in street crime. For example, chemical crime researchers believe that chemical toxins not only have health impacts that relate to disease prevalence and incidence but also may have impacts on learning capabilities, ability to cope with frustration, attention deficit disorder, hyperactivity, and other biological, behavioral, psychological, and developmental factors that have been specified as causes of criminal behavior. Chemical crime researchers argue that the spatial distribution of various chemicals may alter behavior by adversely impacting biological development and elevate crime rates in exposed communities.

See also: Environmental White-Collar Crime; Media Portrayal of White-Collar Crime; Seveso Dioxin Disaster; Union Carbide

FURTHER READING

Del Olmo, Rosa. "The Ecological Impact of Illicit Drug Cultivation and Crop Eradication Programs in Latin America." *Theoretical Criminology* 2 (1998) 28–44.

Fagin, Dan, and Lavelle, Marianne. *Toxic Deception: How the Chemical Industry Manipulates Science, Bends the Law and Endangers Your Health*, 2nd edition. Monroe, ME: Common Courage Press, 1999.

Gibbs, Lois. *Dying from Dioxin: A Citizen's Guide to Reclaiming Our Health and Rebuilding Democracy.* Boston: South End Press, 1995.

Greer, Jed, and Bruno, Kenny. *Greenwash: The Reality Behind Corporate Environmentalism.* New York: Apex Press, 1996.

Lynch, Michael J., and Stretesky, Paul B. "Toxic Crimes: Examining Corporate Victimization of the General Public Employing Medical and Epidemiological Evidence." *Critical Criminology* 10 (2002): 153–172.

Lynch, Michael J., Stretesky, Paul B., and Hammond, Paul. "Media Coverage of Chemical Crimes, Hillsborough County, Florida, 1987–1997." *British Journal of Criminology* 40 (2000): 112–126.

Pearce, Frank, and Tombs, Steve. *Toxic Capitalism: Corporate Crime and the Chemical Industry.* Brookfield, VT: Ashgate, 1998.

Stretesky, Paul B., and Lynch, Michael J. "Environmental Justice and the Prediction of Distance to Accidental Chemical Releases in Hillsborough County, Florida." *Social Science Quarterly* 80 (1999): 830–846.

Stretesky, Paul B., and Lynch, Michael J. "The Relationship between Lead and Homicide." *Archives of Pediatric and Adolescent Medicine* 155 (2001) 579–582.

Stretesky, Paul B., and Lynch, Michael J. "Environmental Hazards and School Segregation in Hillsborough, 1987–1999." *Sociological Quarterly* 43 (2003): 553–573.

PAUL B. STRETESKY
MICHAEL J. LYNCH

CHEVROLET CORVAIR. On October 2, 1959, General Motors' Chevrolet division introduced the 1960 Corvair automobile. This vehicle included an innovative design, similar to some European cars of the time, which placed the engine in the rear of the vehicle. In 1966, a book by a young Harvard Law School graduate named Ralph Nader detailed the dangers of the Corvair as well as the reluctance of the automotive industry to spend money on improving safety. The vehicle's design became the focus of safety issues previously unaddressed by the automotive industry, government, or public.

Prior to the 1960s, the automotive industry operated with minimal government or public oversight. Automobile designs, while similar in body style, varied between make and model and focused on making the car as economical as possible to manufacture, with little emphasis on safety features. Some general features with safety issues included light-colored dashboards that reflected on the windshield, causing the driver's view to be impaired; gear shift patterns with no standardization; dashboard knobs that were identical in appearance and indistinguishable to the driver; steering columns in positions that made them life-threatening in a collision; and a lack of safety restraint systems (unless the purchaser opted to add seat belts for an additional cost).

Nader's book *Unsafe at Any Speed* brought national attention to the automobile industry. The first chapter of the book focused specifically on the Corvair. The Corvair's rear suspension in the 1960–1963 models was alleged to "tuck in," causing the car to fishtail and flip over when cornering sharply. Nader detailed crash incidents that indicated the Corvair was unsafe as well as design flaws that made it so. In response to the publication, General Motors executives hired private detectives to delve into Nader's personal life and follow him. These actions appeared to lend credence to his claims, and revelations of the situation led to GM president James Roche appearing before a congressional committee and publicly apologizing to Nader.

On March 22, 1965, the Senate Subcommittee on Executive Reorganization, Committee on Government Operations, began a long-range series of hearings on the federal role in traffic safety. The Subcommittee Chairman was Senator Abraham Ribicoff. The hearings and resultant public interest contributed to the passage of two new auto safety laws (the National Traffic and Motor Vehicle Safety Act of 1966 and the Highway Safety Act of 1966) and also the creation of the National Highway Safety Bureau, which, under the Highway Safety Act of 1970, was renamed the National Highway Traffic Safety Administration (NHTSA).

The Corvair was a catalyst for consumer protection efforts in the automotive industry and led other industries to follow suit. Ultimately, the automotive industry was scrutinized as a whole for dismissing the necessity of automobile safety and placing blame for accidents primarily on consumers. The circumstances surrounding the Corvair paved the way for corporate change, shifting the industry away from the accepted culture of apathy and toward implementation of vehicle safety measures. Ironically, the NHTSA eventually opened an investigation into the Corvair and concluded that it was no more prone to accidents and rollovers than other cars of that time period.

FURTHER READING

Nader, Ralph. *Unsafe At Any Speed: The Designed-In Dangers of the American Automobile.* New York, NY: Grossman Publishers, 1965.

U.S. Department of Transportation, Federal Highway Administration. *President Dwight D. Eisenhower and the Federal Role in Highway Safety.* May 2005. Federal Highway Administration. Available at http://www.fhwa.dot.gov/infrastructure/safetyep.htm.

SANDRA H. HAANTZ

CITIBANK AND MISDIRECTED RUSSIAN IMF LOANS. After the end of the Cold War, Russia's financial crisis became a catalyst for a variety of white-collar crimes within the United States, and the estimated $500 billion to $1 trillion moved through banks annually from international criminal proceeds increased the vulnerability of American banks. Since the United States was a substantial contributor to international financial aid organizations, it provided its own governmental aid, and private American corporations invested in Russia, the looting of Russia's aid packages resulted in white-collar crimes committed in the United States and generated Congressional and criminal investigations. Major American banks, such as Citibank and Bank of New York, were entangled with Russia's capital flight and money laundering problems and, in the process, violated banking and anti–money laundering laws within the United States.

The Russian Federation experienced an increase in crime, capital flight, banking crises, and destabilization of the ruble during the transition into a capitalist economy. In money laundered related capital flight, Russia lost an estimated $133 billion between 1992 and 1997. To help stabilize the region, Russia and other Central and Eastern European countries received diverse aid packages from the international community. The aid included multinational financial aid, such as loans from the World Bank and International Monetary Fund (IMF), bilateral assistance from nongovernmental organizations (NGOs), and financial and technical support from various governmental agencies and corporations. Russia was plagued with corruption and criminals who fleeced the county.

In 1999, a scandal broke involving Russia, misdirected IMF funds, Western banks, and money laundering. The U.S. Congress began investigating the money laundering allegations and misuse of IMF funding. Oligarchs, businessmen, officials, and criminals moved money and IMF funds out of Russia via money laundering techniques, the Central Bank of the Russian Federation, Western banks, and offshore and private investment firms. Russia provided easy entry ports for illegally gained funds, and the banks reaped profits from the accounts. The siphoned funds and capital flight totaled in the billions. The American bank most associated with the laundered funds from Russia was the Bank of New York; however, there were many other American and Western banks involved, including Citibank, a division of Citigroup.

International Monetary Fund (IMF). The purpose of the IMF loans was to stabilize the Russian ruble, lessen the effects of the economic crisis, enhance infrastructures, and subsidize the government to make up for tax collections shortages. The Central Bank received the aid and then distributed it to the government, Russian banks, and accounts at the Central Bank's offshore firm Fimaco. In 1996, Russia hid part of its currency reserves in Fimaco to mislead the IMF and secure more loans.

The Central Bank issued special licenses to politically connected Russian banks so that the banks and their clients could participate in international banking activities and the distribution of the IMF loans. Many of these banks had substantial ties to organized crime, such as Mikhail Khodorkovsky's Bank Menatep. Three multimillion transfers, marked as a payment for improvements to Russia's automotive industry infrastructure, originated from Bank Menatep and were deposited into American bank accounts. Additionally, Semyon Mogilevich, known as the Godfather of Russian organized crime, used banks in Russia and the northeastern United States to move hundreds of millions of dollars, including funds linked to Russian "quasi-governmental" organizations.

Russia had lax accounting procedures, and IMF loans could not be tracked after the money was transferred to the Central Bank; therefore, conclusively determining whether specific wire transfers from Russian to American banks contained IMF funds is difficult. Additionally, the Yeltsin administration and the Duma were reluctant to pass anti–money laundering laws, thus making the IMF loans vulnerable. As early as 1993, American intelligence believed that the KGB, oligarchs, and corrupt government officials were laundering Western aid and loan money out of Russia as soon as it entered the country by converting it to hard currency and then shipping it to foreign and offshore accounts.

The Central Bank used very little of the financial aid to support the ruble, pay salaries, improve the world's confidence in Russia, or improve infrastructures. Instead, funds were used to help finance President Yeltsin's campaign (linked to corruption and criminals) and were transferred to overseas accounts; at least $2.9 billion of IMF loans may be housed in offshore banks, and a former Russian prosecutor general alleged that $3.9 billion of a 1998 $4.8 billion IMF bailout never reached Russia. Representatives from the IMF and the World Bank could account for 2 to 3 billion rubles that were used to support Russian agriculture. Less than 10 percent of a 1998 $4.4 billion dollar payment was used to support the ruble. The Central Bank transferred the bulk of the $4.4 billion to Russian banks so that the banks could convert short-term loans known as GKOs (for *Gosudarstvennoe Kratkosrochnoe Obyazatelstvo*, "state treasury bonds") to hard currency before the government defaulted on the GKO. At one point the GKO market, characterized as a pyramid scheme, had a rate of return of almost 300 percent and was covered by IMF loans.

More than $10 billion passed through the Bank of New York, and $1.4 billion passed through Citibank of New York and Commercial Bank of San Francisco. After the 1998 bank crisis, IMF lending, in its current form, was suspended. Nevertheless, the IMF stated that there was no evidence to support claims that IMF's loan disbursements, made during the 1998 crisis, were diverted.

Irakly Kaveladze and Citibank. In 1991 Irakly Kaveladze, a Georgian-born businessman, immigrated to the United States and established International Business Creations (IBC). A few years later, Kaveladze created Euro-American Corporate Services, Inc., located in Delaware, to form more than 2,000 corporations for Russian and other Eastern European brokers. Kaveladze charged his clients $350 for each incorporation and $450 to open a bank account. As a formality, employees of IBC/Euro-American visited the Delaware office once every three months. IBC had all phone calls and mail forwarded to an office in New York. From 1991 until 2000, Kaveladze opened approximately 136 accounts for himself or clients of IBC/Euro-American and assisted 50 nonresident aliens to open credit card accounts at Citibank of New York. The addresses listed on the bank and credit card accounts were IBC/Euro-American's business address. The accounts yielded more than $300,000 in profits for Citibank. Kaveladze opened an additional 100 accounts at Commercial Bank of San Francisco for his clients.

The president of IBC/Euro-American stated the purpose of the accounts at Citibank of New York and Commercial Bank of San Francisco was to move money out of Russia. From 1991 to 2000, more than $800 million passed through IBC/Euro-American related accounts at Citibank of New York. Four of IBC/Euro-American's Citibank accounts processed approximately $280 million alone. The funds originated in foreign countries, including Russia, they were deposited into the accounts at Citibank through wire transfers, and then over 70 percent of the funds were transferred out of the U.S. banking system to foreign countries and money laundering havens.

Citibank's Actions and Responses. Citibank agreed to open the questionable accounts based on the assurance that Kaveladze knew the officers of the Russian companies and that they would appear in person to provide the required documents within thirty days of opening the account. Account holders are required to present two forms of identification and incorporation papers when they open the accounts, and financial institutions are to perform background checks on account holders and verify the legality of the funds. IBC/Euro-American had supposedly performed background checks, when required by law, on the companies and the officers. Citibank of New York accepted the word of IBC/Euro-American and did not perform due diligence. The accounts were fully functional, including international wire transfer capabilities, during the 30-day grace period. Moreover, Citibank did not close any of the accounts within four months when account holders failed to appear with the required documentation.

John Reed, then Co-Chief Executive of Citibank, acknowledged that the bank was slow to take appropriate actions, had weak controls, and did not follow their policy to know more about their wealthier clients. Citibank also acknowledged that a U.S. branch allowed $725 million of questionable Russian funds to flow through the accounts associated with Kaveladze. In

1996, the bank's compliance unit detected questionable transactions to or from offshore, high risk jurisdictions and monitored the credit card accounts. The compliance unit closed the credit card accounts. However, Citibank of New York resisted the recommendation of closing most of the bank accounts for four more years.

Citibank failed to conduct due diligence on the IBC/Euro-American accounts, did not follow "know your customer" policies, and violated money laundering provisions of the Bank Secrecy Act, which requires banks to identify and report suspicious activities. Citibank conceded that oversights, such as relying on Kaveladze's word concerning client's background checks, allowing account holders to fail to appear in person, not questioning the large number of the accounts at one address, and not closing the accounts when their own compliance unit advised the closures, occurred in the IBC/Euro-American case. The U.S. Congress had investigated Citibank for similar violations prior to the bank's actions with the Russian and Kaveladze accounts.

Citibank's Additional Russian Activities. Beyond opening accounts in the United States, Citibank was involved in several other activities in Russia. In 1994, Citibank opened the first fully foreign-owned commercial bank in Russia, offering Russian businesses investment banking, financial advisory, financing, and other services. Citibank, along with other major American banks and the U.S. Federal Reserve, provided technical support and had an advisory role with its participation in the Russian-American Bankers Forum. The Forum's purpose was to help with the restructuring of Russia's financial system. Like many other Western banks, Citibank invested in Russia's GKO market. When the market collapsed in 1998, Citibank lost hundreds of millions of dollars. Citibank also participated in nonresident, "S-special" accounts and purchased 4.8 million shares of LUKoil's stock for 1 billion rubles. In order to circumvent tighter controls on limiting capital flight, Russian companies, including companies involved in the controversial loans-for-shares program, would sell shares of their companies, in rubles, to foreign companies and banks. Then the Russian company would buy the same shares back in hard currencies. The funds would remain in overseas, S-Special accounts. The transactions allowed companies to have sizable accounts in foreign banks and to participate in the proliferation of capital flight.

Citibank Private Bank and Its Other Customers. In 1999, Citibank Private Bank had 40,000 clients and accounted for approximately 2.5 percent of Citigroup's business. Private Banks are usually banks within larger banks and offer a one-on-one private banker to manage the assets within the account and provide a variety of services. Clients included honest wealthy individuals, but also corrupt politicians and criminals. Many of the larger and more notorious cases of money laundering and capital flight were through accounts in Private Banks.

The private banking industry is competitive, and returns on the accounts are lucrative. Generally, the accounts usually have more than $1 million in assets ($3 million or more for Citibank Private Bank), which can include property, stocks, arts, or valuables as well as money. The services offered to the client include private trusts, estate planning, tax assistance, financial advice, loans, international wire transfers, offshore accounts, shell companies (known as private investment corporations), secret accounts, and code names. Secrecy and privacy are of paramount importance. Private banking can also conceal the source, routing, and destination of funds that may have been gained through illegal activity. In the United States, banks are forbidden to handle the proceeds of drug trafficking, kidnapping, bank fraud, and other criminal activities. Private banking allows wealthy and powerful clients to conduct business in ways that are permissible abroad and offshore but prohibited in the United States. After the Bank of New York scandal, and after billions of dollars were siphoned out of Russia, the U.S. Senate's Permanent Subcommittee on Investigations and the House's General Accounting Office (GAO) investigated American banks and private banks, in particular Citibank Private Bank, to determine whether they are susceptible to money laundering and whether they may not have failed to report suspicious activities.

Citibank Private Bank has approximately 350 clients that are officials and their families. More notable clients include Asif Ali Zardari, the former Prime Minister of Pakistan's spouse, imprisoned for kickbacks and money laundering; Omar Bongo, President of Gabon, investigated for bribery; Mohammed and Ibrahim Abacha, sons of the former military leader of Nigeria, one of whom was imprisoned for murder and investigated in two countries for money laundering; the daughters of Radon Suharto, the former President of Indonesia who allegedly looted billions of dollars from Indonesia; former Chilean dictator Augusto Pinochet and his family, who had 63 accounts at Citibank New York and Citibank Miami; and Raul Salinas, brother to the former President of Mexico, who, with other members of his family, moved between $80 to $100 million through accounts at Citibank Mexico, Citibank New York, Cititrust (Cayman Islands), Citibank London, and Citibank Switzerland. Citibank assisted Salinas and his wife in setting up an offshore private investigation company, allowed Salinas and his wife to use aliases in Mexico, and wired funds from Citibank Mexico to Citibank New York before moving the funds offshore. Additionally, Citibank failed to generate a financial and banking profile, in accordance to its own "know your customer" policy.

FURTHER READING

Beckett, Paul. "Citigroup Concedes Lapses in Oversight Tied to $725 Million of Russian Funds." *Wall Street Journal* (November 29, 2000): C.1.

Block, Alan A., and Weaver, Constance A. *All Is Clouded by Desire: Global Banking, Money Laundering, and International Organized Crime*. Westport, CT and London: Praeger, 2004.

Bonner, Raymond. "Laundering of Money Seen as 'Easy.'" *New York Times* (November 29, 2000): C.1.

"Citigroup - Russia." May 2005. Citigroup. Available at http://www.citigroup.com/citigroup/global/rus.htm.

Gerth, Jeff. "Citigroup Head Concedes Laundering Controls Were Poor." *New York Times* (November 10, 1999): 6.

O'Hara, Terence. "6 U.S. Banks Held Pinochet's Accounts: Senate Report Details 'Secret Web.'" *Washington Post* (March 16, 2005): E03.

Powell, Bill. "Where Did Russia's Money Go?" *Newsweek International* (October 4, 1999).

Solongo, Dolgor. *Global Programme against Money-Laundering: Russian Capitalism and Money-Laundering*. New York: United Nations, 2001.

United States Congress. House. Committee on Banking and Financial Services. *Russian Money Laundering: Hearings before the Committee on Banking and Financial Services, U.S. House of Representatives, One Hundred Sixth Congress, First Session, September 21, 22, 1999*. Washington, DC: U.S. Government Printing Office, 2000.

United States Congress. Senate. Committee on Governmental Affairs. Permanent Subcommittee on Investigations. *Private Banking and Money Laundering: A Case Study of Opportunities and Vulnerabilities. November 9 and 10, 1999.* Washington, DC: U.S. Government Printing Office, 2000.

U.S. General Accounting Office (GAO). *Suspicious Bank Activities: Possible Money Laundering by U.S. Corporations for Russian Entities.* Washington, DC: GAO, 2000.

Wedel, Janine R. *Collision and Collusion: The Strange Case of Western Aid to Eastern Europe, 1989–1998.* 1st edition. New York: Palgrave, 2001.

SHARON ANNE MELZER

CONTROL FRAUD THEORY. Control fraud theory was developed in the savings and loan debacle. It explained that the person controlling the S&L (typically the CEO) posed a unique risk because he could use it as a "weapon." The theory synthesized criminology (Wheeler and Rothman 1982), economics (Akerlof 1970), accounting, law, finance, and political science. It explained *how* a CEO optimized "his" S&L as a weapon to loot creditors and shareholders. The weapon of choice was accounting fraud. The company is the perpetrator and a victim.

Control frauds are optimal looters because the CEO has four unique advantages. He uses his ability to hire and fire to suborn internal and external controls and make them allies. Control frauds consistently get "clean" opinions for financial statements that show record profitability when the company is insolvent and unprofitable. CEOs choose top-tier auditors. Their reputation helps deceive creditors and shareholders.

Only the CEO can optimize the company for fraud. He has it invest in assets that have no clear market value. Professionals evaluate such assets—allowing the CEO to hire ones who will inflate values. Rapid growth (as in a Ponzi scheme) extends the fraud and increases the "take." S&Ls optimized accounting fraud by loaning to uncreditworthy and criminal borrowers (who *promised* to pay the highest rates and fees because they did not intend to repay, but the promise sufficed for the auditors to permit booking the profits). The CEO extends the fraud through "sales" of the troubled assets to "straws" that transmute losses into profits. Accounting fraud produced *guaranteed record profits—and losses.*

CEOs have the unique ability to convert company assets into personal funds through normal corporate mechanisms. Accounting fraud causes stock prices to rise. The CEO sells shares and profits. The successful CEO receives raises, bonuses, perks, and options and gains in status and reputation.

Audacious CEOs use political contributions to influence the external environment to aid fraud by fending off the regulators. Charitable contributions aid the firm's legitimacy and the CEO's status.

S&L CEOs were able to loot the assets of large, rapidly growing organizations for many years. They used accounting fraud to mimic legitimate firms, and the markets did not spot the fraud. The steps that maximized their accounting profits maximized their losses, which dwarfed all other forms of property crimes combined.

While agreeing that the S&L served as both a "weapon" and a "shield," control fraud theory cast doubt on those metaphors. Weapons and shields are visible; fraud is deceitful. The better metaphors would be camouflage, or a virus. Control fraud theorists rejected the economists' metaphor, "gambling for resurrection" (honest but unlucky risk takers). Gambling cannot explain why control fraud was invariably present at the typical large failure. There were over 1,000 felony convictions of senior S&L insiders. Accounting fraud made control fraud a sure thing—*not* a gamble. Control fraud theory predicts the pattern of record profits and catastrophic failure and the business pattern of deliberately making bad loans. Both patterns are inconsistent with honest gambling.

The identification of the S&L "high fliers" as control frauds and understanding that they were Ponzi schemes relying on accounting fraud led to effective regulatory strategies against the wave of S&L frauds. The Federal Home Loan Bank Board reregulated the industry, curbing growth (a Ponzi scheme's Achilles heel) while the control frauds were still reporting record profits and were praised by top economists.

The second use of control fraud theory was to analyze the structures that produced criminogenic environments that led to waves of control fraud. Deregulation and desupervision of the S&L industry, combined with the industry's mass insolvency, optimized accounting fraud and made "systems capacity" limitations critical. The mass insolvency maximized "reactive" control fraud, and the deregulation, desupervision, and mass insolvency maximized entry into the industry by "opportunistic" control frauds.

Fraud waves can cause financial bubbles to hyperinflate (e.g., Texas real estate during the debacle) and cause regional or systemic injury (e.g., during Russia's "shock therapy," the failures of "the Washington consensus," and the U.S. high-tech bubble). Control frauds cause indirect losses by corrupting politicians and professionals and betraying trust. When control fraud becomes endemic, it can lock nations in long-term poverty.

Control fraud theory poses a fundamental challenge to the core models of finance and economics. The efficient markets (and contracts) hypothesis requires that markets be able to identify and exclude control frauds, and the dominant law and economics model asserts that they do so effectively and quickly. This claim is largely premised on the view that no top-tier audit firm would give a clean opinion to a control fraud. Control frauds have consistently falsified this claim. Deposit insurance was not the key to S&L control fraud. Control frauds deceive "creditors at risk." High reported profits allow them to grow rapidly by borrowing and issuing stock.

To date, most of the work in control fraud discusses looting by the CEO. However, it also exists in government when the head of state uses the government to defraud. It can be used to defraud customers (e.g., "lemons" scams, in which quality or quantity is misrepresented, or cartels) and the public (e.g., tax fraud or a toxic waste firm that gains a cost advantage by dumping in the stream). These forms of control fraud create real profits and, absent effective enforcement, create a dynamic that causes fraud to spread. Systems capacity problems can lead to endemic control fraud in an industry.

See also: Criminogenic Industry; Ponzi, Charles

FURTHER READING

Akerlof, George. "The Market for 'Lemons': Quality, Uncertainty, and the Market Mechanism." *Quarterly Journal of Economics* 84.3 (1970): 488–500.

Akerlof, George A., and Romer, Paul M. "Looting: The Economic Underworld of Bankruptcy for Profit." *Brookings Papers on Economic Activity* 2 (1993): 1–73.

Black, William K. "Reexamining the Law-and-Economics Theory of Corporate Governance." *Challenge* 46.2 (2003): 22–40.

Black, William K. *The Best Way to Rob a Bank Is to Own One: How Corporate Executives and Politicians Looted the S&L Industry.* Austin: University of Texas Press, 2005.

Black, William K., Calavita, Kitty, and Pontell, Henry N. "The Savings and Loan Debacle of the 1980's: White-Collar Crime or Risky Business?" *Law and Policy* 17 (1995): 23–55.

Calavita, Kitty, Pontell, Henry N., and Tillman, Robert H. *Big Money Crime: Fraud and Politics in the Savings and Loan Crisis.* Berkeley and Los Angeles: University of California Press, 1997.

Easterbrook, Frank H., and Fischel, Daniel R. *The Economic Structure of Corporate Law.* Cambridge, MA: Harvard University Press, 1991.

National Commission on Financial Institution Reform, Recovery and Enforcement (NCFIRRE). *Origins and Causes of the S&L Debacle: A Blueprint for Reform, a Report to the President and Congress of the United States.* Washington, DC: Government Printing Office, 1993.

Wheeler, Stanton, and Rothman, Mitchell Lewis. "The Organization as Weapon in White Collar Crime." *Michigan Law Review* 80.7 (1982): 1403–1426.

WILLIAM K. BLACK

CORPORATE CRIME. Corporate crime includes violations of federal or state laws that are committed by employees on behalf of the company rather than simply for their own gain. Employees may commit such violations in order to reduce their companies' costs or to increase sales or prices of products, both of which increase corporate profits. Examples include failing to install or properly operate pollution control equipment as required by environmental laws, defrauding the government on a military supply contract, exposing workers to unsafe workplaces in violation of occupational safety and health laws, selling dangerous or defective products in violation of consumer protection laws, and conspiring with competitor firms to charge higher prices to customers than would be possible under true competition in the marketplace.

Although misconduct in pursuit of business purposes has been committed throughout commercial history, in the United States it first became a matter of wide public concern in the late nineteenth century, during the peak era of American industrialization. The aggressive and often corrupt business practices of the so-called Robber Barons created virtual monopolies (trusts) in such industries as oil and sugar, whereas railroads engaged in price discrimination that favored large companies over small producers. These trusts and behaviors spurred popular opposition that led ultimately to the creation of the first independent federal regulatory agency in 1887—the Interstate Commerce Commission to regulate railroads' rates—and to the passage of the first major corporate crime law in the United States in 1890: the federal Sherman Antitrust Act, which outlawed monopolies and conspiracies that limited competition.

Other early federal legislation included the Pure Food and Drug Act and the Meat Inspection Act, both passed by Congress in 1906. These laws were spurred by scandals in the medicinal drug and food industries and by such exposés as Upton Sinclair's best-selling novel *The Jungle* (1906), which described the unsanitary conditions of production in the Chicago meatpacking industry.

The law of corporate crimes has expanded dramatically in the decades since, typically following either growing recognition of standard business practices that harmed the public interest, or what the media labeled as corporate crime waves of illegal activity by numerous business firms. An example of the first situation is the creation in the early 1970s of the federal Environmental Protection Agency and of new federal laws outlawing air and water pollution in response to growing public concern over industrial pollution. An example of the second is the spur to action caused by such major financial frauds as those discovered at the Enron and Worldcom companies in the early years of the twenty-first century. This pattern of widespread fraud led Congress in 2002 to pass the Sarbanes-Oxley law, legislation that created new standards of top-management responsibility for honest financial accounting and that increased penalties for defrauding investors in shares of corporate stock.

The Study of Corporate Lawbreaking. The systematic examination of lawbreaking by corporations did not develop until the middle of the twentieth century. Although Edward A. Ross, writing in *The Atlantic Monthly* magazine, had drawn attention in 1907 to what he labeled *criminaloids* operating in American business, it was not until the 1949 publication of Edwin Sutherland's pioneering book *White Collar Crime* that the world had its first comprehensive study of corporate offending. The book examined the violations of law by several dozen of the largest American corporations and discovered high rates of offending, typically answered by lenient government penalties. Coming early in an era dominated in the United States by the conservative, anti-Communist culture of the Cold War, the book prompted many in positions of power to call Sutherland's research an unjustified attack on business, and some labeled him a radical. Not surprisingly, his ambitious lead was followed by only a handful of smaller-scale research studies during the 1950s and 1960s.

However, the social conflict and political turmoil of the 1960s and early 1970s provided fertile ground for such research, and the study of corporate lawbreaking took firmer root. In particular, the divisive Vietnam War and the Watergate-era crimes of the Nixon administration and 1972 presidential campaign, including illegal campaign contributions by corporations, focused public concern on abuses of power in both business and government. One consequence of this new political climate was the first federal funding for research on white-collar crime and its regulation. The research arm of the U.S. Department of Justice funded three major research programs in the 1970s, at Yale University and at the universities of Wisconsin and Minnesota. Although the latter project dealt with employee theft from businesses rather than with corporate lawbreaking, the Yale and Wisconsin researchers took up key questions of the misconduct of businesses and of government policies for controlling it. The Wisconsin research produced the first and only comprehensive updating of Sutherland's study, analyses of the violations of federal law by several hundred of the nation's largest industrial corporations that were published in two volumes: *Illegal Corporate Behavior* (1979) and *Corporate Crime* (1980).

Although research in this area has now established its legitimacy in both academic and government circles, it proceeds at a slower pace and at lower levels of government funding than do studies of street crime. While several reasons account for this difference, a principal one is the relatively constant high public and political concern over the dangers posed by such crimes as robbery, burglary, and murder, even when rates of such crimes decline substantially as they did in the 1990s. In contrast, public and political concern over corporate crimes rises and falls with media attention to periodic "crime waves," such as with the recent series of financial frauds in both American and foreign companies.

Another distinction between research on street crime and that on corporate lawbreaking is definitional. Whereas the definition of street crimes is straightforward—violations of criminal laws—definitions have been more controversial for corporate crime. Some scholars argue that researchers should limit their studies only to those cases in which companies have been prosecuted under criminal laws. Others disagree. They argue that, because of the political influence especially of big business, the government treats the vast majority of corporate offenses as noncriminal violations of regulatory or civil laws in order to spare companies the stigma of criminal prosecution. These scholars conclude that there is no fundamental difference between crimes as conventionally defined and corporate violations of law handled by the government as noncriminal offenses. Studies that have used this broader definition of corporate crimes include Sutherland's and the Wisconsin research. Other scholars sidestep this debate by avoiding the terminology of crimes and speaking instead of corporate violations, offenses, and lawbreaking.

Factors in Corporate Lawbreaking. Whatever the definitions used in research, certainly the social harms caused by corporate lawbreaking are massive in the aggregate. Although a single price-fixing conspiracy can net colluding corporations millions of dollars in illegal profits, the financial frauds that led to the bankruptcies of Enron, Worldcom, and other corporations in 2002 alone resulted in dozens of billions of dollars of losses to investors, including many Americans' pension funds. Financial losses of this scale dwarf the annual losses due to conventional street crimes, such as robbery, burglary and auto theft.

Corporate violations can also cause substantial physical harm: to workers on the job, to consumers from unsafe medicines and other consumer products, and to citizens from industrial pollution. For example, each year several thousand employees die from injuries, and several million more are injured or made ill while at work. Tens of thousands of additional deaths from chronic exposure to hazardous work environments are estimated to occur annually. Although it is not known what proportions of these injuries, illnesses, and deaths are caused by companies' violations of worker safety laws, federal Occupational Safety and Health Administration (OSHA) data suggest that corporate violations are responsible for a considerable number. OSHA data show that federal and state inspections during a single fiscal year (2004), discovered more than 121,000 serious violations of worker safety laws, violations in which there was a substantial likelihood of death or serious physical harm.

There is similar uncertainty about the frequency with which corporations break laws and how many offenses they commit annually. Unlike the federal government's annual compilations of street crimes, no regular accounting system tracks corporate violations of law in the United States. What exists instead are a handful of studies, none of recent vintage, that suggest rates at which corporations break laws. They are all limited by their reliance on samples of companies and on available government data on firms found in violation of law. Of necessity, the studies, therefore, do not include offenses unknown to law enforcement officials or not pursued by them.

Sutherland's study in the 1940s of the offense histories of seventy large corporations found that all had committed at least one violation, averaging fourteen violations each over the course of their business lifetimes (which averaged forty-five years), or roughly one case of lawbreaking every three years for the average firm. The violations included price fixing, financial fraud, false advertising, and illegal treatment of workers. His study also found that 60 percent of the companies had been convicted of criminal offenses and that these forty-two firms had averaged four criminal convictions each.

The Wisconsin research compiled legal actions taken by the federal government in 1975 and 1976 against 477 of the largest industrial corporations in the United States. Almost half of the companies were charged with violations of law that were not minor in the areas of unfair competitive practices, worker safety, product safety, and environmental protection, among others; the companies so charged averaged three such cases in the two-year period. Of the enforcement actions taken against these companies, only 3 percent involved criminal prosecutions. Relatedly, a study of more than 1000 major corporations by *Fortune* magazine found that 10 percent of them had committed substantial violations during the decade of the 1970s.

Because corporations break laws at different rates and violate different types of law, and because rates of such lawbreaking vary over time as well, it is apparent that motivations and opportunities for violating laws vary. Understanding these variations has been the goal of considerable social science research. In their search for explanations of corporate lawbreaking, the studies suggest the importance of a number of factors, including the aggressive pursuit of profit, the nature of product markets, the cultural values of individual companies, and corporate officials' perceptions of the legitimacy of the laws that prohibit misconduct. These factors do not operate independently; instead they appear to interact with each other to produce a greater or lesser likelihood that companies will break laws.

For example, there is a slight tendency for companies experiencing relatively low profitability to commit more offenses, but more profitable firms often commit them as well. This tendency suggests that the pursuit of profit is more likely to produce lawbreaking when the corporate culture emphasizes the importance of profitability over other social values, such as corporate responsibility to the community, workers, consumers, and the natural environment. The values established by top corporate executives are key in establishing cultures that are either law-abiding or violation-prone. But executives' values are themselves shaped by such factors as the culture of the industries in which companies compete, the design of compensation systems for management performance, pressure from stock markets to show consistent short-term profit growth, and whether or not the government enforces the laws consistently and aggressively.

The Control of Corporate Offenses. Several mechanisms have been used and proposed to limit lawbreaking by corporations. Legal approaches figure most prominently among these mechanisms, but they also include improved ethics training for both business students and active managers and compliance and ethics programs operated inside companies.

Law may inhibit wrongdoing in either of two ways. It may deter offenses through fear of criminal punishment and costly financial penalties, or it may morally educate citizens to avoid prohibited harmful behaviors. To date, research on the deterrent effects of law for corporate offenses generally suggests that punishment has only modest effects on future compliance with legal rules. Especially for large companies, deterrence will be limited when fines are small relative to the firms' wealth and when companies can use their financial resources and legal expertise to prevent government from provoking or seeking harsh sanctions. Under some circumstances fines and prison terms for individual corporate executives and managers may deter future offenses.

Some scholars, most prominent among them the sociologist John Braithwaite, have advocated the greater use of cooperative methods of legal response to violations in the first instance, rather than an initial reliance on punishment. Such methods include negotiations between government regulators, a law-violating business, and affected third parties (e.g., workers, investors, and community members) toward compliance with legal requirements; if the company continued to violate the laws, the government would then apply increasingly stringent penalties. Advocates of this approach argue that it would produce better compliance with law because company personnel would be more likely to accept the moral importance of socially responsible behaviors. Other scholars are skeptical, and such approaches have yet to be widely applied and assessed for their effectiveness. In the meanwhile, the U.S. Sentencing Guidelines for Organizations, implemented in 1991, have helped spur the development of compliance and ethics programs in many companies; under the guidelines, violating companies that can show good-faith compliance programs may receive reduced penalties upon conviction.

National patterns of enforcement for corporate lawbreaking remain dynamic. These patterns include the imposition of criminal, civil, and regulatory law penalties by both national and state-level government units as well as class-action lawsuits brought by victims of corporate wrongdoing. Over time, enforcement varies in its intensity and in the severity of punishments and costs imposed upon violating companies. Especially in the wake of the numerous financial frauds by corporations in recent years, there have been many cases in which individual companies have paid financial penalties and court settlements of tens and even hundreds of millions of dollars. The effects of such costs on future corporate compliance with law remain to be seen.

See also: Braithwaite, John; Enron

FURTHER READING

Braithwaite, John. *Restorative Justice and Responsive Regulation*. New York: Oxford University Press, 2002.

Clinard, Marshall B., and Yeager, Peter C. *Corporate Crime*. New York: The Free Press, 1980. (Reprint edition with new introduction, New Brunswick, NJ: Transaction Publishers, 2006.)

Clinard, Marshall B., Yeager, Peter C., Brissette, Jeanne, Petrashek, David, and Harries, Elizabeth. *Illegal Corporate Behavior*. Washington, DC: U.S. Department of Justice, 1979.

Coleman, James William. *The Criminal Elite: Understanding White-Collar Crime*, 6th edition. New York: Worth Publishers, 2006.

Corporate Crime Reporter. Available at http://www.corporatecrimereporter.com/.

Simpson, Sally S. *Corporate Crime, Law, and Social Control*. New York: Cambridge University Press, 2002.

Sutherland, Edwin H. *White Collar Crime*. New York: Holt, Rinehart and Winston, 1949. (Reprint edition with new material, New Haven: Yale University Press, 1985.)

Yeager, Peter Cleary. "Understanding Corporate Lawbreaking: From Profit-Seeking to Law-Finding." Forthcoming in Henry N. Pontell and Gilbert Geis (eds.), *International Handbook of White-Collar Crime*. New York: Springer, 2006.

PETER CLEARY YEAGER

CORPORATE WAR CRIMES. Corporate war crimes involve for-profit organizations in the illegal use of military violence. Corporations are routinely involved in supporting state violence in locations in which they face opposition (e.g., oil companies in Colombia and Nigeria), or they may be directly involved in military operations (e.g., the expanding market in private military or *mercenary* companies). The ongoing occupation of Iraq provides us with stark evidence that Western governments are increasingly involving for-profit corporations in combat support, and private military and security companies are playing a key role in military operations.

War crimes are often conceptualized in two ways: as violations of *jus ad bellum* (the legality of the war in the first place) and as violations of *jus ad bello* (how the war is conducted). In the context of corporate war crimes, the former category may include the direct role that for-profit organizations play in the planning and execution of illegal wars. Were the 2003 invasion of Iraq to be considered an illegal war (as many international lawyers have claimed), then several U.S. and UK corporations could be implicated in the logistics and planning of the war. The latter category would include the treatment of civilians and enemy combatants in the course of the war. Private companies implicated in the torture of detainees in Abu Ghraib would fall into this category. The sharp rise in the use of private military companies and mercenary soldiers by governments has also rapidly increased the likelihood of military corporations being involved in both criminal wars and crimes committed in the course of wars.

In addition to war crimes, international criminal law has evolved three broad categories of crime that may also implicate corporations in some circumstances: crimes against humanity (systematic crimes against civilians); genocides (crimes aimed at destroying population groups, e.g., ethnic or religious groups); and terrorism (crimes aimed at spreading terror in civilian populations). At the Nuremberg War Criminal Tribunal, twenty-four IG Farben board members and executives were charged with mass murder, slavery, and other crimes against humanity connected to Hitler's Nazi regime. One accusation was that, during the planning of the invasion of Poland and Czechoslovakia, IG Farben had cooperated closely with Nazi officials in structuring industry to cope with the industrial demands of the Wehrmacht. There was also evidence that IG Farben built a factory for producing synthetic oil and rubber from coal in Auschwitz. This factory is said to have made use of 83,000 slave laborers at the peak of its production in 1944. IG Farben held the patent on the pesticide Zyklon B, the poison used in the gas chambers of Auschwitz for mass murder. Zyklon B was, moreover, manufactured by Degesch, an IG Farben subsidiary.

Fourteen of the IG Farben defendants were convicted for one of the following offenses: committing war crimes and crimes against humanity through the plunder of public and private property in countries and territories that came under German occupation; committing war crimes and crimes against humanity through participation in the enslavement and deportation of civilians for slave labor; and participating in the SS, a criminal organization. In 1951, the company was split up into the original constituent companies. The four largest quickly bought the smaller ones, and today only Agfa, BASF, and Bayer remain. By 1951, all of the IG Farben war criminals had been released from prison.

In a separate case, three officers of the company Tesch and Stabenow were tried for supplying the poison gas used for the extermination of Allied nationals interned in the concentration camps. Between 1942 and 1945, four and a half million persons are estimated to have been killed at Auschwitz with Zyklon B. The prosecution's case was that the commodity was being knowingly supplied to a branch of the state for the mass extermination of civilian nationals. Two senior officers of the company were found guilty; the third was acquitted because he was not in a position in the firm to influence or prevent the transfer of the poison. Both senior officers were hanged for their crimes.

A key issue raised in any discussion of corporate war crimes is that of "victor's justice": the idea that only nationals of the vanquished side are punished for their crimes. In this regard, it is significant that none of the U.S. or European firms that supplied the Nazi regime (among the most widely criticized were IBM, Ford, ITT, and Standard Oil) were ever put on trial. As Geoffrey Robertson points out in his book *Crimes Against Humanity*, the facts surrounding German companies' supplying of nerve gas, subsequently used to massacre Kurds at Halabja, to Saddam Hussein's regime raise issues of culpability that are similar to the Tesch and Stabenow case. Moreover, Hussein would not have been able to carry out his genocidal policies against the Kurds without aircraft supplied by Swiss and French corporations and weapons components and systems supplied by U.S. and British corporations. However, in March 2005, the Netherlands government initiated a case against a Dutch national, Frans van Anraat , who allegedly supplied precursors for mustard and nerve gas used by Iraq.

Movements against corporate crime have recently drawn attention to comparable cases that implicate corporations in the supply of equipment for use in war crimes and crimes against humanity, and collaboration with criminal regimes. For example, the supply of bulldozers by the British firm Caterpillar for use by the State of Israel, which used them to flatten Palestinian villages in the occupied territories, was exposed by the killing of Rachel Corrie, a twenty-three-year-old American peace activist. Corrie was killed when she tried to prevent a Caterpillar D9 bulldozer from destroying a Palestinian home in the Gaza Strip on March 16, 2003. Campaigners in the UK have held a series of protests to prevent Caterpillar from selling more bulldozers to Israel. Human-rights organizations have alleged that corporations operating in Colombia, such as Coca-Cola and BP, have victimized trade union leaders and local opponents of paramilitary units as part of a generalized campaign to suppress opposition to their operations. Questions have also been raised about the role of corporations in the torture, or "disappearance,"of certain individuals.

Corporate war crimes pose particular problems in terms of enforcement and punishment: neither human-rights law nor the laws of war apply directly to corporations. Indeed, corporations are much more likely to enjoy protections under international law than to be held liable for crimes. This point raises a familiar dilemma in the study of corporate and state crime: that Western criminal law, dominated by the concept of individual intent, is inadequately constructed for dealing with the serious crimes committed by states and corporations. International criminal law has evolved with precisely the same emphasis upon individual, rather than collectively produced, crimes. It is, therefore, much more likely that criminal liability for corporate war crimes can be attributed to individual directors or owners of corporations. Those cases are, however, likely to be rare for the same reasons that criminal senior officers are able to escape punishment for other crimes that involve injuring, maiming, and killing (see **Industrial Accidents**).

FURTHER READING

Black, E. *IBM and the Holocaust*. New York: Little, Brown, 2001.
Green, P., and Ward, T. *State Crime: Governments, Violence and Corruption*. London: Pluto, 2004.

Musah, A., and Kayode Fayemi, J., (eds). *Mercenaries: An African Security Dilemma*, London: Pluto, 2000.

Silverstein, K. *Private Warriors*, New York: Verso, 2000.

Whyte, D. "Lethal Regulation: State-Corporate Crime and the UK Government's New Mercenaries." *Journal of Law and Society* 30.4 (2003): 575–600.

DAVE WHYTE

CREDIT LYONNAIS. Credit Lyonnais and the scandal that was associated with this financial institution is a perfect example of how government interference, lax operating management, and poor internal controls can topple a French financial giant. The French firm broke numerous international laws of banking and finance and cost the French people nearly $17 billion. Credit Lyonnais was founded in 1863 and was nationalized in 1945 after World War II, but its problems did not begin until 1988, when the French government made an aggressive move to expand the bank into an international financing powerhouse. It is believed that the bank suffered from a crisis of identity, that it was unsure of whether to serve the needs and interests of the French government preferentially or treat it like any other client. In 1988, President Mitterand appointed Jean-Yves Haberer as CFO. He developed a plan to make Credit Lyonnais rival DeutscheBank and U.S. investment banks by growing existing businesses, opening new offices around the world, and making new investments in real estate. The French government officials liked the grandiose scale of Harberer's plan and gave little oversight to his investments. Unfortunately, with this freedom the bank amassed a great number of poor-quality investments and assets. During the economic boom in the late 1980s, Credit Lyonnais was making millions and the expansion seemed to be working, but this period was cut short by the economic downturn beginning with the Gulf War. It was then discovered that Credit Lyonnais had taken significant equity stakes in businesses and that, in contrast to other banks, these investments were not the result of long-term relationships. The bank often continued to support investments that were poorly managed or were losing money. In fact, by 1992 the French government began to realize that the bank was underreporting its losses, but two of the bank's subsidiaries caused the biggest losses, created scandal, and brought criminal and civil actions from the U.S. Attorney's Office.

Credit Lyonnais had been under the scrutiny of the U.S. Attorney's Office for two scandals. First, it was accused of funding the takeover of MGM Studios by an individual who was both corrupt and criminal while concealing its involvement from the U.S. government. Second, they were accused of playing a role in a scheme to defraud policyholders of the Executive Life Insurance Company and of making off with over a billion dollars from fraudulently acquired junk bonds.

In 1990, Italian businessman Giancarlo Paretti purchased the controlling interest of MGM Studios with $2 billion in loans from Credit Lyonnais and its subsidiary, Credit Lyonnais Nederlands, even though Paretti had a criminal record and a bad credit rating. Paretti was required to report the terms of the acquisition, but he lied in this report, and the U.S. Attorney's Office began to investigate the origin of his finances. In, 1991, Credit Lyonnais was forced to lend Paretti more money to save MGM from financial deterioration and to avoid an investigation from a bankruptcy commission. As security for this new loan, the bank seized control of the company's stock, thus becoming owner of MGM Studios. Such ownership was in direct violation of the Bank Holding Company Act, which prohibits any financial institution from owning a nonfinancial institution. In an attempt to make it seem as though the bank was an unwitting victim of Paretti's schemes, Credit Lyonnais sued Paretti for mismanagement. The U.S. Attorney's Office was not convinced of the bank's victimization and began to investigate how Paretti had been able to request and receive twenty-three loans totaling $50 million from Credit Lyonnais Nederlands without a background check, which would have shown that Paretti had a record of fraud, forgery, and assault. It had also been discovered that Paretti had rewarded Credit Lyonnais's loan officers with shares in his Italian film company and all-expenses-paid trips on yachts and private planes.

While the bank was being investigated, Credit Lyonnais created sham transactions to make it appear as if Paretti were paying down the debt when no such payments were ever made. In 1998, the U.S. Attorney's Office began to prosecute Paretti and his business partner Fiorini, but decided against prosecuting Credit Lyonnais and its officers. A settlement was prepared in which the bank would pay the U.S. government a penalty of $4 million for failing to supervise its employees. The bank also agreed to acknowledge the errors of its officers and promised to commit no further crimes in the United States. However, even before the ink was dry on the settlement, the U.S. Attorney's Office began another investigation into the criminal activities of Credit Lyonnais and its involvement with Executive Life.

Credit Lyonnais had acquired Executive Life Insurance as part of a junk bond portfolio when it bought Altus Finance in 1990. Executive Life had nearly gone under when its junk bonds lost value in the late 1980s. Credit Lyonnais officers figured that a profit could be made when the bonds recovered, so they financially backed Apollo Group Finance, which bought the bonds. But, in order to purchase the bonds, they would also have had to buy Executive Life, which would again put them in violation of the Bank Holding Company Act. To get around this problem, Credit Lyonnais concealed its interest in both the Apollo Group and Executive Life. Then, in 1992, the bank sold part of its interest in the junk bonds to a company called Artemis, whose owner was good friends with the president and other government officials. Credit Lyonnais lent him the money to buy the bonds. The junk bonds did recover and netted about $1 billion in profit while violating U.S. federal law. The violations would have been kept secret, but in 1999 a disgruntled French businessman told the California Department of Insurance that Credit Lyonnais had an illegal relationship with Executive Life. This whistle-blower began an investigation into the deal that would mark the beginning of the end of Credit Lyonnais.

In 2003, the U.S. Attorney's Office presented its evidence to a grand jury, which returned with a fifty-five-count indictment against the bank and it subsidiaries. For the remainder of the year, the two countries fought and negotiated concerning the terms of a plea agreement. Finally, in early 2004, the bank agreed to pay $100,000 to the Federal Reserve (the largest fine ever paid to that institution) and was given three years probation. A package deal required that the parties involved pay nearly $775 million in fines. Although the name Credit Lyonnais is still in existence, the bank no longer exists as a separate entity. Another French bank,

Credit Agricole, bought it for $20 billion in 2002, and it plans to merge Credit Lyonnais into Credit Agricole over the coming years.

FURTHER READING

McClintick, D. "Inside the Credit Lyonnais Scandal." *Institutional Investor Magazine* (November 11, 2003). Available at http://www.dailyii.com/.

SHIYLOH L. DUNCAN

CRIMES AGAINST NATIVE AMERICANS. In the eighteenth century, the U.S. government seized nearly 2 billion acres of land from Native Americans. About half of the land was purchased through treaty at an average price of 65 cents per acre. In addition, the U.S. government confiscated 325 million acres without compensation through acts of Congress and presidential executive orders—often in direct violation of treaties. In the twentieth century, the military acquired land for military bases in proximity to reservations—often on lands that had once been part of reservations. By the end of World War II, the military owned nearly 10 million acres of land. Not only was the land confiscated during the twentieth century for military bases near Native American lands, but these bases often housed dangerous and toxic activities (e.g., bombing ranges and chemical weapons testing). Thus, the broken treaties and theft of land in the nineteenth century have been compounded by environmental threats posed by twentieth-century military activities.

Broken Treaties, Stolen Land. Two well-known episodes—the Cherokee "Trail of Tears" and the Massacre at Wounded Knee—bring into sharp relief the pattern of broken treaties and theft of land that marked the first century of the United States. In perhaps the most well-known violation of Indian rights and treaties, the U.S. government forced the entire Cherokee Nation to relocate, on foot, from their homeland in Georgia and North Carolina to Oklahoma along a route that became known as the Trail of Tears. Lack of food, harsh weather, disease, and harassment by whites along the way resulted in the death of 20 percent of the Cherokee people.

The Cherokee were highly literate, had assisted the colonies in the American Revolution, had signed a binding treaty with the United States, and had many allies in Congress. Moreover, despite the State of Georgia's repeated and deliberate provocation, the Cherokee had responded in a disciplined and nonviolent fashion, thereby removing any pretext for armed invasion. Still the United States broke its treaty with the Cherokee. The Trail of Tears was part of a larger ethnic cleansing in which scores of eastern tribes were forcibly relocated to the western territories, often in violation of treaty obligations.

If the Cherokee Trail of Tears initiated the breaking of treaties and theft of lands, the Massacre at Wounded Knee highlights the completion of this process. As was the case with the Cherokee, the United States broke its treaties with the Sioux and stole lands promised to them. The Great Sioux Reservation included all of western South Dakota, including the sacred Black Hills. Article 12 of the Fort Laramie Treaty, signed in 1868, prohibited further land concessions without consent from at least three-quarters of the adult male Sioux population. With rumors of large gold deposits, miners and settlers streamed into the Sioux Reservation, and George Custer led a large military force into the Black Hills. Just eight years after the signing of the Fort Laramie Treaty, the United States violated its provisions with an "agreement" requiring the Sioux to cede additional lands in exchange for subsistence rations. Ninety percent of the adult males refused to sign this agreement. Nevertheless, in direct violation of the Fort Laramie Treaty, the Sioux reservation was divided into three smaller parcels, and the sacred Black Hills were expropriated.

The theft of Sioux lands set in motion two of the most famous—and infamous—battles of the late nineteenth century. The Battle of Little Big Horn pitted Sioux warriors who would not accept the U.S. treaty violations against General Custer, the military commander who first led troops into the Black Hills in violation of the Treaty of 1868. In this battle, Custer and his troops were defeated and killed. In 1890, after defeating the Sioux and forcing them onto the smaller reservations, the U.S. military committed the Massacre at Wounded Knee. On December 29, 1890, over 300 people—mostly unarmed women and children—were slaughtered by the U.S. military. A century later, a 1980 Supreme Court case concluded that the U.S. Congress had illegally taken land from the Sioux without compensation.

The methods used in acquiring these lands represent white-collar crime because in nearly all instances the United States violated existing treaties signed with Native American tribes, nakedly acquired the land without compensation, and/or violated international law. Over time, the United States claims of land and resources affected Native Americans in unique ways; these impacts are magnified when we consider the environmental consequences facing Native Americans in the contemporary United States.

The Legacy of Land Acquisition: Environmental Inequality. By 1850, the federal government "owned" virtually all land west of the Mississippi River. This ownership was based on the terms of the Louisiana Purchase and terms imposed on Mexico at the end of the Mexican War. Effective control over these lands was realized through a series of Indian Wars that forced western tribes onto reservations. The United States gave away and sold off the lands in its possession to promote the settlement and development of the West. In this manner, railroads were awarded vast tracts of land—both as a right of way for the railroad itself and to subsidize the costs of building and maintaining the railroad. The federal government also sold off lands to white settlers, land developers, and mining interests. In effect, the federal government retained possession of the lands that were least desirable to white Americans. By 1900, both federally owned and Native American lands tended to be in close proximity and concentrated in the states west of the Mississippi where the lands were too dry, remote, or barren to attract the attention of settlers and corporations.

Across the West, the experiences of the Cherokee and Sioux were repeated. Native Americans experienced military defeat, broken treaties, and loss of lands. These white-collar crimes were compounded by the military expansion of the twentieth century. For example, the broken treaties with the Sioux and the Massacre at Wounded Knee provide more than a symbolic backdrop for this discussion. Fifty years after this massacre, the Sioux once again confronted the power of the U.S. military, and once again the issue was land. However, by the 1940s, land acquisition was undertaken as part of the World War II mobilization, and the ceded lands were used by the military rather than white settlers. The U.S. government, for the purpose of constructing a World War II bombing range, confiscated roughly 342,000 acres from the Pine Ridge Reservation in South Dakota. A mere 125 Sioux families were compensated at a rate of three cents an acre. After being forcibly uprooted, the residents of this reservation lived in close proximity to an extremely dangerous bombing range. In fact, after the bombing range was decommissioned in the 1980s, cleanup was long delayed because these lands were too dangerous for cleanup crews due to the presence of excessive amounts of ordnance.

The Western Shoshone also face enormous threats and challenges in the desert Southwest once referred to as the "Bull's Eye" by General Colin Powell, A massive war-game center located in this area includes the Nevada Test Site, Fallon Complex, Yucca Mountain, and China Lake. Open-air testing of nuclear weapons and other military activities have contaminated large areas of the American Southwest. Whereas the military treat the desert Southwest as a wasteland, the Shoshone (and other tribes) claim these lands as both a traditional homeland and religious ground. Once a locale has been seriously degraded, however, it often attracts additional pollution. In some cases, toxic wastes are deliberately directed to locales that are already damaged on the grounds that concentrating toxic wastes in one place is preferable to diffusing them widely. This reasoning stands as a central justification for Yucca Mountain (Nevada) as the selected site to concentrate the nation's high-level nuclear waste.

The Sioux and Shoshone are not the only tribes facing environmental threats. On the contrary, the authors' research (Hooks and Smith 2004) examined all closed military bases, each reservation, and all counties in the continental United States. The authors found that the most dangerous unexploded ordnance is disproportionately located near Native American lands. The evidence then is mounting that the legacy of broken treaties and stolen land goes beyond the obvious material hardships and undermining of Native American culture. The long-term impacts include degraded land and environmental threats.

FURTHER READING

Blumenauer, Earl. "The Threat of Unexploded Ordnances." Available at http://www.house.gov/blumenauer/floor_speeches/fl281.html. Accessed December 27, 2003.

Brown, Dee. *Bury My Heart at Wounded Knee: An Indian History of the American West.* New York: Holt, Rinehart, and Winston, 1970.

Bullard, Robert D., ed. *Confronting Environmental Racism.* Boston, MA: South End Press, 1983.

DeMallie, Raymond. "Introduction to the Bison Book Edition." Pp. xv–xxvi in J. Mooney, *The Ghost-Dance Religion and the Sioux Outbreak of 1890.* Lincoln: University of Nebraska Press, 1991.

Fort Laramie Treaty. *Fort Laramie Treaty, 1868.* Washington, DC: WETA. Available at http://www.pbs.org/weta/thewest/resources/archives/four/ftlaram.htm. Accessed March 27, 2005.

Hooks, Gregory, and Smith, Chad L. "The Treadmill of Destruction: National Sacrifice Areas and Native Americans." *American Sociological Review* 69.4 (2004): 558–575.

Kuletz, Valerie. *The Tainted Desert: Environmental and Social Ruin in the American West.* New York: Routledge, 1998.

Lorenzo, June, and First Peoples Worldwide. "Summary of Land Rights in the United States" Available at http://www.firstpeoples.org/land_rights/united_states/us_summary.htm.

Marshall, Suzanne. "Chemical Weapons Disposal and Environmental Justice." Berea, KY: Kentucky Environmental Foundation, 1996.

Saito, Natsu Taylor. "American Indian Sovereignty" Available at http://law.gsu.edu/nsaito/law7278/AIS/uslaw.htm. Accessed March 2005.

U.S. Supreme Court. *United States v. Sioux Nation of Indians*, 448 U.S. 371 (1980). Certiorari to the United States Court of Claims, No. 79–639. Available at http://caselaw.lp.findlaw.com/scripts/getcase.pl?court=US&vol=448&invol=371. Accessed March 27, 2005.

GREGORY HOOKS
CHAD L. SMITH

CRIMINOGENIC INDUSTRY. The term *criminogenic industry* is understood to refer to an industry that incorporates or relates to characteristics or factors identified by relevant research as predictors of crime and/or related recidivism. This criminogenic net captures not only criminal but civil transgressions as well. In traditional crime, external factors may contribute to the criminogenic nature of individuals; similar reasoning can be applied to white-collar crime and the idea of the criminogenic industry. That is, the commission of white-collar crime may not be due only to the deviant nature of the criminal but also to the workings of the industry in which the crime was committed. And, as a phenomenon, criminogenic industry has been historically linked to numerous instances of white-collar crime, including instances in the automobile, meatpacking, retail, banking, securities, technology, and railroad industries, to name a few.

Rather than attributing criminogenic tendencies in corporations and businesses to flawed leadership practices and influential company executives, the idea of the criminogenic industry points to the acceptance of long-employed and acknowledged practices that are not readily traceable to a managerial event or style but rather to industrywide factors. Before regulations were enacted beginning in the late nineteenth century, criminogenic behaviors were considered a part of normal industry operating practices within the United States. Although many trades have been linked with criminogenic tendencies, one of the most salient and historic examples of a criminogenic industry is that of the meatpacking industry.

With the 1906 publication of Upton Sinclair's controversial novel *The Jungle*, mass corruption and offenses that had long affected both the industry workers and the unwitting public were exposed in the U.S. meatpacking industry. Tales of worker abuses, including lack of compensation and health care, long working hours, poor living conditions, and dangerous working environments, coupled with the inadequate sanitary treatment of the meat product and a lack of product regulation, initiated a societal uproar. In conjunction with these new insights, the Pure Food and Drug Act and the Meat Inspection Act were passed in the same year. The acknowledgment of industry wrongs contributed to the improvement of working conditions and industry practices; however, the meatpacking industry continued to defy law and the implemented standards. Edwin Sutherland's landmark book *White Collar Crime* (first published in 1949) attests to this fact, identifying two meat-processing plants as the top corporate offenders in the United States; Armour and Company and Swift and Company were each cited as having fifty recorded violations of the law, with a majority of the crimes committed involving restraint of trade and unfair labor practices. The public's awareness of wrongs and inhumane treatment in all industries continued to flourish, however, and along with the increased formation of unions and safer labor practices, the meatpacking industry rose to the forefront, touting well-paid, secure jobs that often fostered loyalty among its workers during the mid-twentieth century. Yet, despite marked improvements in industry standards, most of those involved in the meatpacking industry continued to defy the standards set within the industry framework. The well-paid, secure jobs that were evident in the mid-twentieth century diminished in the mid-1980s, into subpar conditions reminiscent of the transgressions that took place in the early part of the century. Estimates now indicate that the meatpacking industry is once again one of the most dangerous jobs in America, employing a largely immigrant workforce functioning with little or no health care or job security.

Although the meatpacking industry illustrates the problems with the cycle of criminogenic industry, it should not be touted as the only example of the problem. Many industries have criminogenic tendencies, with recent examples being the automotive industry (see **Ford Pinto**), the aerospace industry (see **C-5A Transport Aircraft** and **Lockheed Bribing Scandal**) and tobacco industry standards.

Many theories can be associated with factors identified in relation to the cause and perpetuation of the criminogenic industry phenomenon, including (among many others) strain theory, general theory of crime, social control theory, and differential association theory. One universal theme that emerges, however, is the idea of elite or cultural deviance; simply put, that deficient decision making resulting in criminogenic tendencies is tied to a process of individuals "following orders among managerial divisions," orders based on the basic tenet of cost/benefit analyses, with the financial benefits of the commission of criminal-type acts far outweighing the sanctions that would be brought against organizations or individuals due to these acts. Following this central rule, we note that the business code does not always coincide with the legal code, and even with the employment of increasing legislation and sanctions, it seems unlikely that the criminogenic industry phenomenon will be seen less often in the corporate arena.

See also: Control Fraud Theory; Differential Association; Meatpacking Industry; Strain Theory and White-Collar Crime

FURTHER READING

Schlosser, Eric. *Fast Food Nation: The Dark Side of the All-American Meal.* New York: Houghton Mifflin, 2001.
Simon, David R. *Elite Deviance*, 5th edition. Boston: Allyn and Bacon, 1996.
Sinclair, Upton. *The Jungle: The Uncensored Original Edition.* Tucson, AZ: See Sharp Press, 2003 (originally published 1906).
Sutherland, Edwin H. *White Collar Crime: The Uncut Version.* New Haven: Yale University Press, 1983 (originally published 1949).

APRIL D. WALL

CRUISE LINE INDUSTRY. The recreational cruise line industry is a $15 billion-a-year business that has been involved in many environmental crimes. From 1993 to 1998, at least 104 illegal discharge cases were suspected against foreign-flagged cruise ships, those ships that operate out of American waters but are registered to foreign countries, such as Liberia and

Norway. In some of these cases, there were multiple incidents when the discharges occurred, and according to the U.S. Department of Justice, some of these multiple incidents numbered in the hundreds. Of these, eighty-seven cases were handled in the United States; the rest were referred to the country whose flag the ships flew.

Environmental laws and regulations have not kept pace with the enormous rate of growth of the cruise industry. One set of regulating guidelines is called MARPOL (International Convention for the Prevention of Pollution from Ships), a set of standards for all ships to follow regarding the discharge of certain substances and for the building and maintenance of ships and their equipment. Another law governing cruise ship operations is the Clean Water Act, which prohibits the dumping of any pollutant within three nautical miles of the United States and prohibits the discharge of oil and other hazardous substances within twelve nautical miles. The second of two multimillion-dollar criminal fines against Royal Caribbean Cruise Lines originated from direct violations of the Clean Water Act. Another of the U.S. laws instrumental in governing cruise ships is the Federal Act to Prevent Pollution from Ships, which incorporates many of the MARPOL provisions. In 2002, Carnival Cruise Lines was found to be in violation of this law for flushing clean water through sensors instead of bilge water.

Two more recent regulations are Title XIV of the Labor, Health, and Human Services Appropriations Bill and the International Safety Management (ISM) Code. Title XIV, signed and passed in 2000, requires the Coast Guard to develop monitoring and reporting programs for all ship discharges and authorizes the U.S. Environmental Protection Agency (EPA) to establish "No Discharge Zones." The ISM Code, passed in 1998, is an international standard requiring cruise ship owners and operators to establish safety management systems that include an environmental protection policy with procedures for pollution prevention. Although it is not responsible for criminal charges or fines directly, a ship must be certified through the ISM in order to be eligible for insurance.

Several types of pollutants are associated with cruise ships. The first is black water, the sewage from toilets and urinals aboard the ships, and it is estimated that a typical one-week voyage generates as much as 210,000 gallons of black water. Despite strict regulations about the treatment of black water, wastewater expelled from the ships into the sea has been found to contain high levels of fecal coliform bacteria.

A second type of pollutant is gray water; the waste from sinks, showers, galleys, and laundry facilities. The one million gallons of gray water generated on a one-week voyage often contain such contaminants as soaps, detergents, cleaners, oil, grease, metals, pesticides, plastics, hydrocarbons, and even large amounts of fecal wastes. This waste can legally be dumped anywhere, even though the EPA says that gray water may have adverse effects on the environment that are as great or greater than those of black-water waste.

A third type of pollutant includes paint, maintenance materials, and the hazardous waste that comes from the ship's photo-processing labs and dry-cleaning facilities. The chemicals that are produced can be extremely toxic and can have serious adverse effects on the environment. Yet another type of pollutant is solid waste, including food, plastic, paper, wood, cardboard, cans, glass, and other material typically disposed of as garbage. A one-week voyage on a typical ship generates eight tons of garbage, and ships often directly violate the strict disposal regulations by dumping the garbage at sea. One ship, the *Ecstasy*, was found to have dumped 16,000 pounds of garbage at sea.

A final type of pollutant is oily bilge water. The bilge is the lowest point in the ship's hull, where the seawater that seeps into the ship is collected and then pumped back out into the sea. On a typical one-week journey, a ship produces 25,000 gallons of bilge water, and oil from the ship's machinery gets into it. On many occasions, the Coast Guard has been able to prove that ships bypassed antipollution systems, falsified oil record books, and dumped oily bilge water into the ocean.

Of the eighty-seven confirmed U.S. illegal discharge cases, 93 percent (or eighty-one cases) were brought for discharging oil or oil-related chemicals, whereas the remaining six cases dealt with the illegal disposal of solid waste. Royal Caribbean pled guilty to a twenty-one felony charges in one $18-million decision in 1999, only one year after pleading guilty to other criminal charges resulting in a $9-million fine. The $18-million Carnival Cruise Line case was settled on April 19,2002, after Carnival pleaded guilty to criminal charges related to the falsifying of oil records on six of their ships. Holland America Cruises plea-bargained for a $2-million judgment in 1998 after discharging oily water in Alaska's Inside Passage. Seven other cruise lines have also faced criminal fines in the past twenty years, including Norwegian Cruise Lines ($1 million in 2002), Palm Beach Cruises ($500,000 in 1994), Princess Cruises ($500,000 in 1993), Regency Cruises ($250,000 in 1993), American Global Lines ($100,000 in 1994), Ulysses Cruises (two $75,000 fines in 1997), and Seaway Maritime ($75,000 in 1997).

The International Council of Cruise Lines (ICCL), an agency designed to keep member cruise lines in compliance with industry regulations, claims that there has been vast improvement in pollution prevention among member ships. In 2001, the ICCL announced that it had adopted mandatory environmental standards for all members, which covers, but is not limited to, gray-water and black-water discharge, hazardous chemical waste, unused pharmaceuticals, used batteries, and burned-out fluorescent or mercury vapor lamps. Ships must comply with these new standards in order to maintain or gain membership in the ICCL.

See also: Environmental Crime; Hazardous Waste Disposal

FURTHER READING

Brannigan, M. "Royal Caribbean to Plead Guilty in Pollution Case." *Wall Street Journal* (July 22, 1999): A2.

Dessoff, A. "Cruise Ship Discharges Warrant Further Assessment, U.S. EPA Says." *Water Environment & Technology* 12 (2000): 22–26.

Dillingham, G.L. "Marine Pollution: Progress Made to Reduce Marine Pollution by Cruise Ships, But Important Issues Remain." FDCH Government Account Reports B-282376. Washington, DC: U.S. General Accounting Office, 2000.

McPherson, M. "New Mandatory Environmental Standards for Cruise Ships." ICCL press release, June 11, 2001. Available at www.iccl.org/pressroom/press55.cfm. Accessed September 25, 2006.

STEPHANIE E. CARMICHAEL

D

DAIWA BANK, LTD. Prior to 1995, Daiwa Bank, Ltd., was one of the top twenty banks in the world in terms of asset size, and it was Japan's twelfth largest institution. Unfortunately, due to lax internal risk control management, Daiwa Bank and a handful of its employees engaged in illegal securities trading, culminating in extensive losses and a massive cover-up that led to sixteen counts of federal felony charges, a $340 million fine—the largest criminal fine ever imposed in the United States at that time—and political tensions between the United States and Japan. Although Daiwa's losses were some of the largest of its kind in history, the massive cover-up that ensued created the most damage.

On July 13, 1995, the executive vice president of Daiwa's New York branch, Toshihide Iguchi, wrote a thirty-page letter to the president of Daiwa Bank in Japan. In his letter, Iguchi confessed to losing $1.1 billion while dealing in U.S. Treasury bonds over the past eleven years. Daiwa filed an initial report with the Japanese Finance Ministry's Banking Bureau on August 8, 1995. The Bureau told Daiwa to investigate the accusations, and a final report was submitted one month later. On September 18, 1995, six days after receiving the findings from Daiwa, the finance minister reported the findings to the U.S. Federal Reserve. Following the conclusion of the U.S. Federal Reserve Board investigation, Daiwa was fined $340 million—a reduction from the original $1.3 billion fine—and pled guilty to sixteen federal felonies, including two counts of conspiracy to defraud the United States and the Federal Reserve Bank, one count of misprision of a felony, ten counts of falsifying bank books and records, two counts of wire fraud, and one count of obstructing a bank examination. Furthermore, the U.S. Federal Reserve Board forced Daiwa to end all U.S. operations within ninety days of the ruling.

Toshihide Iguchi had been hired by Daiwa in 1977 to manage the back office of the branch's securities business. The New York branch managed the custody of U.S. Treasury bonds, bought by customers and by the bank itself through a subcustody account held by Bankers Trust. In 1984, Iguchi was promoted to trader, but he did not relinquish his back-office duties, thus creating the first breach of internal controls. The scam began when Iguchi lost an initial $200,000 in 1984 and tried to regain his losses by selling off bonds in the Bankers Trust account. Because Iguchi was both a trader and securities manager, he was able to conceal his unauthorized transactions by falsifying the Bankers Trust account statements that he managed through the back office of Daiwa's New York branch. Unfortunately, Iguchi could not recoup the losses, and the debts began to grow even larger. When customers wanted to sell off securities or collect interest on bonds that Iguchi had already sold, he settled their accounts by selling even more securities and falsifying the records. In the course of the eleven-year scandal, Iguchi sold approximately $377 million of Daiwa's customer securities and $733 million of Daiwa's own investment securities; he purportedly forged 30,000 trading slips to cover his losses. Interestingly enough, in the end not one Daiwa Bank customer lost money in this scandal.

During the 1995 federal investigation, Iguchi revealed that two additional unnamed traders had also incurred serious losses totaling approximately $97 million between 1984 and 1987. These losses had been concealed from bank regulators by shifting the losses to Daiwa's overseas affiliates and a shelf company set up in the Cayman Islands. During the investigation, it was discovered that the bank had been operating an unauthorized trading area, which was disguised as a storage room during regulatory examinations. It was also revealed that U.S. regulatory agencies had warned Daiwa in 1993 and 1994 about their poor internal controls; one in particular was Iguchi's dual role as a trader and securities manager.

Perhaps the most damning blow to Daiwa's reputation was the fact that the bank knowingly engaged in a cover-up of the situation. Upon receiving Iguchi's first letter in July 1995, Daiwa began selling off assets before reporting the fraud to authorities, and it seems as though they also attempted to transfer the losses to Japan in order to avoid U.S. scrutiny. Furthermore, U.S. officials were discontented with Japan's finance ministry for belatedly reporting the fraud to U.S. authorities despite regulations requiring immediate notification.

Iguchi pleaded guilty to misapplication of bank funds, false entries in bankbooks and records, money laundering, and conspiracy and was sentenced in New York to four years in prison and a $2.6 million fine, which he will probably never be able to pay. Iguchi requested to serve the first fifteen months in solitary confinement in Manhattan's Metropolitan Correction Center—for fear of what the other prisoners would do to him—before being transferred to a relatively plush minimum-security facility in Pennsylvania. Several of Daiwa's senior managers were forced to resign, and on September 20, 2000, five years after the initial charges, a Japanese court ruled that eleven current and former board members and top executives were to pay the bank $775 million in damages, a decision that was immediately challenged. Today, Daiwa has withdrawn from all overseas banking operations and has instead been focusing on becoming the strongest regional bank in Osaka, Japan.

FURTHER READING

"Daiwa Bank Shuts Down Global Operations." *BBC News Online* (1998, October 25). Available at http://news.bc.co.uk/2/hi/business/201113.stm. Accessed September 25, 2006.

"I Didn't Set Out to Rob a Bank." *Time Magazine Online* (1997, February 10). Available at http://www.time.come/time/magazine/1997/int/970210/interview.i_didnt_set.html. Accessed September 25, 2006.

Jameson, R. "Case Study: Daiwa." *ERisk Online* (2001, August). Available at http://www.erisk.com/Learning/CaseStudies/Daiwa.asp. Accessed September 25, 2006.

"Japan's $1 Billion Scam." *AsiaWeek Online* (October 27, 1995). Available at http://www.asiaweek.com/asiaweek/95/1027/biz2.html.

Mokhiber, R. "Top 100 Corporate Criminals of the Decade." *Corporate Crime Reporter Online* (March 4, 1996). Available at http://www.corporatecrimereporter.com.

Ostrom, D. "Daiwa Bank." *Japan Economic Institute Report* (March 8, 1996).
"Regulators Terminate the U.S. Operations of Daiwa Bank, Ltd. Japan." FDIC press release, November 2, 1995. Washington DC: FDIC. Available at http://www.fdic.gov/news/news/press/1995/ pr9567.html.

ANDREA SCHOEPFER

DALKON SHIELD. The Dalkon Shield, an intrauterine device (IUD) used to prevent pregnancy in the 1970s and early 1980s, was at the center of thousands of lawsuits yielding millions of dollars in settlements. Lawsuits targeted the makers of the Shield, affixing the blame for severe infections, miscarriages, and death on the device's design and questioning the research that surrounded its production and distribution. The Shield was a crab-shaped device with four to five prongs along both sides, a circular hole toward the top, and a tail string with knots at either end. The Shield, like other IUDs, was inserted by a physician into a woman's uterus, with the tail string hanging through the cervix into the vagina. The reason why IUDs in general, and the Shield in particular, work as an effective method of birth control is still undetermined, with popular theories speculating that the presence of a foreign object in the uterus either creates sperm-destroying white cells or keeps a fertilized egg from attaching to the uterine wall.

Despite the uncertainty about how they prevent pregnancy, IUDs have long been used as a method of birth control in both animals and humans. In 1968, Hugh Davis, a Johns Hopkins gynecologist, and Irwin Lerner, an electrical engineer, designed the Dalkon Shield as an improvement over existing IUDs. Lerner was cofounder of Lerner Laboratories, which later became the Dalkon Corporation. Davis and Robert Cohn, a Connecticut attorney, shared ownership in the company.

The new and "modern" design of the Dalkon Shield was considered its major selling point. Its designers believed the new Shield's shape and prongs would help the device resist expulsion, a traditional problem for IUD users. They also believed that its increased surface area and multifilament string would make it easier for physicians to monitor the device's position. After the Dalkon Corporation assumed all rights to the Dalkon Shield and began production, Davis inserted the Shield into 640 patients at a family-planning clinic as a test trial for its effectiveness. Even though the FDA at the time required a test of 1500 subjects over two years for the approval of any drug, IUDs were considered devices rather than drugs, so the regulations did not apply. Davis concluded his twelve-month study with a statement that the Shield yielded an annual pregnancy rate of 1.1 percent (other IUDs reported approximately 3 percent) and reported no adverse side effects.

The study was later criticized for its small sample size and short observation period (the average length of insertion was less than six months). Detractors also objected to the researcher's financial interests in the product being tested. It was later noted that the preemptive pregnancy rates were inaccurate and that additional pregnancies, which Davis discovered after the report was written, would have raised the annual pregnancy rate to over 5 percent. Despite this discovery, the lower percentage rate was published. Davis's financial interests in the success of the Shield were not divulged in his research findings about the Shield and other IUDs.

The A. H. Robins Company, which had never dealt with contraceptive devices before, purchased the rights to the Shield from the Dalkon Corporation on June 12, 1970. Robins, a pharmaceutical corporation in Richmond, Virginia, was headed by E. Clairborne Robins Jr. At the time, Robins provided an international market with such products as Chap-Stick and Robitussin; it was a Fortune 400 company when the Dalkon Shield was put on the market.

Although the company was aware that the published pregnancy rate was incorrect, Robins aggressively marketed the Shield through advertisements in medical journals targeting gynecologists and general practitioners. Advertising was also aimed at the female public. The original 1.1 percent pregnancy rate was reported in marketing, and the product was claimed to be safe and effective. Although Davis had recommended that his trial patients use spermicidal foam for added pregnancy protection in the first several months of Shield use, no mention of this was made in advertising, nor was it considered in rendering the pregnancy rate statistics. In addition, the "nullip" version of the product, an untested version of the Shield designed for use in women who had never borne children, was highly promoted because it was the only IUD of its kind available. Furthermore, the version of the Shield tested by Davis contained no copper; however, adding a heavy metal to a product was thought to increase its effectiveness in preventing pregnancy, so the product that was to be placed on the market had copper mixed into the plastic. No mention of this change in the product's composition was made in the published reports. Some opponents of the Shield speculate that this change was not mentioned because the addition of copper could be viewed as the addition of a drug (due to copper's contraceptive effect), which would have subjected the Shield to FDA drug regulations. Despite these potential complications, the Dalkon Shield hit the market in January 1971.

Between 4.5 and 5 million Shields were distributed before they were pulled from the market in 1974. An estimated 2.2 million of these were implanted in women in the United States. Allegedly, tens of thousands of women worldwide have been injured by using the shield. Included in the injuries are at least eighteen fatalities and many more life-threatening cases of pelvic inflammatory disease (PID), infertility, septic abortions, premature births, birth defects, perforation of the uterus, and ectopic pregnancies.

The string attached to the Shield was thought to be the faulty part of the design that led to numerous infections. Other IUDs on the market used a single-filament string that hung through the opening of the cervix; however, the Shield had a multifilament string wrapped in an open-ended sheath. The string's multifilament design essentially left space between the filaments that could harbor bacteria, and the sheath may actually have held the bacteria in. The string collected and transferred bacteria, creating a pathway into a woman's uterus and fallopian tubes. This phenomenon, termed "wicking," increased the risk of bacteria entering the uterus, leading to a higher incidence of PID, a dangerous type of uterine infection. Additional problems with the string's design also created early concerns among physicians. Problems included sheaths being damaged or broken during production and strings breaking during extraction and deteriorating while in use. Allegedly, tests to assess the string's design and to determine the durability of the sheath were conducted by researchers who both were and were not associated with Robins; purportedly these tests proved the suspicions of a faulty design. Despite these issues, the Shield used the same string design until its production was halted.

Another risk associated with the Shield occurred if the user became pregnant. Despite an early finding by one of Robins' consulting physicians that it was hazardous to leave the Shield in during pregnancy, Robins continued until 1974 to encourage Shield users not to remove the device during pregnancy. In May of that year, after numerous reports of spontaneous septic abortions in Shield users, two deaths of pregnant women who were using the Shield, and an article in the *American Journal of Obstetrics and Gynecology* that associated the Shield with the death of expectant mothers, Robins sent letters to 120,000 physicians urging the removal of the device in pregnant women.

According to analysis conducted by the Women's Health Study, Dalkon Shield users had a relative risk of PID five times greater than women who used other IUDs. Researchers who published the study recommended that all Shields be removed. In 1983, the Center for Disease Control reported that Dalkon Shield users suffered from pelvic infections at rates five to ten times higher than other IUD users and recommended removal. This study was released in time to be used in a case involving Brenda Stempke, a woman who had developed a severe pelvic infection that led to the removal of one of her fallopian tubes and left her infertile. The study influenced jurors to side with Stempke; they awarded her $1.75 million in damages due to the Shield's defective design, Robins' inadequate testing, and the company's failure to warn the public about known risks.

By September 1980, Robins had sent letters to 200,000 physicians recommending they remove the Shield from their patients. The letter said that the risk of infection was higher for long-term users, which at the time included all current users. This letter did not satisfy critics of the Shield, because it failed to mention the risks associated with the multifilament string. In October 1984, the Robins Company began an advertising drive urging women who were still using the Shield to have them removed at the company's expense. In response to the advertisements, thousands of women filed claims for removal, with Robins picking up the cost for removal of over 5000 Shields.

The first lawsuits regarding the Dalkon Shield were filed in 1972, and on February 5, 1975, the first verdict was reached in Kansas, awarding $10,000 in actual (compensatory) damages and $75,000 in punitive damages to a Shield user named Connie Deemer. Deemer, who had become pregnant while wearing the Shield, had suffered a perforated uterus and had to have emergency surgery to have the Shield removed when it became lodged in her abdominal cavity. The decision was not considered to be a large financial loss to Robins, but it set a precedent for future cases that would prove to very damaging to both Robins and its insurer, Aetna Casualty and Surety Company. Distribution of the Shield was suspended in the United States on June 28, 1974, two days after the FDA recognized the high number of Shield-related spontaneous abortions and requested the product be pulled. Sales continued, however, in other countries until April 1975, and there were reports that some doctors continued to insert the Shield for up to six years after that.

In August 1985, a class-action lawsuit was filed on behalf of nearly 2000 claimants against Robins. In the same month, the 120-year-old company sought reorganization under Chapter 11 of the Bankruptcy Code, freezing all monetary claims against it. At that time, the company had paid $530 million for Shield-related cases, but approximately 6000 cases were still pending. Also, the IRS was attempting to claim $63 million in back taxes from the company. In 1989, the American Home Products Corporation acquired A. H. Robins as part of Robins' reorganization plan from bankruptcy andcreated a trust fund designed to cover the rest of the claims against the Shield. Filing for bankruptcy also made it possible for the company to consolidate all the Shield litigation into a Richmond federal court instead of spreading its defenses among many courts. United States District Judge Robert R. Merhige Jr., a native of Richmond, Virginia, and a neighbor of E. Clairborne Robins Sr., was in charge of all the proceedings.

The trust established by American Home was created to pay Shield claimants for the following twenty years. In over a ten-year period, the trust handled over 400,000 claims and paid nearly $3 billion to claimants. Claimants had three options for filing. Option 1 provided $725 to claimants who would sign a sworn statement that they had used the Shield and suffered injury. Option 2 assigned fixed amounts ranging from $850 to $5500 for specific types of injuries to women who could produce medical records verifying Shield use and an injury. Option 3 provided claimants with a settlement that was determined by using adjusted historical values of settlements from before the bankruptcy proceedings. Although the trust made it easier to identify women harmed by the Shield, critics claimed that the settlements women received were inadequate. A claimant who could submit medical records that proved the insertion of the Shield and injury (but did not directly establish cause) received from $850 (if she had suffered uncontrollable bleeding) up to $5500 (if she had had sterilizing surgery).

Robins also came under fire during the bankruptcy proceedings for paying out $7 million in contractor fees and deferred executive compensations, an act some say requires prior court approval. In addition to going after the pharmaceutical company, claimants also filed suits against Robin's insurer, Aetna Casualty and Surety Company, alleging that the insurer attempted to prevent the public from finding out about the dangers of the product.

In recent years, there has been some skepticism regarding the validity of the research against the Shield. Studies finding no increased risk for PID in IUD users (including the Shield) have led some researchers to conclude that IUDs are a safe and effective birth control method and that the indictment against Robins was a mistake. They believe that the Shield itself was not at fault; they contend that the doctors and clinicians who inserted the product caused the problems and that the sexual behavior of users was also a contributing factor.

See also: A. H. Robins; Corporate Crime

FURTHER READING

Couric, Emily. "The A. H. Robins Saga." *ABA Journal* 72 (1986): 56–60.

Mintz, Morton. *At Any Cost: Corporate Greed, Women, and the Dalkon Shield.* New York: Pantheon Books, 1985.

Mumford, S. D., and Kessel, E. "Was the Dalkon Shield a Safe and Effective Intrauterine Device? The Conflict Between Case-Control and Clinical Trial Study Findings." *Fertility and Sterility* 57 (1992): 1151–76.

Sobol, Richard. *Bending the Law: The Story of the Dalkon Shield Bankruptcy.* Chicago: University of Chicago Press, 1991.

STEPHANIE E. CARMICHAEL

DEPOSIT INSURANCE AND THE S&L DEBACLE. The National Commission on Financial Institution Reform, Recovery and Enforcement (NCFIRRE) declared that deposit insurance was the fundamental cause of the savings and loan (S&L) debacle. The conventional wisdom about deposit insurance's culpability for the disaster rested on two related arguments. Deposit insurance created an incentive to "gamble for resurrection," but for insurance, creditors exert "market discipline" that prevents abuses.

The first argument is imprecise. "Moral hazard" theory predicts the perverse incentives that arise when risk and reward are asymmetric and the insured can change his position after he purchases the insurance. The owner of a business insured for twice its market value stands to gain from a fire that burns the business down.

Moral hazard can arise without insurance. "Limited liability" creates it. Risk and reward depart when a corporation is failing. Shareholders capture the gain from fraudulent or risky strategies that increase reported profits. If the strategies fail, the creditors suffer the losses, because the shareholders have no personal liability for the corporation's debts. The value of a share in a failing corporation should be low. Shareholders, therefore, have little or nothing to lose if the strategy fails, but they win big if it succeeds. This activity has nothing to do with deposit insurance. Moral hazard was endemic among S&Ls in the early 1980s because every S&L was insolvent on a market-value basis. The sharp rise in interest rates that began in 1979 left the industry insolvent by $150 billion by mid-1982 (NCFIRRE 1993). Deposit insurance did not cause the industry's insolvency.

Insured U.S. depositories are unusual in that their primary creditors are protected in full by a government insurance fund and the U.S. Treasury. Because insured depositors face no credit risk, they have no incentive to exercise discipline and avoid loaning money to insolvent banks. Insurance is designed to *prevent* depositors from exercising discipline and closing banks through "runs." Insurance removes the incentive for depositors to engage in a "run." False rumors can cause runs that cause uninsured banks to fail.

The conventional economic wisdom asserted that S&Ls responded to the moral hazard through *legal*, though high-risk, investments (gambling). There was no theoretical or empirical basis for this assumption. Moral hazard theorists recognize that it can induce increased fraud or risk (White 1991). In the S&L context, the debate was whether the "high fliers" were honest gamblers or "control frauds." NCFIRRE's study found that control fraud was "invariably" present at the typical large failure (NCFIRRE 1993). NCFIRRE refuted the heart of the conventional economic wisdom about the debacle but adopted its fallback claim that only deposit insurance could explain widespread fraud.

NCFIRRE argued that deposit insurance removed private market discipline and led to the wave of control fraud because the core models of finance and economics (the efficient markets and contracts hypotheses) rest on the *implicit* assumption that such discipline prevents control fraud. Accounting fraud makes markets (and contracts) inefficient. The dominant law and economics model asserted that the markets prevent material control fraud (Easterbrook and Fischel 1993). Economic theory predicts that information asymmetry can produce "lemons" markets in which fraud becomes endemic (Akerlof 1970), but Akerlof and Romer explicitly assumed in 1993 that the government was unique in making inefficient contracts for deposit insurance. Akerlof and Romer were presenting a model of control fraud they described as "looting," and they assumed that financial markets could not suffer from "lemons" problems absent deposit insurance.

The debacle proved that widespread control fraud could occur without deposit insurance. S&L control frauds used accounting fraud to hide losses and report record profits. They were consistently able to get top-tier audit firms to "bless" these financial statements. None of this activity depended on deposit insurance. S&L control frauds were routinely able to attract *uninsured* funds. Shareholders were not insured, but the financial markets did not spot the frauds. Subordinated debt holders were not insured, yet they never spotted an S&L fraud. The conventional economic wisdom is that "sub-debt" holders are the *ideal* disciplinarians because they have the right incentives and they are sophisticated. Accounting fraud allows a CEO to loot the company through normal corporate means. Banks compete to lend to profitable companies so the fraud allows Ponzi schemes (see **Ponzi, Charles**). Accounting fraud is a "sure thing" (Akerlof and Romer 1993). The debacle proved that control fraud was not dependent on insurance. Waves of control fraud in Russia, Latin America, and the United States confirmed this point (Black 2005).

Insurance created an incentive to cover up the industry's insolvency. The insurance fund contained $6 billion to insure an industry insolvent by $150 billion. The shortfall should have been booked as a claim against the U.S. Treasury—which would have increased the national deficit by $144 billion. The administration's top S&L priority was to avoid contributing to a huge growth othe deficit (Black 2005). The cover-up prompted the most destructive regulatory actions (e.g., forbearance, debased regulatory accounting, and the failure to close the worst S&Ls).

See also: Control Fraud; Keating, Charles H., Jr.; Lincoln Savings and Loan Association

FURTHER READING

Akerlof, George. "The Market for 'Lemons': Quality, Uncertainty, and the Market Mechanism." *Quarterly Journal of Economics* 84.3 (1970): 488–500.

Akerlof, George A., and Romer, Paul M. "Looting: The Economic Underworld of Bankruptcy for Profit." *Brookings Papers on Economic Activity* 2 (1993): 1–73.

Black, William K. *The Best Way to Rob a Bank Is to Own One: How Corporate Executives and Politicians Looted the S&L Industry.* Austin University of Texas Press, 2005.

Easterbrook, Frank H., and Fischel, Daniel R. *The Economic Structure of Corporate Law.* Cambridge, MA: Harvard University Press, 1991.

National Commission on Financial Institution Reform, Recovery and Enforcement (NCFIRRE). *Origins and Causes of the S&L Debacle: A Blueprint for Reform, A Report to the President and Congress of the United States.* Washington, DC: Government Printing Office, 1993.

White, Lawrence. *The S&L Debacle: Public Policy Lessons for Bank and Thrift Regulation.* New York: Oxford University Press, 1991.

WILLIAM K. BLACK

DES. Diethylstilbestrol, or DES, was the first artificial estrogen, invented by Dodds in 1938. Between 1950 and 1980, it was marketed worldwide between as a medication with uses in very different therapeutic domains (for example, as a treatment for menopausal complaints, acne, and breast and prostate cancer; as a hair restorer; as a morning-after pill; and as a way to stop early contractions during childbirth). It was also used as a growth hormone in the meat industry. The Smith and Smith cure was a popular application of DES prescribed to billions of pregnant women to prevent miscarriage and spontaneous abortions. Because the inventor didn't apply for patent protection, the product was marketed by more than 250 companies under more than 200 different trademarks. Some experts estimate the number of women who have taken the medicine at 4 million worldwide; others estimate 4.8 million in the United States alone.

Without being fully tested for toxicological effects, the product was marketed worldwide. In the early years of its marketing, scientists had already demonstrated the harmful effects of DES. In 1938, researchers suspected a carcinogenic effect of the product on consumers and their fetuses, while its effectiveness had never been proved. In the early 1970s, researchers led by A. L. Herbst discovered that some women whose mothers had been treated with DES were evidencing a new kind of vaginal cancer. As a reaction to these first alarming results, the publicity for the product was halted. In most countries, governments ordered the product removed from the market, but because the recall happened without drawing a lot of attention to the problem, the product continued to be consumed during the 1980s.

DES has direct and indirect victims. The direct victims are people who have used the product (e.g., women during pregnancy). These women have a higher-than-average risk of breast cancer. Most victims, however, were indirectly contaminated as fetuses when their mothers swallowed the product. Daughters have the most chance of being harmed. Consumption of the product causes a considerable increase in the risk of clear-cell cancer, congenital aberrations, breast cancer, infertility, ectopic pregnancy, and preterm labor and delivery. Sons have more than the average number of congenital aberrations. A recent study in the Netherlands revealed a higher rate of hypospadia (an abnormality of the penis) in boys born to DES daughters.

It is impossible to know exactly how many victims there are, for a number of reasons. The most important reasons are the time that has elapsed between the consumption of the product and presentation of the symptoms and the prevalence with which it was used. Daughters of DES mothers are at highest risk for harmful effects between the ages of fourteen and twenty. Recent research has discovered aberrations in the third generation, meaning that sixty years may have elapsed between the time the product was taken and the development of symptoms. DES has atypical and typical effects. Typical effects include a higher risk of breast cancer and infertility. Atypical effects include a higher risk of clear-cell cancer, a rare kind of vaginal or cervical cancer. Because most effects are atypical, it is impossible to quantify the number of victims, and calculations normally underestimate the effects as well. A strong taboo surrounds the DES product. It is hard for victims to talk about the problems that confront them and to testify publicly about these consequences. Most mothers and daughters no longer remember the trademark of the medicine that was taken. For these and other reasons, it is difficult to estimate the number of victims, and it is impossible to prove the responsibility of a specific company.

In many countries, such as the United States, Canada, France, the Netherlands, Belgium, Ireland, and the United Kingdom, victims have united in DES action groups. The task of these action groups varies and may include providing psychological support, educating health-care professionals, informing members about the possibility of legal action, and even advocating for their members in a judicial procedure. The number of members and the way an action group works depends on the specific context of the country.

In the Netherlands, the DES-Centrum has more than 20,000 members who are sure or relatively certain that they are DES victims. The organization enjoys limited government support. The group formed in 1984 when six Dutch DES daughters suffering from clear-cell cancer lost their civil case and then their appeal because they did not succeed in naming the manufacturer of the product their mother took. The High Court recognized the moral responsibility of all former DES producers and suggested that DES manufacturers should all pay into a fund and that cases should be handled outside the judicial system. After a public appeal, more than 20,000 people announced that they would be seeking compensation. In the spring of 2005, a committee composed of members of DES-Centrum, representatives of the medical community, and lawyers representing the companies were still negotiating compensation. The Dutch Parliament is working on passage of a bill for the collective settlement of mass damage. This bill must protect the responsible companies against legal claims other than the collective settlement and must guarantee a quick settlement for the victims. In France, membership of DES action groups is rather limited, although some victims have already succeeded in civil court cases. The company, however, refuses to accept the verdict.

In Belgium, the DES action group is a one-man organization without any ambition to start judicial actions. In the United States and Canada, action groups are well organized. In the United States, more than 1000 cases have been introduced before civil courts. Judges have exhibited a large degree of creativity in surmounting the problem of not being able to find the responsible company. Until now, class actions have not been accepted because the variety of conditions and injuries caused by DES prohibits certifying plaintiffs as a legal class.

See also: Corporate Crime; Pharmaceutical Companies

FURTHER READING

Bridges J., and Bridges, O. "Hormones as Growth Promoters: The Precautionary Principle or a Political Risk Assessment." In P. Harremoës, D. Gee, and M. Garvin(eds.), *Late Lessons from Early Warnings: The Precautionary Principle, 1896–2000*. OPOCE, 2002.

Chetley A. "The Time Bomb Explodes." Pp. 137–42 in A. Chetley (ed.), *Problem Drugs*. Amsterdam: Health Action International, 1993.

"DES Action USA." Available at http://www.desaction.org. Accessed September 26, 2006.

"DES Daughters." Centers for Disease Control. Available at http://www.cdc.gov/DES/consumers/daughters. Accessed September 26, 2006.

Ibaretta D., and Swan, S., "The DES Story: Long-term Consequences of Prenatal Exposure." In P. Harremoës, D. Gee, and M. Garvin M. (eds.), *Late Lessons from Early Warnings: The Precautionary Principle. 1896–2000*. OPOCE, 2002.

GUDRUN VANDE WALLE

DIFFERENTIAL ASSOCIATION. Psychologists have developed several theories to explain how people learn. One of the more popular theories is called social learning theory. Under this rubric are three subcategories that have been applied to criminology: differential reinforcement theory, neutralization, and differential association. Edward H. Sutherland (1883–1950), a well-known American sociologist, developed the differential association theory to explain the process by which adolescent males become deviant and engage in delinquent behavior, including joining gangs. Later he reformulated and expanded his theory to include the actions of the wealthy, whom he labeled white-collar criminals.

Differential association theory purports that crime is learned behavior that one adopts through affiliating and interacting with others. Favorable attitudes, as well as logistical information about how to commit crimes, are acquired from friends or acquaintances. Additionally, one is socialized into having positive definitions or attitudes about crime. This later process is pertinent to understanding how one comes to regard crime as a viable course of action.

In particular, Sutherland argued that criminal behavior is learned in a process of symbolic interaction with others, primarily in groups. Although nine statements constitute the theory, it is the sixth that Sutherland claimed as *the* principle of differential association. This principle argues that a person commits crimes because he or she learned "definitions" (rationalizations and attitudes) favorable to violation of law in excess of the definitions unfavorable to breaking the law.

Sutherland's theory does not simply claim that association with "bad company" leads to criminality. Rather, he implies that one learns criminal behavior in intimate communication with criminal and noncriminal "patterns" and "definitions." Criminal behavior is explained by one's exposure to others' favorable definitions of crime, which are weighed against one's contact with conforming, noncriminal definitions. The process varies according to the "modalities" of association—that is, persons exposed to law-violating definitions earlier, longer, more often, and more intensity than to law-abiding definitions are more likely to break the law.

Sutherland's theory is able to explain these individuals' actions as learned behavior occurring within an environment that formally and informally instructs them that criminal behaviors are favorable, indeed more desirable than behaviors that do not violate the law.

Differential association theory, in whole or in part, has been used to explain juvenile delinquency, political crime, and property crime and offenders. Undoubtedly, differential association theory has been criticized. Burgess and Akers (1966), among others, argue that differential association theory disproportionately emphasizes mental states that are difficult to measure. They also argue that the way deviant behavior is learned is not precise enough to measure. Consequently, they propose their own theory, "differential reinforcement," which combines elements of differential association and basic patterns of classical conditioning (Pavlov 2001). In short, they argue that deviant behavior is no different from prosocial behavior in that it is learned in the context of rewards and punishments.

Most of the criticism deals with when and how individuals are socialized, particularly where in the socialization process like-minded individuals have an effect on the person committing the deviance or crime. Others suggest that differential association theory and its modifications examine deviance and crime from a middle-class perspective, minimizing a more holistic understanding of this kind of behavior.

FURTHER READING

Akers, R. L., and Sellers, C. *Criminological Theories: Introduction, Evaluation, Application.* Los Angeles: Roxbury Press, 2004.

Burgess, R. L., and Akers, R. L. 1966. "Reinforcement Theory of Criminal Behavior." *Social Problems* 14 (1966): 128–47.

Liska, Allen. *Perspectives on Deviance.* Englewood Cliffs, NJ: Prentice Hall, 1987.

Pavlov, I. P. *Selected Works.* Honolulu: University Press of the Pacific, 2001.

Ross, Jeffrey Ian. *The Dynamics of Political Crime.* Thousand Oaks, CA: Sage Publications, 2002.

Short, James. "Differential Association as a Hypothesis: Problems of Empirical Testing," *Social Problems* 8 (1960): 14–25.

Sutherland, E. H. *Principles of Criminology*, 4th edition. Philadelphia: Lippincott, 1947.

Sutherland, E. H. *White Collar Crime.* New York: Dryden Press, 1949.

Sutherland, E. H., and Cressey, E. *Principles of Criminology*, 10th edition. Philadelphia: Lippincott, 1978.

Sykes, Gresham, and Matza, David. "Techniques of Neutralization: A Theory of Delinquency." *American Sociological Review* 22 (1957): 664–70.

Tunnell, K. *Living Off Crime.* Chicago: Burnham Publishers, 2000.

Warr, Mark. "Dangerous Situations: Social Context and Fear of Criminal Victimization." *Social Forces* 68 (1990): 891–907.

JEFFREY IAN ROSS

DIXON, DON. For a symbol of the savings and loan (S&L) crisis, one can look to Don Dixon. Dixon was a Texas real-estate developer who bought Vernon Savings and Loan Association in 1981 for $6 million. It was a small-town S&L with deposits around $82 million and safe investments with only $90,000 in bad debts. Under Dixon's control, Vernon became a national leader with assets and deposits over $1.7 billion. Vernon lived extravagantly; he owned a $2 million house in Del Mar and a yacht, which he used to host many fundraisers during the mid-1980s for many politicians. Federal investigators insisted that Dixon's books had been cooked to hide millions of dollars of questionable loans. James O'Shea's book *The Daisy Chain* chronicles the $1 billion collapse of Dixon's business.

The root cause of the savings-and-loan crisis lay in the deregulation of the industry in order to allow S&Ls to compete against their unregulated competition, including banks. In the early 1980s, interest rates rose dramatically, rates in the high teens were not uncommon. Prior to this, the thrift industry was almost guaranteed to be profitable. Interest rates on S&L deposits were set by regulation, and competition in the financial services industry (e.g., banks, insurance companies, mortgage brokers, and brokerage houses) took away customers. This created a criminogenic environment. In order for the SLs to compete and survive, the owners and employees came up with very creative ways to keep their customers, while others engaged in systematic looting of the S&L at which they worked.

In the world of S&L fraud, Vernon, under Dixon, looked like a kingpin. Dixon was able to expand his thrift assets quickly by urging top executives to make high-dollar commercial loans, all backed by government guarantees. His business deals included a stud farm and casinos. Dixon often bought property from a person who took out a loan from Vernon and then sold the land to another loan seeker; if that person went bankrupt, Dixon would have the land reappraised and then sell it again. Such a transaction, commonly referred to as "land flipping," occurred over and over. More than $700 million of these loans were later written off as "bad," and Dixon was accused of bank fraud and spending depositors' savings on classic cars, planes, prostitutes, and expensive vacations. Such behavior was created and allowed to persist because of a profound flaw in the Reagan administration's thinking about deregulation: that markets should be liberated not only by writing new laws, but by weakly enforcing existing ones. The system was an open invitation to abuse. Thrift owners, including Dixon, could attract as much money as they wanted by offering interest rates well above the market rate on guaranteed accounts. They were then free to invest in whatever they chose, which was mainly real estate. If the gamble paid off, the thrift owners were laughing; if the investments failed, the government picked up the tab through its guarantees to depositors. Dixon and other thrift owners made vast paper fortunes as they competed fiercely to finance more and more outlandish real-estate deals. Vernon was one of 400 SLs in the state of Texas; all but sixteen of them failed, costing U.S. taxpayers billions. The government declared an astounding 96 percent of Vernon's loans delinquent.

Dixon was eventually indicted, tried, and convicted in 1990 for misappropriating thrift funds to pay for prostitutes and his California beach house. He was facing a possible 120 years in prison but instead received a mere five years in prison, five years probation, 500 hours of community service, and restitution of $611,000. The federal judge was not convinced that Dixon alone caused his thrift's failure; the judge placed the blame on Congress and a lack of diligence by the various regulatory bodies. The scandal was not the crimes themselves, but what was legal. Most of the outrageous high-risk lending activity that Dixon engaged in was not only legal but backed by federal deposit insurance.

See also: Deposit Insurance and the S&L Debacle

FURTHER READING

Brumbaugh, R. D. *Thrifts Under Siege: Restoring Order to American Banking.* Beard Books, 1999.

Calavita, K., Tillman, R., and Pontell, H. N. "The Savings and Loan Debacle, Financial Crime, and the State." *Annual Review of Sociology* 23 (1997): 19–20.

Calavita, K., and Pontell, H. N. (July 1990). 'Heads I Win, Tails You Lose': Deregulation, Crime, and Crisis in the Savings and Loan Industry." Special issue, *Crime and Delinquency* 36 (July, 1990): 309–41.

O'Shea, J. *The Daisy Chain.* Toronto: Pocket Books, 1991.

DEBRA E. ROSS

DREXEL BURNHAM LAMBERT. Drexel Burnham Lambert was one of the most profitable Wall Street investment banking firms during the late 1970s and most of the 1980s. In 1988, the SEC charged Drexel Burnham Lambert for insider trading, rigged takeovers, falsified transactions, and the destruction of records. For its excesses and crimes, Drexel epitomized the "greed is good" decade of the 1980s.

Drexel Burnham was formed in 1973 with the merger of Drexel Firestone and Burnham and Company. The Belgian firm Bruxelles Lambert acquired an interest in 1976. Ignored by former Fortune 500 clients and the prestigious investment banks of Wall Street, Drexel Burnham Lambert struggled to reclaim the reputation Drexel Firestone once had. Clients were leaving for better deals elsewhere; so were many key employees. The firm had suffered losses in the stock market, and its high-grade bond department was also ailing. The only department that was doing well was Michael Milken's noninvestment-grade bond—junk bond—department.

Most in the firm, though, did not like Michael Milken. He was not interested in the high-grade stocks of the Fortune 500 companies that Drexel Burnham Lambert was used to serving. Milken was interested in junk bonds, yet his department was outpacing the others. He complained that, despite his success, the company would not give him much capital. Tubby Burnham decided to take a risk with Milken and gave him $2 million in capital and unlimited authority. Milken was able to keep 35 percent of any of the profits generated from his department. Many of the other departments showed a meager profit, and others showed losses, but the firm as a whole was doing fine. When Milken's department was added to the mix, Drexel saw a windfall. Milken had doubled the $2 million that Burnham had given him.

Milken did not invent junk bonds, but through his work at Drexel he transformed the junk bond market. His department did not just buy and sell bonds; they began issuing new bonds. Milken led the firm into new junk bond issues with $125 million in sales in 1977. Drexel bonds made up 25 percent of the junk market. In 1978, Drexel sold $440 million in junk, with the next strongest rival only selling $150 million.

Michael Milken had started his career trading low-rate bonds floated by marginal firms in the 1970s. He soon learned that he could profit from the bonds of marginal firms that were good candidates for corporate takeovers. Milken aided firms whose assets were below the usual investment standards by helping them raise capital through brokering high-yield bonds. Milken would help float bond issues for such firms and then sell them to other firms interested in hostile takeovers of the companies themselves. Milken and Drexel brokered billions in these junk bonds to interested companies, including those in the savings and loan industry, insurance companies, and banks.

Milken continued to expand the junk bond market by creating junk bond mutual funds. In 1982, he led Drexel into the mergers and acquisitions business. This business was built by recombining, relabeling, and realigning existing materials, not by making anything original. The most expensive restructuring in the history of business did not arise from technological advances or creation of a new industry; it was fueled by having one company take over another, and Milken was a genius at this. Milken found out about forthcoming hostile mergers and used that information to trade stocks illegally and make a whole lot of money for Drexel. He added even more, however, to his personal portfolio. He also sold junk bonds that turned out to be worthless. Milken made an obscene amount of money off these illegal deals. In 1997 alone, he made $550 million in junk bond commissions.

Working for Drexel, Milken had near-total control of the multibillion-dollar junk bond market. He could have made a fortune off his knowledge without breaking the law, but his insatiable desire to expand his power, wealth, and influence seemed to create irresistible temptations. Even though Milken often deceived his clients, his control of the junk bond market gave them little choice but to continue working with him.

Milken was indicted in early 1989 on ninety-eight counts of fraud, racketeering, and illegal insider trading. He was given a stiff ten-year sentence and forced to pay $600 million for his crimes. Milken was also targeted in many civil suits. In March 1992, he agreed to pay $500 million into a compensation fund. This act left him with at least $125 million in his own name and a family fortune well over a half billion dollars. He also received a lifetime ban on associating with any securities broker or dealer.

In 1988, Drexel Burnham Lambert pleaded guilty to six felony counts of wire, mail, and securities fraud; the company also agreed to pay a fine of $650 million, fire Michael Milken, and withhold his bonus for the year (some $200 million). The U.S. Justice Department brought a $6.8 billion civil suit against Drexel in 1989.

Without Milken, Drexel's business soon floundered. The firm continued to underwrite junk bond offerings, including a massive 1989 leveraged buyout (LBO) deal for RJR Nabisco. However, without Milken, the firm had a hard time placing the debt. Increasingly, Drexel had to buy the bonds itself, tying up capital in illiquid, high-risk investments. When junk bond issuers could not make payments on their debt, Milken was no longer there to force investors to accept restructurings. Instead, the issuers defaulted. Drexel's capital was rapidly being depleted. The cost of the legal settlement, attorneys' fees, bonuses paid to keep key employees, and now losses on its own junk bond positions, pushed Drexel over the edge. The huge fines and public loss of confidence were major blows to the firm, and in February 1990 it declared bankruptcy. It was the largest Wall Street investment house failure in U.S. history. Drexel Burnham Lambert became a symbol of Wall Street greed.

See also: Keating, Charles H., Jr.; Lincoln Savings and Loan Association; Milken, Michael

FURTHER READING

Bruck, C. *The Predators' Ball: The Junk-bond Raiders and the Man Who Staked Them*. New York: Simon & Schuster, 1988.
Sobel, R. *Dangerous Dreamers: The Financial Innovators from Charles Merrill to Michael Milken*. New York: Wiley, 1993.
Stewart, J. B. *Den of Thieves*. New York: Simon & Schuster, 1991.
Zey, M. *Banking on Fraud: Drexel, Junk Bonds, and Buyouts*. New York: Aldine De Gruyter, 1993.

DEBRA E. ROSS

E

ENRON. The collapse of the Enron corporation, amid allegations of massive financial misrepresentations and accounting fraud, was the first widely publicized major white-collar crime of the twenty-first century. Some commentators would come to view the Enron collapse as the largest financial and political scandal in American history. The huge scope of Enron's debts and losses was first publicly exposed in October 2001, and it rivaled 9/11 and the war on terror for public attention. In the wake of the Enron case, similar large-scale misrepresentations of the finances of various other major American corporations were also exposed. Although such misrepresentations by corporations were hardly new, the scope and scale of the subsequent losses in these most recent cases were so great that they attracted major attention from the American public and from various political entities. Investors and pensioners were estimated to have lost tens of billions of dollars, and many other adverse consequences for specific communities, and the American economy, also occurred.

Origins of Enron. The Enron Corporation was a product of the merger of the Houston Natural Gas Company with InterNorth, another natural-gas pipeline company, in 1985, to form an interstate natural-gas pipeline company. Whereas the original companies were traditional natural-gas suppliers, the new entity evolved into something quite different. By the year 2000, a mere fifteen years after its formation, Enron was listed as the seventh largest Fortune 500 company, and claimed to be doing some $100 billion a year in business. Kenneth Lay, Enron's CEO or board chair for most of its existence, with a Ph.D. in economics, was the key figure in the transformation of a relatively humble natural-gas company into a "new economy" e-commerce behemoth. Enron acquired many other companies, branching off into many forms of trading activities. And it increasingly operated globally, for example, contracting to produce a multibillion-dollar energy generator in India. Indeed, Enron was featured in many business school lessons as an exemplary case of an innovative new type of corporation, with imaginative leaders successfully exploiting emerging opportunities in a rapidly changing world. Between the beginning of 1998 and the end of 2000, the stock price of Enron experienced a phenomenal rise, and Enron was celebrated as well on Wall Street as an extraordinary investment opportunity. At the beginning of 2001, Enron was still valued at some $60 billion dollars. A year later, the value of its stock had declined by some 99 per cent and was virtually worthless, and the corporation itself had declared the largest bankruptcy in American history up to that time.

Many of the deals that Enron made turned out in hindsight to be based upon wildly optimistic (and unsupportable) projections regarding future supply of and demand for energy, or blatantly exploitative contracts that gouged consumers. With its focus on creative "deals," as opposed to the production of products, Enron no longer took the form of a modern company but was rather a postmodern corporation.

Specific Structure of the Frauds. The frauds carried out at Enron were complex. A major accounting fraud was involved, with Enron's massive debts shifted to off-the-books partnerships—controlled by Enron insiders—that allowed Enron to misrepresent its income flow and profits grossly. Andrew Fastow, Enron's chief financial officer, played a key role in setting up the partnerships—known as "special-purpose entities"—and he and his wife profited greatly from their involvement with these partnerships. Although certain forms of off-the-books partnerships are regarded as a legitimate device to manage financial risk for a corporation, it became clear that in Enron's case these partnerships crossed the line into outright fraudulent entities mainly designed to conceal debt and to enrich those controlling the partnerships. Enron also disguised its immense debt by listing billions of dollars of loans as trades.

For all of the complexity of Enron's financial misrepresentations, some commentators saw Enron as basically a classic "pump-and-dump" operation. This enduring form of investment fraud is characterized by the use of various misrepresentations to drive stock prices up, with insiders then dumping their own stock at the top of the market, leaving the many misled investors to suffer huge losses when the stock inevitably goes into a precipitous decline as misrepresentation eventually comes to light. Other commentators focused on the fact that many of the aggressive accounting practices used by Enron, and its vesting of employee 401(k) retirement plans so largely with Enron stock (with restrictions on employee rights to sell this stock), were actually legal. For example, Enron was allowed to declare immediately profits on highly speculative, long-term energy deals, by a technique known as "mark-to-market" valuation. Such techniques produced a wildly inflated notion of Enron's profitability, pumping up it stock price. Existing laws then too often sanction practices that are inherently deceptive and unethical.

The Complicity of Other Parties. It might be reassuring if Enron's massive financial fraud could be wholly blamed on Enron executives and employees. Unfortunately, many other parties and entities were directly or indirectly complicit in the massive failure of Enron. Its board of directors—including some prominent executives at other major corporations—failed in one of the basic responsibilities of any corporate board: to ensure that the corporation is conducting itself honestly and honorably. But as is true with many such boards, the board members all too often had inherent conflicts of interest, sometimes as well-compensated consultants or contractors for Enron, or they had too many other responsibilities to focus properly on how Enron worked. The Arthur Andersen accounting firm was Enron's auditor, and it should have uncovered and exposed the massive forms of accounting fraud undertaken at this corporation. But Andersen was collecting over $50 million a year in fees from Enron, with more of that amount coming from consulting services than for auditing. Ultimately, as Enron began to collapse, Andersen employees began shredding many of their auditing documents and tampering with e-mail messages. The Andersen firm was indicted on federal obstruction-of-justice charges, and this firm also collapsed following its conviction on those charges.

Investment banking houses and stock analysts were profiting immensely from Enron's business and the dramatic rise in its stock price and failed to question adequately the basis of Enron's claims about its financial performance. Lawyers—including a prominent Houston law firm—either assisted in structuring some of Enron's dubious partnerships and other misleading practices or failed to clearly identify the illegalities involved in such activities. Credit-rating agencies failed to scrutinize Enron's financial claims with sufficient skepticism. Regulatory bodies were too often cowed by Enron's political clout. Altogether, then, many parties contributed in varying degrees to the Enron fraud.

The Role of Political Connections. The political clout of major corporations and their leadership has been an enduring theme of the literature on corporate crime. The ties, or "interlocks," between Enron and top people in the political system were especially striking. Kenneth Lay was a major contributor to George W. Bush's gubernatorial and presidential campaigns—in 2000, for example, he, along with Enron, donated $500,000 to Bush's successful campaign—and had various social contacts with Bush. Vice President Cheney met privately with Lay and other Enron officials to discuss energy policy. Thomas White, the Secretary of the Army, was a former top Enron executive, and various cabinet officers and other high-level Bush administration officials had collected large campaign donations, were consultants and advisors, or had significant investments in Enron. Top leaders in Congress and various influential "power brokers"—some of them top Democrats—also had various ties to Enron. Clearly these ties were helpful in many ways as long as Enron was perceived to be a successful, legitimate enterprise. In the face of its collapse, despite some entreaties from Lay, administration officials inevitably distanced themselves from Enron in various ways and refused to intervene on its behalf.

Consequences for Victims. The Enron fraud victimized an especially large spectrum of people. First, investors in Enron lost billions of dollars in stock value. In addition to those who bought Enron stock outright, these investors included the millions of people who had money in the over five hundred mutual funds that owned Enron stock. Whereas individual losses ranged greatly, the cumulative loss was enormous. Many state pension funds had significant investments in Enron stock, affecting state pensioners. Banks and other financial institutions that loaned money to Enron suffered huge losses. Enron employees in many cases had all their retirement (or 401k) money invested in Enron stock. Some of these employees witnessed declines in their retirement accounts from over a million dollars to less than $20 thousand dollars, with devastating consequences for their retirement plans. Furthermore, these employees were prohibited from moving their money out of Enron stock, while top-level Enron executives were unloading tens of millions of dollars worth of Enron stock. Thousands of Enron employees lost their jobs with the collapse of the corporation, as did employees of other such companies such as Andersen. Other victims included energy consumers in places such as California, who suffered blackouts and predatory energy costs as a consequence of Enron's trading maneuvers. Communities such as Houston and many institutions that counted on economic benefits from Enron's success suffered losses. In a broad sense, the impact of Enron's fraud and failure on investor confidence had harmful consequences as well, even if the specific costs are not so easily measured.

Legal Outcomes. Following the collapse of Enron, both major criminal investigations and massive civil lawsuits were undertaken. On the criminal side, a number of Enron executives agreed to plead guilty to various charges. Andrew Fastow, the chief financial officer, pleaded guilty to two felonies in January 2004 and faced ten years in prison. Indictments on a range of charges of the top executives—for example, former Enron CEOs Kenneth Lay and Jeffrey Skilling—were also eventually announced. Skilling, in testimony before a Congressional committee, and Lay, in an unusual post-indictment press conference, both claimed ignorance of the wrongful conduct at Enron. In the spring of 2006, Lay and Skilling went on trial in Houston on charges related to the collapse of Enron.

The Sarbanes-Oxley Act was passed in July 2002 in the wake of the revelations concerning Enron and other major corporations. Among other provisions, the act calls for increased oversight duties for corporate fraud, requires corporate CEOs and CFOs to certify corporate financial statements personally, and adjusts federal sentencing guidelines to implement longer prison sentences for high-level corporate executives convicted of corporate financial fraud.

Subsequent Corporate Scandals. The revelation of large-scale fraud by Enron in its financial reporting was quite rapidly followed by similar revelations about the finances of a number of other major American corporations, including Global Crossing, Qwest, RiteAid, HealthSouth, and WorldCom, among others. Indeed, the subsequent bankruptcy of WorldCom was even larger than that of Enron. If the exposure of Enron's frauds cast a harsher light on the financial reporting of these other corporations, it remained unclear exactly how widespread the problem of such financial fraud was. Were at least some other major American corporations simply more successful in concealing their fraudulent finances? This possibility could hardly be easily dismissed.

Explaining Enron. A sophisticated understanding of the Enron debacle requires attention to several different layers of explanation. Enron's rise and massive frauds were carried out during the late 1990s, a time when the virtues of a capitalist free market were being especially widely celebrated. The "bull market" of this era created expectations of substantial stock price growth and put CEOs under immense pressure to produce numbers that would promote such price growth or, at a minimum, would not lead to a decline in stock price. As capitalist enterprises began reporting record profits and fortunes large and small were being made by investors, too few people wanted to look very closely at the claims made about the sources of corporate profits. In this environment, deregulation regarding corporate activity was increasingly the norm. One can also argue that an emerging postmodern cultural environment fostered an increasing disconnect between traditional criteria for reality and "hyper-real" orientations, privileging simulations and abstract projections.

Networks and interlocks between Enron executives, board members, accounting firms, lawyers, investment bankers, stock analysts, and politicians created massive webs of conflicts of interest that either fostered fraudulent activity or led to failures to exercise appropriate oversight on corporate financial practices and reports.

On an organizational level, Enron was reported to have exemplified a corporate culture of arrogance and greed. Many within the corporation began to believe their own celebratory press. An environment that included intense competitiveness, intimidation toward compliance with the organizational agenda established by the company's leadership, and promotion of a strong ethos of corporate pride, loyalty, and superiority was also significant. A "rank-and-yank" system of evaluating employee performance meant that jobs of those who failed to comply with management's expectations were in jeopardy. Pay incentive structures encouraged executives to meet inflated numbers by any means possible.

On a dramaturgic level, the Enron corporation was for some time very successful in conveying an image of ultra-respectability that largely insulated it from external challenge and also reinforced an internal legitimation of its business practices. This projection of ultra-respectability was fostered by such maneuvers as Lay's cultivation of and friendship with top political leaders, the construction of an emblematic headquarters in Houston, and conspicuous philanthropy.

On an individualistic level, one should hardly overlook the specific choices and actions of key Enron executives. They have quite uniformly been described as arrogant, greedy, and lacking in basic integrity. They engaged in unwarranted risks. With isolated exceptions, they did not speak out against the fraudulent financial arrangements.

Overall Significance of the Enron Case. Enron is likely to be invoked as the principal symbol for the pervasive and massively costly corporate scandals that surfaced at the outset of the twenty-first century. It inspired a significant level of media and public interest in the unethical and illegal practices occurring within major American corporations. It provided a major impetus for the Sarbanes-Oxley Act. It remains to be seen, however, whether Enron will lead to an enduring transformation in the response to large-scale corporate crimes or will simply be another benchmark in such ongoing patterns of corporate fraud.

See also: Arthur Andersen

FURTHER READING

Bryce, Robert. *Pipe Dreams: Greed, Ego, Jealousy and the Death of Enron.* New York: Public Affairs, 2002.

Cruver, Bryan. *Anatomy of Greed: The Unshredded Truth from an Enron Insider.* New York: Carroll & Graf, 2002.

Elliott, A. Larry, and Schroth, Richard J. *How Companies Lie: Why Enron Is Just the Tip of the Iceberg.* London: Nicholas Brealey, 2002.

Fox, Loren. *Enron—The Rise and Fall.* Hoboken, NJ: Wiley, 2003.

Fusaro, Peter G., and Miller, Ross. *What Went Wrong at Enron.* Hoboken, NJ: Wiley, 2002.

McLean, Bethany, and Elkind, Peter. *Smartest Guys in the Room: The Amazing Rise and Scandalous Fall of Enron.* New York: Penguin, 2003.

Smith, Rebecca, and Emshwiller, John R. *24 Days: How Two Wall Street Journal Reporters Uncovered the Lies that Destroyed Faith in Corporate America.* New York: HarperBusiness, 2003.

Swartz, Mimi, and Watkins, Sherron. *Power Failure: The Inside Story of the Collapse of Enron.* New York: Doubleday, 2003.

DAVID O. FRIEDRICHS

ENVIRONMENTAL WHITE-COLLAR CRIME. Just as street crime is often regarded as a quality-of-life issue, environmental crime is regarded by academics, citizens, and activists alike as having equal or greater importance for our quality of life. Crimes that are committed against the environment for profit often leave unsightly and toxic "crime scenes" that may last for decades or even generations. Despite strong public opinion against such crimes, environmental crimes have been found to be among the most recurrent types of crime committed by corporate organizations. Whereas the problem of corporate and white-collar crime is often portrayed as simply an issue of money and finances, environmental crimes often have lasting physical, even violent, consequences. The human consequences range from debilitating illnesses such as asthma to death from long-term exposure to chemical agents.

The term *environmental crime* has been used quite loosely to describe an array of behaviors ranging from petty littering to large-scale dumping of toxic materials to nation-states subverting pollution control treaties. Mary Clifford (1997) has defined environmental crimes as actions that break any environmental statute that requires police enforcement. Others opt for a broader definition that includes any practice that is harmful to others or is environmentally unsustainable. Frank and Lynch (2002) have proposed that the term *green crime* be applied to the wrongful activities of corporations that break environmental laws. There is considerable debate, however, as to what exactly constitutes an environmental crime. A corporation that fully complies with environmental laws in the United States may be engaging in manufacturing practices that are considered illegal in other countries or that may be environmentally unsustainable in the first place. Furthermore, corporations may move dirty operations to countries without strict environmental standards to engage in behaviors that are illegal in other parts of the world. It is difficult to measure the true extent of environmental crime, as it is clearly global in nature. Studies that have adopted a definition similar to Clifford's description have found that environmental crimes are not only common but routine practices, committed by nearly all manufacturing corporations.

Environmental laws in the United States date back to the Refuse Act of 1899; however, it was not until the late 1960s and early 1970s that comprehensive and federalized environmental laws were on the books and were being enforced. These laws were a product of citizen demands for controls on pollution and biomedical professionals' concerns about the effects of the exponential growth in toxic emissions and exposures to harmful chemicals. These laws include the Clean Air Act, the Clean Water Act, the Resource Conservation and Recovery Act, and the Safe Drinking Water Act. States and municipalities also have laws against various forms of environmental abuses. However, enforcement of environmental laws in the United States and elsewhere appears to be lax at best. The Environmental Protection Agency (EPA), which is charged with enforcing most environmental laws, faces the seemingly contradictory and challenging task of both protecting the environment and promoting the interests of the industries it regulates. When the EPA does find that a corporation or government entity is breaking the law, it does not immediately prosecute but rather allows the facility to correct the problem. Fines are imposed only when the problem continues to persist after repeated warnings. Some have charged that the EPA itself is a deviant organization, claiming that the agency has been politicized and "captured" by industrial interests.

Types of Environmental Offenders. Generally speaking, there are four types of environmental offenders: (1) governments, (2) corporations or legitimate organizations, (3) illegitimate organized crime syndicates, and (4) individuals. The U.S. government is undoubtedly the single largest institutional environmental offender in the world. According to the EPA, the federal government is responsible for more environmental Superfund sites in the United

States than any other organization. The U.S. military apparatus has been identified as the greatest polluter of the seas, land, and water. Arguably, the production and storage of nuclear weapons and waste alone constitutes one of the largest environmental threats to the citizens of the United States and elsewhere. At key federally administered energy and military sites such as Rocky Flats in Colorado and the Idaho National Engineering and Environmental Laboratory, "environmental crimes" are part of the routine practices of the government agencies that administer them. At Rocky Flats, for example, it has been found that radioactive material was burned and groundwater was contaminated in the production and disposal of munitions. State and local governments and other national governments and agencies are also known to be large-scale environmental offenders.

Although governments are responsible for some environmental crimes, the most widespread perpetrators of environmental crimes are corporations. As most pollution and toxics are emitted at the point of production for private gain, most environmental crimes are committed on behalf of corporations. A recent study found that nearly two-thirds of a sampling of manufacturing corporations had committed some kind of serious environmental offence over a six-year period. Highly visible global corporations have committed some of the most infamous and widely reported instances of environmental crimes. These incidents, often reported as accidents or disasters, have become "classic" case studies of environmental offenses. For example, in the late 1970s, it was found that the Hooker Chemical Company had been dumping toxic chemicals into the Love Canal over a thirty-year period. This practice was not discovered until toxic sludge began leaking into a school and the basements of the adjoining residences. A chemical explosion in Bhopal, India, in 1985 that killed at least 2500 residents resulted in criminal charges being filed against the CEO of Union Carbide India; he fled to the United States and has yet to face trial. In 1991, Exxon pled guilty to the largest criminal fine in the history of the U.S. justice system for the 1989 oil spill in Prince William Sound. More than fifteen years later, traces of oily residue still persist on the beaches and shores of Alaska. Carnival Cruise Lines has been convicted of many violations of environmental laws for dumping garbage and waste into open seas in the 1990s. Nothing about any of these incidents suggests that they were accidental events; instead, each of these crimes was the result of premeditated cost-cutting measures that circumvented both environmental laws and common sense.

Organized crime syndicates have been known to be involved in both the legitimate disposal of solid waste and the illegal disposal of toxic and biohazardous materials for other enterprises. Throughout the middle part of the twentieth century, organized crime syndicates controlled the transport and disposal of solid waste in several East Coast cities. Furthermore, the FBI has uncovered actions by members of organized networks to illegally dispose of hazardous waste from manufactures. It is worth noting that each of these first three types of environmental offenders can overlap and engage in crimes that are not mutually exclusive of one another. For example, at Rocky Flats, Rockwell International, a major defense and aerospace contractor, was identified as a coconspirator along with Dow Chemical and the federal government. Likewise, organized crime networks illegally dispose of toxic waste for the private benefit of manufacturing corporations.

Finally, individuals and small businesses break environmental laws for personal gain or because they simply lack awareness of their crimes. Seemingly petty crimes such as littering and illegal dumping have long been unsightly and costly offenses that extract large resources from state and local governments. In nearly every locality in the country, materials such as tires and harmful cleaning solutions are illegally disposed of in public or condemned areas. Similarly, individuals may illegally dispose of hazardous and toxic household materials, such as cleaners, oil, and paint, in landfills. Although these crimes are difficult to detect and are rarely prosecuted, given the scope and frequency of their occurrence, these items pollute groundwater and pose long-term threats to the environment and human health.

Environmental Victimization. Like many types of white-collar crime, environmental crimes are not regarded as seriously as street crimes. Although these acts do not fit the image of "real crimes," the victimization and results of these offenses affect a large proportion of the global population, often disproportionately. Similarly, the victims of environmental crimes are very diffuse, and the people who have been affected may not even know it. Illnesses ranging from cancer to allergies have been traced to substances involved in many environmental crimes. Epidemiologists and medical sociologists have documented alarming trends in the rise of diseases associated with toxic exposure and the release of certain chemicals into the environment. Researchers employing what is known as an "environmental justice framework" have found that victimization from these types of crimes is distributed unequally on the basis of race and class.

See also: Cruise Line Industry; *Exxon Valdez*; Hazardous Waste Disposal; Hooker Chemical Corporation; Seveso Dioxin Disaster; Union Carbide

FURTHER READING

Block, A., and Scarpitti, F. *Poisoning for Profit.* New York: William Morrow, 1985.
Clifford, M. (Ed.). *Environmental Crime: Enforcement, Policy and Social Responsibility.* Gaithersburg, MA: Aspen Publishers, 1998.
Lynch, M. J., and Stretsky, P. B. "The Meaning of Green: Contrasting Criminological Perspectives." *Theoretical Criminology* 7.2 (2003), 217–38.

BRIAN WOLF

EXXON VALDEZ. On March 24, 1989, at a few minutes past midnight, one of the worst cases of aquatic pollution in history occurred when the oil tanker *Exxon Valdez* struck a reef in Prince William, Alaska.

At 9:12 p.m., a fully loaded *Exxon Valdez* departed the Trans-Alaska pipeline and cleared the Valdez Narrows, where the shipping channel narrows to one-half mile. At this point, the local pilot left the vessel and Captain Joseph Hazelwood took command of the wheelhouse, while Helmsman Harry Claar steered the ship into a ten-mile-wide Coast Guard designated shipping lane. There the ship encountered icebergs, and Hazelwood ordered Claar to take the ship out of the designated channel to go around them. At approximately 11:30 p.m., Third Mate Gregory Cousins took control of the wheelhouse, and Helmsman Robert Kagan took over the wheel. They were given instructions on the exact point at which to turn the tanker back into the designated lanes. They failed to do so, and the ship continued on its course under autopilot. At about midnight, a single watch noticed that the *Exxon Valdez* was not on course, and Cousins and Kagan quickly attempted to turn the ship. Because the vessel remained on autopilot, their actions were initially futile. As the wheel was finally being freed from the autopilot, the ship ran into a reef in Prince William Sound. The tanker then traveled about 600 feet, tearing a gash that opened almost half of the holding tanks along one side of the vessel.

Hazelwood immediately notified the U.S. Coast Guard, which notified the Alyeska Pipeline Company, which had the responsibility under the state's oil-spill response plan to deploy containment booms to keep oil from spreading and skimmers to collect oil from the ocean. Neither of these tools, however, was ready to be deployed. Within five hours, 10.1 million gallons of oil had been spilled. Exxon, the Coast Guard, and the State of Alaska worked for two days to get containment equipment to the site, but two days after the spill, a storm hit the spill areas. Containment was impossible during the storm, and the oil spread along 1300 miles of shoreline, heavily oiling 200 shoreline miles of beaches and lightly oiling 1100 miles of beach. After final calculations were made, it was approximated that the spill had covered more than 9000 miles of shoreline.

The Effects. The effects on the region were numerous. More than 350,000 seabirds, 144 bald eagles, 5500 sea otters, 30 seals, and 22 whales died as a result of the spill. The levels of pink salmon and herring also decreased because of the contamination. Although no human lives were lost as a direct result of the disaster, four deaths resulted from the oil spill's cleanup efforts. Approximately thirty resources or species were injured by the spill, and fifteen years later some fish and wildlife species have not fully recovered. Little or no clear improvement has been shown by the common loon, cormorants (three species), the harbor seal, the harlequin duck, the Pacific herring, and the pigeon guillemot.

The environmental damage that resulted from the spill not only significantly affected the ecosystem, it also affected the local communities that were dependent on the area's natural resources, including various fisheries and other subsistence resources. Dependent communities not only suffered economic losses, they experienced social and cultural structure losses as well. The areas most affected by the spill included small Alaska Native villages with community lives that are based on the cultural traditions of harvesting renewable resources. The non-native town of Cordova was also greatly affected, because its primary source of income was commercial fishing. Fifteen years after the spill, progress has been made toward recovering the natural resources on which these communities relied.

After the Spill. After the spill, the State of Alaska had several legal avenues to recover damages. First, the state prosecuted the captain of the ship, Joseph Hazelwood, for criminal negligence and several other smaller charges. He was found guilty only of one misdemeanor. Next the state filed suit against both the Alyeska Pipeline Service Company and Exxon. The State of Alaska claimed that negligent operations and an inferior response caused unspecified damages to the environment. In response, Exxon filed a countersuit claiming that the state had interfered with its ability to clean the oil spill properly. Shortly thereafter, the U.S. Department of Justice filed criminal charges against Exxon, and on October 8, 1991, a settlement was reached. The criminal penalties included a $150-million-dollar fine,; $125 of that amount was remitted on the grounds of Exxon's cooperation. Exxon paid $100 million for criminal restitution, with the federal government and Alaska receiving $50 million each. The civil settlement totaled $900 million and has been disbursed over a ten-year period. This money went into a trust held in a U.S. district court, with the *Exxon Valdez* Oil Spill Trustee Council deciding how the money should be spent.

Since the spill, the trustee council has directed more than $820.5 million in cleanup, restoration, purchase of habitat, research, and monitoring activities. The restoration of the affected region is unprecedented. Today, Prince William Sound, the area where the spill occurred, has one of the best oil transportation systems in the world. Detailed spill plans, as well as spill prevention technology, are continually updated and deployed. There are more than forty miles of containment booms in the area, and the number of skimming systems that can remove oil from the water is now ten times greater than in 1989. The U.S. Coast Guard monitors fully laden tankers via satellite as they pass through Valdez Narrows to assist them in an emergency. Congress has also enacted legislation that requires all tankers in Prince William Sound to be double-hulled by the year 2015. If the *Exxon Valdez* had been double-hulled, the amount of the spill would have been reduced by more than half. Overall, the combination of these factors with regular training exercises and drills has considerably strengthened both the prevention and response of future oil-spill disasters. Today, the *Exxon Valdez* is known as the *Sea River Mediterranean*. It is used to haul oil across the Atlantic Ocean, and it is prohibited by law from ever returning to Prince William Sound.

See also: Environmental White-Collar Crime

FURTHER READING

Gramling, R., and Freudenburg, W. "The *Exxon Valdez* Oil Spill in the Context of U.S. Petroleum Politics." *Industrial Crisis Quarterly* 6 (1992): 175–96.

Haycox, S. *Frigid Embrace: Politics, Economics, and Environment in Alaska.* Corvallis: Oregon State University Press, 2002.

Picou, J., Gill, D., and Cohen, M. "The *Exxon Valdez* Oil Spill as a Technological Disaster: Conceptualizing a Social Problem." In J. Picou, Duane Gill, and M. Cohen (eds.). *The* Exxon Valdez *Disaster: Readings on a Modern Social Problem.* Dubuque, IA: Kendall/Hunt Publishing Co., 1997.

Picou, J., Gill, D., and Cohen, M., (eds.). *The* Exxon Valdez *Disaster: Readings on a Modern Social Problem.* Dubuque, IA: Kendall/Hunt Publishing Co., 1997.

"The Exxon Valdez Oil Spill Disaster." Explore North. Available at www.explorenorth.com/library/weekly/aa032499.htm. Accessed March 2006.

"Then and Now: 15 Years After the Spill." *Exxon Valdez* Trustee Council. Available at http://www.evostc.state.ak.us/. Accessed April 2006.

JILETTA L. KUBENA

F

FALSE ADVERTISING. Corporate crime involving companies misrepresenting products or inducing consumers to purchase worthless goods or services has a long history. For example, in the late nineteenth century, an entrepreneur in London invented what he called a "Magneto-Electrico" bed, which he guaranteed would produce offspring for even the most "barren" of couples. The advertisement for this product claimed, "Any gentleman and his lady desirous of progeny, and wishing to spend an evening on this bed, may, by compliment of a 50-pound bank note, be permitted to partake of the heavenly joys it affords by causing immediate conception."

The roster of contemporary deceptive or false advertising cases is lengthy and involves some of the most prominent companies in the United States. For example, in the 1980s, the Beech-Nut corporation marketed a product that was largely made up of sugar, chemicals, and water as "100 percent pure apple juice." When the Food and Drug Administration (FDA) discovered substantial quantities of fraudulent juice on the market and notified the company, Beech-Nut launched a cover-up operation, ordering executives inside each of their plants to destroy any incriminating evidence. Then, not wanting to sacrifice any profits, the company shipped the remaining 26,000 cases of the so-called "pure" apple juice to Caribbean companies, again selling it as pure apple juice. Beech-Nut, which realized over $60 million in profits from sales of the product, was eventually fined $2 million for this offense (*Consumer Reports* 1989).

Recently, a considerable amount of deceptive advertising has occurred among companies advertising weight-loss products—consumers in the United States spend approximately $38 billion per year on such products. In 2002, the Federal Trade Commission (FTC) reported that 55 percent of weight-loss advertisements included claims that were false or misleading. As an FTC Web site notes with respect to these products: "If the claim looks too good to be true, it probably is" (Federal Trade Commission).

Among the companies most frequently involved in deceptive advertising are those in the pharmaceutical industry. In considering these practices in the pharmaceutical industry, it is important to note that the United States is one of only two countries (the other being New Zealand) that allows companies to market their drugs directly to consumers (DTC) via television and other forms of advertising, and studies have shown that DTC advertising has a significant impact on the consumption of pharmaceutical products. In 2002, the top nine publicly traded pharmaceutical companies in the United States spent $45.4 billion on advertising, and one study estimated that in 1999 Americans viewed an average of nine prescription drug advertisements on television per day.

Although it is certainly not the case that all pharmaceutical advertising is deceptive, there are several examples of such false advertising in this industry. For example, the Warner-Lambert pharmaceutical company (subsequently purchased by Pfizer) was fined $60 million for misrepresenting the safety of its drug Rezulin; advertisements for this drug had referred to its "unparalleled safety." Pfizer was also warned by the FDA about its television and print advertisements for the drugs Celebrex and Bextra. These ads misled consumers, failed to disclose side effects and other risk information, and made unsubstantiated claims regarding the drugs' effectiveness. Although later commercials were not related to a drug per se, Pfizer was forced to replace ads for its Listerine mouthwash product in 2005. The ads had misleadingly suggested that Listerine was as effective as flossing at fighting plaque and gingivitis.

The Regulation of False Advertising. Deceptive advertising in the pharmaceutical industry is regulated through the FDA. One of the first individuals to be charged under the 1906 Food and Drug Act was Robert Harris, manufacturer of a product known as "Cuforheadake BraneFude," which was advertised as a headache cure and "brain food," as the product's name suggests. This product was completely useless with respect to its purported effects and was essentially a painkiller laced with caffeine and alcohol. Presaging the lax treatment of white-collar criminals that persists today, Harris was fined $700 for violations of the Food and Drug Act, even though he made over $2 million on this product (Crossen 2004).

More recently, over the same period in which there has been a tremendous increase in the number of DTC ads for pharmaceutical products, the FDA has reduced its monitoring of these advertisements. In 1998, the FDA sent 158 letters to companies regarding ads the agency believed to be false or misleading, compared to only twenty-six such letters in 2002. Furthermore, from 1999 to 2001, the FDA sent one warning letter to pharmaceutical companies for every 2.8 complaints regarding false advertising, but in the first six months of 2002, it sent one letter for every 13.5 complaints. Even in the context of such lax regulation, pharmaceutical companies frequently choose not to follow FDA recommendations. For example, between 1997 and 2003, the manufacturers of the allergy drug Claritin were informed ten times by the FDA that they had to change their advertisements in order to correct misleading information. Similarly, the manufacturers of two other allergy drugs, Flonase and Flovent, had been cited twelve times by the FDA for misleading commercials and other sales materials.

In the more general context, advertising is regulated by the Federal Trade Commission Act and the Lanham Act, and also through laws in individual states. The FTC Act states that false advertising is a form of unfair and deceptive commerce. The act provides the FTC with the power to order companies to issue "corrective" advertisements, but it does not allow for the punishment, via fines or incarceration, of companies that engage in deceptive practices. In addition, only the FTC has authority to enforce this act. Private parties, such as consumers or competitor companies, can only bring action against a company under the Lanham Act, which was enacted in 1946.

To establish a violation under the Lanham Act, consumers or competitor companies must prove that (1) the advertiser made false statements of fact about its product; (2) the false advertisements actually deceived or had the capacity to deceive a substantial segment of the population to which the advertisement was directed; (3) the deception was material; (4) the falsely advertised product was sold in interstate commerce; and (5) the consumer or competitor initiating the lawsuit suffered a loss or injury as a result of the deceptive advertising.

Although penalties for violations of the FTC Act and Lanham Act have generally not resulted in severe sanctions for companies engaging in false advertising, several companies have been penalized for the violation of state laws. Space does not permit a thorough discussion of various state regulations, but the state of New York provides an instructive example. In that state, consumers who have suffered damages as a result of a business's use of false advertising are entitled to file a civil suit for recovery. In addition, the state attorney general can sue for false advertising on behalf of the State of New York, and companies that are found guilty can be subject to criminal penalties. In recent years, Eliot Spitzer, attorney general for the State of New York, has been particularly aggressive in pursuing companies from a variety of industries, including automobile dealerships and pharmaceutical companies, for false advertising practices.

Deceptive advertising practices affect millions of consumers in the United States and other countries each year. As in other areas of corporate crime, however, regulation of these practices is comparatively lax when compared to the enforcement of street-crime legislation, and even in the rare instances in which violators are identified, the penalties are relatively lax.

See also: Beech-Nut Apple Juice Scandal; Pharmaceutical Companies

FURTHER READING

"Bad Apples in the Executive Suite." *Consumer Reports.* (May, 1989).

Crossen, Cynthia. "Fraudulent Claims Led the U.S. to Take On Drug Makers in 1900s." *Wall Street Journal* (October 6, 2004).

Federal Trade Commission. Available at: http://www.ftc.gov.

Preston, Ivan. *The Great American Blowup.* Madison: University of Wisconsin Press, 1996.

CLAYTON MOSHER

FILM RECOVERY SYSTEMS. Film Recovery Systems, Inc., was a small company situated in a suburb north of Chicago that extracted silver from used hospital X-ray films and other photographic film. Consequent to the death of one of its male workers, the company was successfully prosecuted by the state of Illinois for involuntary manslaughter, and its executives were prosecuted for murder. The conviction of the company's three executives for the criminal homicide of a worker from an industrial accident was believed to be the first of its kind and became the catalyst for similar prosecutions by state attorneys across the country.

Film Recovery Systems, Inc. was a short-lived corporation created in 1979 through a partnership between Steven J. O'Neil and B. R. MacKay & Sons. O'Neil was part owner of a new silver reclamation company called Metallic Marketing Systems in Wheeling, Illinois, north-northwest of Chicago, and MacKay ran a large silver refinery in Salt Lake City, Utah. The price of silver was at a high of fifty dollars an ounce at this time, and early on the partnership proved to be quite lucrative. Under the arrangement, MacKay invested $275,000 into the corporation, and O'Neil became president of both Film Recovery and Metallic Marketing. In order to expand and increase the workforce, he moved operations to a larger building in Elk Grove Village, west-northwest of Chicago. In 1981 he hired Charles Kirschbaum as plant manager, which allowed O'Neil more time outside the plant to negotiate contracts to acquire more used film products. The company was then grossing $13 million a year.

Both O'Neil and Kirschbaum had previously worked for other silver extraction companies and were very familiar with the silver removal process. Used hospital X-ray films and other photographic film were ground up into chips and put into large, open vats containing water and sodium cyanide and then stirred by the workers. The mixture would cause the silver to be dissolved, and the solution containing the silver would be pumped into polyurethane tanks containing electrically charged stainless steel plates, on which the silver would be deposited. Workers would manually remove the plates from the tanks, scrape the silver from the plates, pump out the remaining liquid from the tanks, and then remove the contaminated chips. The silver scraps would be smelted, refined, and then made into silver bullion. This extraction process was performed at the Film Recovery plant, and the scraps were sent to B. R. MacKay and Sons in Salt Lake City to be refined.

Between 1980 and 1982, Film Recovery expanded the number of tanks and vats from less than 10 to over 100 and concurrently increased its workforce, which included mainly non-English-speaking illegal aliens from Mexico and Poland. Daniel Rodriguez was one of these workers. However, he learned enough English to be relied upon by Kirschbaum to communicate with other Mexican workers, and eventually he became foreman and assistant plant manager. Among the new employees was Stephen (Stefan) Golab, a middle-aged Polish worker, who was hired on December 26, 1982, at $4.50 an hour. (See also **Golab, Stephen**.) Golab neither spoke nor read much English. He worked over the large mixing vats, each of which contained 500 gallons of water to which 7.5 pounds of sodium cyanide were added every three days. Within a short time Golab began to develop headaches and sometimes became nauseated; his eyes and skin would burn and itch. Like his fellow employees who had similar symptoms, Golab was unaware that he was working with cyanide and that when cyanide was mixed with water, it produced a poisonous gas that permeated the air that everyone was breathing: hydrogen cyanide, the lethal agent in the Nazis' Zyklon B (see **Corporate War Crimes**) and in gas chambers used for capital punishment. Ceiling fans circulated the contaminated, smelly air but did not ventilate it. When the solution splashed out of the vats onto unprotected hands or arms, the cyanide could be absorbed by the skin quickly. Golab and those he worked with were not issued any specialized gloves, glasses, face masks, or clothing when they stirred the solution in the vats, pumped the liquid from the tanks, or shoveled out the spent film chips.

On the morning of February 10, 1983, after stirring one of the vats, Golab became dizzy and faint, then walked to the lunchroom and proceeded to foam at the mouth, go into convulsions, and pass out. Medical personnel were unable to revive him, and he was pronounced dead upon arrival at a nearby hospital. An autopsy showed that he had died from acute cyanide toxicity. County and federal environmental investigators cited Film Recovery for numerous safety and health violations, but in March 1983 MacKay chose to close down its operations rather than spend money to meet the required workplace standards. The now defunct company was then linked to public hazards when, in mid-May 1983, the Illinois attorney general filed suit against Film Recovery and other companies for illegally storing and disposing of 16 million pounds of chipped X-ray film treated with cyanide in 170 mobile semitractor trailer containers in residential neighborhoods and throughout the state. Officials feared that the chips could cause water and air contamination, and a circuit court judge then ordered the placement of locks on the containers, fences around some container sites, and the posting of twenty-four hour guards at other sites. The attorney general sought cleanup costs and a fine of $25,000 a day for each violation, and contrasted this to the $2.3 million it would have cost Film Recovery had it followed EPA waste disposal standards as a regular business practice. Further investigations by the Environmental Protection Agency similarly implicated other silver extraction facilities in Ohio and New York owned by B. R. MacKay and Sons for improper waste disposal.

Although initially regarded as an industrial accident, the death of Golab plus the extent of the health and safety violations attributed to Film Recovery operations caught the attention of the local Cook County prosecutor, Jay Magnuson. Interviews with former Film Recovery workers and office employees, examination of the plant and previously filed health and safety inspections reports, as well as consideration of current Illinois law, prompted Magnuson to seek approval from then Cook County state's attorney Richard M. Daley to file criminal indictments against Film Recovery for involuntary manslaughter and its officers for murder. He reasoned that Illinois statutes allowed for prosecution of a corporation for involuntary manslaughter because in the Illinois Criminal Code under Articles 2 and 5 respectively, corporations were included in the definition of "person" applicable to all Illinois criminal law, and corporations could be held responsible under the criminal law (1) for misdemeanor offenses, (2) if the legislature intended that an offense applied to corporations, or (3) if the offense had the approval of the board of directors or a high managerial agent acting within the scope of his employment. Article 5 also provided for individual criminal liability for conduct done for the benefit of the corporation. Either way, liability for death or serious bodily injury had to include proof that the defendant (as a reasonable person) must have been able to foresee that his reckless conduct could result in death or great bodily harm. Magnuson knew his prosecution of corporate officials for a worker's death would be breaking new legal ground: a murder conviction needed proof that the individual defendant's conduct was done with the knowledge that there was a high probability that it would result in death or great bodily harm. He would hold the officials, as well as the corporation, accountable for the death of Golab. He would show that by not telling Golab about his work with cyanide, not training him or giving him protective equipment, the corporation knowingly created a strong probability of his death.

On October 18, 1983 the grand jury indicted Film Recovery Systems president Steven J. O'Neil, plant manager Charles Kirschbaum, plant foreman Daniel Rodriguez, and vice-presidents Gerald Pett and Michael MacKay (who was also president of B. R. MacKay and Sons) for the murder of Stefan Golab. It also indicted Film Recovery Systems, Inc., its sister company Metallic Marketing, and B. R. MacKay and Sons, Inc. for involuntary manslaughter of Golab. All the defendants were indicted for reckless conduct regarding 20 other Film Recovery employees.

The joint bench trial began April 15, 1985, and lasted eight weeks. Many former workers attested to the conditions in the plant and the physical problems they experienced, as well as the extent to which each of the companies' executives had been present in the extraction areas of the plant and made aware of the workers' physical complaints. Halfway through the trial, Judge Ronald J. P. Banks dismissed the charges against Pett. MacKay, at home in Salt Lake City, did not stand trial because the governor of Utah refused requests for extradition. On June 14, 1985, the companies and executives were found guilty as charged. The individuals were sentenced to 25 years imprisonment and fourteen concurrent 364-day imprisonment terms for reckless conduct. O'Neil and Kirschbaum were each fined $10,000 for the murder and $14,000 for the reckless conduct, and the companies were each fined $10,000 for involuntary manslaughter and $14,000 for reckless conduct. This was a huge victory for the State of Illinois. The trial and its verdicts received national attention from the press, academics, and like-minded state prosecutors across the country.

In January 1990 the Appellate Court of Illinois reversed the convictions on the basis of legally inconsistent verdicts. It agreed with the arguments of O'Neil, Kirschbaum, and Rodriguez that because murder requires a mental state of knowing and intentional act, but reckless conduct does not, they could not be convicted of both offenses, since the same conduct was used to establish the guilt for both crimes. Similarly, the court agreed with O'Neil, Kirschbaum, and Rodriguez that they could not be convicted of murder as individual defendants and of involuntary manslaughter as corporate defendants because murder requires a mental state of knowing and *intentional* act, whereas involuntary manslaughter requires proof of *unintended* conduct that is reckless. Nevertheless, both crimes had been prosecuted on the basis of the same conduct by the individual defendants: under state criminal statutes, the mind and mental state of the corporation needed to be determined by the "collective" mind and mental state of the members of the board of directors or high managerial agents. However, in summarizing the testimonial evidence given at trial indicating the dangerous working conditions endured by the Film Recovery employees as well as the events surrounding Golab's death—at a time when O'Neil, Kirschbaum, and Rodriguez were responsible for plant operations—the court concluded that evidence was not sufficient for a retrial.

At the beginning of his opinion, Judge Lorenz noted that consideration of the appeal had been delayed from 1987 to allow for the resolution of a case before the Illinois Supreme Court that included an argument similar to the defendants'. In *People v. Chicago Magnet Wire Corp* (1989) the Court determined that state prosecutions against individual and corporate defendants for conditions in an industrial workplace were not preempted by the federal Occupational Safety and Health Act. This ruling was welcomed by the Cook County State's Attorney's office as well as state's attorney Magnuson, because he had also worked on the indictments for that case. Few prosecutions had been initiated by the Occupational Safety and Health Administration (OSHA) since its creation, and *Chicago Magnet* opened the door for states to fill this void and thereby benefit workers and the public at large in holding corporations accountable for providing safer work environments.

Kirschbaum, O'Neil, and Rodriguez later pleaded guilty to involuntary manslaughter in the death of Golab prior to the start of their retrial in September 1993. O'Neil and Kirschbaum were sentenced to prison for three and two years, respectively, while Rodriguez received two years probation. In exchange for a guilty plea to one misdemeanor charge of reckless conduct in the injury of another plant worker, the murder charge and the 22 counts of reckless conduct against MacKay were dropped in May 1995. He was fined $1,000 and ordered to perform

100 hours of community service. Seven years earlier, in response to a state civil suit, he had agreed to pay $265,000 cleanup costs to reimburse the state for disposing of the cyanide-contaminated film chips from the Film Recovery plant.

Despite the high expectations, state criminal prosecutions of individual corporate officials for workplace deaths and injuries have not proliferated since the *Film Recovery* case. They compete for time and resources with other more pressing threats to the public's safety, require more investigation and business-related expertise, and involve elements of crimes more difficult to prove when applied to each individual if the conduct required in the law was done in part by different individuals who did not exhibit the same mental state. Other considerations include whether the conduct resulted from cost/benefit analysis in the business model; whether decisions were left to lower-level officials; whether deterrence or punishment is the real goal behind the prosecution; whether the state is realistic in trying for a larger punishment for a crime with elements such as specific intent that are more difficult to prove; and whether a "corporate reckless endangerment" statute is available, or worth lobbying the legislature for. On the other hand, Golab's death from acute cyanide poisoning was unusual in a legitimate, yet more highly regulated, industry such as metal reclamation that used hydrogen cyanide in its operations. However, one could speculate that the extraordinary rise in the value of silver, the quick plant expansion to take advantage of the market, the hiring of illegal aliens (older, non-English-speaking men such as Golab) who needed employment and would work without questioning the conditions, as well as the irregularity of regulatory plant inspections, provided an environment in which such a fatal accident could occur.

See also: Golab, Stephen

FURTHER READING

Broussard, Judy. "The Criminal Corporation: Is Ohio Prepared for Corporate Criminal Prosecutions for Workplace Fatalities?" *Cleveland State Law Review* 45 (1997): 135.

Gibson, Ray. "A Worker's Death Spurs Murder Trial." *The National Law Journal* (1985, May 20): 6.

"Illinois Says Waste with Cyanide Was Illegally Stored Near Homes." *The New York Times* (1983, May 14).

Magnuson, Jay C., and Leviton, Gareth C.. "Policy Considerations in Corporate Criminal Prosecutions after *People v. Film Recovery Systems, Inc.*" *Notre Dame Law Review* 62 (1987): 913.

People v. Chicago Magnet Wire Corp., 126 Ill.2d 356, 534 N.E.2d 962 (1989).

People v. O'Neil, 194 Ill. App. 3d 79, 550 N.E.2d 1090 (1990).

People v. Film Recovery Systems, Inc., No. 83-11091 (Cir. Ct. of Cook County, Ill. June 14, 1985) (consolidating *People v. O'Neil*, No. 84-5064).

Rosoff, Stephen, Pontell, Henry, and Tillman, Robert. *Profit Without Honor: White Collar Crime and the Looting of America*, 3d edition. Upper Saddle River, NJ: Pearson Education, 2004.

Samuels, Anne D. "Reckless Endangerment of an Employee: A Proposal in the Wake of *Film Recovery Systems* to Make the Boss Responsible for His Crimes." *University of Michigan Law Journal of Law Reform* 20 (1987, Spring): 873.

Shipp, E. R. "Can a Corporation Commit Murder?" *The New York Times* (1985, May 19): 2.

Siegel, Barry. "Officers Convicted Murder Case a Corporate Landmark Series: First of Two Parts." *Los Angeles Times* (1985, September 15): 1.

KATHLEEN M. SIMON

FIRE IN GOTEBORG, SWEDEN. Fire raced through a crowded second-floor dance hall in Goteborg, Sweden, on October 30, 1998, killing sixty-three persons and injuring 213. Most of the attendees at the dance, and most of the victims, were teenagers whose families had immigrated to Sweden from various countries. Aside from the deaths and injuries, the fire resulted in several indirect harms. For instance, claims of a hate-motivated attack against those at the dance hall fueled racial tensions in Sweden. At the time of the incident, Sweden was experiencing a degree of culture clash following the entry of many immigrants from Asia, Africa, and Eastern Europe. Further, the psychological effects of such a tragedy extend beyond those directly associated with the incident, as research noted a high level of post-traumatic stress among a sample of Goteborg students seven months after the fire (Dyregrov et al., 2003).

It was unclear how the fire started, although some initially suggested an electrical spark was the cause. The aggressiveness with which the fire spread led investigators to suggest arsonists were responsible. In addition to the quickness with which the fire consumed the building, it was argued that the actions, or inactions, of others contributed to the high death toll. Some questioned the timeliness of emergency response teams summoned to the burning dance hall. The response time of roughly six minutes after the first call to emergency crews includes a three-minute delay due to difficulty in understanding the caller, who spoke with a thick accent. However, fire rescue personnel stated that even an instant response would have been too late given the ferocity of the fire.

Attention also focused on the dance organizers and the owners of the dance hall. The dance hall had been inspected and approved for occupancy of 150 persons. The event, organized by a group of teenagers and the owner of the dance hall, was attended by an estimated 400 individuals. The ticket till noted that 320 tickets were sold. Further, the building lacked a sprinkler system. Moreover, some survivors stated that speaker equipment blocked one of the two stairwells leading from the upstairs of the building and that an open door that should have been closed contributed to the spread of smoke and the fire.

Some claimed the fire was the result of arson, motivated by conflict between native Swedes and the immigrant students who organized and attended the dance. Those claims were dismissed following the identification of four naturalized Swedes found to be responsible for the fire. An investigation determined that the four youths, who immigrated from Iran, started the fire because they were upset at not being permitted to enter the dance free of charge. Three of the four offenders had prior criminal records.

The four youths were convicted and sentenced on charges of aggravated arson in 2000. The alleged leader of the group, Shoresh Kaveh, who later admitted to being involved with the incident and apologized for his role, received a sentence of eight years in prison. Kaveh stated that he did not intend to cause such destruction; he only wanted to create additional work for the dance hall employees who would not let him enter without paying. Two others, Housein Arsani and Mohammad Mohammadamini, each received six years in prison. Meysam Mohammadyeh, the fourth member of the group, was under age 18 at the time of the offense and received three years in juvenile detention. No charges were filed against the building owners or the organizers of the dance.

Closer examination of the case suggests that culpability is not restricted to the arsonists, because corporate wrongdoing contributed to what was deemed "the worst (fire) in living memory in Sweden" (Austin 2000: 17). Although the arsonists in this case are primarily responsibility for the fire and subsequent harms, one must question the lack of official attention directed toward the organizers of the dance and the building owners. These individuals were cleared of charges, even though the Goteborg Chief Prosecutor said he might consider charges against the party organizers. Although they were not directly involved in setting the fire, the organizers' and owners' negligence certainly contributed to the resulting harms. The absence of a sprinkler system, a building containing roughly 250 more people than permitted, and inaccessible emergency exits certainly contributed to the high number of deaths, but officials failed to charge those responsible for these violations. Their avoidance of culpability reflects the widespread argument that white-collar crimes often go unrecognized by public officials (e.g., Lynch et al. 2000; Friedrichs 2004).

The Goteborg fire contains elements of traditional crime (the arson) and white-collar crime (owner/organizer negligence), rendering it ideal for evaluation. For instance, in assessing U.S. newspaper coverage of the incident, Burns (2002: 145–146) found that emergency response "personnel were over three times more likely than the owners/promoters to be deemed responsible for the deaths, even though rescue personnel arrived within six minutes of the first call for assistance, and the owners/promoters violated multiple regulations." The disproportionate attention devoted to the arson-related aspect of the incident, particularly from a media standpoint, supports the notion that street crime is far more often recognized by the media, public officials, and the public in general than white-collar crime is.

Recent events, such as the arrests of several high-profile white-collar criminals, and the United States claiming a crackdown on corporate crime as evidenced in passage of the Sarbanes-Oxley Act, hint that a change in perceptions of—and actions toward—white-collar crime may be forthcoming. Such changes, however, offer little in the way of justice for those associated with the devastating fire in Goteborg.

FURTHER READING

Austin, Tony. "Four Convicted for Disco Deaths." *The Guardian.* (2000, June 9): 17.

Burns, Ronald, and Orrick, Lindsey. "Assessing Newspaper Coverage of Corporate Violence: The Dance Hall Fire in Goteborg, Sweden." *Critical Criminology* 11 (2002): 137–150.

Dyregrov, Atle; Frykholm, Ann-Margret; Lilled, Lars; Broberg, Anders; and Holmberg, Ingvar. "The Göteborg Discothèque Fire, 1998." *Scandinavian Journal of Psychology* 44 (2002): 449–457.

Friedrichs, David. *Trusted Criminals*, 2nd edition. Belmont, CA: Wadsworth Publishing, 2004.

Lynch, Michael; Michalowski, Raymond; and Groves, W. Byron. *The New Primer in Radical Criminology: Critical Perspectives on Crime, Power and Identity*, 3rd edition. Monsey, NY: Criminal Justice Press, 2000.

Wright, John; Cullen, Francis; and Blankenship, Michael. "The Social Construction of Corporate Violence: Media Coverage of the Imperial Food Products Fire." *Crime and Delinquency* 41 (1995): 20–36.

RONALD BURNS

FIRESTONE 500 TIRES. The Firestone 500 radial tire, manufactured in the early 1970s, required one of the largest product recalls in history. In the 1970s, competition between

Firestone, Goodrich, and Goodyear was at an all-time high. Car companies such as General Motors and Ford were demanding steel-belted radial tires. Firestone rapidly expanded its radial tire production, and within two years of being introduced the Firestone 500 Steel Belt was the most recognized brand in the industry. Although Firestone's decision to leverage existing manufacturing processes allowed rapid market penetration, it also contributed to quality problems with the tire's steel cords, which failed to adhere properly to the rest of the tire. Although other companies also experienced quality problems with their radials, Firestone's were the most severe, and the company came under heavy pressure from consumer groups and the National Highway Traffic Safety Administration (NHTSA).

In 1977, Firestone recalled 400,000 similar tires made in Decatur, Illinois, the location that also made the 500 radial. In 1978, the company agreed to a voluntary recall of 8.7 million Firestone 500 tires at a cost of $150 million after taxes—an action that constituted the largest consumer recall in U.S. history. Although Firestone had stopped producing the tire in 1977, the NHTSA had over 2,000 complaints about the tires. These complaints generally involved multiple complaints about more than one tire. The complaints generally involved the steel cords coming out, bubbles ballooning out of the side of the tires, or an all-out tire blow. At the time of the congressional hearings, 27 deaths and 31 injuries were related to blowouts of the Firestone 500. Firestone, much like many other tire companies at the time, was also making tires for other private brand companies such as Kmart, Montgomery Ward, LaMons, Union, and Atlas Golden Aire.

Firestone, at the time, expressed surprise at the NHTSA decision. A Firestone spokeswoman said, "We cannot believe that the NHTSA has prejudged this case before the investigation is completed. Firestone is confident that a full and fair hearing will demonstrate that the steel belted radial 500 tire has no safety defects and that a recall of the tire would be unwarranted." The NHTSA sued the company in an attempt to force Firestone to give up certain death and injury rate documentation as well as information on the number of tires the company had taken back from consumers. A mere four years later it would seem that the executives at Firestone had a new position. In 1981 the chairman and chief executive officer of Firestone, John J. Nevin, believed that Firestone should have recalled its Firestone 500 tires prior to the 1978 government-mandated recall. Nevin contended that the tire did not cause more accidents than other brands but that 15 to 20 percent of the 30 million tires manufactured developed problems, giving both the government and consumers reason for pause. Nevin felt that it would have been sound business practice and would have given the consumer more confidence in Firestone's commitment to quality products. The NHTSA ordered the recall on the ground that the 500 tires were unsafe, not on the ground that they were defective.

The cause of the problem with the Firestone 500 tires was never publicly determined. Firestone stopped making the 500 altogether and made changes. The 500 episode, however, was a financial blow to the company that it could not overcome on its own, and the tire giant was bought out by Bridgestone in 1988. After that Firestone remained a known and respected brand for over a decade.

After such a large recall and financial loss, most would never have expected to see Firestone in the limelight again. This could not have been farther from the truth. In 2000 Firestone, ironically, once again had problems at its Decatur plant, which made tires for sport utility vehicles (SUVs) such as the Ford Explorer. The problem, twenty years later, was tread separation.

Tread separation is the result of failure of the polymer adhesives in the tire to bond the tread to the rest of the tire. The Firestone 500 tire recall made America examine the tire industry and its commitment to safety, yet Firestone, because of another mass tire recall, is once again facing scrutiny for problems with its tires.

FURTHER READING

Claybrook, Joan. "Statement of Joan Claybrook on Firestone Tire Defect and Ford Explorer Rollovers Before the Transportation Subcommittee, United States Senate Committee on Appropriations." *The Public Citizen* (2000, September 6). Available at http://www.citizen. org/autosafety/suvsafety/ ford_frstone/articles.cfm?ID=5413. Accessed September 26, 2006.
Sull, Donald N. "The Dynamics of Standing Still: Firestone Tire & Rubber and the Radial Revolution." *Harvard Business School Working Knowledge for Business Leaders* (2000, November 27). Available at http://hbswk.hbs.edu/item/1832.html. Accessed September 26, 2006.

KELLY ANN CHEESEMAN

FIRST ALLIANCE CORPORATION HOME EQUITY. First Alliance Corporation (FACO) of Irvine, California, was founded in 1971 as a consumer finance company by Brian Chisick. The corporation, including the First Alliance Mortgage Company (FAMCO) of Irvine and a wholly owned subsidiary, also named First Alliance Mortgage Company but headquartered in Bloomington, Minnesota, flourished as it pursued the subprime market during the home equity loan boom of the 1980s and 1990s. Unlike typical subprime lenders, whose borrowers are without collateral, which makes them increased credit risks, First Alliance faced little or no risk, because its loans were guaranteed by the borrowers' homes.

The risks First Alliance confronted came from accusations of predatory lending. In the end, lawsuits and negative publicity from a March 2000 joint investigation by the *New York Times* and *ABC News 20/20* that exposed First Alliance's predatory lending practices forced it to close offices and file for Chapter 11 bankruptcy.

Subprime Lending or Predatory Lending. Subprime lending is not necessarily bad, predatory, or criminal. Subprime loans often provide social and economical benefits by allowing individuals closed out of the traditional loan market to obtain financing, albeit at much higher interest rates, which are intended to compensate creditors for the increased risk. Subprime lending becomes predatory or criminal when lenders intentionally use misleading marketing practices, prey on vulnerable borrowers' inexperience, fraudulently misrepresent the terms of loans, hide important information, or charge excessive fees and interest.

First Alliance's Predatory Practices. The First Alliance's direct mail solicitations and aggressive, high-pressure telemarketers targeted senior citizens and poor inner-city borrowers who had equity in their homes but who may have had difficulty securing conventional loans. Sales personnel encouraged homeowners to refinance mortgages, consolidate debt, or finance home improvements or other big-ticket items using their homes as collateral. They misled consumers about the existence and amount of loan origination fees or points (which ranged from 10 to 25 percent of the loan, whereas most other lenders charged no more than 2 percent)

105

and penalties for prepayments, misrepresented prepaid finance charges as part of interest payments on loans, and enticed consumers with low initial interest rates on adjustable-rate mortgages (ARMs) that were not tied to the market but automatically increased as much as 1 percent every six months regardless of market conditions. Loan terms were designed to strip wealth from borrowers, who soon found themselves unable to afford monthly payments when they ballooned too high. The home-secured credit card that First Alliance offered through an arrangement with Fidelity Federal Bank, F.S.B, had the same effect. It put the consumer's home equity at risk for credit card purchases.

The first indication of the company's illegal business practices came to light in 1988, when California state regulators sued the company for using deceptive sales pitches and discriminating against borrowers from neighborhoods with high concentrations of minorities, charging minorities higher rates than whites. Eventually, the Federal Trade Commission (FTC); the states of Arizona, Florida, Illinois, Massachusetts, Minnesota, New York, and Washington; the American Association of Retired Persons (AARP); and attorneys representing class action plaintiffs and private individuals filed lawsuits against the company for fraudulent and unlawful business practices, including violations of the of the Federal Trade Commission Act, the Truth in Lending Act, and the 1994 Homeownership and Equity Protection Act. Seeking to avoid convictions, the companies paid over $7.2 million to settle several lawsuits between 1989 and 1994. In September 1999, First Alliance settled the Minnesota consumer protection lawsuit by paying each Minnesota customer between $4,000 and $6,000 without admitting any wrongdoing. The three First Alliance companies, executive officer Chisick, and his wife, Sarah, reached what was then the largest settlement in a predatory lending case ($60 million) with the FTC, AARP, and various states and consumers in March 2002.

Criminogenic Environment. Several structural conditions facilitated First Alliances' predatory lending practices. First, clients from underserved communities were easily discredited, which provided conditions that allowed abuse and misconduct to slip under the regulatory radar. Second, laws created opportunities for banks and Wall Street institutions to reap huge profits at the expense of the poor, while projecting the image that they were helping provide services to these individuals and communities.

Although First Alliance initially obtained money for its operations by selling loan bundles to private investors, it turned to Wall Street investment banks for a less expensive source of capital in 1993. The banks profited handsomely from the arrangement. Not only did they receive approximately a third of a penny for every dollar raised, they also gained a steady supply of high-yield mortgage notes to sell to their institutional customers. To meet Wall Street's increasing demand for bundled loans and to increase its own profits, First Alliance made as many loans as possible.

The federal Community Reinvestment Act, which was designed to combat redlining, requires federal bank supervisors to determine whether and how depository institutions serve the credit needs of the entire community, including members with low and moderate incomes. Banks buying high-interest loans from predatory lenders easily boosted their lending statistics and appeared to be involved in minority communities.

Despite increasing legal difficulties, First Alliance received support that allowed it to continue its predatory practices. MBIA Insurance guaranteed that principal and interest would be paid to investors, and Lehman Brothers continued its relationship with the corporation even after others discontinued. By 1999, Lehman Brothers was First Alliance's sole underwriter and lender. In 2003, a federal judge concluded that Lehman Brothers knew of and substantially assisted First Alliance in defrauding homeowners and ordered it to pay customers $5 million.

See also: Criminogenic Industry

FURTHER READING

Consumers Union West Coast Regional Office. "Consumers Union Hails Withdrawal of Expansion Plan for First Alliance Lending Company." Press release, February 11, 1998. Available at http://www.consumersunion.org/finance/allwc298.htm. Accessed July 26, 2006.

Doe, et al. v. First Alliance Corp., Brian Chisick and Lehman Brothers, Inc., No. 01-CV-971 (C.D. Cal., 2003). Available at http://www.morelaw.com/verdicts/case.asp?n=01-CV-971&s=CA%20%20%20%20%20%20%20&d=25089. Accessed July 26, 2006.

Henriques, Diana B. "Lehman Aided in Loan Fraud, Jury Says." *New York Times* (2003, June 17): C1.

Henriques, Diana B., and Lowell Bergman. "Mortgaged Lives: A Special Report: Profiting from Fine Print with Wall Street's Help." *New York Times* (2000, March 15): A1.

Lopez, Frank. "Using the Fair Housing Act to Combat Predatory Lending." *Georgetown Journal on Poverty Law & Policy* 6 (1999 Winter): 73–109.

SUSAN WILL

FORD PINTO. In 1980, in *State of Indiana v. Ford Motor Company*, a northern Indiana jury returned not guilty verdicts on three counts of reckless homicide against Ford Motor Company. This has been considered a landmark case because it was one of the first instances of a corporation's being charged in criminal court, rather than sued in civil court, for an allegedly faulty product.

This was not the first time Ford had run into problems because of an alleged design problem with the Pinto. In 1977, *Mother Jones* published an article titled "Pinto Madness," in which Mark Dowie alleged that Ford was aware of a design defect in the Pinto that increased the likelihood of the fuel tank rupturing following a rear-impact collision. The article stated that Ford had conducted a cost-benefit analysis in which a human life was valued at $200,000. On one side of the analysis, the company would not fix the defect, resulting in an estimated 180 burn deaths, 180 serious burn injuries, and 2,100 burned vehicles and costing the company $49.5 million in settlements. On the other side of the analysis, the company would fix the problem at an approximate cost of $11 per vehicle or a total of $137 million. According to "Pinto Madness," Ford made the decision, based on the cost-benefit analysis, not to fix the problem because it would be cheaper to settle claims.

At the time of the criminal trial, about 50 active lawsuits involving the Ford Pinto were pending in civil court. Just six months prior to the accident that led to the criminal case, a jury in California awarded a record settlement in a lawsuit following a 1972 accident in which a Pinto stalled on a highway and was rear-ended, rupturing the gas tank and badly burning the two occupants. The driver, 52-year-old Lilly Gray, died several days later; the passenger, 13-year-old Richard Grimshaw, underwent more than 60 operations to repair damage caused by his burn injuries. Grimshaw was awarded more than $128 million in the lawsuit, though damages were later reduced to less than $8 million.

The criminal trial in Indiana resulted from an accident that killed three teenage girls, sisters Judy and Lyn Ulrich and their cousin Donna, on August 10, 1978. The three girls were traveling in a 1973 Pinto when the vehicle was rear-ended and burst into flames, killing two of the victims immediately; the third died later. Elkhart County Prosecutor Michael Cosintino took the case to a grand jury and secured an indictment on three counts of reckless homicide against Ford Motor Company. Part of the reason Cosintino was able to charge Ford with homicide was that Indiana's reckless homicide statute had recently been changed to include corporations in the definition of persons. The Ford Motor Company hired high-profile attorney James Neal, and a change of venue was granted to Winamac, Indiana. On January 16, 1980, the criminal trial began and lasted for ten weeks. After 25 hours of deliberation, the jury returned verdicts of not guilty on all three counts. In August 1980, Ford settled out of court with the Ulrich family for $7,500 for each of the three victims.

See also: Corporate Crime; Iacocca, Lee

FURTHER READING

Becker, Paul J., Jipson, Arthur, and Bruce, Alan S. "*State of Indiana v. Ford Motor Company* Revisited." *American Journal of Criminal Justice* 26.2 (2002): 181–202.

Birsch, Douglas, and Fielder, John H. (Eds.) *The Ford Pinto Case: A Study in Applied Ethics, Business, and Technology.* Albany: State University of New York Press, 1994.

Cullen, Francis T., Maakestad, William J., and Cavender, Gray. *Corporate Crime under Attack: The Ford Pinto Case and Beyond.* Cincinnati, OH: Anderson, 1987.

PAUL J. BECKER

FUNERAL INDUSTRY FRAUD. Fraud in the funeral industry (euphemistically known today as the death care industry) is the deliberate deception by a representative of the industry in order to secure unlawful monetary gain by inducing a person to give up a valuable pre-need funeral insurance contract belonging to the policy beneficiary, thereby inducing that individual to surrender his or her legal right through deceit. Such fraudulent practices have cost consumers over millions of dollars in unnecessary and fraudulently obtained funeral expenses by representatives of the death care industry.

The most common example of funeral industry fraud is the failure to honor pre-need funeral insurance contracts. Such acts of fraud include but are not limited to conspiracy to defraud, breach of contract, omission of material facts, fraud in the inducement by omission, unfair trade practices in violation of insurance codes, and violation of unfair trade practices and consumer protection law.

Pre-need funeral insurance plans represent one of the most profitable and aggressively marketed tools in the death care industry and are a favorite priority of corporate funeral service chains to earn profits. Consumers purchase prearranged funeral plans in the belief that they are being ensured future coverage of their funeral/burial expenses. Upon need, however, the insurer provides an inferior-quality casket that the policy beneficiary, who is responsible for funeral arrangements, cannot accept. On the grounds of the beneficiary's refusal, the original insurance plan is voided in its entirety by the insurer and not honored by the funeral service (both entities often operating under the same corporate structure). The beneficiary is then charged additional thousands of dollars for the funeral services originally covered under the now-voided pre-need insurance contract, as well as additional costs to cover an acceptable casket.

Such practices engaged in by representatives of the death care industry involve a *conspiracy to defraud* its consumers, because the purchaser of the policy and the policy beneficiary are victims of a conspiracy involving both the funeral homes/services that sold the pre-need insurance policy and the insurer that provides an unsuitable, inferior casket and then voids the entire insurance contract upon customer's refusal to accept the casket. The beneficiary receives a minimal amount of compensation, equal to the face value of the policy, but the funeral home then charges the beneficiary the full amount of the much larger present-day cost of the funeral services, plus the price of an "upgraded" casket, amounting to thousands of dollars above the insured price guaranteed by the original pre-need insurance policy.

Breach of contract consists of the failure on the part of death care industry representatives to provide services as stipulated in the pre-need insurance contract or to provide services of equal value. The casket that is provided is inferior in quality to the casket described in the contract. Policyholders are not notified that the casket specified in the contract is no longer available, nor that a suitable replacement equal to that provided under the contract would be made available under the terms of the contract. Policyholders are "forced" to accept the inferior casket or forgo the terms of their insurance policy.

Omission of material facts occurs as death care industry representatives fail to disclose to the purchasers of pre-need burial insurance relevant facts as to the quality of the casket, which, if revealed at time of purchase, would result in purchasers not agreeing to the terms of the contract. Here, representatives are deemed negligent in disclosing the unfit and unacceptable condition of the casket purchased through the pre-need burial insurance as well as negligent in disclosing other unwritten severe limitations of the policy imposed by funeral industry representatives on policyholder beneficiaries.

Fraud in the inducement by omission is the practice in which death care industry representatives conceal or fail to disclose the fact that the casket described in the pre-need insurance contract, although inferior in quality, must be accepted by the beneficiary or else, according to interpretation by death care service representatives, the beneficiary loses all benefits and services described in the policy, and the original terms of the policy are voided.

Unfair trade practices in violation of insurance codes are engaged in by death care insurance representatives when they provide advertising information that misrepresents the terms of the pre-need insurance policy. Policy conditions, benefits, advantages, and other provisions are misrepresented by the insurance representatives to the purchasers, and facts are concealed regarding benefit payments of the insurance policy.

Because such unethical and illegal practices are extremely injurious to consumers, representatives of the death care industry have been shown to engage in unfair business practices in *violation of unfair trade practices and consumer protection legislation.*

These fraudulent practices in the funeral industry are commonly referred to as "bait and switch" scams, used to swindle policyholders out of their fully paid funeral expenses. It is estimated that more than 10,000 young and elderly consumers have been victims of insurance industry fraud by being deprived of millions of dollars through fraudulent pre-need funeral insurance plans. Additionally, more than 10,000 policyholders of such plans will be future victims of death care industry schemes to defraud them out of millions of dollars in years to come. Loopholes and flaws in both state and federal laws regulating the death-care industry, as well as lax enforcement of those laws that do exist, are considered the major reasons for such fraudulent practices.

See also: Bait and Switch; Insurance Industry Fraud

FURTHER READING

Roberts, Darryl J. *Profits of Death: An Insider Exposes the Death Care Industries.* New York: Five Star Publications, 1997.

Wasik, John F. "Fraud in the Funeral Industry." *Consumers Digest* 34.5 (1995, September/October). Available at http://ajibay.com/freefuneralhelp/articles/cdsep95.htm.

BERNADETTE JONES PALOMBO

G

GOLAB, STEPHEN (1923–1983). Stephen (Stefan) Golab was a Polish immigrant whose death from acute cyanide poisoning while working for a suburban Chicago silver extraction company became the focus of the first American criminal case in which a company and its corporate executives were found guilty of homicide in a state prosecution of corporate activities. (See **Film Recovery Systems**.) Golab, a steel construction laborer by trade, came to the United States in December 1981 on a passport and a visitor's visa, leaving his wife and son in Poland. He lived in Chicago with his sister-in-law, Jadwiga Popek, and remained in Illinois after his visa expired. On December 26, 1982, he began working for Film Recovery Systems, Inc., at its silver reclamation plant, located northwest of Chicago in Elk Grove Village, for $4.50 an hour. Like many of the company's Polish and Mexican employees, he neither spoke nor read much English. Also like fellow employees, he began not to feel well, and he told his sister-in-law that he was experiencing headaches, nausea and vomiting, and burning eyes. What he did not know was that the air that he was breathing inside the plant contained hydrogen cyanide.

Film Recovery Systems, Inc. extracted silver from used photographic and hospital x-ray film in a process that involved grinding up the film into chips, which were put into large, open vats containing water and sodium cyanide and then stirred by the workers. The mixture caused the silver to be released, and the solution containing the silver was then pumped into polyurethane tanks containing electrically charged stainless steel plates. After the silver attached to the plates, individual workers manually performed the following tasks: removing the plates from the tanks, scraping the silver from the plates, pumping out the remaining liquid from the tanks, and then removing the contaminated chips. The silver scraps were then sent to B. R. MacKay and Sons, Inc. in Salt Lake City, Utah, to be smelted and refined and then made into silver bullion. The workers did not receive protective clothing, safety glasses, or special gloves. There were no covers on the vats and there was no ventilation system other than ceiling fans.

Golab and Roman Guzowski (an employee who regularly stood next to Golab) tended some of the large vats. On Thursday, February 3, 1983, they both felt sick while at work. The next day, Guzowski stayed home, and Golab, through an interpreter, went to Plant Manager Charles Kirschbaum and requested job relocation within the plant. However, Kirschbaum did not immediately grant that request. Shortly after arriving at work a week later, on Thursday, February 10, 1983, Golab disconnected a pump on one of the tanks, picked up a rake, and began to stir the contents of the vat with a rake. He became dizzy and light-headed, and Guzowski encouraged him to go to the lunchroom to rest. After seeing Golab tremble, foam at the mouth, and then faint, other workers took him outside. Paramedics, called to the plant, could not revive him. They took him to the nearby Alexian Brothers Medical Center, where he was pronounced dead. There was a discrepancy as to whether he was age fifty-nine or sixty-one at the time of his death.

Cook County Medical Examiner Dr. Robert J. Stein performed an autopsy on February 11, 1983. Based on the toxicology report, he determined that Golab had died from acute cyanide poisoning through the inhalation of cyanide fumes in the plant air (*People v. O'Neil* 1990: 82). This was consistent with the smell of bitter almonds coming from the inside of Golab's body during the autopsy. Further testing indicated that Golab's blood cyanide level was 3.45 micrograms per milliliter, enough to kill a person.

Within a month of Golab's work-related death and the release of the autopsy findings, both county and federal environmental investigators began a few routine governmental inspections. The Director of the Cook County Department of Environmental Control determined that the company had failed to get the state and federal environmental and operating permits necessary to assure that emission and other safety controls were provided on the equipment used for the silver extraction process, and also that the hydrogen cyanide levels in the plant's operations area were double the federal Occupational Safety and Health Administration's (OSHA) maximum standard. A federal OSHA inspector issued seventeen citations for numerous violations, including the company's failures to supply proper training, to issue various adequate safety and protective gear to the workers, and to give proper oral and written warnings about air and equipment hazards in languages understood by the foreign workers. Rather than spend the money to renovate its operations, Film Recovery Systems closed down its plant in March 1983.

In the fall of 1983, after further investigation into the plight of the workers at Film Recovery Systems, Cook County State's Attorney's Office Prosecutor Jay Magnuson got approval from Richard M. Daley, the Cook County state's attorney, to seek indictments against the company and its officials. On October 18, 1983, the grand jury indicted Film Recovery Systems president Steven J. O'Neil, plant manager Charles Kirschbaum, plant foreman Daniel Rodriguez, and vice-presidents Gerald Pett and Michael MacKay (who was also president of B. R. MacKay and Sons) for the murder of Stefan Golab. It also indicted Film Recovery Systems, Inc., Metallic Marketing (the sister company of Film Recovery Systems), and B. R. MacKay and Sons for involuntary manslaughter of Golab. All the defendants were indicted for reckless conduct regarding twenty other Film Recovery Systems employees.

The bench trial began April 15, 1985, and lasted eight weeks. Fifty-nine witnesses were called, including Golab's sister-in-law and his friend Guzowski, who was brought back from Gdansk, Poland. Many former workers attested to the conditions in the plant and to the physical problems they experienced, as well as to the extent to which each of the company's executives had been present in the extraction areas of the plant. Halfway through the trial, Judge Ronald J. P. Banks dismissed the charges against Pett. MacKay, at home in Salt Lake City, did not stand trial because the governor of Utah refused requests for extradition. On June 14, 1985, the companies and executives were found guilty as charged. In January 1990 the Appellate Court of Illinois reversed the convictions on the grounds of legally inconsistent verdicts. Kirschbaum, O'Neil, and Rodriguez later pleaded guilty to involuntary manslaughter in the death of Golab prior to the start of their retrial in September 1993, and in exchange for a guilty plea to one misdemeanor charge of reckless conduct in the injury of another plant worker, murder charges against MacKay were dropped in May 1995.

Although a 1930 Illinois statute allowed for prosecution of a corporation for involuntary manslaughter, the murder charges against company officials for the death of a worker on the job were unprecedented. Historically, the legal remedies available to deal with matters such as work-related death and workplace conditions could be found in state workers' compensation, labor, and environmental laws as well as in the federal OSHA workplace safety laws and regulations, which provided for fines and very short-term imprisonment sanctions. Also, individuals could sue corporations for negligence and seek compensation in the event of personal injury or wrongful death. The idea that the threat of fines or large awards would be a deterrent factor in worker-safety-related business decisions generally has been countered with the argument that the potential for such monetary losses would become part of a typical cost/benefit analysis. Such a cost would be added to the price of doing business for the company, and fines imposed upon the actual persons responsible for questionable conduct may be covered by the company. However, the potential for corporations and individuals actually being prosecuted under the criminal law and punished with incarceration for such misconduct (including homicide) may have a more deterrent and humbling effect upon such persons.

By the late 1980s, a few successful state criminal prosecutions for death and injuries to workers in Texas, Wisconsin, and, again, in Illinois were upheld by state appellate courts despite challenges that only OSHA had the authority to bring such criminal cases. More recently, the trend is for state prosecutors to use reckless homicide, criminally negligent homicide, or variations of manslaughter statutes as charges in employment-related deaths (provided that the state statutory definition of a person includes corporations). Alternatively, some states have specific corporate–criminal liability statutes that can be used as a last resort for work–related injuries or deaths caused by a corporation (Broussard 1997).

In addition to prosecution, data collection is another method that spotlights occupational safety and health matters. Each year since 1992, the Bureau of Labor Statistics (BLS), U.S. Department of Labor, releases findings from both the Survey of Occupational Injuries and Illnesses and the National Census of Fatal Occupational Injuries (CFOI). Data from the federal Mine Safety and Health Administration, the Federal Railroad Administration, as well as from thousands of private employer reports collected and processed by agencies in the fifty states and the District of Columbia, are used for the Survey. To ensure accuracy, data for CFOI come from a variety of sources across the fifty states and the District of Columbia. The data provides the most authoritative count of deaths in the workplace, as well as the manner in which fatalities occur, what kinds of work-related deaths are most frequent, and information on the gender, ethnicity, and age of the deceased. Because of these programs, workers are better informed of job-related hazards, and employers are more likely to provide job safety training and improve safety standards. Census data indicates that between 1992 and 2004, the most frequent work-related fatal events were highway accidents, falls, homicides, and being struck by objects. Between 1994 and 2004, the number of workplace homicides decreased by almost half, from a high of 1,080 down to 551; however, cause-of-deaths categories are shootings, stabbings, or self-inflicted injuries. Between 1999 and 2003, the number of deaths from exposure to harmful substances or environmental hazards averaged 508, with exposure to caustic, noxious, or allergenic substances accounting for an average of 105 deaths, fifteen of which were attributed to substance inhalation. Put in perspective, in 2004 there was a total of 5703 recorded work-related fatalities (4.1 per 100,000 workers) in the United States, the third lowest annual total since 1992. The 5703 fatalities in 2004 included 1374 highway incidents (25 percent), 815 falls (14 percent), 596 workers struck by objects (18 percent), 551 homicides (10 percent), and 114 substance exposure incidents (2 percent) (National Census 2004).

Golab's death from acute cyanide poisoning was unusual in the metal reclamation industry. In the United States, industries that use hydrogen cyanide in their operations are allowed to operate, but they are more highly regulated than other industries. Silver reclamation requires specialized employee protective gear, adequate plant ventilation, hooded vats, careful maintenance and cleaning of work areas, regular monitoring of the air, workers' training in the handling and dangers of the substance, and particular waste disposal methods. Both O'Neil and Kirschbaum had worked in places that maintained some, if not all, of these standards. However, one could speculate that the quick plant expansion required to take advantage of the silver market, the use of uneducated and undocumented workers as cheap labor, and the irregularity of government plant inspections provided an environment in which a fatal accident could occur. In addition, there was the isolated incident of the hiring of Golab. He was fifty-nine and had been a steel worker for twenty years; chemical hazards associated with that occupation could have affected his body. A pre-existing medical condition may have prevented him from taking the job had he known about the exposure to cyanide, but the workers were not instructed that they were using cyanide and not told how to protect themselves from direct inhalation of the gas—the same gas first used in America by several states to carry out death–penalty executions. The plant's first aid kit was not supplied with the antidote for cyanide poisoning, and the local medical rescue teams were not informed about the cyanide use at the plant, which could have had a bearing on how other workers might have responded to Golab's immediate symptoms. All of these factors contributed to the proverbial "accident waiting to happen." The accident happened with fatal results.

Few people actually knew Stefan Golab, yet the name of this once relatively obscure Polish immigrant became nationally known. Because of his tragic death, his name was linked with employees' outcry for more powerful legal remedies against their employers for the redress of serious workplace health and safety grievances.

See also: Film Recovery Systems

FURTHER READING

Broussard, Judy. "The Criminal Corporation: Is Ohio Prepared for Corporate Criminal Prosecutions for Workplace Fatalities?" *Cleveland State Law Review* 45 (1997):135.
Greenhouse, Steven. "A Responsibility for Job Safety." *The New York Times* (June 25, 1985): 2.
Magnuson, Jay C., and Leviton, Gareth C. "Policy Considerations in Corporate Criminal Prosecutions after *People v. Film Recovery Systems, Inc.*" *Notre Dame Law Review* 62 (1987): 913.
National Census of Fatal Occupational Injuries in 2004. Bureau of Labor Statistics (BLS), U.S. Department of Labor. Available at http://www.bls./lif/oshcfoi1.htm.

People v. O'Neil, 194 Ill. App. 3d 79, 550 N.E.2d 1090 (1990) (consolidated with *People v. Film Recovery Systems, Inc.*).

People v. Film Recovery Systems, Inc., No. 83-11091 (Cir. Ct. of Cook County, Ill. June 14, 1985) (joined with *People v. O'Neil*, No. 84-5064).

Rosoff, Stephen, Pontell,Henry, Tillman, Robert. *Profit Without Honor: White Collar Crime and the Looting of America*. 3rd edition. Upper Saddle River, NJ: Pearson Education., Inc., 2004.

Samuels, Anne D. "Reckless Endangerment of an Employee: A Proposal in the Wake of *Film Recovery Systems* to Make the Boss Responsible for His Crimes." *University of Michigan Law Journal of Law Reform* 20 (1987, Spring): 873.

Shipp, E. R. "Can a Corporation Commit Murder?" *The New York Times*, (May 19, 1985): 2.

KATHLEEN M. SIMON

H

HADACOL. Hadacol was a wildly popular patent medicine that swept through the American South and then much of the nation in the late 1940s and early 1950s. Although it was little more than vitamin B and alcohol, sales of Hadacol exceeded $24 million a year in its heyday, making Hadacol the best-selling patent medicine in history. The success of Hadacol was largely due to the often ingenious, and at times fraudulent, advertising claims and schemes of its inventor, Dudley LeBlanc. "Coozan" LeBlanc was a Louisiana Cajun born to a family of poor sharecroppers. LeBlanc relied on his charm and significant powers of persuasion in his, at times, overlapping careers as a politician, a salesman, and a "medicine man." Although at least reasonably successful in all of these ventures, it was patent medicine that made LeBlanc his fortune.

LeBlanc's initial efforts in the patent medicine business included the production and sale of Dixie Dew Cough Syrup and Happy Day Headache Powder, which were both reasonably successful, despite the fact that shipments of the headache powder were seized by the U.S. Food and Drug Administration (FDA) for fraudulent labeling in 1941. Soon after this LeBlanc was afflicted with a disease that caused his legs to swell, rendering him unable to walk by 1943. LeBlanc saw several doctors regarding his condition, all of whom diagnosed him with gout, severe arthritis, or beriberi (a nerve disease). Becoming desperate, LeBlanc went to a local doctor who administered a series of shots of a solution that was mostly B vitamins. His symptoms subsided and eventually disappeared. Perhaps he really did have beriberi, a vitamin B_1 deficiency disease; in any case, LeBlanc became convinced of the healing powers of vitamin B. He read everything he could find regarding vitamins, bought samples of every patent medicine available, and began to conduct experiments in his barn with the intention of creating the next great patent medicine. LeBlanc mixed his ingredients in two old wine barrels, stirring the concoctions with old boat oars, and eventually produced a tincture of vitamin B_1 (thiamine hydrochloride), vitamin B_2 (riboflavin), vitamin B_6 (pyridoxine), pantothenic acid, iron, manganese, calcium, phosphorus, hydrochloric acid, honey, citric acid, and 12 percent alcohol. He called it "Hadacol."

Initially LeBlanc noted that the name "Hadacol" was derived from the initials of his earlier headache powder company—The HAppy DAy COmpany—with an "L" added on the end for LeBlanc. However, LeBlanc later claimed the concoction was dubbed "Hadacol" because he "haddah call it somethin." Between 1944 and 1947, sales of Hadacol were roughly $60,000 per year, as it remained a regionally popular, though largely unknown patent medicine. However, as

LeBlanc became more aggressive in advertising Hadacol, sales rapidly increased to over $20 million per year in the late 1940s and early 1950s. In marketing Hadacol, LeBlanc read testimonials of satisfied customers over the radio, those who claimed Hadacol had helped relieve anemia, arthritis, asthma, diabetes, epilepsy, heart trouble, blindness, paralytic stroke, tuberculosis, chronic fatigue, and insomnia among dozens of other ailments. Although LeBlanc was careful never to claim directly that Hadacol was a cure for these ailments, he never denied its potential as a cure either, and he even told the Federal Trade Commission that "The writers of the testimonials are the best judge of the effect that the preparation Hadacol has upon them" (as quoted in Brigham and Kenyon 1976: 525).

In spite of an American Medical Association statement strongly denouncing Hadacol, and a mandate from the FDA forcing LeBlanc to remove advertising that claimed the substance would "restore youthful feeling and appearance" and promote "good health," sales of the patent medicine continued to increase rapidly as a result of LeBlanc's marketing schemes. LeBlanc expanded his publication of customer testimonials to hundreds of major newspapers, using full- and double-page ads, and he also broadcast advertisements through hundreds of radio and TV stations. LeBlanc continued his massive advertising push of Hadacol to the point that by 1950 there were over one and a half million Hadacol commercials per year, costing LeBlanc an estimated million dollars a month. LeBlanc also had two songs, "Hadacol Boogie" and "Everyone Loves That Hadacol," written, recorded, and placed in jukeboxes throughout the South, and there was even a Captain Hadacol comic book. As testimony to LeBlanc's desire to market to all segments of the population, in one issue of the comic Captain Hadacol gives eight bottles of Hadacol to a young boy, telling him to drink them down to get "immediate super strength"—despite the fact that the alcohol content in eight bottles of Hadacol would be roughly equivalent to a pint of 80-proof liquor! LeBlanc also came up with the idea of giving kids "Captain Hadacol Credit Cards," which enabled children to get a bottle of Hadacol on credit from their local drugstore. Children could sell the bottle, keep the boxtop, and return the money from the sale to the druggist. With enough boxtops, children could then earn prizes such as an air-rifle or roller skates.

LeBlanc's final and most ambitious promotional effort, however, was the Hadacol Caravan. As a result of the massive sales of Hadacol, and in part because much of the money spent on advertising Hadacol was taxable, LeBlanc had accumulated a substantial tax debt. LeBlanc was thus put in the difficult position of balancing his desire to expand Hadacol's sales territory and continuing his aggressive marketing strategy while also offsetting his tax debt. He came up with the idea of the Hadacol Caravan—a massive, circus-like medicine show involving floats, dancing girls, clowns, comedy acts, and musical performances by some of the biggest names of the day in entertainment, such as Bob Hope, Andy Rooney, George Burns, and Hank Williams. The caravan mainly targeted areas where Hadacol was not widely sold, and it often involved more than seventy trucks, three airplanes, air-conditioned buses for the entertainers, and at times a train (called "The Hadacol Special"). Everything LeBlanc spent on the caravan was tax-deductible because admission was technically free—requiring only Hadacol boxtops. LeBlanc's marketing strategy also involved heavily advertising the coming of the caravan prior to its arrival in the next city. As people eagerly anticipated the caravan's arrival, LeBlanc arranged contests during which radio stations would play well-known songs and challenge people to "name that tune" to win a bottle of Hadacol. Hundreds of thousands of "winners" would name the easily recognized songs and then receive a coupon for their free bottle of Hadacol. However, as LeBlanc was well aware, these were areas where Hadacol was not widely sold, so people would flock to their local drug stores trying to redeem their prizes and there would be no Hadacol on hand. LeBlanc once even hired scores of housewives to canvass their local drug stores requesting Hadacol, further encouraging the perception that Hadacol was in high demand. As demand for Hadacol surged, druggists would frantically try to stock the product, and just about that time the caravan would arrive in town. LeBlanc would then send salesmen out to the eager local druggists and quickly fill large and lucrative orders from his caravan's stock trucks. For example, within four days of the caravan's arrival in Atlanta, Le Blanc sold ten full trucks' worth of Hadacol, equating to approximately $225,000 in sales.

However, despite the massive sales of Hadacol generated by the caravan and other advertising efforts, the company was losing millions because LeBlanc spent money faster than he was earning it. In 1951 LeBlanc announced he had sold Hadacol to a group of Eastern businessmen for $8,000,000 and fifteen years' guaranteed employment at a salary of $100,000 a year, but in actuality Hadacol was sold for only $250,000, with the remainder contingent on profits that would never materialize, and LeBlanc was not offered a role in the company. When it was sold, Hadacol was over $8,000,000 in debt, there were fourteen lawsuits pending against the firm, and in 1954 the new owners were forced to declare bankruptcy.

See also: Pharmaceutical Companies

FURTHER READING

Anderson, Ann. *Snake Oil, Hustles and Hambones: The American Medicine Show.* Jefferson, NC: McFarland & Company, 2000.

Brigham, J., and Kenyon, K. "Hadacol: The Last Great Medicine Show." *Journal of Popular Culture* 10 (1976): 520–533.

Young, James. *The Medical Messiahs: A Social History of Health Quackery in Twentieth-Century America.* Princeton, NJ: Princeton University Press, 1969.

SCOTT AKINS
JANE FLORENCE GAUTHIER

HALLIBURTON. Halliburton was first established in 1919. Since that time the corporation purchased several subsidiaries including Brown and Root (the consortium of Devonport Management Ltd.), Dresser Industries (M.W. Kellogg, a subsidiary of Dresser, merged with Brown and Root after both were acquired by Halliburton, forming KBR), Landmark Graphics Corporation, Wellstream, Well Dynamics, Eventure, and Subsea 7. The success of the Halliburton Corporation is the consequence of a range of strategic practices. Since the mid-1990s, many of Halliburton's corporate actions have come under scrutiny of several U.S. governmental oversight organizations (such as the Security Exchange Commission, U.S. General Accounting Office, and congressional committees), the international society, and criminologists. The investigations of Halliburton's actions focused on a series of its practices that can be classified as white-collar crime. Halliburton's actions of systematically overcharging the U.S. Government for contracted work, utilizing bribes to attain foreign contracts, and using subsidiaries and foreign joint ventures to bypass U.S. law restricting trade embargoes are examples of this corporate crime. The financial ties and vested interests between Vice President Dick Cheney and Halliburton exemplify practices that incorporate a form of white-collar crime called state/corporate crime.

International Bribery Charges. In 2005 Halliburton came under investigation for international bribery charges by the French Government. The bribes occurred from the mid 1990s through the year 2000 and were made to a Nigerian state official. In a separate but related inquiry by the U.S. Justice Department and the Securities and Exchange Commission (SEC), additional systematic use of bribery to attain foreign oil contracts was revealed. In a 2002 filing with the SEC, Halliburton acknowledged that one of its foreign subsidiaries operating in Nigeria made improper payments of approximately $2.4 million (U.S.) to an entity owned by a Nigerian national. The payments were made to obtain favorable tax treatment in violation of the U.S. Foreign Corrupt Practices Act and the convention adopted by the Organization for Economic Cooperation and Development (OECD) prohibiting offering bribes in the course of commercial transactions.

Foreign Trade Barred under International Sanctions. As Halliburton's subsidiary, Dresser, Inc., did substantial business with Iraq from 1997 through the summer of 2000, closing $73 million worth of deals with Saddam Hussein. Many of these deals were joint ventures with the Ingersoll-Rand Company (known as the Dresser-Rand and Ingersoll Dresser Pump Companies) that occurred under the subsidiary of Dresser Inc. and were disguised under the United Nations' Oil for Food program. During this time U.S. law forbade trade with Iraq; however, U.S. firms routinely used foreign subsidiaries and joint ventures to avoid the opprobrium of doing business directly with Baghdad, thus not in direct violation of U.S. law.

The Treasury Department opened an inquiry in 2001 to examine the legality of Halliburton's business dealings with Iran during the 1990s, when Vice President Dick Cheney was CEO. The Treasury Department charged the company with using loopholes that allowed Halliburton to get around the sanctions on Iran by doing business through foreign subsidiaries. Under legal standards used to define crime, Halliburton would not be culpable of illegal trade with Iraq or Iran; however, from a criminological perspective, both may be classified as state-corporate crime.

Systematic Overcharges to the U.S. Government. The U.S. General Accounting Office (GAO) brought charges against Halliburton in 1997 for billing the U.S. Army for questionable expenses for work in the Balkans, including charging $85.98 per sheet for plywood that cost Halliburton $14.06 a sheet and charges for "cleaning" offices up to four times a day. A 2000 follow-up report by the GAO regarding Halliburton's contract in the Balkans found continuous systematic overcharges in the form of inflated costs submitted in Halliburton's billings to the U.S. Army.

In February 2002 Halliburton paid $2 million in fines to resolve fraud claims for work done at Fort Ord, California. The Defense Department Inspector General and a federal grand jury had investigated allegations that KBR, a subsidiary of Halliburton, had defrauded the government of millions of dollars through inflated prices for repairs and maintenance.

A Pentagon audit found that Halliburton (specifically, KBR) was overcharging the U.S. Government for approximately fifty-seven million gallons of gasoline delivered to Iraqi citizens under a no-bid contract during the "war on terror" from 2002 through 2004. Further exacerbating the problem, part of the money for the KBR gas service contract came from the UN Oil for Food program (now the Iraq Development Fund). Under the terms of UN Security Council Resolution 1483, an independent board, called the International Advisory and Monitoring Board, was to be created to ensure that Oil for Food funds were spent for the benefit of Iraqi citizens. This agency was to be the primary vehicle for ensuring that the Iraqi Development Funds were used properly. However, the international oversight agency was never created. Thus, the U.S. (Coalition Provisional Authority) use of the funds to pay inflated prices to Halliburton ($600 million out of $1 billion was transferred to Halliburton) remained unchecked.

Halliburton systematically overcharged the state for services rendered (and not rendered) under the logistics contracts it obtained from the U.S. Department of Defense. Many of these services were subcontracted out by Halliburton. When Halliburton submitted costs for military dining services to the U.S. government, they included charges totaling more than $67 million over the amounts that the corporation paid to the actual subcontractors.

Halliburton was charged with improprieties surrounding a joint venture with Morris Corporation, an Australian catering company (a $100 million contract to supply meals to U.S. troops in Iraq). Halliburton canceled the contract six weeks after it was signed when it was revealed that an employee sought kickbacks worth up to $3 million during the negotiations of the subcontract work. A Pentagon report released in March 2004 found that Halliburton failed to inform the military that the Morris contract to supply meals had been canceled. Yet, Halliburton continued to use the contract to estimate costs and render charges of more than $1 billion for catering services it was not providing.

See also: Criminogenic Industry; State-Corporate Crime

FURTHER READING

Chambliss, William. "State Organized Crime." *Criminology* 27.2 (1989): 183–208.
Clinard, Marshall. "Criminological Theories of Violations of Wartime Regulations." *American Sociological Review* (February, 1946): 258–270.
Friedrichs, David. *State Crime: Volumes I and II*. Aldershot, UK: Ashgate/Dartsmouth,1998.
Kramer, Ronald, Michalowski, Raymond, and Kauzlarich, David. "The Origins and Development of the Concept and Theory of State-Corporate Crime." *Crime and Delinquency* 48.2 (2002): 263-282.
Rothe, Dawn. "War Profiteering and the Pernicious Beltway Bandits." Pp. 333–370 in Ronald Kramer and Raymond J. Michalowski, (ed). *State-Corporate Crime: Wrongdoing at the Intersection of Business and Government*. Piscataway, NJ: Rutgers University Press, 2005.
U.S. Department of Defense. "United States Department of Defense Contracts." (October 2004). Available at http://www.defenselink.mil/contracts.

DAWN L. ROTHE

HAZARDOUS WASTE DISPOSAL. Understanding the requirements for proper hazardous waste disposal is important to the study of white-collar crime, because businesses have a legal and social obligation to dispose of hazardous waste safely. Moreover, there are substantial risks to the environment and human health if waste is disposed of illegally. Hazardous waste pollutes the environment and wreaks havoc on ecosystems. Human exposure to hazardous waste has been associated with cancer, genetic damage, neurological disorders, liver damage, birth defects, respiratory problems, and numerous other health issues. To ensure proper management of hazardous waste, Congress passed two federal statutes: the Resource Conservation and Recovery Act (RCRA) in 1976, and the Comprehensive Environmental Response, Compensation, and Liability Act (CERCLA) in 1980. The Environmental Protection Agency (EPA) is the federal agency responsible for the administration and enforcement of RCRA and CERCLA as well as for determining which industrial wastes are hazardous.

The EPA estimates that one million generators of hazardous waste produce more than forty million tons of hazardous waste annually in the United States. A small percentage of chemical, petroleum, and metal manufacturers produce the majority of this waste; however, local dry cleaners, auto repair shops, hospitals, exterminators, and photo processing centers also generate a considerable amount of toxic waste.

RCRA. In the past, most companies disposed of hazardous waste by dumping it in landfills or by discharging it directly into the air or water. RCRA prohibits open dumping and regulates the transportation, treatment, storage, and disposal of hazardous wastes. The statute utilizes a life cycle management process, otherwise referred to as a "cradle to grave" approach, to make the disposal of hazardous waste a safer process. This means that wastes are regulated and tracked from the time they are generated until they are disposed.

Generators of waste are required to consult with the EPA to determine whether the waste is hazardous. If the waste is hazardous, the generator must send the waste to a treatment, storage and disposal (TSD) facility within ninety days or apply for a TSD permit to handle the waste on site. Approximately 98 percent of hazardous waste is managed on location by generators with TSD permits. Generators must keep records regarding the quantities and constituents of hazardous waste, accurately label and use proper containers to store hazardous waste, provide information about the chemical composition of the waste to transporters and TSD facilities, and comply with RCRA permit reporting requirements.

If a generator chooses to transport waste offsite, the entity must select a reputable transporter to deliver the waste and follow manifest procedures set forth by RCRA and the Hazardous Materials Transportation Uniform Safety Act of 1990. In 1999, 17,914 transporters moved over eight million tons of hazardous waste. Given the problems that can occur during the shipping/transportation process, Congress set forth strict standards under RCRA. In addition to having an EPA identification number, transporters can transport waste only with proper labels and must comply with the federal manifest system.

A manifest is a form with multiple copies pertaining to each participant involved in a shipment process. For a shipment of hazardous waste, the manifest details the type and quantity of waste, the points for delivery, and the dates and time of delivery. The form includes the names of the generator, transporter, and the TSD. Throughout the transportation process, the manifest must accompany the hazardous waste. The manifest system also requires transporters to deliver hazardous wastes only to the designated TSD. Upon delivery, the transporter must verify that the designated receiving facility has a TSD permit. Once the waste reaches its final destination, the generator is sent a copy of the manifest as verification that its waste arrived at the specified facility.

Three aspects of hazardous waste management include storage, treatment, and disposal facilities with a TSD permit have authorization to perform any one or all three of these functions. The EPA reports that there are over 300,000 organizations that manage waste in the United States. *Storage facilities* are most common, and they simply hold hazardous waste until it is treated or disposed of later. *Treatment facilities* alter the physical, chemical, or biological character/composition of hazardous waste in order to neutralize it, to make it nonhazardous, or to recover energy or resources from it. *Disposal facilities* employ numerous techniques to dispose of waste that include incineration, detoxification, recycling, and direct deposit/discharge into the ground, water, or air. Although the practice is strongly discouraged, approximately 70 percent of hazardous waste is land-disposed in underground injection wells, landfills, or surface impoundments.

CERCLA. RCRA attempts to address most hazardous waste disposal issues, but it applies only to facilities in current operation and does not apply to abandoned waste sites, which often contain the most toxic of wastes. Thus, Congress passed CERCLA to remedy improper and careless waste disposal practices that were prevalent in former decades. CERCLA places responsibility for clean up costs on primary responsible parties (PRPs) who were previously associated with abandoned sites. If there is no identifiable PRP, CERCLA provides federal monies (commonly known as the Superfund) to assist state and local governments with clean up efforts.

Most Superfund sites were former locations of manufacturing facilities, mines, federal ammunition dumps, landfills, and chemical storage ponds. The most notorious Superfund site involved Hooker Chemical Company in Love Canal, New York. Current estimates indicate that there are over 50,000 known abandoned hazardous waste sites, and many of them threaten groundwater supplies. Given the vast number of abandoned sites, the government uses a National Priorities List (NPL) to prioritize cleanup efforts in the most dangerous locations. In 2004 there were 1240 sites on the NPL.

Responding to Illegal Hazardous Waste Disposal. Unfortunately, there is no reliable system to track the nature and extent of environmental crimes as the Uniform Crime Reports do for street crime. At present one must rely on rough estimates that do not accurately represent the problem. Corporations, small businesses, and even the U.S. Government are common RCRA/CERCLA offenders. Some entities/individuals engage in violations on their own, while others conspire with each other. RCRA/CERCLA violations are often due to profit–seeking behavior, negligent behavior leading to an accident, and lack of knowledge regarding RCRA and CERCLA requirements.

RCRA Violations. There is a wide range of violations committed under RCRA; however, most offenses involve the illegal disposal or management of hazardous waste (NIJ 2004). For example, some facilities operate without a TSD permit, while others illegally dispose of waste into the air, water, or land. To cut businesses expenses, generators have hired "gypsy" transporters (who have no EPA identification numbers) to engage in "midnight dumping" at remote locations. Some transporters even bribe landfill employees to accept hazardous waste onto the location. Another type of RCRA violation is "cocktailing," in which a generator, TSD facility, or transporter dilutes hazardous waste with nonhazardous waste to mask it as nonhazardous to save money. Some even forge manifests to hide their illegal practices. For example, some generators and transporters will falsely record that waste was sent to a TSD facility when in reality, it was disposed of at a remote location.

Should the EPA determine that any person/facility has violated a provision of RCRA or is in current violation of it, EPA can issue administrative orders that impose enforceable legal requirements. There are four types of administrative orders, including compliance, correcting, monitoring, and imminent endangerment orders. Administrative orders can also include suspension or revocation of any EPA- or state-issued permit. If necessary, EPA can also issue fines. When assessing the penalty, the EPA considers the seriousness of the violation and any good-faith efforts taken to comply. Once an order is final and penalties are assessed, should a violator not take corrective action, the entity can be charged additional fines of as much as $25,000 per day of noncompliance and can have its permit revoked.

When a person or facility violates RCRA or fails to comply with an administrative order, EPA will often take civil action. When doing so, the EPA turns to a U.S. District Court to seek relief for repeated violations, noncompliance, or for activities that present an imminent and substantial endangerment to human health or the environment. Relief can include temporary or permanent injunctions and fines not to exceed $25,000 for each violation; however, each day of a violation constitutes a separate violation.

RCRA has two major criminal provisions—*knowing violations* and *knowing endangerment*. The activities that constitute knowing violations often include knowingly: transporting hazardous waste to a facility without a TSD permit; treating, storing, or disposing hazardous waste without a permit or in violation of a permit; omitting material information or making false material statements or representation in any written document (e.g., application, records, manifest, permits); generating, storing, treating, transporting, disposing of, exporting, or otherwise handling any hazardous waste without abiding by RCRA's recordkeeping and reporting requirements; transporting hazardous waste without a manifest; and exporting a hazardous waste without the consent of the receiving country. RCRA provides that any person who knowingly engages in any of these activities is subject (upon conviction) to: (a) a maximum fine of $50,000 for each day of the violation, (b) imprisonment for not more than two years, or (c) both fine and imprisonment. If the person is a repeat offender, fines and imprisonment can be doubled.

RCRA provides stricter criminal sanctions for activities that qualify as knowing endangerment. Thus, any person who engages in any of the aforementioned activities and who knows that they place another person in imminent danger of death or serious bodily injury is subject to (a) a maximum fine of $250,000, (b) imprisonment of up to 15 years, or (c) both fine and imprisonment if convicted. If the defendant is a corporation, then the maximum fine is one million dollars.

Consider the following case as an example of a RCRA violation. According to the EPA, in 2002 a well-known oil corporation illegally disposed of benzene-contaminated wastewater near New York City Harbor without a permit. Benzene is a hazardous waste that has been linked to cancer. As a result, the company was ordered to pay an $8.2 million penalty in addition to $3 million for restoration costs.

CERCLA Violations. Most violations of CERCLA apply retroactively to dumping activities committed by industry and small businesses prior to 1980. In other words, CERCLA makes PRPs liable for past hazardous waste disposal practices. Under CERCLA, the EPA can either (a) require a PRP to finance and conduct cleanup activities or (b) seek reimbursement for removal and remediation activities undertaken by the government (RCRA

2003). The sanctions imposed under CERCLA vary based on the cleanup costs associated with a specific site.

Consider the following case as an example of a CERCLA violation. The EPA reports that from 1954 to 1971 numerous companies dumped an estimated 700,000 pounds of polychlorinated biphenyls (PCBs) into the Fox River in Wisconsin. PCBs were used as lubricants and coolants in electric transformers, motors, and appliances, but exposure to PCBs can cause cancer, birth defects, liver disease, and genetic mutations. As of 2006, the EPA estimates that there are still 65,000 pounds of PCBs left in the river sediment, of which 620 pounds are flushed into Green Bay annually. The EPA reached a settlement agreement with two companies who were designated as the liable PRPs. The settlement requires PRP to pay $25 million each into an escrow account to be used to finance the cleanup process as determined by the EPA.

Enforcement Trends. Scholars believe that most violations of environmental laws are never detected because of a lack of enforcement resources. When the EPA is aware of a violation, it relies heavily on administrative actions and rarely utilizes criminal sanctions. Indeed, the chances of criminal sanctions are rare—one researcher found that only 0.03 percent of hazardous waste generators were criminally convicted for various environmental crimes. The lack of convictions is due to numerous factors related to politics, to poor identification of responsible parties, to the lack of proof/evidence, and to high costs. In fact, the EPA and the Department of Justice (DOJ) consider a variety of factors before pursuing criminal prosecution that include the degree of harm caused by the offense; the presence of criminal intent, the evidence of voluntary disclosure; the degree and timeliness of cooperation; the presence of preventative measures and compliance programs; the pervasive history of non-compliance; the presence of disciplinary systems to punish employees who violate company policies; and subsequent compliance efforts. Given these factors, some scholars have concluded that violators are typically allowed to "negotiate compliance" and avoid serious sanctions for their illegal behavior.

See also: Cruise Line Industry; Environmental Crime; Hooker Chemical Corporation; Polychlorinated Biphenyls (PCBs)

FURTHER READING

Blabolil, Sandee, Cho, Ines, Haenni, Scott, Kuffler, Joe, Leach, Susan, and Kara Little. "Environmental Crimes." *American Criminal Law Review* 34 (1997): 491–554.

Drielak, Steven. *Environmental Crime*. Springfield, IL: Charles C. Thomas, 1998.

Environmental Protection Agency. "Fiscal Year 2003 Case Highlights." EPA, 2003. Available http://www.epa.gov/compliance/resources/reports/endofyear/eoy2003/fy2003casehighlights.pdf. Accessed January 27, 2004.

Findley, Roger, and Farber, Daniel. *Environmental Law: In a Nutshell*. 3rd edition. St. Paul, MN: West Publishing Company, 1992.

Glicksman, Robert, Markell, David, Mandelker, Daniel, Tarlock, Dan, and Frederick Anderson. *Environmental Protection: Law and Policy*. 4th edition. New York: Aspen Publishers, 2003.

Hunter, Susan, and Waterman, Richard. "Determining an Agency's Regulatory Style: How Does the EPA Water Office Enforce the Law?" *The Western Political Quarterly* 45 (1992): 403–417.

Katz, Rebecca. "Hazardous Waste." Pp. 387–391 in Lawrence Salinger (ed.) *Encyclopedia of White-collar and Corporate Crime, Vol. 1*. Thousand Oaks, CA: Sage Publications, 2005.

National Institute of Justice. *Environmental Crime Prosecution: Results of a National Survey*. Washington, DC: U.S. Department of Justice, 1994.

"RCRA." Pp. 699–809 in *Selected Environmental Law Statutes 2003–2004 Educational Edition*. St. Paul, MN: ThomsonWest Publishing Company, 2003.

Ross, Debra. "Corporate Dumping." Pp. 213–235 in Lawrence Salinger (ed.) *Encyclopedia of White-collar and Corporate Crime, Vol. 1*. Thousand Oaks, CA: Sage Publications, 2005.

Ross, Debra. "A Review of EPA, Criminal, Civil, and Administrative Enforcement Data: Are the Efforts Measurable Deterrents to Environmental Criminals?" Pp. 55–76 in Sally Edwards, Terry Edwards, and Charles Fields (eds.), *Environmental Crime and Criminality*. New York: Garland Publishing, 1996.

Wagner, Travis. *The Complete Guide to Hazardous Waste Regulations*, 2nd edition. New York: John Wiley and Sons, 1991.

Wolf, Sidney. "Hazardous Waste Trials and Tribulations." *Environmental Law* 13 (Winter 1983).

TARA O'CONNOR SHELLEY

HEALTH CARE INDUSTRY. The U.S. health care industry presents an attractive target for white-collar criminals, corporations, and criminal organizations to commit fraud and other malfeasance. As one of the fastest-growing sectors of the U.S. economy and essentially the largest business in the country, health care drew $1.5 trillion of national spending in 2002, an average of $2350 per person. It is estimated that between 3 and 10 percent of national expenditure on health care is lost to fraud and abuse.

The health care industry is diverse with respect to both recipients of health care and service providers. Consumers are in need of a range of health services—treatments for injury and sickness, access to hospice as well as preventative care, education for patients, and provisions for a broad range of prescription drugs and medical products. Of the $1.5 trillion spent on health care in 2002, 33 percent was spent on hospital care, 23 percent on physician and clinical services, 11 percent on prescription drugs, and 7 percent on nursing home care. Over the past three decades, these four categories constituted 70 percent of the growth in national health care expenditure. The number of persons employed in the health services industry increased by 47 percent from 8.6 million in 1990 to 12.7 million in 2003. The growing ranks include persons employed as physicians, nurses, dentists, and pharmacists as well as people in the fields of health plan administration, merchandise sales, and research and development.

The delivery of health care services has changed markedly over the last three decades. Notable shifts have occurred in health care delivery, patient demographics, cost and payment for services, and industry regulation and enforcement. Technology has played a central role in advancing diagnostic and health care service delivery, resulting in improvements in treatment, though adding to the cost of health care. Costs associated with hospital utilization increased steadily over this period. At the same time, many procedures that previously required a stay in the hospital were provided on an outpatient basis—the number of outpatient visits increased steadily from 368 million in 1990 to more than 640 million in 2002. Advances in health care have come at a greater expense as health care companies seek to recover years of investment in medical research and development through increased costs of prescription and specialized treatment services.

An important component of future growth in the health care industry is the changing demographics of the recipient population. As people live longer, the need for health care services increases. Greater spending on health care accompanies the growth in the elderly population as health costs increase with age. The average life expectancy increased from 70.8 years in 1970 to a record 77.6 years in 2003. The U.S. Census projects that by the year 2050, the number of persons 65 and over will grow to 86.7 million, comprising 21 percent of the total population. This compares with 36.3 million in 2004 (12 percent of the population). National expenditure on nursing home and home health care was $139.3 billion in 2002, an increase of 32.5 percent from 1995. As the baby boom generation ages in the coming years, the expense associated with meeting the health care needs such as nursing homes for the elderly will continue to rise.

The health care industry presents a complex environment for regulation and enforcement. This complexity is due in part to the varied arrangements for payment for service, the multitude of potential victims, and the variety of schemes used for fraud. Also, health fraud offenses tend to cross state lines and enforcement jurisdictions. Perpetrators of fraud in the health care industry target the growing pool of health care money available through private and public insurers as well as monies from the consumers' own checkbooks. About one-half of the nations' health care expenditure in 2002 ($762 billion) was spent through private insurance purchased by consumers (72 percent) and the remainder from out-of-pocket payments by consumers (28 percent). The U.S. government, the largest single insurer, spent 46 cents of each health care dollar in 2002 (an expenditure of $713 billion); approximately three-fourths of the total government expenditures were used for Medicare and Medicaid. Fifteen percent, or 43.6 million, of U.S. citizens were not covered by health insurance in 2002.

A common form of health care fraud is the deliberate submission of false claims to private or public health insurance programs. Fraudulent schemes include double billing for services rendered, charges for unnecessary or unperformed tests, misrepresenting services or quality, fraudulent medical equipment sales, nursing home abuses, and self-referrals/kickbacks. Victims of fraud and abuse in the health care industry include the vulnerable such as the elderly, the disabled, and the poor. In addition to placing recipients at risk of suffering or death, medical fraud and abuse adds to the rising costs of insurance for businesses and individuals and places recipients at risk of cutbacks in services offered.

The problem of fraud in the health care industry impacts the general public as costs are passed on to consumers through increased premiums and rising out-of-pocket expenses, as well as increased taxes. In 1996 Congress passed the Health Insurance Portability and Accountability Act (HIPAA), which strengthened the coordination between federal, state, and local governments in enforcement and prosecution of health care fraud. At the state-level the State Attorney General, the Medicaid Fraud Units, the Fraud Bureau, and insurance departments receive fraud referrals from private-sector payers such as health maintenance organizations (HMOs), commercial insurers, and self-insured employers. State Medicaid Fraud Control Units conduct investigations and prosecute cases involving provider fraud, patient abuse fraud, and program administration fraud in entities funded by Medicaid. At the federal level, the FBI, the Office of the Inspector General for Health and Human Services, and the Fraud section of the Criminal Division in the Department of Justice investigate and prosecute health care industry fraud through civil (e.g., False Claims Act) and criminal (anti-kickback) statutes. An additional sanction is exclusion of the service provider from future participation in Medicare/Medicaid programs. Over the last decade, criminal and civil penalties have been enhanced for fraud, waste, and abuse in the health care industry with penalties including up to 20 years in prison and sizable civil monetary penalties.

See also: Nursing Home Fraud

FURTHER READING

Government Accountability Office, *Medicare: Health Care Fraud and Abuse Control Program for Fiscal Years 2000 and 2001.* Washington, DC: U.S. Government Printing Office, 2002.

National Health Care Anti-Fraud Association. Available at http://www.nhcaa.org. Accessed September 26, 2006.

Rosoff, Stephen M., Pontell, Henry N., and Tillman, Robert. *Profit without Honor: White-Collar Crime and the Looting of America.* Upper Saddle River, NJ: Prentice Hall, 1998.

U.S. Census Bureau. *Statistical Abstract of the United States: 2004–2005.* Washington, DC: U.S. Department of Commerce, 2004.

MARK MOTIVANS

HEAVY ELECTRICAL EQUIPMENT ANTITRUST CASES OF 1961. The Heavy Electrical Equipment Antitrust Cases of 1961—as they have been labeled by sociologists—were the focus of a large amount of research. Some experts claim that no other white-collar crime in American history, except Watergate, has been analyzed more comprehensively. In addition, although the Heavy Electrical Equipment Antitrust Cases have often perceived of as a single crime, in reality they consisted of a cluster of interrelated conspiracies—as did Watergate (Rosoff et al. 2004: 72–73).

The Organizational Offenders and the Offenses. These cases involved forty manufacturers of heavy electrical equipment, including General Electric and Westinghouse, their top executives, and twenty distinct product lines (Rosoff et al. 2004: 73). In total, forty-five defendants from twenty-nine corporations were indicted for criminal conspiracy to fix prices, rig bids, and divide markets on the sales of heavy electric equipment. All of them either admitted their guilt or pleaded *nolo contendere* (no contest)—taken as basically an admission of guilt. This case involved "the most serious violations of the antitrust laws since their time of passage" in 1890 (as cited by Gies 1995: 151).

These antitrust violations were discovered in 1959, when identical but supposedly competitive bids for electrical equipment were submitted to the Tennessee Valley Authority (TVA)—the largest generator of electricity in the United States at the time. This story was covered in the press and drew a great deal of attention. The Justice Department subsequently examined records of the TVA for a three-year period and uncovered twenty-four other instances of similar "competitive" bids (as cited in Rosoff et al. 2004: 73). The federal government then initiated grand jury investigations into the alleged violations.

The grand jury hearings, which led to the criminal indictments, were not made public. This decision was made on the grounds that the secrecy of grand jury proceedings was more important

127

than the public interest in obtaining information about the conspiracy and that this secrecy was more important than the interests of the numerous purchasers of heavy electric equipment in obtaining information that would serve as the foundations of civil suits against the violating corporations (Geis 1995: 152).

These corporations also conspired to divide markets and rig bids. That is, the "competitors" agreed among themselves which of them would "win" each "secret" bid for a specific type of electrical equipment (e.g., electric generators for hydroelectric dams). Then the other corporations would agree to bid higher than the designated company in the closed bidding process, ensuring that the designated corporation would win the contract.

Another component of these conspiracies was price-fixing. That is, the corporate executives would agree among themselves what to charge for certain products. These actions, of course, also subvert the intent of the closed bidding process. The secret bidding process is intended to increase competition and provide the purchaser of the electrical equipment with the best price for the product.

The Sanctions. The corporations were eventually fined $1,787,000, and the individual defendants were fined $137,000. What drew the most attention at sentencing were the 30-day jail terms that were levied against seven defendants.

Under antitrust regulations, those entities that were harmed by these illegal actions were allowed to pursue civil suits for three times the amount of financial damages they suffered (i.e., treble damages). These civil suits resulted in the most serious financial consequences for the corporations in violation of the antitrust statutes. By mid-1964, General Electric alone had settled 90 percent of the 1,800 claims against it for an estimated $160 million. However, given the corporation's immense revenues, these losses were comparable to a traffic ticket, equivalent to a $320 fine for an individual with an income of $175,000 per year (Geis 1995: 153–154). It has also been noted that most of the costs of these civil suits were tax-deductible as business expenses (see Friedrichs 2004).

The Corporate Executive Offenders. Top corporate executives carefully planned their illegal activities. They held secret meetings to discuss these activities, did not travel together at these times, took on fictitious names, used public telephones for their communications, used secret codes for their meetings, did not leave wastepaper in the meeting rooms, and took various other concealment actions. These behaviors are obvious evidence of their knowledge that their activities were illegal. One antitrust violator said, "I didn't expect to get caught, and I went to great lengths to conceal my activities so that I would not get caught" (Geis 1995: 154).

Despite going to great efforts to conceal their illegal practices, these antitrust violators did not think of themselves as criminals. One Westinghouse executive, when asked by a Senate Subcommittee on Antitrust and Monopoly attorney whether he knew that these meetings with competitors were illegal, said: "Illegal? Yes, but not criminal." One official of General Electric said, "It had become so common and gone on for so many years that I think we lost sight of the fact that it was illegal" (Geis 1995: 156–157).

Like "street" criminals, these white-collar criminals used techniques of neutralization to excuse their illegal actions to themselves and others. One official of the Ingersoll-Rand Corporation said, "It is against the law" but "I do not know that it is against public welfare because I am not certain that the consumer was actually injured by this operation." Others said it was an expected part of the culture and standard practices of the corporation—that is, it was part of normal business practices. Others stated that they were only stabilizing prices for heavy electrical equipment—that is, they blamed the market instead of themselves or their corporations. Another convicted corporate officer said, "We did not fix prices. . . . all we did was recover costs" (Geis 1995: 156–159).

Subsequent Antitrust Violations. Despite the wave of attention paid to these cases by the courts, congressional committees, and scholars, bid-rigging continues to be common. For example, over one half of the criminal cases filed by the antitrust division of the U.S. Department of Justice in the 1980s were about rigging of sealed bids (see Rosoff et al. 2002). Antitrust violations continue to be a major problem today.

See also: Bid Rigging Cartels; Price Fixing; Techniques of Neutralization

FURTHER READING

Friedrichs, David O. *Trusted Criminals: White Collar Crime in Contemporary Society,* 2nd edition. Belmont, CA: Thomson Wadsworth, 2004.

Geis, Gilbert. "The Heavy Electrical Equipment Antitrust Cases of 1961." Pp. 151–165 in Gilbert Geis, Robert F. Meier, and Lawrence M. Salinger (eds.) *White-Collar Crime: Classic and Contemporary Views,* 3rd edition. New York: The Free Press, 1995.

Herling, John. *The Great Price Conspiracy: The Story of Antitrust Violations in the Electrical Industry.* Washington, DC: Robert B. Luce, 1962.

Rosoff, Stephen M., Pontell, Henry N., and Tillman, Robert H. *Profit Without Honor: White-Collar Crime and the Looting of America,* 2nd edition. Upper Saddle River, NJ: Pearson Education, 2004.

ERIC L. JENSEN

HERALD OF FREE ENTERPRISE. The English Channel, between England and continental Europe, is one of the world's busiest waterways. During the 1980s passenger ferries were facing the threat of new competition. Sealink UK Ltd was privatized by the neoliberal Thatcher Government in 1984, opening the market up to greater competition between operators. Reductions in crew numbers; modernization of port facilities to speed ferry turnaround time; building of new, larger roll-on, roll-off (ro-ro) ferries (so called because vehicles drive in through doors in the bow before departure and out through the stern after arrival); and a range of cut-price fares began to characterize the market. After 1986 such trends were exacerbated when the British and French governments agreed to construct the Channel Tunnel, to be operative by 1994.

The Herald of Free Enterprise was one of the largest ro-ro sea ferries. One of the *Herald*'s service points was the Belgian port of Zeebrugge, where turnaround time was longer than on other routes because of the design of loading facilities. To save time, the *Herald* commonly left the port while the bow doors were still open. When the ferry did so on March 6, 1987, water began to flood through the open bow doors across the main car deck, which, as in other ro-ro ferries, lacked dividing bulkheads. The *Herald* quickly became unstable and capsized in about 90 seconds. The sea was calm, and there was only a light breeze. One hundred and ninety-three passengers and crew members died.

The findings of the Court of Formal Investigation into the *Herald* capsizing, held in 1987, were remarkable for their content and tone. It is worth quoting one key, and infamous, passage at length:

> [A] full investigation into the circumstances of the disaster leads inexorably to the conclusion that the underlying or cardinal faults lay higher up in the company. The Board of Directors did not appreciate their responsibility for the safe management of their ships. They did not apply their minds to the question: What orders should be given for the safety of our ships?
>
> The directors did not have any proper comprehension of what their duties were. There appears to have been a lack of thought about the way in which the *Herald* ought to have been organized for the Dover-Zeebrugge run. All concerned in management, from the members of the Board of Directors down to the junior superintendents, were guilty of fault in that all must be regarded as sharing responsibility for the failure of management. From top to bottom the body corporate was infected with the disease of sloppiness. . . . It is only necessary to quote one example of how the standard of management fell short. . . .
> It reveals a staggering complacency. (Department of Transport 1987: 14.1)

The disaster had significant legal consequences. The inquest into the capsizing, which was held later in 1987, returned verdicts of "unlawful killing"—despite the coroner's instruction that such a verdict was inadmissible—and created the possibility of a criminal prosecution. A manslaughter case against P&O European Ferries, owners of the *Herald*, and seven other individuals did follow, but the judge closed the proceedings before the prosecution had finished presenting its case on the basis that the legal test under current manslaughter law could not be met in this case. Indeed, in addition to avoiding criminal sanction, the chairman of P&O European Ferries, Sir Jeffrey Stirling, became Lord Stirling in Prime Minister Thatcher's 1990 resignation Honours.

This case was significant for several reasons. It had a symbolic significance in several respects: the sheer scale of the tragedy, the media's images of this enormous, everyday piece of technology, capsized; and also the irony of its name—*the Herald of Free Enterprise*—that seemed, following the sinking of the vessel, emblematic of the problems created for public and worker safety by a Government-led enterprise culture that seemed to valorize profit and risk taking. Further, the failure of the prosecution to advance its case raised political and popular concerns regarding the problems of successfully holding large, complex organizations to account for the production of death. The ensuing outcry was one factor leading in 1996 to new proposals for a new law on "corporate killing"—though at the time of this writing (2006), this law had not yet passed through the UK parliament.

Design changes to ro-ro ferries had been called for in 1985, following the capsizing of the *European Gateway* off Harwich in 1982. Six people were killed in that incident. Following Zeebrugge, the United Nations body, the International Maritime Organisation (IMO), convened a special conference and eventually passed the Safety of Life at Sea Regulations (SOLAS 90). Regulation 8 of SOLAS 90 states that all roll-on, roll-off ferries must be able to stand upright long enough for passengers to evacuate. Although this applied automatically to vessels built after April 1990, it did not apply to those built before that date—it was argued that the cost of installing bulkheads on existing craft would, if passed on to passengers, increase fares by up to 35 cents per ticket. The standards agreed as suitable in SOLAS 90 were repeatedly postponed. They were due to be fully operative in 2005.

Yet ro-ro ferries seem inherently unsafe. Between 1989 and 1994, *Lloyds Register* recorded 4583 lives lost at sea—a third (1544) of which were lost in incidents involving ro-ro ferries, even though these ferries were but a small fraction of the world's fleet. Then, infamously, on September 28, 1994, the ro-ro ferry *Estonia* capsized in the Baltic Sea, killing—officially—852 people (small children were not registered as passengers, so the toll could have been significantly higher). Water entered the vessel through defective bow doors. Most of these people died in the vessel because they did not have sufficient time to get onto the upper deck. Six weeks after this sinking, a report from the Department of Transport's Marine Safety Agency discovered that of the 107 roll-on, roll-off ferries it had inspected, bow door faults were found in one of every three vessels.

In 2002 P&O announced a widespread reorganization, cutting its fleet of ships from twenty–four to seventeen and ending several "uneconomic routes"—including services from Dover to Zeebrugge. P&O's ferry services director, Graeme Dunlop, stated at that time, eight years after the opening of the Channel Tunnel, that "We knew the tunnel was going to open and we knew it was going to grab a share of the market. Our strategy was to increase the size of the market, so we each got a slice of a bigger pie" (Clark 2002).

See also: Industrial Accidents; *Piper Alpha*

FURTHER READING

Bergman, David. *The Case for Corporate Responsibility: Corporate Violence and the Criminal Justice System.* London: Disaster Action, 2000.

Boyd, Colin. "The Zeebrugge Car Ferry Disaster." Pp. 498–511 in William Frederick, Keith Davis, and James Post (eds.), *Business and Society.* Hightstown, NJ: McGraw Hill, 1992.

Clark, Andrew. "Shape Up or Ship Out." *The Guardian Unlimited* (June 4, 2002). Available at http://www.guardian.co.uk/transport/Story/0,2763,727258,00.html. Accessed September 26, 2006.

Crainer, Stuart. *Zeebrugge. Learning from Disaster.* London: *Herald* Families' Association, 1993.

Department of Transport. *The Merchant Shipping Act 1894, Mv* Herald of Free Enterprise, Report of Court No 8074 (Sheen Report), London: Her Majesty's Stationery Office, 1987.

Slapper, Gary, and Tombs, Steve. *Corporate Crime.* London: Longman, 1999.

Wells, Celia. *Corporations and Criminal Responsibility.* Oxford: Clarendon, 1993.

STEVE TOMBS

HERITAGE USA/HERITAGE PARK. See Bakker, Jim and Tammy Faye

HOOKER CHEMICAL CORPORATION. Hooker Chemical provides an important case study of corporate involvement in environmental abuses and crime. Hooker originated in Brooklyn, New York. In 1905 Hooker moved to Niagara Falls to establish a large industrial base for production of agricultural chemicals, fertilizers, plastic, and assorted industrial chemicals. In 1968 Occidental Petroleum Corporation (OPC) purchased Hooker and renamed it. The Occidental Chemical Corporation (OCC) in 1982.

Prior to the passage of environmental laws, Hooker's hazardous waste disposal practices were careless and dangerous; however, the company was following customary practices of the time. Indeed, the actions of Hooker and other companies prompted the passage of environmental laws and triggered the creation of the Environmental Protection Agency (EPA) in 1970.

Niagara County, NY. Hooker has been identified as a responsible party in several Comprehensive Environmental Response, Compensation, and Liability Act (CERCLA) cases involving abandoned/formerly owned waste sites (commonly known as Superfund sites) and for violating a number of other environmental laws. CERCLA retroactively holds companies liable for irresponsible hazardous waste disposal practices.

Hooker is best known for its involvement in the infamous Love Canal incident. From 1942 to 1952 Hooker disposed of 22,000 tons of chemical waste into the canal. In 1953, Hooker closed the landfill, covered it, and sold it to the Niagara Falls Board of Education for one dollar. Hooker had reservations about selling the property; however, it eventually succumbed to political pressure to sell. Given its reservations, Hooker disclosed that chemicals were present at the site, inserted a clause in the deed of sale releasing the company from future liability, and cautioned against excavation or development of the site.

Despite these warnings, the Board constructed a school, and developers built over 200 homes, on and near the Love Canal property. Shortly thereafter, residents complained of peculiar odors and strange substances leaking into their homes, and many experienced health problems ranging from skin rashes and burns to cancer—problems that some experts attribute to toxic substances migrating from the site. In 1978 and again in 1980, the area was declared a national emergency.

In 1979 the U.S. Government brought action against Hooker under CERCLA and the public nuisance law to seek reimbursement for cleanup costs and to ensure public safety. Although the court did not award any punitive damages, Hooker/OCC paid approximately $227 million for cleanup efforts as part of various settlements and consent decrees.

Hooker owned and operated three other chemical dump sites (in S-Area, on 102nd Street, and in Hyde Park) in Niagara County. From 1942 to 1975, these sites (in addition to Love Canal) were used to dispose of 199,900 tons of chemical wastes that subsequently emitted 82 toxic chemicals into the environment. The disposal of chemical wastes resulted in the migration of harmful chemicals onto adjacent properties as well as into the Niagara River, Lake Ontario, and local groundwater supplies. In 1979 the Justice Department and the EPA brought action against Hooker for violations of CERCLA, the Clean Water Act, the Safe Drinking Water Act, the Resource Conservation and Recovery Act, the Rivers and Harbors Act, and general nuisance law. After a lengthy legal process, Hooker agreed to initiate and finance clean up activities.

Other Incidents. Hooker and the Ruco Polymer Corporation manufactured plastics, latex, and esters in Hicksville, New York. From 1956 to 1975, Hooker/Ruco annually discharged two million gallons of toxic waste into dry wells, resulting in the contamination of drinking water in surrounding areas. The EPA is working with Hooker/Ruco to address the contamination problem.

In 1979 Michigan sued Hooker for the chemical contamination of White Lake and nearby sources of groundwater. Hooker stored approximately 20,000 barrels of toxic wastes on its property. Toxic chemicals eventually leaked from these barrels, polluting White Lake and contaminating groundwater supplies. Hooker was issued a court order to clean contaminated soil and groundwater, excavate contaminated materials, and provide alternative drinking water to residents whose wells were polluted. Hooker's actions also resulted in the EPA issuing numerous advisories and bans against drinking water and consuming fish. The EPA continues to monitor the site as an area of concern.

Conclusion. Many of Hooker's past disposal practices were not illegal until the passage of environmental laws in the 1970s and 1980s. However, many of the disposal practices in which companies such as Hooker engaged were socially irresponsible. It can be argued that companies that disposed of hazardous wastes in the past reasonably knew their actions were (or could be) dangerous and even lethal to human health and the environment. As a result, the government passed environmental laws to legally coerce corporations to adopt safe and responsible disposal practices. Hooker's environmental record has improved as a result of these reforms, as is evident by cleanup initiatives at the afore mentioned sites and the removal of Love Canal from the EPA's Superfund list in 2004.

See also: Chemical Crimes; Environmental White-Collar Crime; Hazardous Waste Disposal

FURTHER READING

Crawford, Mark. (ed.) *Toxic Waste Sites: An Encyclopedia of Endangered America.* Santa Barbara, CA: ABC-Clio, 1997.

"Environmental Protection Agency." NPL Site Narrative for Hooker Chemical/Ruco Polymer Corp (1986). Available at http://www.epa.gov. Accessed February 2005. "U.S. Sues Hooker Chemical at Niagara Falls." New York Environmental Protection Agency (1979). Available at http://www.epa.gov. Accessed February 2005.

Katz, Rebecca. "Hazardous Waste." Pp. 387–91 in Lawrence Salinger (ed.) *Encyclopedia of White-Collar and Corporate Crime.* Thousand Oaks, CA: Sage, 2005.

"Love Canal." Pp. 501–503 in Lawrence Salinger. (ed.) *Encyclopedia of White-Collar and Corporate Crime.* Thousand Oaks, CA: Sage Publications, 2005.

Robinson, Erin. "Community Frame Analysis in Love Canal: Understanding Messages in a Contaminated Community." *Sociological Spectrum* 22 (2002): 139–169.

Ross, Debra. "Corporate Dumping." Pp. 213–35 in Lawrence Salinger. (ed.) *Encyclopedia of White-Collar and Corporate Crime,* Vol. 1. Thousand Oaks, CA: Sage Publications, 2005.

U.S. v. Hooker Chemicals & Plastics Corporation, 540 F. Supp. 1067 (1982).

U.S. v. Hooker Chemical & Plastics Corporation, 607 F. Supp. 1052 (1985).

U.S. v. Hooker Chemicals & Plastics Corporation, 641 F. Supp. 1303 (1986).

U.S. v. Occidental Chemical Corporation, 965 F. Supp. 408 (1997).

"White Lake Area of Concern." (2001) Available at http://www.epa.gov. Accessed February 2005.

Wolf, Sidney. "Hazardous Waste Trials and Tribulations." *Environmental Law* 13 (1983, Winter): 367.

TARA O'CONNOR SHELLEY
SHARON ANNE MELZER

I

IACOCCA, LEE (1924–). The **Ford Pinto** debacle of the 1970s is one of the most notorious examples of white-collar crime because it illustrates how powerful corporations such as Ford are able to kill with impunity. It is well documented that Lee Iacocca, the former president of Ford Motor Company, had an unhealthy obsession with cornering the emerging subcompact market. Iacocca insisted that the Pinto could not weigh even an ounce over 2000 pounds or cost as much as a cent over $2,000. Under Iacocca, Ford executives did not even consider extra safety features to be installed in the Pinto because these increased both the weight and price of the vehicle. Iacocca instructed his employees that "safety did not sell," and this negligent attitude quickly permeated the entire organization.

One way in which safety was flagrantly disregarded was by Iacocca's decision to cut the production time for the Pinto in half. This inevitably led to many uncorrected problems. It was discovered that there were major deficiencies with the Pinto's fuel tank, yet Ford employees still refused to correct this problem. Rather than fixing the defective fuel tanks (at a cost of $11 per Pinto), Iacocca chose to ignore what was obviously an extremely dangerous defect. In perhaps the most startling aspect of this case, Ford executives conducted a detailed cost-benefit analysis and determined that it would be more cost-efficient to allow the defective Pinto to kill and injure people, and to pay $200,000 in damages for each death and $67,000 for each burn injury, than to fix the fuel tank. This conclusion was summarized in the infamous 1973 "smoking-gun memo" represents white–collar crime at its worst.

The "smoking gun memo" illustrates that upper-level employees at Ford were willing to let their consumers die rather than correct a design flaw in the Pinto. The car was so dangerous that a collision at less than 40 miles per hour had the potential to be fatal. After many deaths and an article in *Mother Jones* that detailed the defects in the Pinto, the Ford Motor Company was charged with reckless homicide in the State of Indiana. The "smoking-gun memo" was never admitted as evidence during the trial, and eventually the company was acquitted.

See also: Ford Pinto

FURTHER READING

Cullen, Francis T., Maakestad, William J., and Gray, Cavender. *Corporate Crime under Attack: The Ford Pinto Case and Beyond*. Cincinnati: Anderson Publishing Co., 1987.

De George, Richard T. "Ethical Responsibilites of Engineers in Large Organizations: The Ford Pinto Case." From *Business Ethics*, 3rd edition. New York: Macmillian Publishing Company, 1981.

Dowie, Mark "Pinto Madness." *Mother Jones* (1977). Available at http://www.motherjones.com/news/feature/1977/09/dowie.html. Accessed August 21, 2006.

Lenhoff, Alan S. "Just Folks: Ford's Lawyer Playing the Hick for Rural Jurors," *Akron Beacon Journal* (1980): B-1.

Rosoff, Stephen M., Pontell, Henry N., and Tillman, Robert H. *Profit Without Honor: White-Collar Crime and the Looting of America*. Upper Saddle River, New Jersey: Prentice Hall, 2004.

Strobel, Lee Patrick. *Reckless Homicide?* South Bend, Indiana: And Books Publishing Company, 1980.

Zeisel, Hans, and Kalven., Harry, Jr. *The American Jury*. Boston: Little, Brown and Company, 1966.

ROBERT WORLEY

IDENTITY THEFT. The Identity Theft and Assumption Deterrence Act of 1998 defines identity theft as:

> Knowingly transfer[ing] or us[ing], without lawful authority, a means of identification of another person with the intent to commit, or to aid or abet, any unlawful activity that constitutes a violation of Federal Law, or that constitutes a felony under any applicable State or local law.

Restated, identity theft is the unlawful acquisition and/or use of any aspect of an individual's personal information to be used for the commission of some form of criminal activity. The latter definition is intended to encompass all forms of crime that fraudulently and/or illegally utilize the victim's name, social security number, address, bank account number, credit card number, or biometric characteristics.

In the year 2004 alone, over 9.3 million Americans reported having been victims of varying levels of identity theft. In addition, recent research has estimated that the cost of identity theft in the United States in 2004 was $52.6 billion, a figure that continues to rise.

Identity theft is a broad category of criminal activity. Statutes have been developed to break down the act of identity theft for more efficient prosecution. The act can involve crimes such as identification fraud, credit card fraud, computer fraud, mail fraud, wire fraud, or financial institution fraud. Currently many agencies are responsible for investigating identity theft, including the United States Secret Service, the U.S. Postal Inspection Services, and the Federal Bureau of Investigation (FBI) in addition to state and local authorities.

Types of Identity Theft. While scholarly attention to identity theft in general is currently in its infancy, much work has been focused on describing the different forms of identity theft as reported by victims. Identity theft can be separated into three separate categories, including *financial identity theft*, *nonfinancial identity theft*, and *criminal records identity theft*.

Financial identity theft is crime based on the illegal acquisition of financial data through the abuse of a victim's personal information. For this form of identity theft, the offender may open a false bank account in the victim's name, open new credit card accounts, or even file for bankruptcy using the personal information of another. *Nonfinancial identity theft* occurs when the offender uses the victim's information to open fraudulent utilities accounts, including basic utilities and telecommunications accounts. Finally, *criminal records identity theft* involves the offender using the victim's personal information for the purpose of avoiding legal sanctions (i.e., acting as an imposter).

Methods of Identity Theft. Specific methods by which an identity theft offender may gather or assemble information on a potential victim are virtually limitless and may vary from extremely simplistic techniques to tremendously complex operations. One of the more basic methods includes what is termed *dumpster diving.* This method of involves simply looking, or digging, through available refuse with the hope of finding some piece of information that can serve as a key to access a victim's personal information. The potential criminal who utilizes this technique has the intention of finding information revealing the victim's social security number, driver's license number, financial account numbers, medical records, bank statement, or other revealing information. Any and every piece of personal information may make it easier for the thief to be successful in his or her criminal acts.

A related form of identity theft is referred to as *data mining.* This activity involves using computer technology to access sensitive personal information about a victim. Advances in technology have benefited the potential identity thief with an easy and affordable means to gathering information. *Shoulder surfing* is the act of watching the victim in public places to gain information during the transaction of a legitimate activity, sometimes simply looking directly over the victim's shoulder. For example, the identity thief may watch what numbers the victim types while using an ATM or while punching in the code to a calling card. Recent advances in the capabilities of cellular phones may have also increased the effectiveness of some identity thieves. It is now common for personal cell phones to include a digital camera and video feature. The identity thief may use such a device to gather information from checks or ID cards or even take a photo of a potential victim's signature and credit card number, then email the information to a partner and begin abusing the victim's credit; even before the victim reaches home.

In recent years the Internet has become an increasingly attractive source of information for the potential identity thief. Email "spam" is becoming a common factor in the increase of identity theft; however, the majority of victims who are aware of how they became a victim report having lost, or having had stolen, physically sensitive documentation such as credit card receipts, driver's licenses, or checks. Additionally, computer users often receive email messages that pose as legitimate sources requesting personal information. The recipient of such an email who follows the links supplied unknowingly discloses vast amounts of information directly into the hands of the criminal instead. Such techniques are commonly referred to as *phishing* scams.

Identity theft may also include criminal activity which is based on gaining employment or residence by those who enter the United States illegally. From this observation, it may be possible for potential terrorists to enter the United States via similar means. Cases have been uncovered in which such information is readily available on the black market for a premium price.

See also: Internet Fraud

FURTHER READING

Buba, Nicole M. "Waging War against Identity Theft: Should the United States Borrow From the European Union's Battalion?" *Suffolk Transnational Law Review* 23 (2000): 633.

Hoar, Sean B. "Identity Theft: The Crime of the New Millennium." *Oregon Law Review* 80 (2001):1423.

Identity Theft and Assumption Deterrence Act of 1998. 18 U.S.C. 1028. Available at http://www.ftc.gov/os/statutes/itada/itadact.htm. Accessed September 26, 2006.

"Identity Theft and Fraud." U.S. Department of Justice. Available at http://www.usdoj.gov/ fraud/ idtheft.html. Accessed March 24, 2004.

Mandebilt, Bruce D. "Identity Theft: A New Security Challenge." *Security* 38 (2001): 21–24.

Perl, Michael W. "It's Not Always About the Money: Why the State Identity Theft Laws Fail to Adequately Address Criminal Records Identity Theft." *Journal of Criminal Law and Criminology* 94 (2003): 169–208.

Slosarik, Katherine "Identity Theft: An Overview of the Problem." *The Justice Professional* 15 (2002): 329–343.

ROBERT G. MORRIS

IMPERIAL FOOD PLANT FIRE. In the morning hours of September 3, 1991, a fire erupted at the Imperial Foods plant in Hamlet, North Carolina. The fire and resulting heavy smoke would claim the lives of twenty-five employees and would injure another fifty-four. In total, seventy-nine individuals, out of the approximately ninety who were working, were killed or injured. Almost all the casualties and most of the serious injuries could have been avoided entirely had critical exit doors not been locked from the outside—locked, as further investigations found, under the orders of the plant owner, Emmett Roe.

Food processing plants dot the southeast United States, where the cost of labor is cheap and governmental oversight limited. Indeed, North Carolina advertised limited regulatory oversight as a way to attract businesses of this type. In the year preceding the fire, for example, North Carolina took the unusual step of returning to the federal government money aimed at increasing the number of State Occupational Health and Safety investigators. These decisions would have dire consequences.

Housed typically in small, rural communities, meat processing factories are frequently located in buildings too old to be in compliance with contemporary building codes. So it was with the Hamlet plant. The building that housed the machinery, including large frying vats filled with grease maintained at 375°F, was over 100 years old. It had no windows, had no plantwide sprinkler system, and had not been inspected by State Occupational Health and Safety inspectors once in its eleven years of operation.

The fire ignited after a hydraulic hose burst, spraying combustible fluid into a cooking vat. After-action reports found that fifty to fifty-five gallons of hydraulic fluid provided the fuel for the fire to burn. Out of the cooking vat emerged an enormous fireball and heavy, hydrocarbon-charged, thick black smoke that spread quickly throughout the plant. Because the plant was kept cool to preserve meat, the humidity was very high. The heavy smoke, in interaction with the high humidity and heat from the fire, engulfed the entire 30,000 foot plant in less than two minutes. Surviving employees reported that they were blinded by the smoke and found their way out only because they were close to an unlocked door at the time of the fire, because all of the exit signs were covered by the heavy smoke.

Workers immediately converged on the exit doors in a panicked attempt to escape the smoke and fire. As they pushed on the doors, they found them chained and padlocked from the outside. Unable to escape through the exit doors, workers sought protection in one of two large coolers. The smoke, however, eventually filled the coolers.

The majority of fatalities were located in the coolers; others were found near the exit doors. Firefighters on the scene reported seeing finger gouges in the steel doors where frightened workers tried to escape, only to succumb to the smoke.

The fire destroyed the plant, the largest employer in the town of Hamlet, and left many without employment. In the aftermath, officials and townspeople alike sought to understand how such a tragedy could occur. The investigation inevitably focused on the padlocked exit doors. Because Emmett Roe suspected some employees of stealing small amounts of chicken nuggets and taking unauthorized coffee breaks, he directed the plant manager, James Hair, and his son, Brad Roe, to padlock the exit doors. The two complied with the elderly Roe's demand and directed the janitors to make certain the exit doors were locked. Emmett Roe later admitted that he had approved locking the only escape route available to the workers.

Authorities arrested Emmett Roe and initially charged him with twenty-five counts of involuntary manslaughter. Charges against James Hair and Brad Roe were dropped, largely because investigators found that Emmett Roe was in charge of the day-to-day operations of the plant, and because Emmett Roe agreed to plead guilty if the charges were dropped against his son and Hair. North Carolina also levied the largest fine in its history against Imperial Foods and Mr. Roe: $808,150.

The plea bargain resulted in Emmett Roe being found guilty of two counts of involuntary manslaughter. Under the law, Roe could have received ten years for each count of involuntary manslaughter, or 250 years if found guilty of all twenty-five counts. In return for his plea, however, he was found guilty on two counts and was sentenced to nineteen and one half years in prison. The judge stopped short of sentencing Roe to twenty years because North Carolina law stipulated that, for a sentence of that length, a majority of prison time would have to be served before consideration for parole. Roe, with a nineteen and one-half year sentence, would be eligible for parole in just three years. After two unsuccessful attempts to gain parole, Roe was released from prison after serving only four and one-half years.

At least two lessons were learned from the Imperial Food Processing plant fire. First, some level of governmental oversight is necessary to help ensure workers' safety. North Carolina was heavily criticized for its unwillingness to take workers' safety seriously. Although the federal government threatened to take over North Carolina's Occupational Health and Safety responsibilities. In the end, a deal was struck, and North Carolina hired more inspectors and expanded their oversight.

Second, although some argue that using the criminal law, as opposed to regulatory law, against businesses and their owners and managers is too burdensome, the Imperial Plant fire demonstrated that it can be used effectively under at least some circumstances. No longer would owners and managers be shielded from prosecution for behaviors that placed workers in clear jeopardy. Indeed, the prosecution of Emmett Roe may have cleared the way for the criminal law to be used in cases in which lives were not put in jeopardy but managers stole millions of dollars from investors and employees. In the world of white-collar crime, WorldCom, Enron, MCI, and Martha Stewart may have Emmett Roe and a fire that occurred in a small town in North Carolina to thank for their criminal charges.

See also: Industrial Accidents; Meatpacking Industry; Media Portrayal of White-Collar Crime

FURTHER READING

"3 Surrender in Plant Fire." *The New York Times* (March 13, 1992). Available at http://query.nytimes.com/gst/fullpage.html?res=9E0CEFDE1731F930A25750C0A964958260. Accessed September 26, 2006.
Wright, John, Cullen, Francis T. Blankenship, Michael B. "The Social Construction of Corporate Violence: Media Coverage of the Imperial Food Products Fire." *Crime and Delinquency* 41.1 (1995): 20–36.

JOHN PAUL WRIGHT

INDUSTRIAL ACCIDENTS. The term "industrial accident"—usually used to refer to deaths and injuries to workers, consumers, passengers, and local communities arising out of industrial contexts—is a common misnomer, with significant consequences.

The term "accident" implies an aberrant phenomenon, yet industrial deaths and injuries are ubiquitous. Deaths, for example, occur across all industries, all types of companies, in all economies. And the collective scale of such deaths is almost incomprehensible. In May 2002, the International Labour Organisation (ILO) estimated that two million workers die each year through work-related accidents and diseases, a figure that is referred to as the tip of the iceberg because for every fatal accident there are another estimated 500–2000 injuries, depending on the type of job. Twelve thousand children die each year working in hazardous conditions.

Industrial deaths and injuries are thus a major social problem—one not "merely" involving *physical* harms but also having widespread, if often unrecognized, financial, psychological, as well as social effects. Yet these deaths, injuries, and their various effects are unequally distributed, with a particularly heavy toll of dead and injured occurring in developing countries, where large numbers of workers are concentrated in primary and extraction activities such as agriculture, logging, fishing, and mining. And *within* the most developed economies, there is also good evidence to indicate that these deaths and injuries fall disproportionately upon members of the lowest socioeconomic groups. The *impacts* are also differentially distributed. Thus, for example, occupational health and safety compensation schemes differ enormously—whereas workers in Nordic countries enjoy nearly universal coverage, only ten per cent or fewer of the workforce in many developing countries is likely to benefit from any sort of coverage.

None of these observations supports either the aberrant or random features associated with the term "accident." The language of accidents is one that focuses upon specific events, abstracting them from a more comprehensible context. It evokes discrete, isolated, and random events and carries with it connotations of the unforeseeable, unknowable, and unpreventable, despite the fact that any examination of a range of incidents reveals common, systematic, foreseeable, and eminently preventable causes and consistent locations of responsibility. Such language of course, carries with it particular connotations of causation (and thereby appropriate modes of prevention and regulation) and effects (seriousness). The language of accidents often invokes events or phenomena in which victims are implicated via their carelessness, apathy, or poor lifestyles (use of alcohol or banned substances, poor sleeping habits, and so on).

An associated key feature of this term is that its widespread use—or its derivatives reserved for multiple fatalities or serious injuries, namely "disaster" or "tragedy"—is one of a series of social processes that seek to remove work-related harms from the sphere of crime and law.

Thus the vast majority of industrial deaths and injuries remain cast as "accidents," which is likely to mean that there has been little or, usually, no investigation of their circumstances, nature, and relationship to law and legal duties. Indeed, the term "accident" carries with it assumptions regarding intentionality, or the lack of it, that are crucial obstacles to thinking about such events as possible crimes. Certainly in the United Kingdom—and there is no good reason to think that the United Kingdom is idiosyncratic in this respect—a whole series of studies has indicated that "management failure" is the cause of about 70 percent of occupational fatalities and injuries. This indicates that such events might at least warrant consideration as crimes. Yet this happens in only a small minority of cases in the United Kingdom and beyond, and, where legal processes are invoked, any sentences that follow are overwhelmingly lenient, usually in the form of monetary fines. In other words, the linguistic term "accident" supports, and is in turn reinforced by, the failures of most criminal justice systems, politicians, and forms of media across the world to treat physical harms that occur as a result of work-related activity as actual, or at least, potential crimes. This is but *one* specific instance of the ways in which corporate crime and harm tends to be decriminalized, either formally through law, or informally through their treatment by legal institutions—though this is best viewed more as the result of a complex interplay among a range of social processes rather than any intentional manipulation.

Although occupational safety and health protection falls squarely within the criminal law, criminalization, in practice, has never formed a central part of states' agendas. In general, across developed and developing economies, the records of legal protection in relation to workers' and the public's safety have been, and continue to be, poor. The label, and consequent logic, of "industrial accident" is one part of this general process. If the idea of "accident" is a neutral, "anesthetizing" one, then by contrast, alternative terms, such as "industrial killing," "industrial wounding," or "industrial violence," would carry with them quite different connotations and logically be related to quite different legal, political, and social responses.

See also: Film Recovery Systems; *Herald of Free Enterprise*; Imperial Food Plant Fire; *Piper Alpha*

FURTHER READING

Bergman, David. *The Case for Corporate Responsibility: Corporate Violence and the Criminal Justice System.* London: Disaster Action, 2000.

Goldman, Laurence. "Accident and Absolute Liability in Anthropology." Pp. 51–99 in Gibbons, J., (ed.), *Language and the Law.* London: Longman, 1994.

Glasbeek, Harry. "Why Corporate Deviance Is Not Treated as Crime." Pp. 126–145 in Caputo, T. et al. (eds), *Law and Society: A Critical Perspective*. Toronto: Harcourt Brace Jovanovich, 1989.

Hills, S. *Corporate Violence. Injury and Death for Profit*. Totowa, NJ: Rowman and Littlefield, 1987.

Reiman, Jeffrey. *The Rich Get Richer and the Poor Get Prison*, 7th edition. Boston: Allyn and Bacon, 2004.

Slapper, Gary and Tombs, Steve. *Corporate Crime*. London: Longman, 1999.

Wells, Celia. *Corporations and Criminal Responsibility*. Oxford: Clarendon, 1993.

STEVE TOMBS

INDUSTRIAL ESPIONAGE. Industrial espionage, the theft of trade secrets, predates the Industrial Age. A trade secret is information that, when kept confidential, gives a measure of economic advantage to its possessor. The Chinese process for silk fabric is an example of a trade secret that dates to at least 3,000 BC. The exportation of silkworms, their eggs, and mulberry tree seeds were prohibited by imperial decree and the penalty for disclosure of the process was death by torture. In the second century B.C., a Chinese princess risked torture to please her new husband, an Indian prince, by concealing silkworms and mulberry seeds in her headdress when leaving China. Another example of a trade secret is the metal alloy used in making the Zildjian cymbals, long regarded as the standard of quality sound by musicians, which were first produced by the Zildjian family of Constantinople in 1623. Although the cymbals are now produced in Quincy, Massachusetts, the alloy composition remains a trade secret.

The dawn of the Industrial Age in the latter half of the eighteenth century spurred competition to produce better products and to do it at less cost than competitors. John Foley was an English ironmaster and also a talented violinist. He traveled through Europe playing violin, while collecting information on making steel. Once back in England, he put this information to use to such an effective degree that the ironmasters' guilds of Europe attempted to have him assassinated, and when that failed, they tried to sabotage his factories.

Just as Foley's family fortune rested on his skills as an industrial spy, another family fortune remaining to this day, that of Friedrich Krupp, rests in part on industrial espionage activities. Alfred Krupp, Friedrich's son, is credited with developing a network of spies to perfect his steel-making process in Germany during the nineteenth century. Recognizing the value and danger of the industrial spy, Krupp instituted a code of behavior for his own employees. "Whatever the cost, workers must at all times be watched by energetic and thoroughly experienced men, who will receive a bonus whenever they arrest anyone guilty of sabotage, laziness or spying," wrote Alfred Krupp in 1872. Today Krupp, now Thysen Krupp AG, is a huge European conglomerate, one of the largest steel producers in the world, and Germany's fifth largest firm.

The development of electricity, the automobile, and aircraft leading up to World War II created a focus on technology and competitive strategy. However, it was after World War II that the skills of former military intelligence officers were refocused on competitive intelligence. A presenter at the World Future Society Conference on Communications and the Future in Washington, DC, in 1982, speaking on the "Realities of the Information Age," noted that markets had globalized to the extent that foreign competitors' market share was growing and this would lead to an increase in industrial espionage. Ironically, that day the *Washington Post* headline read "FBI Arrest Agents of Hitachi for Stealing IBM Trade Secrets." During the following twenty years this forecast held true, as the "Trends in Proprietary Information Loss Survey Report" for 2002 confirmed. Of the 138 companies responding to the survey, the estimated total loss due to information theft, to the 40 percent of respondents reporting a loss, was between $53 and $59 billion. The average dollar value per incident was $404,000 for research and development information and $356,000 for financial data. The area of greatest concern of those experiencing an incident was a loss of competitive advantage. When the loss included financial data, management's concern was embarrassment and reputation.

Targets of Industrial Espionage. According to the 2002 Survey Report, customer lists and related data were the most sought-after information, followed by strategic plans and roadmaps, financial data, research and development, merger/acquisition, manufacturing data, unreleased product specifications, prototypes, and second-party information.

Legal Protection of Trade Secrets. Following the Hitachi-IBM incident and other incidents involving foreign companies that impacted American semiconductor, computer, and pharmaceutical firms, Congress passed the Economic Espionage Act of 1996. Section 1831 of the Act addresses "any foreign government, foreign instrumentality or foreign agent." In Section 1832 the Act addresses theft of trade secrets "related to or included in a product produced for or placed in interstate or foreign commerce." This section provides an alternative to plaintiffs who, until 1996, had only state laws addressing theft of trade secrets, usually modeled on the Uniform Trade Secrets Act. Now plaintiffs have a choice of federal or state law to pursue their claim.

The *Restatement (First) of Torts*, published in 1939, provides the definition of a trade secret commonly referred to in U.S. courts: "A trade secret may consist of any formula, pattern, device or compilation of information which is used in one's business, and which gives him an opportunity to obtain an advantage over competitors who do not know or use it. It may be a formula for a chemical compound, a process of manufacturing, treating or preserving materials, a pattern for a machine or other device, or a list of customers."

Requirement of Secrecy. In order to pursue an action against one accused of stealing a trade secret, one must show that everything reasonable and prudent had been done to maintain its secrecy. Judge Taft, who later became Chief Justice of the U.S. Supreme Court wrote in a decision in 1887: "There can be no property in a process, and no right of protection if knowledge of it is common to the world." What was or was not done to keep an alleged trade secret secret is often the center point of litigation in a trade secret case.

Roger Milgrim, author of *Milgrim on Trade Secrets*, the primary legal reference work, notes seven prerequisites for a trade secret:

- Having agreements with employees and others
- Informing employees upon hiring and termination of their obligation to protect trade secrets
- Limiting access
- Marking information, use of signs at entrances to sensitive areas
- Informing employees how to identify trade secrets
- Reviewing speeches, articles, etc., for sensitive information
- Auditing compliance

Contemporary Protective Measures for Trade Secrets. Two benchmark studies were conducted of major Fortune 500 companies to ascertain what specific measures they took to avoid being a victim of industrial espionage. The first study was conducted in 1992–1993 and involved twelve companies; some of the participants were DuPont, GE, IBM, and Motorola. All companies had written policy and procedures on protection of proprietary information, and all classified and marked information using the terms *confidential* or *proprietary* and the name of the company. Eleven of these companies had a security education program. The second study in 1999 included six companies, three of which were Alcoa, Caterpillar, and Monsanto. All had a written policy and procedures, four classified and marked information, and five had a security education program.

The Entrepreneurial Trade Secret Thief. The past thirty years have seen the emergence of entrepreneurial trade secret thieves, employees who take the risk of attempting to sell their employers' trade secrets to competitors in anticipation of a large payment for the information. Recognizing a sudden improvement in a competitor's product, and identifying its probable source, is usually not difficult. Knowing this and the significant penalties for accepting stolen trade secrets, many competitors know the risk of accepting unsolicited trade secrets and refuse them.

When competitors of Medtronic, Coca-Cola, and Warner-Lambert were contacted by an individual offering proprietary information, they rightly contacted these companies. In each case, the FBI eventually apprehended those responsible. Occasionally, envelopes of stolen trade secrets have been returned to the legal owner with a letter stating that the unsolicited information was not circulated and would not be used.

How sad it must have been for a young girl attending high school to face her friends after her father's photo appeared on the front page of the *Minneapolis Star and Tribune* when arrested by the FBI for attempting to sell his company's (Medtronic) trade secrets. Entrepreneurial trade secret theft is a very high-risk enterprise.

STEPHEN A. CARLTON

INFANT FORMULA. Since the 1970s or so the marketing of infant formula, or breast milk substitute, in the developing world has been the object of considerable critical attention by health experts and activists. After a widely publicized campaign against infant formula marketing—practices variously described as irresponsible, inhumane, and murderous—national and international public health agencies now characterize the marketing of infant formula in developing countries as unethical. The World Health Organization of the United Nations (WHO) has established infant formula marketing guidelines for the developing world, where poor women are especially vulnerable to such marketing. Infant formula marketing continues to be monitored by intergovernmental organizations and activists.

Infant formulas, or breast milk substitutes, are cow- or soy-milk-based products that seek to approximate the nutritional role of breast milk. Major producers include the Swiss corporation, Nestlé, which is the world's largest producer of infant formula; Mead Johnson, Ross Pediatrics (a division of Abbott Laboratories), Wyeth Nutrition, Bright Beginnings, Gerber, and Similac. The availability of industrially produced breast milk substitutes has led to considerable medical, social, scientific, and public debate in Europe and North America about the relative virtues of breastfeeding as opposed to substituting other products for infant nutrition.

Breast milk substitutes cannot replicate the superior nutrition of breast milk, in part because breast milk is not fully scientifically understood. Infant formula cannot replicate the key beneficial health effects of breastfeeding. Breast milk composition changes in response to infants' breastfeeding patterns, adjusting in coordination with the baby's individual course of development. As the result of immunoglobulins found in breast milk, infants who are breastfed for the first six months demonstrate enhanced immunity from childhood diseases including pneumonia, botulism, bronchitis, staphylococcal infections, influenza, ear infections, and rubella. These infants also have lower levels of diabetes, arguably better developmental outcomes, and lower levels of infant mortality from diarrhea and sudden infant death syndrome (SIDS). Even poorly nourished mothers can adequately nourish their breastfed infants. And, because lactation delays fertility, breastfeeding functions as a natural, free, and passive form of contraception with health benefits for both women and infants.

International public health experts agree that in most circumstances, breastfeeding exclusively for six months and then breastfeeding in coordination with complementary foods is the best nutritional prescription for most children in the developing world. When breastfeeding is unavailable or particularly unsafe, breast milk substitutes offer an imperfect alternative for infant nutrition; however, the WHO recommends that no breast milk substitutes be used for infant nutrition unless the substitutes are acceptable, feasible, affordable, sustainable, and safe (AFASS).

Infant Formula in the Developing World. Conditions in the developing world are particularly incompatible with safe use of infant formula. The WHO estimates that 1.5 million infants die each year because they are not breastfed. Poor education and illiteracy among caregivers mean that printed safety warnings and instructions for safe use of breast milk substitutes are widely ineffective. Users (usually but not always, mothers) often lack the facilities or education needed to sterilize water, bottles, and nipples and to maintain their sterility. In hot climates, formula stored without refrigeration fosters bacterial growth.

Infant formula is expensive for poor people, especially as compared with breast milk, which is free. Desperate economic conditions lead users of breast milk substitutes to try to "stretch" what powdered infant formula they are able to acquire, presenting an enormous risk to infants. Diluted infant formula offers inadequate nutrition for infant development, and contaminated water used for dilution gives infants diarrhea, which is a significant source of infant mortality in the developing world. Formula-fed infants are estimated to be twenty-five times more likely to die of diarrhea than breastfed infants.

Because of the risk of HIV transmission during breastfeeding (demonstrated by infection rates increasing with age among breastfed children born to HIV-infected mothers), the WHO has developed HIV-specific infant feeding recommendations. The WHO suggests that HIV-negative and untested mothers breastfeed exclusively from the birth of their children until the children reach six months of age and then continue to breastfeed in coordination with other foods (complementary feeding). The WHO encourages HIV-positive mothers to use only breast milk substitutes that are AFASS.

The WHO currently recommends that health workers, or other community workers if necessary, demonstrate the use of appropriate breast milk substitutes for infants who are not breastfed only to the mothers and other family members who need to handle the substitutes; and workers should include adequate instruction for appropriate preparation of the substitutes as well as the health hazards resulting from inappropriate preparation and use. The WHO places nonbreastfed infants in a risk group and recommends that they receive special attention from health and social workers.

In the United Nations system, formulations appropriate for infant nutrition—whether industrially produced infant formula or home prepared formulas with micronutrient supplements—are specified in the *Codex Alimentarius*, prepared by a commission of the United Nations' Food and Agriculture Organization (FAO) and the WHO in which more than 160 countries, including the United States, participate. Extensive regulation of the legal market for breast milk substitutes does not afford protection to those who consume infant formula distributed through the illicit infant formula market, in which cans of infant formula are deceptively labeled to simulate acceptable infant formula products prior to distribution.

Marketing in the Developing World. Marketing infant formula in the developing world encourages mothers to switch from what the WHO recognizes as the safest, best source of infant nutrition to an inferior and profoundly hazardous alternative. Thus, companies marketing infant formula have been criticized not only for their marketing methods but also for the decision to market infant formula in the developing world at all. Critics of infant formula marketing in the developing world show that material and social circumstances in developing countries make the use of infant formula there particularly inappropriate, and make consumers there especially vulnerable to infant formula marketing methods.

Three marketing methods in particular have received the greatest critical attention: distributing free samples, dressing female marketing representatives in what appear to be white nursing uniforms, and using pictures of healthy European babies on product labels. Free samples pose a serious danger to infants in the developing world because lactation continues only while babies breastfeed. When mothers use all of the free samples of infant formula that they are given, they find they can neither breastfeed nor afford to buy substitutes. Distributing infant formula using "milk nurses" suggests the preference of medical professionals for breast milk substitutes. This falsely suggests, to poor women who lack the sophistication to distinguish marketing from science, that infant formula is superior. Product labels depicting fat, healthy, light-skinned babies falsely suggest that using breast milk substitutes will lead to the better infant health enjoyed by wealthy children and even to the development of lighter skin, which is a marker of social and economic success worldwide.

International Opposition. During the early 1970s, a period of high attention in the developed world to health and safety conditions in the developing world, activists employed economic rather than legal strategies to affect infant formula marketing practices. Companies marketing infant formula in the developing world were exempt from the strict consumer protection regulations common in developed countries. International public health experts showed that the switch from breastfeeding to formula feeding was an unmitigated disaster for the affected children. The activists argued that the marketing practices employed by infant formula marketers were unusually deceptive in light of the social circumstances of developing-country consumers, who were usually poorly educated and often illiterate, and that infant formula marketing was, unfortunately, effective in persuading mothers to substitute infant formula for breastfeeding.

A Swiss court fined Arbeitsgruppe Dritte Welt (Third World Action Group), based in Berne, Switzerland, for circulating informational pamphlets describing Nestlé's infant formula marketing practices under the heading "baby killers," yet Nestlé's conduct did not violate Swiss criminal law. Activists in the United States launched an international consumer boycott of Nestlé products in 1977. The Nestlé boycott called attention to the shocking discrepancy between advertisers' characterization of infant formula as a safe and helpful product and the disastrous results that breast milk substitution presented for infants in the developing world.

International Standards. On May 21, 1981, the WHO's general assembly, the World Health Assembly, approved the International Code of Marketing of Breastmilk Substitutes (the Code) by a nearly unanimous vote. This instrument forbids marketing of breast milk substitutes to the general public for consumption by infants younger than six months and making any public claim of the health benefits or superiority of infant formula to breast milk. Product labels may not depict mothers or children or use certain terms such as "motherly," and they must present simple information in local languages, including statements that breastfeeding is the best way to feed babies and that substitutes should be used only after consultation with health professionals. Companies may not distribute free samples, bottles, or promotional gifts to hospitals, health workers, or other public health service providers. The Code restricts communication by infant formula companies with pregnant women, mothers, and health workers.

The Code's existence does not guarantee adherence to its guidelines. The Code carries the strongest legal force in sixty countries in which it has been incorporated to various extents into local law. The WHO monitors and reports on Code compliance and makes implementation recommendations for international organizations and member states. Advocacy organizations also monitor infant formula marketing practices. Current advocacy organizations include the International Baby Food Action Network (IBFAN), a network of more than 200 groups in 100 countries, which monitors compliance in sixty–nine countries; Baby Milk Action in the United Kingdom, the current secretariat of the International Nestlé Boycott Committee; and, Aktionsgruppe Babynahrung e.V. The Nestlé boycott ceased in 1984 after Nestlé agreed to comply with the Code. Citing Nestlé's noncompliance, the organizers relaunched the boycott in 1988. Nestlé's activities are monitored by Corporate Watch.

See also: Pharmaceutical Companies

FURTHER READING

Aguayo, Victor M., Ross, Jay S., Kanon, Souleyman, and Ouedraogo, Andre N., "Monitoring Compliance With the International Code of Marketing of Breastmilk Substitutes in West Africa." *British Medical Journal* 326: (2003): 127.

"Breaking the Rules, Stretching the Rules, 2004: Evidence of Violations of the International Code of Marketing of Breastmilk Substitutes and Subsequent Resolutions." International Baby Food Action Network. Available at http://www.ibfan.org/english/pdfs/btr04.pdf. Accessed September 26, 2006.

Gerber, Jurg. "Enforced Self-Regulation in the Infant Formula Industry." *Social Justice* 17 (1990): 98–112.

"Global Strategy for Infant and Young Child Feeding." World Health Organization. (2003). Available at http://www.who.int/nutrition/publications/gs_infant_feeding_text_eng.pdf. Accessed September 26, 2006.

"Infant Formula." Federal Drug Administration. Available at http://www.cfsan.fda.gov/~dms/inf-toc.html. Accessed September 26, 2006.

"Infant Formula and Related Trade Issues in the Context of the International Code of Marketing of Breast-Milk Substitutes." World Health Organization. (2003). Available at http://www.who.int/nutrition/ infant_formula_trade_issues_eng.pdf. Accessed September 26, 2006.

"International Code of Marketing of Breast-milk Substitutes." World Health Organization. (1981).

"Promoting Proper Feeding for Infants and Young Children." World Health Organization. Available at http://www.who.int/nutrition/topics/infantfeeding/en/index.html. Accessed September 26, 2006.

"WHO Report On Infant and Young Child Nutrition: Global Problems and Promising Developments." World Health Organization. (2003). Available at http://www.who.int/nutrition/publications/ code_english.pdf. Accessed September 26, 2006.

JUDITH WISE

INSIDER TRADING. Illegal *insider trading* is a form of securities fraud that consists of the purchase or sale of a security while the purchaser is in possession of material, confidential information concerning that security, and/or passing the information to others, who then trade. When corporate insiders trade prior to the public release of important information, they breach the fiduciary duty they owe to shareholders to act in the shareholder's best interests. Individuals outside the company may also be liable if they trade on the basis of nonpublic information to which they have been given access as part of their employment (e.g., lawyers, accountants, bankers, brokers, printers, and government employees). Such individuals violate their employer's or client's confidence when they misappropriate the information entrusted to them.

Insider trading legislation rests on the premise that the act undermines the confidence and integrity of the marketplace. The offense derives its legitimacy from Section 10(b) of the Securities Exchange Act of 1934, promulgated in the wake of the 1929 stock market crash and the subsequent depression. The corresponding Securities and Exchange Commission (SEC) Rules 10b-5, 10b5-1, and 10b5-2 specify the elements required for civil and criminal insider trading action, namely the intentional omission of important facts in connection with a security's trade. Corporate insiders are prohibited from using their inside information to their advantage in their trades. Insiders may trade only when that information becomes publicly available. Unless the confidential information is disclosed to the public prior to the trade, insiders may not trade in the security.

Finally, SEC Rule 14e-3 prohibits anyone from trading a security while in possession of nonpublic information related to a merger or acquisition or passing that information on to others. Typically, the price of the stock increases considerably when the merger or acquisition is announced publicly. Because numerous individuals from various professions work behind the scenes to put together such a deal, the opportunity to commit insider trading is expanded. Rule 14e-3 prevents those who are privy to the confidential information from profiting unfairly.

The SEC, the primary regulatory agency enforcing insider trading rules, has jurisdiction over administrative and civil proceedings, but it refers cases for criminal prosecution to the Department of Justice. The SEC receives leads on possible violations from numerous sources, including informant tips, individual complaints, securities-related organizations such as the

New York Stock Exchange, and the SEC's own proactive surveillance activities. To encourage informant tips, individuals who provide information in civil cases may be awarded a bounty from the recovered profits.

Insider trading is quite difficult to prove at trial. Unless the defendant confesses, cases are based on circumstantial evidence such as meetings, telephone calls, trading patterns, and interpersonal relationships. Consequently, a cooperating witness or informant is often crucially important in a case.

Insider traders may be vulnerable to administrative, civil, and criminal sanctions. Administratively, the SEC may issue a "cease and desist" order, require disgorgement of (returning) illegal profits, revoke or suspend the registration of an offending broker, and bar or suspend violators from employment. In civil suits, the Commission invariably seeks an injunction prohibiting future violations; violators of an injunction are subject to criminal or civil contempt proceedings. Additionally, the SEC typically orders the violator to disgorge illegal profits and to pay a fine equal to that profit. The SEC has the power to impose a maximum fine of up to triple the illegal profits, although such fines are rarely imposed. The Commission may also bar or suspend offenders from positions as corporate officers or directors. In civil proceedings, most violators settle without admitting or denying guilt.

The U.S. Attorney's Office decides whether a violation calls for criminal prosecution. Under the Insider Trading and Securities Fraud Enforcement Act of 1988, insider traders may receive a maximum prison sentence of ten years and a maximum fine of $1 million. The maximum fine for corporations is $2.5 million.

The SEC sporadically enforced insider trading until the 1980s when the SEC dramatically increased its enforcement efforts. This decade of greed and decadence was witness to the passage of two Acts to increase the penalties attached to insider trading: the Insider Trading Sanctions Act of 1984 and the Insider Trading and Securities Fraud Enforcement Act of 1988. The latter Act was passed in the aftermath of the Levine-Boesky-Milken insider trading scandals. The charges against "junk bond king" Michael Milken and his subsequent criminal conviction for securities fraud shook the securities industry in the late 1980s.

Dennis Levine was a managing director of mergers and acquisitions for Drexel Burnham Lambert when he was arrested for insider trading in 1986. He had cultivated a ring of associates from different Wall Street firms to feed him information concerning upcoming mergers and acquisition deals. Using this inside information, Levine brought and sold securities under a fictitious name through a Swiss bank in the Bahamas. By the time he was arrested, he had accumulated over $11 million in illegal profit. In exchange for a lighter sentence, Levine agreed to cooperate with the government, turning over his network of co-conspirators, including arbitrageur Ivan Boesky. He pled guilty to securities fraud, tax evasion, and perjury and received a fine of $11.6 million and a two-year prison sentence.

Boesky was a risk arbitrageur who made his money by investing in companies that were rumored to be targets for takeovers. If his information was accurate, and he could buy the stock prior to others at a relatively low price, then his profit margin was secured. Like Levine, Boesky cultivated a network of insiders to provide information on potential takeover targets. By relying on information from those working on the deals, rather than amorphous rumor, he violated the insider trading laws. Once Boesky was implicated in the Levine insider ring, he likewise agreed to cooperate with the government providing incriminating evidence against his associates, one of whom was Milken. Boesky pled guilty to criminal securities fraud charges, received a fine of $100 million and a three-year prison sentence, and was barred by the SEC for life from working in the securities business.

Milken was the most noted individual connected with the insider trading scandals of the late 1980s. Milken has been vilified for his role in the rise of hostile takeovers and leveraged buyouts, made possible through his high-yield, high-risk "junk" bonds. The layoffs and heavy corporate debt associated with leveraged buyouts made Milken a target for resentment.

Milken created and ran the high-yield bond market, which financed corporate endeavors that were deemed too risky by traditional banks and underwriters, at Drexel Burnham Lambert. His department was the most profitable for the firm, and he was richly rewarded for his work. For instance, in 1987 when he was generating virtually all of Drexel's profits, his bonus was $550 million. In 1988, based on information supplied by Boesky, the SEC filed a complaint against Milken alleging violations involving billions of dollars. Included in the SEC complaint were charges of insider trading. As part of his consent agreement with the SEC, Milken was barred for life from the securities business. In 1990 following a guilty plea for criminal charges, he was fined $600 million and sentenced to ten years in prison, a term which was later reduced. He served less than two years and was released in 1993.

In 1996 while Milken was still on probation, the SEC investigated his actions to determine whether he violated his consent decree in connection with his role on deals involving such major corporations as MCI, Turner Broadcasting, and Time Warner. To settle the case, Milken agreed to disgorge the $42 million he received for his work on the deals.

Drexel itself settled with the SEC in 1988, pleading guilty to mail, wire, and securities fraud and paying a $650 million fine. Without Milken its fortunes declined, and in 1990 it filed for bankruptcy protection.

Previous high-profile convictions have not deterred others from committing the profitable crime. In 2002 Sam Waksal, CEO of the biopharmaceutical company ImClone Systems Inc., was charged in civil court with insider trading. This incident was soon followed by the 2003 insider trading complaint against Martha Stewart, the CEO of Martha Stewart Living Omnimedia, Inc.; Stewart and Waksal shared the same Merrill Lynch broker, Peter Bacanovic. After receiving advance notice that the Food and Drug Administration (FDA) planned to refuse to review ImClone's application to market a new, highly publicized cancer treatment called Erbitux, Waksal and his daughter placed orders to sell all the ImClone stock held in their Merrill Lynch accounts. The civil complaint alleges that Bacanovic instructed his assistant to warn Stewart that the Waksals were selling their stock. Acting on the information, Stewart sold all of her ImClone stock. She and Bacanovic later contrived a story to conceal from the SEC and criminal investigators the true reason for her sale. The criminal indictments of Stewart and Bacanovic stem from these false statements. After ImClone publicly announced that the FDA had refused to review ImClone's application, the price of ImClone stock dropped. By selling before the public announcement, the civil complaint alleges, Stewart avoided losses of approximately $46,000.

Both Stewart and Bacanovic were convicted of the criminal charge of obstruction of justice in a jury trial and each was sentenced to a five month prison term and two years of supervised release—five months of which must be spent under house arrest. Waksal pled guilty to criminal securities fraud, among other charges, and was sentenced in 2003 to just over seven years in prison.

See also: Boesky, Ivan; Drexel Burnham Lambert; Enron; Junk Bonds; Milken, Michael; Levine, Dennis; Stewart, Martha

FURTHER READING

Frantz, Douglas. *Levine & Co.: Wall Street's Insider Trading Scandal.* New York: Henry Holt, 1987.
Prud'homme, Alex. The *Cell Game: Sam Waksal's Fast Money and False Promises—and the Fate of ImClone's Cancer Drug.* New York: Harper Business, 2004.
Stewart, James B. *Den of Thieves.* New York: Simon & Schuster, 1991.
Stewart, James B. "The Milken File." *The New Yorker* (January 22, 2001): 47–61.

Elizabeth Szockyj

INSURANCE INDUSTRY FRAUD. Fraud in the international insurance industry is massive in its proportions and severe in its impact on individual consumers. Although much public attention focuses on claimant fraud, which involves false claims submitted to insurance companies, those losses are far outweighed by the losses inflicted upon consumers who unwittingly purchased worthless insurance policies sold to them by the operators of fraudulent insurance companies. Insider insurance fraud has been facilitated by several factors: the structure of the industry itself, deregulatory policies, and broader changes in the insurance industry.

Industry Structure. Unlike other industries that produce tangible products or provide immediate services to customers, the business of insurance involves, in essence, the selling of promises: "promise(s) to pay all or a part of the costs associated with some future event." In some cases the consumer may rarely use the services for which he or she paid. Transactions in the industry are characterized by what is known as a "long tail": a long period of time often elapsing between the date when a customer begins paying for future services (coverage of health care costs) and the date that those services are actually demanded (when a claim is filed). In the interim, unscrupulous insurance company owners and operators have ample time to abscond with their clients' premiums.

Changes in the Industry. One of the long-term trends in the U.S. insurance industry has been the departure of many of the largest insurance carriers from a number of markets deemed to be unprofitable. Over the last several decades, insurers have abandoned the small-business health insurance market, the high-risk auto insurance market in California, the small-business product liability market, as well as others. These changes have left consumers in these markets desperate for insurance and thus easy marks for the purveyors of bogus insurance policies.

Deregulation. Despite the fact that U.S. insurance companies currently hold over $5 trillion in assets, there is no federal regulation of the industry. Instead, regulation varies among the fifty states. This regulatory structure has been further weakened by deregulatory policies. Beginning in the 1970s, policy-makers attempted to open up markets by allowing companies other than insurance companies in certain sectors of the industry to sell insurance products outside the regulatory requirements imposed on traditional insurance companies.

One of these sectors was the small-business health insurance market. Federal legislation enacted in the 1970s allowed small employers to band together to form Multiple Employer Welfare Arrangements (MEWAs) to purchase health insurance for their employees at favorable rates and to do so without adhering to the standards imposed on insurance companies. White-collar criminals quickly saw the potential in this situation and began organizing fraudulent MEWAs, which they operated as Ponzi schemes—initially paying claims in order to keep the scheme going, then delaying payments, and eventually paying no claims as they had diverted much of the premiums to themselves. The General Accounting Office (GAO) estimated that between 1988 and 1991, fraudulent MEWA schemes left more than 400,000 individuals with $133 million in unpaid medical claims. Similar schemes have involved the use of phony employee-leasing companies and bogus labor unions to achieve the same end of defrauding health insurance policyholders. A GAO report in 2004 identified 144 of these fraudulent entities that operated between 2000 and 2002 and failed to pay over $252 million in medical claims to over 200,000 policyholders.

Another problematic area of the insurance industry has been the offshore sector; insurers whose primary market is the United States but that are officially domiciled in foreign countries and thus not fully subject to American regulatory and tax standards. By 1994, 10 percent of all U.S. insurance premiums went to foreign insurers. Unscrupulous operators of offshore insurance companies have moved into markets that are underserved by legitimate insurance carriers and in which consumers are desperate for coverage. They lure unsuspecting victims with low rates and minimal requirements, take their premium dollars, and then vanish when the claims roll in.

One group that was targeted by offshore insurance crooks consisted of small-business owners in the inner city of Los Angeles in the early 1990s. After being redlined (denied coverage because of their location) by major insurance carriers, they were forced to turn to little-known offshore companies for their insurance needs. After the riots of 1992, many of these business people (a large proportion of whom were Korean-American immigrants) found their stores and shops had been damaged or destroyed. After they filed claims to begin rebuilding their businesses, they eventually realized that they were never going to be paid. More than simply suffering monetary losses, many of the victims found that their whole lives had changed. A significant number were unable to reopen their businesses and ended up unemployed or underemployed. The victims also suffered disproportionate rates of mental illness and divorce, and several even attempted suicide.

Corrupt practices in the offshore insurance industry are linked to the increasing globalization not only of the insurance industry but also of financial services industries in general. Just as insurance companies, banks, and securities firms have discovered the benefits of operating outside U.S. borders—in countries where taxes and regulatory oversight are low—so too have white-collar criminals. As this pattern of globalization continues, one can expect the incidence of this form of white-collar crime to increase as well.

See also: Victoria Insurance Company

FURTHER READING

Private Health Insurance: Employers and Individuals are Vulnerable to Unauthorized or Bogus Entities Selling Coverage. U.S. General Accounting Office GAO-04-3142. Washington, D.C., 2004.

Tillman, Robert. *Broken Promises: Fraud Among Small Business Health Insurers.* Boston: Northeastern University Press, 1998.

Tillman, Robert. *Global Pirates: Fraud in the Offshore Insurance Industry.* Boston: Northeastern University Press, 2002.

ROBERT H. TILLMAN

INTERNET FRAUD. The growth of the Internet, especially over the last ten years, has led to a rise in the amount of fraud that occurs online. Criminals are increasingly adopting Internet technologies and using them to commit more traditional fraudulent schemes. The number of consumer victims continues to grow every year.

Because of the Internet's global reach, jurisdictional issues compound difficulties in the investigation of crimes and prosecution of offenders. In addition, both law enforcement capabilities and legal protections lag behind as the technology advances, further adding to the problem.

Types of Internet Fraud. Internet fraud is an umbrella term, and it encompasses a variety of different criminal acts. The following are the most prevalent:

Auction Fraud. This is the most commonly reported type of Internet fraud and is seen on online auction sites such as eBay. This crime normally is committed by a seller who might offer goods or services that he or she does not have, might not ship the goods or services paid for by the buyer, might not provide refunds to the buyer in a timely fashion, or might provide goods and services that have been falsely advertised.

Investment Fraud. Offenders create a fake company web site or send out unsolicited e-mail (spam) offering an investment opportunity. After the victim sends money to become involved, the offender will disappear (i.e., stop responding to e-mails or other means of contact), or the web site will vanish.

"419" or Advance Fee Scams. The sender in this type of scam often purports to be a high-level government official (stereotypically, in Nigeria or some other African country) or other professional businessperson. The offender is looking for individuals to handle a large sum of money in exchange for receiving a percentage of it. The offender claims that he or she will handle all necessary documentation, which is designed to look official. However, the victim is requested to provide some money to the offender in advance to cover the expenses of the transaction. The offender then takes the advance money and disappears, possibly after a couple more rounds of milking the victim. Overseas travel may be required of the victim. The name "419" comes from the section of the Nigerian criminal code that outlaws this activity.

Phishing. This fraudulent act usually takes the form of e-mail, seemingly from a major financial institution, requesting that the recipient reenter his or her account information under pain of losing the account privileges. The e-mail contains a link that looks like a link to the company's Web site but actually leads to a fake Web site created by the offender. If the recipient of the e-mail takes the bait and follows the link, he or she is asked to enter personal information, such as name, address, phone number, credit card number, bank account number, and Social Security number, which the offender collects. Armed with this information, the offender can then use it to commit identity theft, credit card fraud, or other financial fraud. Similar phishing scams pretend to come from organizations seeking charitable donations, often referring to major domestic and international disasters (e.g., the December 2004 tsunami in Asia or Hurricane Katrina).

Business Fraud. Senders of certain unsolicited (spam) e–mails may be offering goods and services that they do not deliver after buyers pay, or they may misrepresent the items for sale. In addition, other online sellers of goods or services who advertise on Web pages or in online catalogs may not deliver after buyers pay, or they may misrepresent the goods or services.

Identity Theft. Although not strictly an Internet-based offense, identity theft is the fastest-growing crime in the United States. It consists of two parts: the theft or procurement of the victim's personal information, and the fraudulent use of that information. In certain jurisdictions, offenders may be charged who merely have possession of the information with the intent to use it, even if a fraudulent act does not occur. Offenders misuse a victim's Social Security or credit card number in order to commit credit card, bank, loan, employment, or benefits frauds. The victim's information may be obtained over the Internet or may be obtained offline and later used on the Internet.

Adoption of Technology. Technology is an important tool that can be used for both legal and illicit purposes. Electronic mail, especially, has been used in Internet fraud schemes. Offenders can easily send these mails in bulk, using programs that exist to harvest e-mail addresses that are publicly available online. Other personal information is also available on the Internet, including names, addresses, phone numbers, Social Security numbers, and dates of birth, which has also made it easy to commit Internet fraud.

Response to Internet Fraud. The United States has recently used the Controlling the Assault of Non-Solicited Pornography and Marketing (CAN-SPAM) Act to directly target unsolicited e-mails that are often attempts to commit Internet fraud. However, because the law is still new and because of the difficulty in investigating crimes, few individuals have been arrested and prosecuted under this law. The Identity Theft and Assumption Deterrence Act, passed in 1998, makes identity theft a federal crime against consumer victims, and while it has had more success in the courts than other legislation, many offenders are charged with fraudulent crimes other than identity theft.

Organizations formed to handle and track consumer complaints of Internet fraud include the National Fraud Information Center's Internet Fraud Watch Program, the Internet Fraud Complaint Center (a collaboration between the U.S. Federal Bureau of Investigation and the National White Collar Crime Center), and the Federal Trade Commission's Consumer Sentinel. These organizations refer cases to local, state, and federal law enforcement agencies and provide yearly statistics on the fraud trends in the United States. However, because the Internet is a global entity, crimes do not always occur neatly within a single jurisdiction or geographical area. More often, law enforcement and investigators from different areas must work together, especially when the victim and offender live in separate locations. Although some countries are cooperating to solve computer crime, this is not true for all of them. These issues are compounded by the lack of resources in many law enforcement agencies, which impedes investigations of crimes involving Internet fraud. Lack of enforcement is due in part to the tendency to view crimes involving money as less serious than crimes involving violence.

153

As Internet threats become better understood, both laws and law enforcement resources must be vigilant in addressing how to stop these types of crimes.

See also: Identity Theft

FURTHER READING

Internet Fraud Complaint Center. Available at http://www.ifccfbi.gov. Accessed December 2004.

National Internet Fraud Watch Information Center. Available at http://www.fraud.org. Accessed February 2005.

U.S. Federal Trade Commission. "Consumer Sentinel." Available at http://www.consumer.gov/sentinel. Accessed December 2004.

SARA E. BERG

IRAN-CONTRA. The roots of the Iran-Contra affair date back to the foreign policy agenda of the Reagan administration in 1981. It was President Reagan's announced intention to encourage the removal of the Marxist Sandinista government in Nicaragua and to aid the Contras, a pro-American rebel army engaged in a guerrilla war against the Sandinistas. Congress, however, was less than willing to authorize funding for an interventionist policy and passed the Boland Amendments between 1982 and 1986, which severely limited or prohibited the appropriation of funds on behalf of the Contras. By that time, however, the White House had committed itself to backing the Contras at all costs. Since this policy could not be carried out without defying Congress, the administration formulated two schemes for achieving it covertly. The first entailed letting the National Security Council (NSC) arm the Contras since Congress had proscribed the use of funds for such a purpose by the CIA and the Defense Department. The NSC was not technically an intelligence agency, so it allowed the administration to evade the spirit of the law, if not the letter. The second method was to use either private or third-party funds on the assumption that only official U.S. funds had been prohibited. This plan would also be carried out by the NSC, which, at the time, was headed by Robert McFarlane. He assigned the task to his chief "action officer," Marine Lieutenant Colonel Oliver North, a decorated Vietnam veteran, who would become the designated "contact" between the NSC and the Contras, and whose job it was to recruit others to help fund the Contras.

Two major figures to whom North turned for funding were international arms dealers: retired Air Force Major General Richard Secord and his business partner Albert Hakim. They sold over $11 million worth of arms to the Contras. In order to pay for the arms and to deceive Congress, funds had to be raised privately. This was done primarily through nonprofit conservative foundations and by pressuring governments of other countries to contribute in exchange for political favors.

At the same time, events on the other side of the globe were to complicate an already Byzantine enterprise. Another item on the Reagan foreign policy agenda was the conflict with the Iranian regime led by the ferociously anti-American Ayatollah Khomeini, on whose behalf Iranian students had held American hostages at the U.S. embassy in Tehran for 444 days. In

1984 another group of hostages were captured and held in Lebanon by Islamic extremists under Khomeini's control. While promising the public that no deals would be made for the release of hostages, the administration orchestrated the sale of weapons to Iran through Israel for their release. After a series of sales through 1985, one hostage was released. McFarlane resigned and was replaced by his deputy, Vice-Admiral John Poindexter. The secret arms sales produced secret profit, which the NSC used as a source of funding for the Contras.

In 1986 the covert operations began to unravel after a supply plane was shot down over Nicaragua, and North was linked to fund-raising activities on behalf of the Contras. Later in a speech drafted by North, President Reagan addressed the nation and stated, "We did not—repeat—did not trade weapons or anything else for hostages, nor will we." Later he admitted that a small amount of arms had been traded, but that he was terminating all such sales. Following additional blunders before the press, Reagan fired Poindexter and transferred North out of the NSC in an attempt at damage control. Working with his secretary, former fashion model Fawn Hall, North altered and shredded documents from his files. When she later testified before Congress, the intensely loyal Hall was asked whether she realized that what she had done was wrong. "Sometimes," she said, "you have to go above the written law."

Reagan had Attorney General Ed Meese acknowledge the diversion of funds from Iranian arms sales to the Contras. He implied that North may have been guilty of violating the law—without presidential authorization. In May 1987, Congress held hearings on the Iran-Contra affair, at which time the colorful North took center stage. McFarlane pleaded guilty to four misdemeanor counts of withholding information from Congress and received two years of probation and a $20,000 fine. A federal grand jury returned criminal indictments against North, Poindexter, Secord, and Hakim. All of them received probation in exchange for their cooperation except Poindexter, who received a six month sentence for lying to Congress. Later, North's and Poindexter's convictions were overturned on technical grounds by a divided appeals court. North became popular on the lecture circuit, was an unsuccessful Republican nominee for a U.S. Senate seat in Virginia in 1994, and became the host of a nationally syndicated radio program.

FURTHER READING

Bradlee, Ben, Jr. *Guts and Glory: The Rise and Fall of Oliver North.* New York: Donald Fine, 1988.

Cohen, William S., and Mitchell, George J. *Men of Zeal: A Candid Inside Story of the Iran-Contra Hearings.* New York: Viking, 1988.

Draper, Theodore. *A Very Thin Line: The Iran- Contra Affairs.* New York: Hill and Wang, 1991.

Rosoff, Stephen M., Pontell, Henry N., and Tillman, Robert. *Profit Without Honor: White-Collar Crime and the Looting of America,* 3rd edition. Upper Saddle River, NJ: Prentice Hall, 2004.

HENRY N. PONTELL
STEPHEN M. ROSOFF

J

JOHNS-MANVILLE CORPORATION. The Johns-Manville Corporation (hereafter referred to as Manville) was notorious for being one of the largest processors and manufacturers of asbestos-containing products. In fact, in 1982 Manville claimed to be *the* largest processor of asbestos in the world. However, things took a turn for the worse for the asbestos industry early in the twentieth century when the medical world began to acknowledge a strong link between asbestos exposure and severe health complications (see **Asbestos**). In the 1930s Manville, along with other industry leaders, conspired to keep any negative publicity (e.g., medical research with adverse findings) from reaching their employees and the general public and decades later vehemently denied knowledge of adverse health affects during lawsuit proceedings. Perhaps what the Johns-Manville Corporation is most notorious for is the unusual way in which they protected themselves from the millions of dollars in claims and litigation costs. Manville was the first Fortune 500 company to file for bankruptcy while still unmistakably solvent and profitable.

Henry W. Johns founded the H. W. Johns Manufacturing Company in 1858 to market asbestos commercially as a fire-resistant roofing material. In 1901 the company merged with the Manville Covering Company to form the H. W. Johns-Manville Company (later dropping the "H. W." in 1926). The newly formed company focused most of its production on asbestos roofing and pipe insulation. Business climbed steadily, and by 1925, Manville reported annual sales of approximately $40 million. Manville continued to excel, dominating its market in the U.S. and expanding production and sales abroad.

When researchers in the United Kingdom began suggesting a strong link between asbestos exposure and pulmonary diseases in the 1930s, top executives at Manville argued that individual factors played a role in the UK findings and thus had no bearing on the U.S. situation. In a 1935 letter to Summer Simpson, who was the president of Raybestos Manhattan, the second largest asbestos producer, Manville's general counsel, Vandiver Brown, stated that "Our interests are best served by having asbestosis receive the minimum of publicity" (Calhoun and Hiller 1988: 310). In fact, the asbestos industry was very successful at impeding publication of adverse findings in trade journals and keeping pertinent health information from employees. However, the asbestos industry needed to do more than simply minimize public awareness.

In 1928 Manville began sponsoring its own research examining links to cancer (not asbestosis) using nonhuman subjects. Then in 1936 Brown and Simpson proposed a research plan in which Manville executives would review unpublished medical research on asbestos and decide what could be released and what should be kept under wraps; the research that was released was often misleading. Amazingly, the medical professionals were all too willing to cooperate. Unfortunately for the asbestos industry, this plan did not last long. By the mid 1960s, independent medical professionals were publishing unedited research on the dangers of asbestos exposure. Finally, in 1964, due to growing public knowledge, Manville began placing warnings on all asbestos-containing products.

Prior to 1964, Manville maintained that there was not enough evidence of health complications related to asbestos exposure. However, in 1977, one plaintiff's attorney discovered the "Summer Simpson Papers," which contained correspondence dating back as early as the 1930s. These letters written by industry executives proved that the companies not only knew about the dangers associated with asbestos but also aggressively tried to suppress that information.

This information, combined with the latent effects of asbestos exposure, led to an avalanche of asbestos lawsuits from the mid 1960s to the early 1980s. It has been estimated that Manville was named as a defendant in 13,000 out of the 20,000 suits industrywide between 1968 and 1982. One of the first blows to the industry came in 1973, when an appellate court ruled that asbestos manufacturers were liable for failing to test for and warn others about the dangers associated with their products. The next major blow came in 1974 when Reba Rudkin, a twenty-nine-year employee of Manville's Pittsburgh, California, plant, was diagnosed with asbestosis and filed a precedent-setting civil suit against her employer. Normally worker's compensation insurance covers instances of employees suing employers, but Rudkin's attorneys argued that Manville should not be allowed to be shielded from the fraud and conspiracy charges. Rudkin's lawyers succeeded, and the California Supreme Court ruled that workers could sue their employees when circumstances like those of the Rudkin case applied. This ruling opened the door for even more litigation, leaving Manville with a $606 million defense cost for litigations between the early 1970s and 1982.

In 1976 Manville's insurance company refused to renew its policies, forcing Manville to self-insure and become fully responsible for its own defense costs. In the face of pending litigations, Manville sought financial help from the federal government. When that attempt proved to be unsuccessful, Manville's executives decided to seek protection by filing for bankruptcy in August 1982. This came as a shock not only to the industry but also to the business world. As of December 1981, Manville's assets totaled $2.3 billion; it was clearly not bankrupt, and, because of its earlier moves to phase out asbestos, the company was still highly profitable. It was not long before other leaders in the industry followed Manville's example and filed for protection in the bankruptcy courts as well. In 1983 Manville proposed a plan to put asbestos health claimants on equal footing with all creditors and to provide a fair, systematic way of handling health claims. This plan was successful, and on November 28, 1988, Manville emerged from Chapter 11 bankruptcy. Today the Johns-Manville Corporation is still a leading manufacturer in the insulation and roofing business, having permanently switched from asbestos to fiberglass.

See also: Asbestos

FURTHER READING

Calhoun, C. and Henryk, H.. "Asbestos Exposure by Johns–Manville: Cover-Ups, Litigation, Bankruptcy, and Compensation." Pp. 305–329 in *Corporate and Governmental Deviance*. New York: Oxford University Press, 1996.

"Johns-Manville Company History." Johns-Manville Company. 2005. Available at http://www.jm.com/corporate/56.htm. Accessed September 26, 2006.

"The Firm's Role in Asbestos Litigation." *Mesothelioma Facts & Information Newsletter*. 2005. Available at http://www.mesothelioma-facts.com/history.cfm. Accessed September 26, 2006.

ANDREA SCHOEPFER

JUNK BONDS. Junk bonds, more formally known as high yield bonds, are bonds that rate below BBB on the Standard and Poor's credit rating index. The Standard and Poor Corporation performs financial research and analysis on stocks and debt instruments as well as ranking the credit–worthiness of borrowers through the use of a standardized ratings scale. These ratings are determined by the issuing company's credit risk, or likelihood of its defaulting on the loan amount. A rating of BBB is a medium-grade bond, whereas a rating one grade below (a rating of BB) is described as a low-medium-grade bond, is somewhat speculative in nature. The lowest possible rating for any bond under the Standard and Poor's index is a bond rating of D, or, "in default." Junk bonds—bonds between these ratings—are below investment grade and present a great deal of risk to those who invest in these types of debentures because of their speculative nature. The lower the rating, the more risk involved and the greater the rate of return offered to the investor, making the bond profitable—provided the company does not go into default or file for bankruptcy. Investors can expect to earn pennies on the dollar if such debentures fall into default; thus the risk involved can greatly outweigh the gains to unsuspecting or inexperienced investors.

Junk bonds are often associated with securities frauds that occurred during the late 1980s and early 1990s, particularly those cases involving Ivan Boesky and Michael Milken. Prior to the eighties, junk bonds had little if any market in which they could viably be sold and, as such, were usually bonds from once-prominent companies whose fortunes had taken a turn for the worse. Hence these bonds were sometimes called "fallen angels." Until Drexel Burnham Lambert came on the scene as a major investor in below-investment-grade bonds under Milken's guidance, junk bonds were grossly untapped as to their potential value. Milken's premise was that if he could find buyers for these bonds and change the existing attitudes toward the bonds, returns on such them would be high, and all sides could make substantial profits. Unfortunately, as the junk bond mark grew, so too did the unscrupulous behavior of the junk bond dealers. The lure of fast money and greed began to consume many who participated extensively in the junk bond market.

Trading and issuing junk bonds is not, in and of itself, a criminal act; however, companies that issue such bonds are, in some instances, in dire need of an influx of capital and will go to great lengths to secure these funds. In many instances the insuring/lending institution will require companies to issue options or give up assets as collateral to make the bond issuance more enticing to investors on the open market. It is because of these requirements that frauds are most likely to arise.

This was precisely the case with American Tissue, the fourth largest tissue manufacturer in the United States in 1999. In order to secure the funds necessary to continue acquiring smaller firms and for everyday operations, American Tissue was told that it must bolster its balance sheet. To accomplish this, the company's parent company, Middle American Tissue, sold millions of dollars worth of bonds back to the lending agency, Donaldson, Lufkin, and Jenrette, and injected those funds onto American Tissue's balance sheet, also agreeing to place members of the investment bank on the board of directors. Ironically, the investment bank was also accused of fraud by protecting its investment through using the board to recoup potentially lost funds and failing or ignoring other outstanding creditors' claims. Also, the purchase of bonds from the parent company, whose only asset was American Tissue, made American Tissue solely responsible for the debt amount, which—as, it claimed, Donaldson, Lufkin, and Jenrette knew—it could not repay in accordance with the terms of the loan. As a result, numerous frauds were perpetrated by both companies, and the lending agency received a very high rate of return on the bonds themselves even as American Tissue went into bankruptcy.

Today, junk bonds are traded on an active market at unprecedented levels and have afforded many smaller companies the ability to compete with larger conglomerates. Essentially, access to capital through the issuing of junk bonds has leveled the playing field. As such, many of the bonds are bought and sold at near or above par value, thus making the high yield or rate of return negligible. This has not deterred many inexperienced investor and mutual fund companies from continuing to invest in these high-risk debentures in hopes of earning a considerable high rate of return.

See also: Boesky, Ivan; Drexel Burnham Lambert; Milken, Michael

FURTHER READING

Dinehart, Mason III. "High Yield or Junk Bonds, Haven or Horror." Expert Law Web Site. Available at http://www.expertlaw.com/library/business/junk_bonds.html. Accessed May, 2005.

"Junk Bond." Available at http://www.riskglossary.com/articles/junk_bond.htm. Accessed May 2005.

Metcalfe, Liz. "Junk: Not Your Father's Bonds." *Money Sense*. Available at http://www.moneysense.ca/investing/stocks_markets/article.jsp?content=512270. Accesed May 2005.

Vardi, Nathan. "DLJ Junk Bonds Jilt Credit Suisse." *Forbes* (September 10, 2003). Available at http://www.forbes.com/2003/09/10/cx_nv_0910tissue.html.

Yago, Glenn. "Junk Bonds." *The Concise Encyclopedia of Economics*. The Library of Economics and Liberty. Available at http://www.econlib.org/library/enc/junkbonds.html. Accessed May 2005.

ADRIAN M. MASCARI

K

KEATING, CHARLES H., JR. (1923–). The collapse of Lincoln Savings and Loan of Irvine, California, in 1989, the most expensive thrift failure (approximately $4 billion in costs to taxpayers) of the savings and loan crisis of the 1980s, is infamous not only for its massive losses, but also because it serves as a prime example of the excesses and corruption that plagued the industry during that time period. The case of Lincoln Savings and its flamboyant owner, Charles Keating, Jr., was characterized by Representative Henry Gonzalez as nothing less than a "mini-Watergate." Keating, who at that time was a Phoenix real estate developer, had an eclectic past. Once a national champion swimmer, Keating became a major anti-pornography crusader who traveled the country battling smut for the Nixon administration. In 1980 he served as campaign manager for John Connally's unsuccessful campaign for the Republican presidential nomination. President Reagan nominated him for an ambassadorship, which was soon withdrawn after it came to light that Keating had settled charges brought by the Securities and Exchange Commission that alleged illegal and fraudulent transactions regarding bank loans in his home state of Ohio.

Keating bought Lincoln Savings and Loan in 1984 and quickly transformed it from a traditional small thrift that made home mortgage loans into his own personal money machine. The institution began trading in junk bonds, in giant tracts of undeveloped land, and in Keating's "masterpiece"—the Phoenician Hotel in Scottsdale, Arizona. The resort was financially doomed from the start given Keating's lavish spending, which involved $260 million of other people's money. Keating also used Lincoln Savings to provide a steady stream of income to his real estate company, American Continental Corporation, and violated numerous federal regulations regarding direct investments and loans made to individual borrowers in the process. The thrift became involved in a series of fraudulent real estate deals designed to pump money into American Continental. Keating and his family benefited both directly and indirectly. Among numerous immediate family members on the payroll, his son, a twenty-eight-year-old college dropout and former busboy, was named chairman of the board of Lincoln Savings and was paid an annual salary of one million dollars. In total, nearly $34 million was paid directly to the Keating family in terms of salaries and bonuses from both Lincoln Savings and American Continental.

When government regulators discovered the violations at Lincoln, Keating decided to fight back using his political clout. A friend of Presidents Ford and Reagan, Keating managed to have his close business associate, Lee Henkel, appointed to the Federal Bank Board in an effort to change the direct investment rule as it applied *only to Lincoln Savings and one other savings and loan.* Henkel, too, was to become embroiled in scandal and resigned soon thereafter. Keating went on to hire a slew of prestigious law firms and a major accountant to prove that Lincoln Savings was on sound financial footing. He paid Alan Greenspan, who would become the Chairman of the Federal Reserve, to prepare an economic report showing that Lincoln Savings was financially sound. Within three years, sixteen of them would be bankrupt. Keating also attempted to "buy" the chief S&L regulator, Ed Gray, out of his job. Gray refused Keating's offer.

Finally, and perhaps most ignominiously, Keating contributed $1.4 million to the campaigns and causes of five U.S. Senators, who would later become known as the "Keating Five." They were Alan Cranston, Democrat from California; Dennis DeConcini, Democrat from Arizona; Don Riegle, Democrat from Michigan, the Chair of the Senate Banking Committee; John McCain, Republican from Arizona; and John Glenn, Democrat from Ohio and former astronaut. In 1987 Gray was called to a meeting in DeConcini's office, where he found Senators DeConcini, McCain, Cranston, and Glenn. Arguing for their "friend," Keating, DeConcini offered a deal in which Lincoln would make more traditional home loans if Gray would ease up on the direct investment rule and leave Lincoln Savings alone.

Another meeting took place a week later with the full Keating Five, which also included the San Francisco regulators who were putting together the case against Lincoln. One of the regulators, Bill Black, took meticulous notes at the meeting, which clearly indicate that the senators were attempting to thwart the government agency's actions regarding Lincoln. The regulators informed the senators that they were going to file a criminal referral with the Justice Department. Gray later stated that the Keating Five meetings "were exercises in naked political power on behalf of a major political contributor."

When Ed Gray's term as Bank Board Chairman expired, M. Danny Wall, a self-described "child of the Senate," was appointed as his replacement. Wall had reportedly met with Keating several times and later took the San Francisco regulators off the Lincoln case. Lincoln remained in operation for two more years, during which time it continued to hemorrhage big losses. In testimony before the House Banking Committee in 1989, before which Keating had refused to testify by invoking the Fifth Amendment, Wall admitted that he had bungled the Lincoln case: "We have all learned some tough lessons from this case. We made some mistakes." This weak concession seemed to take the matter rather lightly. In testimony given by the two chief regulators in San Francisco, whom Wall had removed from the Lincoln case, Wall and other top officials were accused of undercutting regulatory actions against Lincoln Savings despite strong evidence of wrongdoing.

In April 1989 the government seized Lincoln Savings and uncovered what was described as "a web of fraud and deceit with few parallels in the history of finance." New accountants, after careful review, concluded that Lincoln, through a series of phony real estate transactions, had been showing "profits" by giving its money away. Later that year, the government filed a $1.1 billion racketeering lawsuit against Lincoln.

The Senate Ethics Committee held lengthy hearings on the actions of the Keating Five but found no impeachable offenses, although Cranston received the strongest reprimand. In a deposition given to investigators, Cranston, a liberal Democrat, stated that Keating, a conservative

Republican, had donated nearly $1 million to his political activities because Keating was a "patriot who believes in democracy." In 1991 the Senate Ethics Committee found Cranston to have violated Senate rules by intervening on Keating's behalf while soliciting large campaign contributions from him.

M. Danny Wall was later forced to resign as a result of his handling of the Lincoln Savings case. Calling for Wall's removal as chief S&L regulator, Congressman Gonzalez blamed him and other federal regulators for not stopping the looting of Lincoln Savings by officials of American Continental and for allowing Lincoln to become Charles Keating's personal "cash machine." Just days before Lincoln was seized by the government, Wall was still expressing confidence in Keating and arguing for alternatives to a federal takeover.

In that same year, another more disturbing scam perpetrated by Keating came to light. It involved the illegal sale of junk bonds in Lincoln Savings' parent real estate company, American Continental Corporation, also controlled by Keating. Over 20,000 customers, mostly elderly or poor, were tricked into buying the bonds at Lincoln Savings branch offices through high-pressure sales tactics, which had led them to believe that the bonds were government-insured. Some of the victims had invested their life savings, thinking that the soon-to-be-worthless bonds were a safe haven for their retirement funds. One elderly man, who was distraught over losing his $200,000 life savings in the Lincoln collapse, killed himself.

In the meantime, Keating not only offered no apologies but also went on the offensive, campaigning against the "injustice" which government regulators had perpetrated against him. Claiming that overzealous regulators had left him impoverished, Keating denied claims that he had hidden funds in foreign bank accounts. Regarding his namesake senators, he said that they "had done darn well and should be congratulated." Despite his cry of indigence, a few months later, regulators filed a $40.9 million claim for restitution against Keating, charging him and associates with using phony tax shelters and shady land deals to plunder Lincoln Savings.

Keating legally challenged the government's takeover of his thrift. In denying Keating's claims, U.S. District Judge Stanley Sporkin ruled that the government was "fully justified" in seizing Lincoln and noted that the thrift was "in an unsafe and unsound condition to transact business." Judge Sporkin added that Keating and his accomplices had "abused their positions through actions that amounted to a looting of Lincoln."

Finally, in September 1990, Keating and three others were indicted by a grand jury in Los Angeles on charges of securities fraud regarding the sale of almost $200 million in American Continental bonds at Lincoln Savings branches. A superior court judge refused to reduce Keating's $5 million dollar bail, arguing that given his pursuit by regulators, creditors, and prosecutors, "he has significant reasons not to stay around." Bail was reduced, however, for Keating's co-conspirators, Judy J. Wischer, former American Continental president, and Robin S. Symes and Ray C. Fidel, both former Lincoln presidents. After a month long stay at the L.A. County Jail, Keating finally was released when a federal judge lowered his bail to $300,000. Keating was convicted on December 4, 1991, his 68th birthday. Still strongly proclaiming that the regulators were to blame for the demise of his financial empire, Keating was found guilty on seventeen of eighteen counts related to the sale of junk bonds at Lincoln Savings branches.

Just eight days after his conviction on state charges, Keating again pleaded innocent after a federal grand jury indicted him and four associates on 77 counts of racketeering, bank fraud, and other charges, culminating a two-and-one-half-year investigation into the failure of Lincoln Savings and Loan. On April 10, 1992, Charles Keating was sentenced to the maximum term of 10 years in prison by Judge Lance Ito for duping Lincoln Savings' depositors into buying his uninsured bonds. In the biggest fraud trial ever, federal prosecutors rested their case against Keating in December 1992. In January 1993, he and his son were found guilty of racketeering, conspiracy, and fraud. Keating was convicted on seventy-three counts, while his son was found guilty on sixty-four. The verdict exposed Keating, who was already incarcerated at the time on his state conviction, to a maximum of 525 years in prison. The younger Keating was slightly less vulnerable, facing only 475 years.

While the prospect of having the Keatings locked up for the rest of their lives no doubt gratified some of their defrauded investors, Keating's victims, who lost much or all of their life savings, had more immediate concerns. Government efforts to recoup Keating's loot were largely fruitless, however. Keating's 20,000-acre dream community, Estrella, the single largest real estate venture of Lincoln, was valued at less than ten cents on the dollar.

Before his sentencing on the federal charges, prosecutors had asked for a relatively stiff term of 25 to 30 years in prison, claiming that Keating had shown no remorse, despite convictions in two trials, and that he had perjured himself repeatedly and thus deserved extra punishment for obstructing justice. As one Assistant U.S. Attorney explained: "Despite the findings of two criminal juries that he is guilty of fraud beyond a reasonable doubt, defendant Keating still refuses to shoulder any of the blame for the devastation his conduct caused. . . . Instead, he continues to blame everyone but himself." In calling Keating's fraud "staggering in its proportion," a U.S. district judge sentenced him to 12 years and 7 months in prison for looting Lincoln Savings and Loan and defrauding investors in American Continental of more than $250 million.

The state and federal convictions did little to make Charles Keating repentant. In fact he has remained steadfast in his refusal to deliver the standard *mea culpa* declaration. That defiance set Keating apart from most of his upper-world criminal counterparts. Not only was he not sorry, he would not even pretend that he was. He again asserted that Lincoln's failure and his own legal and financial demise were due to vindictive regulators who were out to get him.

In 1996 Keating won his appeal on the state securities fraud conviction, which meant that he "only" had to serve his twelve-year federal sentence. In overturning the state conviction, a federal appeals judge ruled that Keating's constitutional due process rights were denied because his state conviction was based on "nonexistent legal theory" and erroneous jury instructions from Judge Ito.

Three years later, Charles Keating received more good news. On December 2, 1996, an appellate court overturned his federal convictions, finding that jurors in the case had improperly learned about his prior state court conviction. On November 9, 2000, the decade-long criminal case against Keating finally ended quietly as prosecutors formally withdrew fraud charges, representing the final act among state and federal cases and civil and government lawsuits against him. Still unrepentant, he said he had learned his lesson: "Stay . . . out of the government's way. . . . Don't mess with the regulators." It was reported that prosecutors dropped the case for practical reasons, including the deaths and old age of witnesses, the four and one-half years Keating had already served in federal prison, and his guilty plea in federal court.

Whether a bank or thrift failure and investor loss of the magnitude of Lincoln Savings and Loan could happen again is doubtful. Observers were stunned at the scale of the losses. One thing is certain, however. As Michael Manning, a lawyer involved in unraveling Keating's "deals," noted: "[N]o thrift operator rivaled Keating's combination of risky investments, political influence, multi-million-dollar payments to family and friends and sheer, bold arrogance." Charles Keating indeed earned the title of "poster boy" of the savings and loan debacle.

See also: Lincoln Savings and Loan Association

FURTHER READING

Black, William K. *The Best Way to Rob a Bank Is to Own One.* Austin: University of Texas Press, 2005.

Calavita, Kitty, Pontell, Henry N., and Tillman, Robert H. *Big Money Crime: Fraud and Politics in the Savings and Loan Crisis.* Berkeley: University of California Press, 1997.

Rosoff, Stephen M., Pontell, Henry N., and Tillman, Robert H. *Profit Without Honor: White-Collar Crime and the Looting of America,* 3rd edition. Upper Saddle River, NJ: Prentice Hall, 2004.

HENRY N. PONTELL
WILLIAM K. BLACK

KERR-McGEE. Kerr-McGee, as of 2006, is involved in oil and gas exploration and production and is the third largest producer of titanium dioxide pigment, which is the preferred whitener for paint, plastics, and other products. The Kerr-McGee name, however, may be best known for the controversy surrounding the contamination and death of Karen Silkwood in the early 1970s.

Kerr-McGee was originally named the Anderson and Kerr Drilling Company by its founders, James L. Anderson and Robert S. Kerr, in 1929. The pair formed the company in Ada, Oklahoma, to take advantage of the booming oil business in the 1920s. In 1937 Dean A. McGee joined the company, and in 1946 the company changed its name to Kerr-McGee. Kerr-McGee drilled the world's first commercial oil well out of sight of land in the Gulf of Mexico in 1947, and in 1952 it became the first oil company to enter the search for uranium when it purchased the Navajo Uranium Company. In 1968 the company opened the Cimarron uranium Plant in Crescent, Oklahoma, which produced uranium pellets that were put in fuel rods for light-water nuclear reactors. Then, in 1970, Kerr-McGee opened the Cimarron River plutonium plant, where plutonium fuel pins were fabricated.

Karen Silkwood was hired at the Cimarron plutonium plant in 1972 and worked there as a technician until the time of her death in 1974. As an employee at the plant, Silkwood became aware of safety and health infractions and joined the Oil, Chemical, and Atomic Workers Union (OCAW). She was later elected to a three-person steering committee within the union and was responsible for investigating the health and safety violations occurring at the plant. The steering committee testified in front of the Atomic Energy Commission (AEC) about thirty-nine violations that had occurred at the plant. The violations included storing plutonium in desk drawers and on shelves; neglecting to perform routine surveys of respirators;

allowing a contaminated employee to walk through the facility, spreading radioactivity; failure to provide personnel to repair instruments except during the day shift; and telling employees to ignore criticality alarms. After their testimony, the AEC promised to investigate.

Not convinced that the AEC would follow up with the investigation, Steve Wodka, an OCAW representative from Washington, told Silkwood to continue investigating from inside Kerr-McGee. During her investigations, Silkwood allegedly found evidence that photographic negatives were being touched up to hide defects and that quality control data were being manipulated so that fuel rods would pass inspection.

Sometime during a three-day period in November 1974, Silkwood was contaminated by plutonium. Silkwood submitted several urine and fecal specimens to Kerr McGee officials, and all of her samples were contaminated. Subsequent tests at the AEC facility in Los Alamos, New Mexico, showed that Silkwood had internal contamination. Kerr-McGee officials went to Silkwood's apartment and found that her apartment was also contaminated. The exact source of the contamination, however, was unknown. Some people have speculated that Silkwood contaminated herself, while others have speculated that she was intentionally contaminated by Kerr-McGee officials.

On November 13, 1974, Silkwood attended a union meeting, after which she planned to drive to Oklahoma City to meet with Steve Wodka and a New York Times reporter, supposedly to hand over incriminating documents about quality control tampering. On her way to the meeting, Silkwood died in a single-car accident, and no documents were found at the scene. The autopsy report showed that Silkwood's blood contained more than the therapeutic dosage of methaqualone (Quaalude), suggesting that she may have fallen asleep while driving. The Oklahoma Highway Patrol, and later the FBI, ruled her death an accident. Yet A. O. Pipkin, an accident investigator hired by the OCAW, found that there was enough evidence to suspect that Silkwood had been forced off the road. The Oklahoma Highway Patrol, however, stated that there was no evidence to substantiate these findings and maintained that her death was an accident.

Three months after Silkwood's death, the AEC reported on the allegations that had been raised by Silkwood and the other union members. In the report twenty of the thirty-nine violations had been substantiated, but they concluded that only three were violations of AEC rules. The AEC violations included Kerr-McGee's failure to notify the AEC when it had shut down for forty-eight hours to decontaminate the plant; Kerr-McGee's officials placing plutonium in work areas in quantities exceeding safety regulations; and Kerr-McGee's using plutonium in a purer form than the AEC allowed. The AEC report also concluded that a lab analyst had touched up forty quality control negatives with a felt-tipped pen (but without the knowledge of Kerr-McGee officials), however, the changes did not cover up any flaws in the fuel rods. In addition, the AEC found that Silkwood had been contaminated outside the plant and that she had been contaminated deliberately, but it was unclear who contaminated her.

Almost immediately there was speculation surrounding Silkwood's death. Three days after her death, the New York Times reported that the AEC was involved in a massive cover-up regarding the hazards of nuclear power and that for a decade it had been suppressing studies suggesting that plutonium and nuclear reactors were far more dangerous than it had been willing to admit. Other stories by NPR, ABC, Ms., and Rolling Stone all challenged Kerr-McGee, the AEC, and the Oklahoma Highway Patrol. Although none of these stories offered any new evidence, they helped to prompt FBI and Congressional subcommittee investigations. In the end, the FBI investigation concluded with a report that Silkwood's death was an accident, but the subcommittee investigation was never completed.

A memo written by the subcommittee, however, touched on many of the important issues. First, the subcommittee found no evidence that a plutonium-smuggling ring existed at the Kerr-McGee plant (as had been suggested by some of the magazine articles). In addition, it found no evidence that Silkwood had incriminating documents at the time of her death. However, it also stated that the FBI had failed to conduct an adequate investigation, especially into Silkwood's contamination. Although the investigation did not reveal much about Silkwood's contamination and death, it did establish that Kerr-McGee was an unhealthful and unsafe facility. The plant closed in 1975, but twenty-five years later, the grounds of the Cimarron plant were still being decontaminated.

Silkwood's father, Bill Silkwood, filed suit against Kerr-McGee trying to recover damages for the contamination injuries to Silkwood and her property. The trial court awarded him $500,000 for personal injuries, $5,000 for property damage, and $10 million in punitive damages. Kerr-McGee appealed, and the Tenth Circuit Court of Appeals affirmed the $5,000 in property damage but overturned the personal injury and punitive awards, claiming that only the federal government could regulate radiation hazards within plants and that any state remedy would conflict with federal regulations. Bill Silkwood appealed the punitive damages to the Supreme Court. In a 5-4 decision, the Court determined that state tort law did not conflict with federal safety regulation of nuclear power plants, and it overturned the appeal court's judgment and remanded the case back to the Tenth Circuit. While the case was awaiting retrial, it was settled out of court for $1.3 million.

FURTHER READING

Ezell, John Samuel. *Innovations in Energy: The Story of Kerr-McGee*. Norman, OK: University of Oklahoma Press, 1979.

Rashke, Richard. *The Killing of Karen Silkwood: The Story Behind the Kerr-McGee Plutonium Case*. Boston: Houghton Mifflin, 1981.

Silkwood v. Kerr-McGee Corp. 464 U.S. 238 (1984). Available at http://caselaw.lp.findlaw.com/cgi-bin/getcase.pl?court=US&vol=464&invol=238. Accessed September 6, 2006.

JANE FLORENCE GAUTHIER
SCOTT AKINS

KREUGER, IVAR (1880–1932). Ivar Kreuger gained control of a huge portion of the world's production of matches and, in the process, accumulated a massive fortune. At his death in 1932, Kreuger owned factories, forests, mines, and real estate, including a penthouse apartment on New York's Park Avenue. His company represented one of the earliest and most extensive enterprises with a global reach. Kreuger loaned more than $300 million to financially strapped countries throughout the world in exchange for monopoly privileges in the production of matches. He appeared to prosper during the severe worldwide economic depression marked by the 1929 stock market crash in the United States, but, ultimately, he overextended himself and began to employ crooked accounting practices, hiding losses in the more than 400 subsidiaries that his *Svensktrusten* (Swedish trust) controlled.

Kreuger himself was the only person who was aware of the details of the empire he had built, which aided him greatly in pulling off fraudulent deals. In one instance, he arranged financing from several New York banks, using some of his company's stock as collateral for the loans. However, he arranged the transaction so that he could substitute other securities for his original pledge. After his death, the holdings he had subsequently deposited with these banks were found to be Yugoslavian bonds hardly worth the paper on which they were printed.

Ivar Kreuger appears in a brief roster presented by Edwin H. Sutherland in his 1939 presidential address to the American Sociological Society when he introduced the term "white-collar crime." Sutherland maintained that the upper-class crooks of that time, Kreuger among them, were more suave and deceptive than the "robber barons" of the previous century. A popular account of Kreuger's machinations calls attention to what was said to be his peculiar insensitivity to pain, an item claimed to be a key to his personality. There is the further observation that the more he was tempted, the more contemptuous he became of those who were so easily duped, and the more he came to believe that they deserved nothing better than to be deceived.

Kreuger and His Empire. Ivar Kreuger was born in 1880 in Kalmar, a city in southeast Sweden near the Baltic Sea. His father, in partnership with an uncle who lived in London, owned two small match factories in the area of Kreuger's birth. An unexceptional student, Kreuger graduated as a civil engineer from the Royal Technical College in Stockholm, and then, only twenty years old, moved to New York City, where he worked as a construction engineer on the building of Macy's Department Store, the Plaza and the St. Regis Hotels, and the Syracuse University Football Stadium . He also served as an engineer on projects in Vera Cruz, Mexico, and Johannesburg, South Africa.

In 1907 Kreuger returned to Sweden and formed a construction company in partnership with Paul Toll, earning sizable profits by introducing a new process for reinforcing concrete, which he had learned in the United States. Six years later, he established Aktiebolaget Sveriges Förande Tändstrickfabrikeer (the Swedish Match Company), which began as a small family-owned operation and grew into a $600 million global enterprise with branches in thirty-six countries. In sixteen of these countries, Kreuger's company enjoyed a monopoly on the match market. The stocks and bonds in his company paid stunning annual interest rates between 16 and 20 percent, but the money was coming not from profits but from capital. In essence, Kreuger was operating a gigantic pyramid scheme, paying off one group of investors with money entrusted to him by another group.

There were no audits and no penetration of the veil of secrecy that Kreuger had put in place around his business affairs. The tightening money market in a depression year, however, forced Kreuger to sell a telecom venture he had started to International Telegraph and Telephone (ITT), which insisted on examining the books of Kreuger's companies before consummating the deal. ITT auditors were shocked to discover the glaring discrepancies between what Kreuger claimed and the truth, and they sought to cancel the deal until Swedish banks bailed Kreuger out with loans secured only by securities of uncertain worth in his company. There also were a range of underhanded deals that Kreuger cooked. On his death, for instance,

Italian banknotes with a face value of $150 million were found in his vault. Swedish banks had refused to loan funds on these notes, and when they later were shown to Benito Mussolini, the Italian dictator, for possible redemption, he called in his finance minister, whose signature was on them. The minister pointed out that the forgery was self-evident: his name on the notes had been misspelled; in fact, it had been spelled in three different ways.

Kreuger, his economic world collapsing around him, was found dead on March 12, 1932 in his Paris apartment across from the Grand Palais. There was a note in his New York penthouse reading, "I'm too tired to continue." The autopsy said that he had shot himself with a 9 mm Browning pistol, though the gun disappeared shortly thereafter. The suicide finding continues to be challenged by persons who maintain that the weapon was purchased by someone who had forged Kreuger's signature and that Kreuger was at a meeting elsewhere at the time the gun was acquired. His body was cremated almost immediately after it was returned to Sweden, and his diaries burned. When the true state of Kreuger's financial affairs was revealed, the company went bankrupt. A writer today, examining the regulation of the New York Stock Exchange, says that the answer to an important question requires but two words. The question is, "Why did the Exchange initiate stringent oversight rules?" The two-word answer is "Ivar Kreuger."

FURTHER READING

Churchill, Alan. *The Incredible Ivar Kreuger*. London: Weidenfeld and Nicholson, 1967.

Kreuger, Torsten. *The Truth about Ivar Kreuger*. Stuttgart, Germany: Seewald, 1968.

Lindgren, Hâkan. *Corporate Growth: The Swedish Match Industry in Its Global Setting*. Michael Callow, trans. Stockholm: Liber, 1979.

Shaplen, Robert. *Kreuger, Genius and Swindler*. New York: Knopf, 1960.

Wells, Joseph T. "Keeper of the Flame: Ivar Kreuger." Pp. 71–112 in *Frankensteins of Fraud: The 20th Century's Top Ten White-Collar Criminals*. Austin, TX: Obsidian, 2000..

Willander, Ulla. *Kreuger's Match Monopolies, 1925–1930: Case Studies in Market Control through Public Monopolies*. Julie Sundquist, trans. Stockholm: Liber, 1980..

GILBERT GEIS

L

LEVINE, DENNIS (1953–). Dennis Levine's insider trading case launched one of the most famous probes into the industry and brought to light such people as Ivan Boesky, Michael Milken, and the investment firm Drexel Burnham Lambert. Dennis Levine began his career earning $19,000 as a Citibank trainee in 1978. Later, Levine was a highly placed merger and acquisition specialist with the Wall Street firm of Drexel Burnham Lambert. Levine epitomized the classic American Dream, a middle-class boy who made good, or so it seemed. He grew up in a middle-class family in Bayside, Queens, and graduated from New York City's Baruch College.

He became an expert at gathering and trading on insider information. At thirty-three, Levine seemed to have it all, including a Ferrari, a luxurious New York apartment, and a million-dollar annual salary from his employer. His success story stopped when he was charged with using inside information to make $12 million in illegal profits. He was trading in the stocks of fifty-four companies, most of them takeover targets. He earned his fortune based on information concerning the takeovers, together with other important corporate developments of which he was aware but that had not been publicly announced. This is known as a form of insider trading.

Levine was a master at developing an insider trading ring of professionals working at various Wall Street firms. After receiving inside information, Levine would place his trades through an account maintained under an assumed name at various offshore accounts. Many of these were located in the Bahamas. These offshore banks executed transactions through several brokerage firms, including Merrill Lynch. In May 1985, Merrill Lynch detected suspicious activity and conducted an internal investigation, which they passed onto the Securities and Exchange Commission (SEC).

The SEC and the U.S. Attorney's office found a web of relationships among Wall Street professionals who were trading information and other favors. The SEC was tipped off to Dennis Levine's activities related to using inside information to collect over $12 million in illegal profits. Levine was granted immunity by the SEC in exchange for pleading guilty to four felony counts of insider trading. Levine pleaded guilty to perjury, securities fraud, and tax evasion and received a meager two-year prison term and a $362,000 fine. His plea agreement was due to his cooperation with the authorities to implicate others involved in his insider-trading schemes. He repaid almost $12 million and gave authorities many names, including that of Ivan Boesky.

The fallout from the Levine case and his named associates has shaped many changes. Many major securities firms and banks now have new rules of conduct for their employees. Several laws have been implemented to tighten securities laws and to curb corporate takeovers. The issue of business ethics, or lack thereof, has sparked much debate and instigated many changes in the business environment and curriculum at business schools across the nation.

See also: Boesky, Ivan; Drexel Burnham Lambert; Insider Trading; Milken, Michael

FURTHER READING

Bruck, C. *The Predators' Ball: The Junk-Bond Raiders and the Man Who Staked Them.* New York: Simon & Schuster, 1988.
Sobel, R. *Dangerous Dreamers: the Financial Innovators from Charles Merrill to Michael Milken.* New York: Wiley, 1993.
Stewart, J. B. *Den of Thieves.* New York: Simon & Schuster, 1991.
Zey, M. *Banking on Fraud: Drexel, Junk Bonds, and Buyouts.* New York: Aldine De Gruyter, 1993.

DEBRA E. ROSS

LINCOLN SAVINGS AND LOAN ASSOCIATION. Lincoln Savings (Lincoln) is the most expensive insured financial institution failure in U.S. history, costing over $3 billion. It turned the S&L debacle into a political scandal because Charles Keating (see **Keating, Charles**) used its resources and apparent legitimacy to secure political intervention to fend off the regulators and delay Lincoln's closure by two years at an additional cost of $2 billion. Lincoln turned the debacle from an abstract financial issue into a flesh-and-blood story by selling worthless, uninsured junk bonds issued by its parent, American Continental Corporation (ACC), to retirees—creating sympathetic, individual victims (primarily widows).

Lincoln was a classic looting control fraud (see **Control Fraud Theory**) (Black 2005). The person controlling the company uses it as weapon to defraud creditors and shareholders. Accounting fraud is a looter's weapon of choice. It provides guaranteed record profits and allows the CEO to use normal means (e.g., options) to convert company assets to his benefit. The CEO optimizes accounting fraud by investing in assets that are easy to inflate, lending to the worst borrowers, entering into phony deals with nominees (straws) that hide losses and create false gains, and growing rapidly (a Ponzi scheme). Real estate investments were ideal for control fraud because they had no clear market value and could be used to create fictional income even under generally accepted accounting principles (GAAP). Appraisers and accountants valued them. S&L control frauds "shopped" for professionals who transmuted real losses into accounting gains (NCFIRRE 1993; Calavita et al. 1997; Black 2005). Junk bonds, similarly, had no clear market value, given Drexel's dominant role in setting nonmarket prices and understating the default rate (Akerlof and Romer 1993; NCFIRRE 1993, Black 1993 a,b,c). Lincoln optimized so well that it reported it was the most profitable S&L.

Keating acquired Lincoln, a California chartered S&L, on February 22, 1984. Lincoln was a traditional S&L making home loans with $1.2 billion in assets. On a market value basis, it was insolvent by over $100 million, thus Keating paid $51 million to acquire a *net liability*. That would be irrational for an honest buyer. Drexel Burnham Lambert's de facto leader, Michael Milken, recruited Keating and funded his acquisition through the issuance of $125 million in ACC junk bonds. Keating owned a controlling block of shares in ACC, which was Lincoln's sole owner.

ACC was a troubled real estate developer that had once operated in several states. By 1984 it operated only in Arizona, having ceased operations in other states because of construction and design defects (Black 1985).

By recruiting and providing Keating's (over) financing, Milken gained domination over Lincoln. It functioned as Milken's "captive" (Akerlof and Romer 1993; Black 2005; Mayer 1990). Lincoln soon owned over $1 billion in junk bonds, overwhelmingly issued by Drexel. Drexel controlled the portfolio without any decision making by Lincoln; it advised Lincoln at the end of the day what junk bonds it now owned. Drexel churned the portfolio to maximize its fees (it typically represented both the seller and the buyer and set the price) and dumped increasingly poor-quality junk in Lincoln's portfolio. This caused serious losses to Lincoln and eventually led to a series of criminal acts to attempt to deceive the S&L regulators.

Keating, in applying for permission to acquire Lincoln, had promised that it would continue to make home loans in its home territory in southern California. However, Lincoln promptly ceased making home loans and began making direct investments and acquisition, development, and construction (ADC) loans almost exclusively in its real estate operations. Ultimately, it made roughly $5 billion in real estate investments and purchased $1 billion in junk bonds. The real estate investments were overwhelmingly in Arizona. Lincoln became ACC's "cash cow." Keating was never an officer or board member of Lincoln, but he dominated it and made its real estate decisions.

Federal Home Loan Bank Board Chairman Ed Gray began to reregulate the industry in late 1983 and proposed rules limiting direct investments, increasing capital requirements, and restricting growth in early 1984. Keating immediately understood the threat posed by the rules to his plans and used the resources, and apparent legitimacy of Lincoln's resources, to seek to block reregulation and control the agency.

In November 1986, the Federal Home Loan Bank of San Francisco (FHLBSF) supervisors informed Lincoln that the examiners had found that it had (1) engaged in a massive ($600 million) violation of the direct investment rule, (2) had serious losses, (3) as a result, failed its capital requirement, and (4) was not to pay dividends to ACC. Gray had ordered staff to take effective action against all S&Ls that failed their net worth requirements and/or were in material violation of rules. The Bank Board had begun targeting control frauds for early takeovers ("conservatorship") prior to proving that they were insolvent, and the agency's rules provided it with substantial powers over S&Ls that failed capital requirements. Gray's actions threatened all the S&L control frauds, but Keating had a special concern. Keating and many members of his family received lucrative salaries from ACC. ACC was insolvent, unprofitable, and deeply in debt because of its junk bond issuance. If Lincoln could not pay dividends, ACC would fail and end the family's income, wealth, and prestige. It would also cause the regulators to take over Lincoln, give them full access to ACC and Lincoln's records and employees, and lead to prosecutions. Keating used ten stratagems to continue to upstream Lincoln's cash to fund ACC and to delay the agency's takeover of Lincoln:

- Preventing the agency from learning of the full direct investment violations
- Transmuting the real estate losses into gains, thereby upstreaming funds to ACC through a "tax sharing" agreement
- Funding ACC through the sales of junk bonds (primarily from Lincoln's branch network in southern California retirement communities)
- Blocking reregulation
- Taking control of the Bank Board
- Using a "mole" to seek to immunize its violation of the direct investment rule
- Using the five senators who became known as "the Keating Five" (Alan Cranston, Dennis DeConcini, Don Riegle, John McCain, and John Glenn) to immunize its violation of the rule
- Using the Keating Five to help prevent passage of the Federal Savings and Loan Insurance Corporation (FSLIC) recapitalization legislation while Gray was in office (because the bill had a provision that would restore a lapsed power to appoint a conservator for a state chartered S&L prior to insolvency and allow Gray to act)
- Driving Gray from office
- Intimidating Gray's successor (M. Danny Wall) to remove the FHLBSF"s jurisdiction and ignore its recommendation to appoint a conservator for Lincoln

Lincoln's efforts were blunted while Gray was Chairman, but they were successful once Speaker of the House James Wright and Treasury Secretary James Baker met secretly and agreed that Gray would not be reappointed. The Texas S&L control frauds had convinced Wright to hold the FSLIC's funding "hostage" to extort Gray to act favorably. The bill that would have restored the Bank Board's lapsed conservatorship power was not passed until Gray's term ended.

On September 2, 1987, in response to Lincoln's threat to sue, Wall's senior staff ordered a halt to the investigation of Lincoln. On January 28, 1988, after Keating had Senator Glenn arrange a luncheon meeting with Speaker Wright and had Senator Cranston arrange a meeting that afternoon with Wall—which Keating began by stressing Wright's rage at the FHLBSF—Wall ordered an "amicable resolution" (Black 2005: 200). Political pressure from Speaker Wright and the Keating Five and litigation threats led Wall to capitulate.

On May 20, 1988, Wall removed the FHLBSF's jurisdiction, refused to consider its conservatorship recommendation, and signed agreements that, effectively, represented a cease-and-desist order *against the agency*. These actions were unprecedented and led to Lincoln's becoming the most expensive U.S. depository failure.

Prior to the removal of its jurisdiction, Lincoln used deceit to obtain approval of a tax sharing agreement that Lincoln interpreted as allowing it to send cash to ACC for tax payments to the IRS that were *not due* (and might never be due). Any profitable transaction by Lincoln triggered a "tax payment" by it to ACC. Lincoln entered into a series of huge real estate "sales" that produced "profits" so large that Lincoln upstreamed $94 million to ACC. ACC did not pay any of these funds to the IRS—no tax payments were due because of its enormous loss carryforwards. The field examination that Wall had terminated focused on these sales. Wall's new examination team did not examine these suspicious transactions, because Lincoln argued that its deal with Wall precluded such a review. Fortunately, the top California S&L regulator, Bill Crawford, convinced Wall's top supervisor to look at the tax sharing deal and the Bank Board ordered the illegal upstreaming of funds halted in September 1988.

Accountants hired by the Bank Board ultimately determined that the sales were false. Lincoln lent each of the buyers the money they used to buy its real estate; each of the buyers defaulted on those loans; and far from being profitable, each of the real estate properties caused a huge loss to Lincoln. The buyers were "straws"; Enron would later use the same mechanism to inflate values and hide losses.

The order to stop tax-sharing payments put ACC and the Keating family in a crisis. ACC decided to defraud retirees. Lincoln had Southern California branches near retirement communities. ACC, which was deeply insolvent and unprofitable and used fraudulent financial statements to claim the opposite, sold worthless junk bonds to retirees through Lincoln's branches—where depositors would consider them safe. Lincoln sold nearly $250 million in junk to over 18,000 customers. ACC billed the junk bonds as safe and paid a tiny premium relative to insured deposits. This was not a matter of greedy investors buying assets too good to be true. ACC advertised high interest rates on long-term insured deposits. When callers inquired about the insured CDs, they were told that if they wanted higher rates, they could buy ACC bonds—bait and switch. The seller (ACC found that young, clean-cut, and polite males sold best to the widows) added that Lincoln's assets stood behind ACC's bonds. One of the nation's top bond experts called them (prior to ACC's failure) the worst bonds in America. The bond sellers were so young and financially unsophisticated that some of them sold to their parents.

ACC's and Lincoln's top priority, after the tax sharing payments were ended in September 1987, was maximizing sales of ACC junk bonds. ACC created incentive systems for the top bond sellers, including "bond buster" T-shirt awards and holiday skits deriding the elderly purchasers.

Examiners warned the Bank Board of the junk bond sales and pointed out that it was a Ponzi scheme—ACC could pay interest to old purchasers only by bringing in new junk bond buyers. Keating told the examiners that if Lincoln were taken over, it would cost the taxpayers $2 billion. The effective examiners on the team were finding large losses and fraud in every transaction they reviewed. The Department of Justice was, finally, investigating Lincoln Savings for a wide range of frauds. The Bank Board, however, waited for months—taking no enforcement action, taking no depositions, taking no action to stop the sale of ACC junk bonds, and deferring appointing a conservator. Closing Lincoln Savings would amount to an admission that the agency had erred and would damage its leaders' reputations. Wall expressed the hope, after learning that Lincoln was clearly massively insolvent, that Keating could use his political connections and "pull a rabbit out of the hat" (Black 2005: 236).

ACC used the opportunity for a final raid on Lincoln's assets. Lincoln gave its most valuable real estate assets to its subsidiaries. It had already upstreamed its cash to ACC. ACC, and Lincoln's direct subsidiaries, then filed for protection of the bankruptcy laws the day before the Bank Board put Lincoln in conservatorship on April 14, 1989 (almost two years after the FHLBSF recommended doing so). Lincoln was left holding the vast bulk of the liabilities but stripped of control over its assets. It took the federal government roughly a year to recover full control. The result was an immediate liquidity crisis that required the Federal Reserve to lend to Lincoln.

Lincoln's lending and direct investments were so large that, in conjunction with other control frauds investing in Arizona, they hyperinflated a real estate bubble that caused market prices to rise even as vacancy rates soared—Akerlof and Romer (1993) discuss a similar pattern in Texas. This caused a severe regional recession that contributed to the failure of even honest banks and helped push Lincoln's losses over $3 billion.

Lincoln's collapse led to judicial and legislative hearings. House Banking Committee Chairman Henry Gonzalez, over his party's objections, led a vigorous investigation. Democratic leaders knew the hearings would embarrass the Keating Five—four of whom were of their party. The Gonzalez hearings led Wall to resign. The hearings marked the first time that individual S&L fraud victims were presented to C-SPAN viewers. Deposit insurance diffuses losses and victim-ization among all taxpayers, but ACC's fraudulent sales of junk bonds to widows created sym-pathetic individual victims. One told of how she cared for her adult daughter, the victim of severe brain damage. She told the bond salesman that her goal was to save enough money to purchase a van with a wheelchair assist so she could take her daughter on trips out of the care facility. The salesman advised her to use all her savings to purchase ACC bonds. The public perception of the S&L debacle as an unfathomable finance mess changed. Humans empathize most easily with the plight of sympathetic individuals. The Gonzalez hearings focused on the Bank Board, not the Keating Five, but they convinced the public that the scandal was as much political as financial.

Lincoln's legal challenge to the Bank Board's appointment of a conservator also became a *cause celebre*. U.S. District Court Judge Stanley Sporkin, the famous former head of SEC enforcement, blasted Lincoln as a criminal enterprise, but he changed the perception of the debacle by asking, "Where were these professionals?" He caused the public to focus for the first time on the key role professionals play in aiding control fraud.

The Senate ethics investigation of the Keating Five was weak. The members reached unity at the beginning of the hearings—attacking the citizens' group Common Cause for filing the ethics complaint that had led to the hearings! The committee ended on a similar note—delaying the release of their report until the day the allies launched their land attack in the first Gulf War, which, of course, pushed the S&L story off front pages and TV screens. The committee reprimanded Cranston (who had announced his retirement) and criticized the other senators' poor judgment.

See also: Keating, Charles H., Jr.

FURTHER READING

Akerlof, George A., and Romer, Paul M. "Looting: The Economic Underworld of Bankruptcy for Profit." *Brookings Papers on Economic Activity* 2 (1993): 1–73.

Black, William K. 1993c. "Thrift Accounting Principles and Practices." *NCFIRRE Staff Report No. 20.* Reprinted in U.S. House of Representatives, *1989 Investigation of Lincoln Savings & Loan Association.* 101st Cong., 1st Sess., Part 2: 370–386 ("Lincoln Hearings").

Black, William K. *The Best Way to Rob a Bank Is to Own One: How Corporate Executives and Politicians Looted the S&L Industry.* Austin: University of Texas, 2005.

Calavita, Kitty, Pontell, Henry N., and Tillman, Robert H. *Big Money Crime: Fraud and Politics in the Savings and Loan Crisis.* Berkeley and Los Angeles: University of California Press, 1997.

Mayer, Martin. *The Greatest-Ever Bank Robbery: The Collapse of the Savings and Loan Industry.* New York: Macmillan, 1990.

National Commission on Financial Institution Reform, Recovery and Enforcement (NCFIRRE). *Origins and Causes of the S&L Debacle: A Blueprint for Reform. A Report to the President and Congress of the United States.* Washington, DC: Government Printing Office, 1993.

Pizzo, Stephen, Fricker, Mary, and Muolo, Paul. "Lincoln Hearings." In *Inside Job: The Looting of America's Savings and Loans,* 2nd edition. New York: HarperCollins, 1991.

WILLIAM K. BLACK

LOCKHEED BRIBING SCANDAL. The Lockheed bribing scandal came to light in the United States on February 6, 1976, when the vice chairman of the Lockheed corporation told a U.S. Senate subcommittee that the Japanese prime minister had accepted $1.8 million in bribes during his term in return for requiring Japan's parastatal airlines, All Nippon Airways (ANA), to purchase Lockheed's L-1011 aircraft. This wide-ranging scandal enveloped politicians at the top of the U.S. and Japanese governments and sparked several investigations into the foreign business practices of American corporations, ultimately resulting in the creation and passage of the Foreign Corrupt Practices Act (FCPA).

The Lockheed scandal began in July 1972 when Kakuei Tanaka, an embittered and controversial Japanese politician already suspected in previous bribery and corruption scandals, became the prime minister of Japan. Lockheed was facing stiff competition in the aircraft industry from McDonnell Douglas and Boeing and was in a difficult financial situation. Lockheed had only recently avoided bankruptcy in 1971 with a $250 million federal loan guarantee and was struggling to promote and sell its flagship aircraft, the TriStar L-1011, which represented state-of-the-art commercial aircraft manufacturing. The Japanese airline market was very lucrative, and it was clear that ANA would need to expand its fleet to keep up with its national demand.

In August 1972, Archibald Carl Kotchian, then president of Lockheed Aerospace Industry, made a trip to Tokyo with the goal of selling the L-1011 aircraft to All Nippon Airways. Knowing that Tanaka was about to leave for a visit with U.S. President Richard Nixon to discuss trade issues between the two countries, Kotchian asked Toshiharu Okubo, a representative of Marubeni Corporation, to arrange a meeting with the prime minister to discuss a sale of Lockheed's TriStar L-1011 aircraft to ANA.

Okubo informed Kotchian that a "pledge" of 500 million Japanese yen (approximately $1.6 million) would be required to set up the meeting; he did not state where the money would go. In testimony before Congress in 1976, Kotchian stated that he assumed it was intended for the prime minister's office. Shortly after the meeting with Kotchian, Tanaka met with Nixon and announced that ANA would be exploring purchasing aircraft from Lockheed. Lockheed and ANA commenced negotiations and, after more than two months, announced that ANA was about to order six planes with an option to buy eight more. On October 29, Okubo called Kotchian and told him that the deal would be secured if $400,000 was available the next morning, with $300,000 to go to the president of ANA and $100,000 to be divided among six Japanese politicians.

Eight months later, in August 1973, Okubo contacted Kotchian and informed him that it was time for Lockheed to honor its pledge to Prime Minister Tanaka. Okubo said that dishonoring that pledge would prevent Lockheed from ever getting contracts in Japan again. Lockheed made the payment to Tanaka.

Once Lockheed had gained entry into the Japanese aircraft market, it used bribery and corrupt business practices to maintain and expand its market share. Investigations by the U.S. Congress revealed that Lockheed had enlisted Yoshio Kodama, a Japanese businessman linked to the Yakuza, a Japanese organized crime group, to help Lockheed increase its market share in the region.

Kodama was later recognized as a notorious figure in both the United States and Japan when it emerged in 1976 that Lockheed had paid Kodama more than $2 million to influence the Japanese market away from McDonnell Douglas and Boeing and toward Lockheed. Kodama, using classic Yakuza extortion tactics, sent a gang of *sokaiya* ("shareholders' meeting men") to disrupt a meeting of ANA stockholders. The *sokaiya* spread rumors of an illegal million-dollar loan made to the president of the company, Tetsuo Oba, who had rejected Lockheed's bid for a new fleet of passenger aircraft. The pressure mounted on Oba, and he was soon forced to resign. His replacement was handpicked by Kodama, and the new president was more favorably disposed to purchasing Lockheed's wide-body jets such as the L-1011. Though the police could not uncover enough proof to prosecute Kodama on charges stemming from the Lockheed incident, they found that he had evaded taxes on more than $6 million.

On February 6, 1976, Kotchian, then Lockheed's vice chairman, took the stand in Washington, D.C., before the U.S. Senate Subcommittee on U.S. Corporations Overseas Operations and disclosed the bribery. In June 1976, former Tanaka was arrested on charges of accepting those bribes. In the United States, the scandal was heightened by the fact that Lockheed had paid a total of $22 million to Japanese and other foreign government officials, and before this was known, Lockheed had received a $250 million emergency loan guarantee from the U.S. government.

When Japan's Ministry of Foreign Affairs asked the United States for the names of officials and other evidence concerning the Lockheed case, Henry Kissinger reportedly tried to prevent release of the information, maintaining that the political stability of U.S. allies would be threatened if the scandal were to spread abroad.

A resolution asking the U.S. Senate for information was quickly passed by the Japanese Diet. One of the Japanese opposition party leaders declared that he would write a personal letter to President Gerald Ford asking for the evidence. As a consequence, Japanese prosecutors were able to get all the material they needed.

The Lockheed trial ended on October 12, 1983. Tanaka was found guilty and sentenced to four years in jail, but he filed an appeal and announced that he would not leave the Japanese Diet as long as his constituents supported him. The appellate process went on for more than ten years and was never resolved; it was concluded only when Tanaka died in 1993.

The Lockheed bribing scandal was a major embarrassment for the Lockheed corporation and the Japanese and U.S. governments. The U.S. Congress used the Lockheed bribing scandal as a springboard to launch investigations into the foreign business dealings of several U.S.

firms. In 1977, the U.S. Congress passed the FCPA, largely in response to the Lockheed bribing scandal.

See also: Corporate Crime; State-Corporate Crime

FURTHER READING

Friedrichs, David O. *Trusted Criminals: White-Collar Crime in Contemporary Society*, 2nd edition. Belmont, CA: Wadsworth, 2004.

DANIEL MABREY

M

MARTIN COUNTY COAL SLURRY SPILL. On October 11, 2000, a coal impoundment pond failed in Inez, Kentucky, near the West Virginia state line, releasing over 300 million gallons of coal slurry into two Martin County streams. Even though the release was larger than a similar spill that had caused the Buffalo Creek Flood, there were no immediate casualties (see **Buffalo Creek Flood**). The seventy-two-acre impoundment pond, which was built over an abandoned coal mine, contained a combination of water and waste from the mining process. When coal is mined, it is broken into pieces and placed in water. The clean coal floats to the top while impurities, including mercury, lead, and arsenic, sink to the bottom. Afterward the coal is removed, and the mixture of water and impurities, referred to as slurry, is stored in ponds known as impoundments. Eventually the water evaporates and the impoundment is covered with dirt.

The Martin County Coal Company, a subsidiary of the A. T. Massey Coal Company, claimed that there was a seventy-foot barrier between the bottom of the impoundment and the abandoned coal mine; however, after the pond collapsed into the mine, it was determined that the barrier was closer to ten feet. The coal slurry then exited the mine through two separate mine shafts into Wolf Creek and Coldwater Fork, eventually polluting over a hundred miles of rivers and streams.

In 1994, there had been a smaller leak at the same impoundment, and inspectors from the U.S. Mine Safety and Health Administration made recommendations for making the impound safer. The Martin County Coal Company failed to follow those recommendations, and in 1997 the agency identified the impound as having a moderate risk for failure.

When the impound pond failed in 2000, the governor of Kentucky was forced to declare a state of emergency in ten eastern counties because of water shortages. The spill also had a negative impact on wildlife, with an estimated 385,000 fish killed. Federal inspectors determined that the Martin County Coal Company could have prevented the spill, and the company was fined by a number of agencies. They were forced to pay $225,000 to the Kentucky Fish and Wildlife Service and over $600,000 in fines to various agencies in West Virginia, which was also affected by the spill. In addition, the Federal Mine Safety and Health Administration issued two federal violations and imposed the maximum fine of $55,000 for each; however, in a controversial move, an administrative judge dismissed one of the offenses and reduced the fine for the second to $5600. The Martin County Coal Company is also involved in a number of civil suits as a result of the spill and has spent over $46 million in cleanup costs.

Currently there are over 700 coal slurry impoundments nationwide, and in 1997 over one-third were classified as having a high risk of failure. Because of the Martin County coal slurry spill, there have been increased efforts to find alternative ways to deal with coal waste other than storing the slurry in coal impoundments.

See also: Buffalo Creek Flood

PAUL J. BECKER

MEATPACKING INDUSTRY. Corporations in the meatpacking industry (including beef, pork, and chicken producers) are among the most notorious of all companies with respect to their violation of societal norms and formal legislation. The practices of these companies include: the creation of workplace conditions that lead to high rates of injury and death, the violation of antitrust and immigration legislation, inhumane treatment of animals, and the introduction of unhealthy microbes into the human food chain. Despite a lengthy and well-documented record of transgressions with respect to each of these issues, companies in the meatpacking industry have been relatively immune from experiencing serious consequences for their actions at the hands of local, state, or federal governments.

The most well-known account of the meatpacking industry is Upton Sinclair's 1906 book *The Jungle.* Although critics have noted that Sinclair's account was at least partially fictional, his documentation of the treatment of slaughterhouse workers in Chicago and his graphic descriptions of the actual content of the meat consumed by humans has interesting parallels when one considers the meatpacking industry some 100 years later.

Working Conditions. Although work in the meatpacking industry has always been arduous and dangerous, between 1930 and 1970 employees in the industry were relatively well paid. The rise of the Iowa Beef Packers (IBP) company in the 1960s, however, started the industry on the path to greater consolidation, mechanization, and the relocation of meatpacking plants from urban to rural locations. In 1980, the top four meatpacking companies controlled 36 percent of the market, but by 2004 this figure approached 80 percent. Borrowing from assembly line techniques used in other industries, IBP also implemented changes in meat processing that virtually eliminated the need for skilled workers and emphasized speed in the meat production process. The other large meatpacking companies adopted similar practices, and these changes had profound implications for the wages and safety of workers in the industry. Although workers in the industry were paid close to $30,000 a year in the 1980s, many currently work for $6 to $9 per hour (roughly $13,000–19,000 per year). In 2002, meatpacking workers earned 24 percent less than their counterparts in other manufacturing sectors.

The decrease in wages of meatpacking workers has also been driven by the fact that the workforce is largely composed of immigrant laborers (many of them illegal immigrants), who are reluctant to join unions. Some of the meatpacking companies have also actively engaged in activities that prevent the formation of unions among workers at their plants, thereby decreasing the amount of worker compensation that the companies must pay. And even though wages in the meatpacking industry have been declining over time, some companies engage in additional practices that further decrease the take-home pay of their workers. Such practices include deducting pay for supplies, including knife sharpeners, nonslip rubber boots, hairnets, and earplugs—all items that are essential for their work. Surveys by the United Food and Commercial Workers organization have shown that many meatpacking employees have hundreds of dollars deducted from their wages each year for such supplies.

Not only are workers in the meatpacking industry underpaid, but these jobs are among the most dangerous in the United States, with an injury rate of more than twice the national average for industrial workers. The Bureau of Labor Statistics estimates that approximately 32 percent of meatpacking workers are injured each year, and a recent Human Rights Watch report concluded that health and safety conditions in the industry violated international laws regarding basic worker and human rights. Many of the injuries (and deaths) are the result of the speed of disassembly lines and the presence of sharp knives and dangerous equipment in the processing plants. For example, the following are some of the accidents experienced by meatpacking workers and reported by the Occupational Safety and Health Administration (OSHA): "employee killed when arm caught in meat grinder"; "employee killed when head crushed in hide-fleshing machine"; "employee caught and killed by gut-cooker machine"; "employee's legs amputated by meat-blender blades." Because of the repetitive motions involved in meatpacking work, nearly 12 percent of workers in this industry experience cumulative trauma injuries, such as carpal tunnel and tendonitis—a rate that is thirty-seven times the rate for all industries.

It is also known that at least some of the major meatpacking corporations systematically underreport injuries experienced by their workers. In 1987, for instance, IBP was fined $2.6 million by OSHA for underreporting injuries at its Dakota City plant. Further evidence of this systematic deception was provided by Edward Murphy, former safety director for a Monfort meatpacking facility, in testimony before Congress in 1992. Murphy claimed that Monfort maintained two injury report records, that the company continuously deceived OSHA, and that documents requested by OSHA were routinely shredded. In his testimony, Murphy further noted that the dangers associated with working in Monfort plants were the result of systematic procedures in which profit took precedence over worker safety, even if the pursuit of profit resulted in injuries to workers.

Violations of Antitrust and Immigration Laws. The roster of cases with respect to violations of antitrust and immigration law violations by meatpacking companies is also lengthy. In 1974, IBP was convicted of bribing both union leaders and meat wholesalers and was forced to pay a $7000 fine. In 1989, ConAgra, another major company in the meatpacking industry, systematically tampered with trucks and scales in order to mislead local retailers in the amounts of meat products delivered. These actions resulted in a $17.2 million fine against ConAgra. In 1995, the same company paid $13.6 million to settle a class-action lawsuit alleging a scheme of colluding to fix prices in the catfish industry. In 2004, a jury in Alabama issued a $1.25 billion verdict against Tyson Foods in response to its manipulation of markets that allowed the company to purchase cattle for significantly lower prices than its competitors. Although these fines appear to be substantial, they must be placed in the context of the overall sales and profits of the respective companies. It is also important to note that, in contrast to the penalties associated with the violation of laws addressing "street crimes," officials of meatpacking companies have not been incarcerated for the violation of these antitrust laws.

As noted earlier, a high percentage of workers in the meatpacking industry are immigrants, many of them undocumented immigrants. There is evidence to suggest that meatpacking companies have been complicit in hiring undocumented immigrants; for instance, in 1996, U.S. Immigration and Naturalization Service (INS) officials apprehended 147 illegal immigrants who were working at Swift and Company's pork-processing plant in Marshalltown, Nebraska. Meatpacking companies routinely send recruiting teams to Los Angeles and other locations where there are established immigrant communities; they have also advertised on radio stations along the Mexican border and sent buses to pick up individuals as they cross into the United States. It has also been documented that some meatpacking companies have provided their workers with false immigration documents.

Environmental and Health Consequences. Prior to their arrival on the slaughterhouse floor, animals are confined to factory farms that house tens of thousands of animals in relatively small areas. For example, the largest confinement facilities in Iowa contain up to 10,000 hogs, and such confinement centers produce more fecal matter than 40,000 humans. Similarly, two cattle feedlots in Greeley, Colorado, house 100,000 head of cattle each and produce more waste than the cities of St. Louis, Atlanta, Denver, and Boston combined. Not surprisingly, the foul-smelling emissions from these large-scale animal containment centers have been connected to upper respiratory and mucous membrane problems among residents who live near these centers. In addition, most of the confinement centers and meat-processing factories have inadequate sewage systems that remove the waste by storing it in artificial lagoons. The large concentrations of manure contained in these lagoons result in leakages into groundwater and irrigation systems, leading to contaminated water, polluted lands, and fish kills. Tyson Foods, which reported sales of $24.5 billion in 2003, was fined $18,400 for wastewater spills occurring at one of its plants in the Washington, D.C., area.

Because of the crowded condition of the animals in these confinement centers, large outbreaks of diseases are common. The implications of these conditions for human health are significant because these feedlots serve as the perfect breeding ground for common human pathogens such as *E. coli* and *Salmonella*. Largely because the meatpacking industry now processes extremely large quantities of ground beef on site, the number and severity of food-poisoning outbreaks have increased dramatically in recent years. Although the fear of bovine spongiform encephalopathy (BSE), better known as "mad cow disease," has slightly increased the oversight of the meatpacking industry, the U.S. Department of Agriculture (USDA) lacks the authority to recall contaminated meat or to enforce compliance with regulations through the issuance of fines. Furthermore, outgoing Secretary of Health and Human Services Tommy Thompson recently acknowledged that the poisoning of the food chain, especially in the meatpacking industry, stands as one of the major terrorist threats facing the United States. Given the lack of regulatory oversight accorded the USDA, these problems in the meatpacking industryappear to be a legitimate threat to the health of United States citizens.

Conclusion. The impacts of the corporate crime documented above become clear only when one considers the amount of meat consumed in the United States. In 2004, the average

American consumed 221 pounds of meat. Most of these meat-eating consumers are unaware, however, of the working conditions, violations of international law, and environmental and health concerns associated with the meatpacking industry.

See also: Imperial Food Plant Fire; Industrial Accidents

FURTHER READING

Bell, Michael. "Money and Machines." Pp. 65–101 in Michael Bell (ed.), *An Invitation to Environmental Sociology*. Thousand Oaks, CA: Pine Forge Press, 1998.

Cook, Christopher. "Hog-Tied." *The Progressive* (1999, September): 28–32.

Human Rights Watch. "Blood, Sweat, and Fear: Workers' Rights in U.S. Meat and Poultry Plants." Human Rights Watch Web site. Available at http://www.hrw.org/reports/2005/usa0105/usa0105.pdf. Accessed March 2005.

Schlosser, Eric. *Fast Food Nation: The Dark Side of the All-American Meal*. New York: Perennial, 2002.

Sinclair, Upton. *The Jungle*. New York: New American Library , 1971.

CHAD L. SMITH
CLAYTON MOSHER

MEDIA PORTRAYAL OF WHITE-COLLAR CRIME. Media coverage of crime and deviant behavior largely involves violent behavior, usually perpetrated by poor minorities; organizational actors rarely appear in media images of crime and deviance. Such coverage of crime results in media consumers maintaining media-generated images of crime as consisting primarily of street crime, despite the significant impact of white-collar crime. Ermann and Lundman (1996) note that organizational actions absent from common images of deviance "are frequently more personally and socially important than the individual deviance on which most people concentrate."

C. Wright Mills earlier identified the military, government, and large corporations as "the Power Elite" that shapes the United States. He also recognized the role of the media, suggesting that very little of what we know, our social reality, is shaped from first-hand accounts. He added: "[W]e often do not really believe what we see before us until we read about it in the paper or hear about it on the radio. The media not only give us information; they guide our very experiences" (Mills 1956: 311). His comments of half a century ago hold true, even though the media to which he referred was not nearly as powerful as today's media.

As times have changed and with the advent of the Information Age, one could clearly add the media to the power elite. Those people in the media who control what we see, read, and hear certainly influence our perceptions of crime. Media emphasis on street crime ultimately affects perceptions of crime from both a quantitative and qualitative standpoint. Disproportionate coverage of street crime news results in citizens being unnecessarily fearful of street crime victimization. This fear involves victimization by violent crime, although it is well established that minor crime constitutes the overwhelming majority of criminal victimization. Furthermore, limited media coverage of white-collar crime contributes to the public's failure to recognize the frequency and significance of such acts. Researchers recognize the harms associated with white-collar crime as more severe than those associated with traditional crimes.

Media coverage of crime news is affected by the manner in which media personnel gather information. Much of the information appearing in printed and televised news originates from police reports. Such information typically excludes white-collar crime, given the overwhelming attention devoted to street crime by local police departments. Relying on police reports also results in the public being unaware of the sentencing outcomes of white-collar crime cases, which typically involve civil penalties as opposed to the criminal penalties imposed on street criminals.

The hesitancy of media outlets to cover white-collar crime may result from a fear of litigation or a withdrawal of advertising funds should the media provide disparaging information regarding powerful corporations. One could also point to the inability of media consumers to comprehend the nature of many white-collar crimes or to their disinterest in such offenses as further reasons for limited media coverage.

One must bear in mind that the media do not have an obligation to cover crime precisely as it exists in our society, and media consumers are certainly permitted to use sources other than media outlets to form perceptions and beliefs. Media consumers are free to choose their sources of information; however, ownership of media outlets is increasingly shrinking to the point where a few powerful organizations own multiple outlets, leaving identifiable restrictions on freedom of choice. Media mergers have resulted in fewer corporations owning more media sources. Bagdikian (2004) used the term *media monopoly* to describe this situation in which more media outlets are being controlled by fewer groups. Media mergers have resulted in fewer gatekeepers and a tighter control of information dissemination, particularly with regard to white-collar crime.

Evidence of the media's limited portrayal of white-collar crime is found throughout the research literature on white-collar crime. For instance, Swigert and Farrell (1980) analyzed media coverage of claims regarding faulty Ford Pintos. In particular, they researchers found that newspaper reporters were reluctant to recognize Ford's behavior as deviance, and media coverage of the situation affected the State of Indiana's enforcement efforts against Ford. People familiar with the Ford Pinto case are aware that overwhelming evidence pointed to Ford's culpability. The news media are not the only media sources neglecting white-collar crime. For instance, Lynch et al. (2004) recently noted the dearth of information on white-collar crime in criminology and criminal justice textbooks and journals. They also identified limited course offerings dealing with whitecollar crime in criminology doctoral programs in the United States.

Recent media coverage of several white-collar offenses suggests that the media's historic neglect of white-collar crime may be changing. Several incidents involving high-profile corporate officials from Tyco, Firestone, Ford, Enron, and WorldCom, among others, recently received widespread coverage in the news media. Tumber (1993) identifies increased investigative reporting, the more prominent role of advocacy groups, and enhanced media efforts toward integrity as reasons for the increasing media attention to white-collar crime.

The change, however, may be stimulated by the media's historical overrepresentation of sensationalized crimes. For instance, the nature of the crimes associated with the corporations noted in the preceding paragraph include such identifiable actions as employees losing their retirement savings, automobile tires exploding and resulting in fatal accidents, and lavish spending on behalf of corporate executives. The harm caused by these crimes were identifiable to the media and to the public, whereas the bulk of white-collar crime is not as easily identifiable. In other words, the indirect harms associated with most white-collar crimes are not easily covered by the media and are thus inaccessible to media consumers.

See also: Enron; Ford Pinto

FURTHER READING

Bagdikian, Ben H. *The New Media Monopoly.* Boston: Beacon, 2004.

Cullen, Francis T., Maakestad, William J., and Cavender, Gray. *Corporate Crime Under Attack: The Ford Pinto Case and Beyond.* Cincinnati, OH: Anderson, 1987.

Ermann, M. David, and Lundman, Richard J. "Corporate and Governmental Deviance: Origins, Patterns, and Reactions." Pp. 3–44 in David Ermann and Richard Lundman (eds.), *Corporate and Governmental Deviance*, 5th edition. New York: Oxford, 1996.

Friedrichs, David. *Trusted Criminals*, 2nd edition. Belmont, CA: Wadsworth Publishing, 2004.

Grabosky, Peter, and Wilson, Paul. *Journalism and Justice: How Crime Is Reported.* Leichhardt, Australia: Pluto, 1989.

Lynch, Michael J., McGurrin, Danielle, and Fenwick, Melissa. "Disappearing Act: The Representation of Corporate Crime Research in Criminological Literature." *Journal of Criminal Justice* 32 (2004): 389–98.

Mills, C. Wright. *The Power Elite.* New York: Oxford University Press, 1956.

Reiman, Jeffrey. *The Rich Get Richer and the Poor Get Prison*, 7th edition. Boston: Allyn & Bacon, 2004.

Swigert, Victoria, and Farrell, Ronald A. "Corporate Homicide: Definitional Processes in the Creation of Deviance." *Law and Society Review* 15 (1980): 161–82.

Tumber, Howard. "Selling Scandal: Business and the Media." *Media, Culture and Society* 15 (1993): 345–61.

Wright, John, Cullen, Francis, and Blankenship, Michael. "The Social Construction of Corporate Violence: Media Coverage of the Imperial Food Products Fire." *Crime and Delinquency* 41 (1995): 20–36.

RONALD BURNS

META-REGULATION AND THE CONTROL OF WHITE-COLLAR CRIME. Although there is no universally accepted definition of the term *meta-regulation*, it can embrace two meanings. The narrower of the two refers to state supervision of the self-regulatory activities of a company or other regulated entity. The basic idea involves companywide or industrywide development and implementation of its own codes (usually subject to approval by some governmental authority), with state-imposed sanctions in the event of noncompliance. The model envisaged by this definition is still hierarchical and state-centered, although it consciously harnesses the knowledge and capacity of the regulated entity to a greater extent than would be the case in a traditional "command and control" framework based on state prescription of specified conduct, rulebook inspection, and prosecution for violations.

There is, however, much more to the regulatory process than the activities of governments. A second, much broader conception of meta-regulation would embrace activities occurring in a wider regulatory space under the auspices of a variety of institutions, including the state, the private sector, and public-interest groups. These institutions may operate in concert or may function independently.

The role of the state in this pluralistic regulatory space can vary. At one extreme, the state can be an active director. Private actors may be commanded by law to assist in the regulatory process. In most Western nations, banks have been transformed into agents of the state and have become instruments of policy to combat tax evasion, drug traffic, and money laundering. To this end, banks are required by law routinely to report transactions over a certain threshold and those transactions that are of a suspicious nature, regardless of their amount, to a governmental authority.

In addition to mandating certain conduct on the part of the regulated entity, the state may require that it interact with a number of external institutions that are in a position to exercise a degree of vigilance and control over its behavior. These controls might include, for example, requiring the company to obtain certification by an independent auditor or requiring that the company be insured.

Less coercively, the state may proffer rewards and manipulate incentives in order to induce compliance by a regulated entity. Incentives may be conferred upon a specified target of regulation or upon third parties for assistance in achieving compliance on the part of the regulatory target.

States may also delegate regulatory authority to private parties. In many common-law jurisdictions, the investigation and prosecution of alleged cruelty to animals is conducted not by government employees but by societies for the prevention of cruelty to animals. Licenses to practice medicine or to deal in securities may be conferred and revoked by professional associations. Regulatory activity, from motor vehicle inspection to tax collection, may also be contracted out to private institutions.

A less state-centered approach would see the state act as a facilitator or as a monitor of corporate social control exercised by nongovernmental institutions. Governments have begun to "steer" rather than to "row," structuring the marketplace so that naturally occurring private activity may assist in furthering public policy objectives. The term *leverage* can refer to this approach. For example, through their own acquisitions or by the strategic use of industry subsidies, governments may create markets for recycled products. Governments may confer standing on private citizens to sue polluters or fraudulent contractors.

At the other extreme, the role of government would be that of a passive observer with regulatory functions performed to a greater extent by nonstate institutions. The role of the state may be limited to being a playing field on which nonstate regulatory institutions can operate.

For example, the state may play a role in ensuring the integrity of information that is conducive to the functioning of a healthy market. Governments may develop labeling and organic certification schemes and allow consumer preferences to dictate producer behavior. Securities regulators may, for example, require disclosure of significant information to stock markets.

Market forces may themselves be powerful regulatory instruments. Consumer preferences for certain products may dictate corporate behavior. Large retailers are in a position to register their products and process preferences with suppliers, and the very substantial purchasing power that large retailers command often carries considerable influence. A buyer for a large supermarket chain may, for example, seek to examine the pesticide application audit records of a winery's contract grape growers. If the buyer is not satisfied with the kinds of chemicals used, the concentration at which they were used, and the length of time between application and harvest, the buyer will go to another winery. Buyers are thus in a position to wield more regulatory power than government officials do.

Similarly, large fast-food chains are in a position to assess their suppliers and to refuse to purchase an animal that has been administered hormones or antibiotics to promote its growth. Industry associations can withdraw accreditation or certification from a member who does not conform to required performance standards. In industries such as organic agriculture or meat export, certification may give a producer a competitive edge. Indeed, where certification is essential for access to a market, denial of such certification by an industry's self-regulatory regime can put a company out of business.

Institutional investors, such as banks, insurance companies, and pension funds, may require standards of corporate governance and environmental management by the companies in which they invest. In addition to their activities as institutional investors, banks and insurance companies may exercise considerable influence over their clients. Lenders and insurers now recognize the risk to their own commercial well-being posed by questionable practices on the part of a borrower or policyholder. Beyond the lender's obvious interest in the commercial viability of the borrower, banks must now be concerned about the environmental risks posed by any assets that they might hold as security for a loan. In the event of foreclosure, banks could end up owning a liability rather than an asset. The pressures that the banking and insurance industries can exert in furtherance of corporate citizenship can be considerable. An environmental audit report is increasingly becoming an integral part of a loan application. Banks may refuse to lend to a prospective borrower with a poor record of health, safety, or environmental performance; insurers may refuse to insure such borrowers against loss.

Entire industries have developed to assist businesses in achieving compliance. Many can justifiably claim that they can increase profit as well. Susan Shapiro refers to "private social control entrepreneurs for hire," whereas Reinier Kraakman refers to "gatekeepers." This is perhaps nowhere more evident than in the environmental services industry, in which consultants are able to assist clients in reducing the use of raw materials and energy and in reducing emissions and waste. Not only do they help client companies achieve a better bottom line; they can contribute to a positive corporate image that may be valuable in its own right.

The state in its role as regulator may itself be subject to oversight by governmental agencies, by the press, or by public interest groups. Among the significant contributions of Ian Ayres and John Braithwaite are the attention that they give to the concept of regulatory tripartism and to the constructive role that they envisage for nongovernmental actors, particularly public interest groups, to monitor the behavior not only of businesses, but also of government regulatory agencies. Ayres and Braithwaite demonstrate how an active public interest sector can energize state regulatory authorities and thereby reduce the likelihood of capture by the private sector. Third parties can also bring influence directly to bear upon companies by mobilizing adverse publicity in the aftermath of a significant violation or by dealing in a constructive manner with the firm beyond the regulatory gaze of government.

One could perhaps look to a metaphor from the prevention and control of street crime to illustrate the wider conception of meta-regulation that has been outlined here. Criminologists have recognized for quite some time that the criminal justice system is a very imperfect instrument of social control. They remind us that there are other more effective institutions of social control within society, such as the family, the educational system, the neighborhood, and the church, which constitute the first line of defense against crime. Indeed, the problem of crime and the role of the criminal justice system are likely to intensify when the influence of these other more fundamental social institutions weaken. The state may seek to intervene more or less intrusively to improve the functioning of these institutions, or it may step aside, let them fend for themselves, and then mobilize the criminal process if and when they fail. As Donald Black so elegantly put it, law varies inversely with other forms of social control. This wider conception applies to white-collar crime no less than to street crime.

FURTHER READING

Ayres, Ian, and Braithwaite, John. *Responsive Regulation: Transcending the Deregulation Debate*. New York: Oxford University Press, 1992.

Braithwaite, John. "Enforced Self-Regulation: A New Strategy for Corporate Crime Control." *Michigan Law Review* 80 (1982): 1466–1507.

Grabosky, Peter. "Using Non-governmental Resources to Foster Regulatory Compliance." *Governance* 8 (1995): 527–50.

Grabosky, Peter. "Regulation by Reward: On the Use of Incentives as Regulatory Instruments." *Law and Policy* 17 (1995): 256–81.

Grabosky, Peter. "Inside the Pyramid: Towards a Conceptual Framework for the Analysis of Regulatory Systems." *International Journal of the Sociology of Law* 25 (1997): 195–201.

Kraakman, Reinier. "Gatekeepers: The Anatomy of a Third-Party Enforcement Strategy." *Journal of Law, Economics and Organization* 2 (1986): 53–104.

Morgan, Bronwen. "The Economization of Politics: Meta-Regulation as a Form of Nonjudicial Legality." *Social & Legal Studies* 12 (2003): 489–523.

Parker, Christine. *The Open Corporation: Self-Regulation and Democracy*. Cambridge, UK: Cambridge University Press, 2002.

Shapiro, Susan. "Policing Trust." Pp. 194–220 in Clifford Shearing and Philip Stenning (eds.), *Private Policing*. Beverly Hills, CA: Sage Publications, 1987.

PETER GRABOSKY

MILKEN, MICHAEL (1946–). Michael Milken was born in the city of Encino in southern California's San Fernando Valley in 1946. His father was a successful accountant. Milken graduated Phi Beta Kappa from the University of California, Berkeley, then studied business at the Wharton School at the University of Pennsylvania. While at Wharton, he worked part-time for two years in the Philadelphia office of Drexel Harriman Ripley. After leaving Wharton in 1970, he was offered a full-time position in the research department at the Wall Street office of the firm, which had just been renamed Drexel Firestone.

Milken soon gravitated to the company's bond-trading department. Since his undergraduate days, he had been entranced by a small, arcane corner of the bond market—high-yield, low-grade bonds. These would later be renamed, reportedly by Milken himself, "junk bonds."

Most of the bonds being traded at the time Milken landed on Wall Street were investment grade and rated AAA. They were virtually risk free, but they barely yielded more than U.S. Treasury bonds. Milken's specialty, however, became the subinvestment-grade, deep-discount bonds, rated BB+ or lower. One of his professors at Berkeley had published a twenty-year study maintaining that a portfolio of low-grade bonds—if it was sufficiently large and diversified—would consistently outperform a higher-grade portfolio. Even though some of the low-grade bonds inevitably would default, the greater overall yield of the nondefaulting bonds would more than compensate, or so the theory went.

In the mid-1970s, there was little market demand for junk bonds. Investors were reluctant to go near unrated debt. In addition to the intrinsic risk, many of the bonds were issued by relatively obscure companies about whom comprehensive financial research was seldom available. Junk bonds were thus trapped in a spiral in which light trading would translate into low liquidity, which would then retranslate into light trading, and so on. But Milken, a "workaholic" of seemingly limitless energy, began to find a niche for junk bonds.

In addition to his flair for the creative nonuse of cash, Milken's success in reshaping the junk bond market can be credited to that market's almost complete lack of regulation. In 1977, Milken convinced his firm (now renamed Drexel Burnham) to underwrite new issues of high-yield bonds from heavily leveraged companies and market them directly to the public. In 1978, Milken decided to move his operation to his native Los Angeles. This move removed him from any day-to-day control by Drexel management and allowed him to expand his domain from trading and underwriting into investment banking and mergers and acquisitions. Indeed, by this time, Milken was generating almost 100 percent of Drexel's profits.

In 1987, Milken's empire began to fall. Ivan Boesky had been enrolled in a program of the Securities and Exchange Commission (SEC), derided by some as the SEC's "Frequent Liars Program," and was preparing to help build prosecutable cases against some of his associates at five major brokerage houses. He was instructed to place phone calls to everyone he had implicated and to arrange meetings. The plan was to "wire" him at those meetings and tape-record incriminating evidence. One call went to Michael Milken. Milken agreed to meet with Boesky, and in mid-October they dined in Boesky's sumptuous Beverly Hills hotel suite. The Milken–Boesky relationship had begun in 1981 when Boesky was seeking sufficient capital to become a "merchant broker"—Boesky's preferred term for a corporate raider. Boesky was after Vanguard, his late father-in-law's company, whose holdings included the Beverly Hills Hotel, where Boesky was staying (and where Boesky would secretly tape-record Milken years later).

In 1983, Milken arranged $100 million for the Vanguard (now known as the Northview) deal. Boesky began traveling regularly to Beverly Hills to oversee his interest in the hotel, so he and Milken became closer. It is no quirk that of the six charges for which Milken eventually would be convicted, four involved dealings with Boesky. The two men engaged in a number of reciprocal "parking" arrangements, in which one investor buys and holds stock for another in order to conceal the true owner's identity. The titular buyer typically is guaranteed against loss by the true owner. Parking stock with Milken allowed Boesky to circumvent SEC regulations requiring public notification of the acquisition of a 5 percent or greater stake in a company. In other words, Boesky could buy just under 5 percent himself and then buy more through Milken. For Milken, parking a stock with Boesky was useful if the purchase involved a Drexel client, restricting Milken (or anyone at Drexel) from buying it. Either way, the practice of parking stock is illegal.

In 1985, plans were drawn up for the largest arbitrage organization in history. Boesky would dissolve his corporation and raise $220 million from a new group of limited partners. Then Milken would raise $660 million with junk bonds. These funds would provide Boesky with the resources to mount a raid on almost any company. Boesky, as usual, had little trouble attracting partners to put up $220 million. Milken, on the other hand, was hard-pressed to sell investors on a $660 million arbitrage fund. Eventually, however, the money was raised. It is worth noting that $100 million of the debt was purchased by Charles Keating's Lincoln Savings and Loan, which was to figure so prominently in the S&L debacle a few years later.

Thus, when Milken and Boesky met in Boesky's hotel suite in 1987, they brought to the table a tangled history of collusion. Boesky had been coached by prosecutors on where to direct the conversation, but Milken had heard rumors of Boesky's impending hearing and behaved circumspectly. For instance, when Boesky mentioned an illegal $3.5 million kickback that he owed Milken from the arbitrage fund deal, Milken told him to keep it. At one point, Milken even warned Boesky, who was wearing a hidden recording device taped to his body, to be wary of electronic surveillance.

By mid-1988, however, Boesky was in prison, and the Milken case seemingly had stalled. Milken, moreover, had hired an aggressive public relations firm that had begun packaging him to the American people as a "national treasure." Milken, who had always been a very private man, started giving self-serving interviews to selected journalists. He even took a group of 1700 underprivileged children to a baseball game. The public was seeing a philanthropic Michael Milken at his carefully orchestrated best.

That same public saw a very different picture when Milken was subpoenaed to testify before a congressional subcommittee later that year. He immediately invoked the Fifth Amendment and refused to answer a single question. After adjournment, the chairman held an angry press conference in which he excoriated Milken, flatly accusing him of insider trading and market manipulation.

In September 1988, Milken's top salesman defected to the government in exchange for immunity from prosecution. That same month, the government filed a lawsuit against Milken and Drexel. In November, federal racketeering (RICO) charges were filed—a clear precursor to a criminal indictment. Drexel entered a plea bargain, agreeing to acknowledge wrongdoing, pay a $650 million fine (an all-time record), and suspend Milken, withholding his enormous annual bonus. On March 29, 1989, Milken was indicted by a federal grand jury on ninety-eight felony counts and RICO charges. Six months later, the junk bond market collapsed. In February 1990, Drexel filed for bankruptcy. Milken agreed to plead guilty to six counts and to pay a fine of $600 million. On November 21, 1990, Michael Milken received a ten-year prison sentence. One observer described the courtroom scene: "Milken broke down completely. He began to shriek and wail so loudly that it attracted the attention of people throughout the courthouse. Fearing that he would faint, federal marshals rushed in with an oxygen tank. Milken's hysteria had subsided only slightly by the time he got to the airport for his chartered flight back to Los Angeles: During the entire trip, he lay in his wife's arms sobbing."

Milken's sentence was later reduced to two years. After his parole in 1993, he began teaching a business course at UCLA under the oversight of Professor Bradford Cornell. The class consisted mainly of case studies of Milken's deals. One student described the class and Milken's input: "He had to win every point. . . . He would debate Cornell and, to make sure he'd won, he'd make some dig like, 'Now that kind of thinking is why Bradford is a professor.' The implication was, 'I made a billion dollars. Who are you going to listen to?'"

"Professor" Milken probably never addressed the issue of motivation in his lectures. Many people may wonder why persons earning incomes in seven, eight, or even nine figures would cheat and steal. Jaded respondents likely would counter that the question answers itself: that cheating and stealing are precisely how these individuals accumulated so much money. Greed, no doubt, is a reasonable explanation of insider trading. To Milken and his fellow travelers—indeed to so many white-collar criminals—the question "How much is enough?" is not only unanswerable, it is unworthy of consideration. One might just as well ask, "How high is up?"

See also: Boesky, Ivan; Drexel Burnham Lambert; Junk Bonds; Lincoln Savings and Loan Association; "Parking" Stock

FURTHER READING

Bruck, Connie. *The Predators' Ball: The Junk Bond Raiders and the Man Who Staked Them.* New York: Simon and Schuster, 1988.
Rosoff, Stephen M., Pontell, Henry N., and Tillman, Robert H. *Profit Without Honor: White-Collar Crime and the Looting of America*, 3rd edition. Upper Saddle River, NJ: Prentice Hall, 2004.

STEPHEN M. ROSOFF
HENRY N. PONTELL

N

NASA. The National Aeronautics and Space Administration (NASA) was created in 1958 with the mission of advancing flight-related and space technology. Throughout the years, NASA has played an important role in the advancement of science, technology, and space exploration. A federal agency unlike any other, NASA faces a number of unique challenges and difficulties. The complexity and evolution of NASA's mission, along with the political context within which it exists, place NASA in the position of being vulnerable to a variety of divergent types of behaviors that can be classified as white-collar crimes. These activities vary in terms of the entity involved (e.g., individual, organization), the nature of the offense, and the extent of fraud involved. The white-collar crimes associated with NASA are complex, difficult to define, and are not always criminal. As with other forms of white-collar crime, establishing intent is not always easy.

Detecting Offenses. White-collar crimes resulting from fraud, waste, and mismanagement are detected from a number of different sources. Much of the information on white-collar crimes comes from governmental audits and investigations conducted by agencies such as the NASA Office of Inspector General (OIG) and the Government Accountability Office (GAO). Reports conducted by presidential commissions, mishap investigation committees, and transcripts from congressional hearings on NASA present another source for identifying cases. Additional sources of information include data on criminal and administrative charges, media reports, and whistle-blower accounts. To enhance efforts to identify problems of waste and mismanagement, whistle-blower protection programs, and governmental fraud reporting hotlines have been established. The diverse sources for documenting and identifying white-collar crimes both within and against NASA demonstrate the complexity of this category of white-collar crime.

Types of Activities. Various types of white-collar crimes are associated with NASA. Although the following typology is not exclusive, it demonstrates the range of activities that can be classified as white-collar crimes. These categories include state-corporate crime, contract procurement and financial fraud, inspection failures, environmental contamination, and other offenses. For many of these activities, assessing blame and responsibility is complex. Activities often involve a complex sharing of responsibility between NASA, other federal agencies, and private contractors and corporations with which NASA conducts business.

The significance of these interrelationships complicates attempts to assess blame, determine accountability, and assign responsibility.

State-Corporate Crime. The *Challenger* disaster in 1986 and the *Columbia* disaster in 2003 have been identified as forms of state-corporate crime. State-corporate crime occurs when a harmful act results from the actions of both governmental agencies and private-sector entities working together to achieve a goal. Presidential commissions and congressional investigations following these disasters determined that the causes of these disasters went beyond mechanical failure. In both instances, responsibility and blame were placed on both NASA and the private corporations involved in designing and building the shuttle or its parts. In general, these disasters were caused by faulty parts, risky decision making, flawed communication, and an organizational culture supportive of risk taking. Although the primary cause of the *Challenger* disaster was identified as faulty O-rings in the boosters manufactured by Morton Thiokol, there is evidence that both Morton Thiokol and NASA management failed to respond adequately to problems in the O-ring design leading up to the disaster. A similar pattern of events led to the loss of the *Columbia* shuttle. The primary cause of the *Columbia* disaster was damage to the wing resulting from a piece of foam that broke off when the shuttle launched. Following the *Columbia* disaster, the *Columbia* Accident Investigation Board (CAIB) placed partial blame on NASA for maintaining an organizational environment in which safety information was not effective communicated and differences of opinion were stifled. Foam loss and the resulting damage had occurred on every previous Space Shuttle flight and the majority of other missions. Although the evidence suggests NASA was aware of the foam loss problem, NASA failed to correct the problem before the loss of *Columbia*.

Contract Procurement and Financial Fraud. Many opportunities for fraud and mismanagement exist in NASA's contract procurement and financial management processes. Because of its complex mission and structure, NASA relies heavily on the work of contractors to achieve its goals. NASA is one of the largest civilian-contracting agencies within the federal government; the agency spends more than $12 billion of its annual budget on space hardware, research, and development. Contract management remains an area at risk for fraud because of ineffective systems and processes for overseeing contractor services. Both internal management reviews and audits by the Inspector General have found that NASA's procurement and contract management processes are vulnerable to mismanagement and waste. Problems associated with the contract procurement process include inadequate cost analysis capabilities, lack of data to assess contract progress, and poor contractor oversight.

Financial auditing problems within NASA have also been documented. In 2003, a PricewaterhouseCoopers audit revealed significant errors in NASA's planned reporting schedule. The most significant errors were identified as an inability to reconcile the fund balance with the treasury, an unexplained $204 million line item in a principal financial statement, and the inability to classify transactions properly on key statements. In an attempt to deal with the financial issues, NASA has made several attempts to create an integrated system to assist with the tracking of financial transactions. The agency is, as of 2006, on its third attempt to establish a system that will effectively address controls in the areas of financial management, procurement, human resources, and logistics. In a 1997 attempt, NASA awarded a $186 million financial management contractl however, the project experienced problems, and work on it ceased in March 2000. It is estimated that the current effort will not be fully functional until 2007. Until that time, NASA remains vulnerable to mismanagement and fraud.

Financial problems continue to plague NASA with regard to the International Space Station project. In 2001, the Office of Management and Budget (OMB) placed the NASA space station project on probation, giving the organization two years to improve the credibility of the program. The decision followed an external review of the redesigns and schedule slips that delayed the launch of the space station service module. Although achievements of the space station program were exceptional, the estimated costs associated with the program grew to $4.8 billion.

Part of the credibility issue was caused by concern over Russia's difficulty in completing the propulsion module. Out of concern, NASA contracted with an independent contractor to develop a backup system. The backup system contract was canceled when it failed to meet mission requirements. The economic losses associated with the redundant system were $300 million. Contributing factors to the failed effort included a lack of contract management oversight, an incorrect definition of requirements, and lack of an early systems analysis. In July 2000, Russia was successful in launching the module.

In an effort to bring credibility to the program, NASA has reassessed and reduced projects associated with the space station program. Reductions include the cancellation of many research projects, and limitations have been placed on the number of crew members and hours devoted to on-board research.

Inspection Failure. Inspection failure occurs when NASA employees, management, other federal employees, or private contractors override, or fail to conduct, mandatory inspections of a product, process, or a mechanical part. Quality assurance problems and lack of oversight have contributed to losses of portions of NASA's products and, in some cases, entire missions. The economic losses and consequences of such inspection failures and oversight can be significant. In 2003, the National Oceanic and Atmospheric Administration (NOAA) N-Prime satellite fell as it was being moved from a vertical to a horizontal position, because a Lockheed Martin operations team had failed to secure the satellite with bolts. The NASA Mishap Investigation Board criticized both Lockheed Martin Space Systems Co., the corporation that had built the satellite, and NASA, which was responsible for overseeing the project for NOAA. As a result of the mishap, the $239 million satellite suffered damages that would cost an estimated $135 million to repair. In this case, human error and lack of oversight were key causes of the accident.

In another incident, the Mars Climate Orbiter, a $75 million system designed to observe and collect data on Mars, was destroyed upon entering Mars's atmosphere. According to the NASA Mishap Investigation team in charge of looking into the cause of the mission loss, the loss occurred because English rather than metric units were mistakenly entered in the navigation software. As a result, the trajectory was computed incorrectly, and the spacecraft was lost.

There is evidence that such inspection failures are not isolated but continue to plague the agency today. Cultural barriers exist regarding the sharing of negative lessons. In some cases, inspection failures have led to criminal charges being filed against the individuals involved. For example, in 2004 a federal criminal indictment was filed against a former NASA quality assurance specialist, charging him with eighty-three counts of fraud involving space shuttle parts and eighty-three counts of making false statements.

Environmental Contamination. Environmental pollution includes violation of federal and state environmental laws and activities that result in harm to the environment or individuals as a result of improper disposal or handling of hazardous or toxic wastes. As with other federal agencies, NASA is required to abide by federal environmental regulations. NASA is involved in several projects at its various sites in the United States where toxic and dangerous materials are produced and mishandled or disposed of improperly. Given NASA's reliance on services provided by private contractors, assessing cleanup responsibility and managing disposal of wastes is complicated. An investigation by the GAO in 1997 reported that NASA identified 913 sites that were potentially contaminated at twenty-two field facilities in ten states. The report also found that in many instances of environmental violations, NASA failed to pursue potentially responsible parties to share in cleanup costs. In some of these instances, the environmental contamination was discovered only after individuals exposed to the materials developed illnesses or other health problems.

Aside from environmental damage and health risks posed to humans, the economic costs of environmental contamination are significant. For example, the GAO cited the John F. Kennedy Space Center as having one of the largest inventory of potentially contaminated sites, the estimate to clean up the contaminated sites at this single location was $379.6 million. Although NASA is currently in the midst of determining how to handle environmental contamination at its various sites, environmental pollution remains an area of significant concern.

Other Offenses. Other types of white-collar crimes associated with NASA include occupational white-collar crimes committed by its employees either for organizational or personal gain, and unrelated offenses committed by individuals associated with NASA. With an organization as complex as NASA, many opportunities exist for white-collar crimes by employees and contractors alike. Occupational crimes that occur within NASA differ from other types of occupational crimes to the extent that NASA is unique from other types of organizations. Different forms of occupational crimes include employee theft, bid rigging, misuse of governmental property, tax evasion, filing false statements, and fraud.

NASA as a Victim. Weaknesses in the financial management system and delays in reporting have left NASA operations vulnerable to negligent behaviors and criminal fraud. A six-month investigation in 2004 conducted by the OIG led to the recovery of $3,004,370 and resulted in eleven indictments and fifteen convictions or pretrial diversions for incidents of false claims, false reporting, inappropriately charged costs, and failure to report taxable income. The OIG criminal investigations impact report in September 2004, included suspensions or debarments from government contracting of five individuals and one firm as well as eleven administrative disciplinary actions that included four NASA employees.

Responsibility and Accountability. The types of offenses associated with NASA that can be identified as forms of white-collar crime illustrate the complex, diverse types of activities that occur on both organizational and individual levels. Fraudulent activities occur both by and against NASA, victimizing the agency, the government, and taxpayers alike. Offenders include the organization, employees, corporations, and private contractors. In many instances, multiple parties are responsible. NASA's complexity, its mission, and its structure make the agency particularly vulnerable to waste, fraud, and mismanagement. When mistakes occur, regardless of the party at fault, losses can be great. NASA continues to face a number of challenges associated with identifying problems and holding the responsible parties accountable. In most cases, the losses incurred by NASA, whether due to fraud, to mismanagement, to human error, or to mistake, are absorbed and paid for by U.S. taxpayers.

See also: State-Corporate Crime

FURTHER READING

Columbia Accident Investigation Board. *Columbia Accident Investigation Board Report.* Vol. 1. Washington DC: U.S. Government Printing Office, 2003.
Kramer, Ronald C. "The Space Shuttle *Challenger* Explosion—A Case Study of State-Corporate Crime." Pp. 214–43 n K. Schlegel. and D. Weisburd, D. (eds.), *White Collar Crime Reconsidered.* Boston: Northeastern University Press, 1992.
United States v. Billy Thomas Thornton, Case No. 6:04-cr-183-ORL (M.D. Fla.), Orlando Division.
Vaughan, Diane. *The Challenger Launch Decision.* Chicago: University of Chicago Press, 1996.

RASHI K. SHUKLA
E. ELAINE BARTGIS

NEGATIVE OPTION BILLING. Negative option billing is a little-known practice, but it victimizes millions of consumers each year. Also known as negative option cancellation, repeated automatic billing, or continuous billing, the practice is widespread and occurs across a number of industries. Anyone with a telephone service, cable television, or a credit card has probably received some sort of negative option offer in the last few years. This entry discusses the practice of negative option billing, provides several examples of it, and discusses government regulation of the practice.

The Practice of Negative Option Billing and Examples. In the typical exchange between companies and consumers, the company offers a product or service for sale, and the consumer accepts that product or service through an affirmative or positive statement. In contrast, with negative option billing, the company essentially infers a buyer's acceptance of the product or service unless the buyer explicitly rejects the offer. In essence, this process inverts the generally perceived notion of what constitutes a consumer transaction.

The negative option billing plan was first introduced by the founders of the Book of the Month Club in the 1920s. The initial idea of Max Sackheim and Harry Scherman was to send a new book each month to members of the club; the book could be returned, with postage paid by the club, if the member was not satisfied with the book. In the early period of this scheme, the number of books returned and the associated postage costs resulted in reduced profits, so the club began sending members a card announcing the monthly selection. Members could then decline that month's book by returning the card before the book was mailed (Spriggs and Nevin 1996). The practice initiated by Sackheim and Scherman spawned several similar club-type plans to sell books, music, and other products.

Other examples of businesses using negative option billing include direct marketers who automatically renew subscriptions to magazines (frequently at a rate higher than the one originally agreed-upon) without the customer's explicit authorization. Internet service providers have also engaged in repeated automatic billing: for example, the Internet companies America Online, CompuServe, and Prodigy Services offered customers "free" introductory online computer services without informing them that they would be subject to automatic billing when their trial period had ended. Although the Federal Trade Commission (FTC) eventually ruled against this practice, the companies in question were not fined or otherwise penalized for their activities.

In Canada, negative billing practices on the part of cable television companies sparked a consumer revolt in the 1990s and eventually led to changes in legislation to regulate these practices. In this case, the companies began offering their subscribers seven new specialty channels. After receiving these new channels free for several weeks, customers were billed for the services unless they formally notified the companies that they wanted to cancel the channels. As is typical of the response of corporate executives responsible for these practices, the president of Rogers Cablesystems commented, "We made a mistake, and we apologize." Legislation was introduced in Canada to outlaw negative billing, providing fines of up to $25,000 for companies that engaged in the practice.

Negative billing has also been used widely by a number of companies in the United States. For instance, a radio advertisement for the "natural male enhancement product" Enzyte, made by Berkeley Premium Neutraceuticals, informs potential customers that they can receive a thirty-day free trial of the product by calling a toll-free number. Individuals who call the number are requested to provide their credit card number to pay for three months' supply of the substance, and those individuals who provide their credit card numbers receive Enzyte each month at the cost of $35 per month. Although Berkeley Premium Neutraceuticals is legally required to stop shipments to consumers who wish to have them stopped, evidence suggests that the company does so only if a consumer agency intervenes by sending a letter (Wallace 2005). A similar example involves a company selling panty hose that mailed "free" pairs of panty hose to customers. If the customer did not cancel the order after receiving the first pair of panty hose, she would begin receiving additional pairs of panty hose each month.

An additional example of negative billing involves the Sprint Spectrum phone company, which in 1997 announced that it would begin charging $4 a month to customers for insurance against loss or damage to its telephone handsets. Previously, the company had offered this insurance free of charge as part of a twelve-month service plan offered to businesses and government agencies. As one customer poignantly commented in reaction to the company's change in policy, "How can they have me sign a contract to stay with them for a year and then remove one of the reasons why I decided to sign?" (Mills 1997).

Sears, Roebuck and Company and the telemarketing firm Memberworks, Inc., agreed to pay a $2 million fine to settle a lawsuit accusing them of deceiving customers about automatic billing programs for discount services. In this case, the companies offered consumers a range of products and services, from health care to travel, without making it clear that the customers would be charged annual fees of $49 to $89 after a thirty-day trial period—customers' memberships were automatically renewed every year unless they called to cancel. Although, as mentioned, the companies were forced to pay a $2 million fine for their actions, as often happens in cases of corporate crime, neither of the two companies admitted any wrongdoing.

Regulation of Negative Option Billing. In the 1970s, the FTC held hearings to address concerns that negative billing plans serve to exploit consumers' tendencies toward inattentiveness and procrastination, thereby allowing companies to sell products without the requisite informed choice that should be the fundamental basis of all consumer transactions. Under the current federal legislation in the United States, the FTC enforces what is known as the prenotification negative option rule, which requires companies to provide consumers with information about their plans clearly and conspicuously in any promotional materials that consumers receive. Companies are thus required to inform consumers (1) whether there is a minimum purchase obligation, (2) how and when consumers can cancel their membership, (3) how many announcement and rejection forms customers will receive each year, (4) the deadline for returning the rejection form in order to avoid shipment of the merchandise (or receipt of service) in question, and (5) where relevant, whether billing charges include postage and handling. The FTC regulations further specify that if a consumer wishes to cancel his or her membership and sends a request in writing to do so, the company will be required to cancel the membership promptly. If the company sends additional merchandise after receiving the written cancellation notice from the consumer, the consumer should return the first item sent. Any additional items received can be considered unordered merchandise and can be kept as a gift by the consumer (FTC 2001).

Although these FTC rules would seem to protect consumers from being victimized by negative option billing, government regulation is incredibly lax, as in other areas of corporate crime. As of 2004, only some thirty cases of negative billing had been brought under the legislation, and it is important to note that continuity plans, which automatically send merchandise or provide services until the consumer requests they be stopped, are not covered under the FTC prenotification negative option rules.

Negative option billing is widespread in the United States and is frequently promoted in publications that cater to businesses. For example, one marketing magazine noted that negative option billing "can result in increased profitability [and] can make doing business smoother, faster, and more pleasant for customers. . . . In a busy world, consumers appreciate obtaining products and services they want in a pain-free way. . . everyone's a winner" (Rossi and Eremin 2000). It is certainly questionable whether negative option billing is "pain-free" for the millions of consumers victimized by these practices; although the loss to any individual consumer as a result of such victimization may seem relatively trivial, the profits that companies realize through these practices are enormous. If a street criminal shoplifted $3 items several thousand times from a department store, it is likely that he would eventually be incarcerated. Apparently, the same principles do not apply in the regulation of corporate crime in general and negative option billing in particular.

FURTHER READING

Federal Trade Commission. "Prenotification Negative Option Plans." 2001. Available at http://www.ftc.gov/bcp/conline/pubs/products/negative.htm. Accessed January, 2006.

Mills, Mike. "Customers Must Say No or Pay New Sprint Spectrum Charge." *Washington Post* (1997, February 28).

Rossi, Arleen, and Eremin, Don. "Continuous Billing." *Target Marketing* 23 (2000): 72–73.

Spriggs, Mark, and Nevin, John. "Negative Option Selling Plans: Current Forms versus Existing Regulations." *Journal of Public Policy and Marketing* 15 (1996): 227–37.

Wallace, David. "Host." *Atlantic Monthly* (2005, April).

CLAYTON MOSHER
CHAD L. SMITH

NIKE V. KASKY. In 1996, Nike faced growing public allegations that it ran overseas sweatshops to produce its myriad of sporting goods and apparel products. To manage its public image and maintain lucrative relationships with its various publics, Nike undertook a communication campaign, sending letters, press releases, faxes, and ads to editors, athletic directors, and university presidents across the country. The ads, letters, and press releases refuted allegations that Nike products were made in factories with unsafe working conditions and subpar wages, and they claimed that the company paid "on average, double the minimum wage" and protected its workers from abuse.

In April 1998, California consumer Mike Kasky sued Nike for unfair and deceptive practices under the state's Unfair Competition Law and False Advertising Law. Kasky claimed that "in order to maintain and/or increase its sales," Nike made false statements and engaged in "omissions of fact." He did not claim any personal damages but brought the suit on behalf of the "General Public of the State of California."

At issue in this case was the boundary for First Amendment protection of freedom of commercial speech. The First Amendment has been interpreted as protection for a diversity of opinions, especially with regard to political speech. Commercial speech has repeatedly been granted only very limited protection under the First Amendment. In this case, Kasky claimed that Nike engaged in nine different kinds of commercial speech, including its letters to university presidents, full-page ads in various publications, press releases, letters to newspapers and athletic directors, and so forth. As commercial speech, those communications would be granted limited First Amendment protection, and Nike could be held accountable if its statements were false.

Nike claimed that those communications were noncommercial political speech because they addressed matters of larger political public concern and were not advertisements designed to communicate specific commercial transactions. Nike argued that any commercial speech that addresses matters of public concern should be granted full First Amendment protection.

Decades earlier, the United States Supreme Court defined commercial speech as "speech that does no more than propose a commercial transaction" and "expression solely related to the economic interests of the speaker and its audience."

Commercial speech, if it is defined primarily in terms of advertising, is subject to various regulations specially designed to protect consumers from false or misleading claims. The case does not consider Nike's actual practices or whether its statements were false or misleading; it addresses the question of whether companies can claim First Amendment protection for statements regarding their own business practices where they involve matters of public debate. Was Nike's public relations campaign commercial speech, for which it should be held accountable?

Should companies engaging in public debate on environmental issues, for example, be exempt from the commercial speech doctrine for that communication even though it contributes to image-making efforts, investor confidence, and so forth? Should press releases, letters, and other new and novel forms of corporate communication be held to advertising standards? Are they commercial speech, too?

Despite corporate acknowledgments that nearly all decisions and actions a company makes are to boost its bottom line, California state and appellate courts ruled that Nike's statements were protected noncommercial speech. In May 2002, however, the California Supreme Court overturned those rulings, deciding that Nike's public relations effort was commercial speech and therefore entitled to only limited First Amendment protection. The court wrote, "When a corporation, to maintain and increase its sales and profits, makes public statements defending labor practices and working conditions at factories where its products are made, those public statements are commercial speech that may be regulated to prevent consumer deception." The court declared that it did not matter that Nike was responding to public allegations—its statements contributed to its image, sales, and profits and were therefore commercial speech. In 2003, the U.S. Supreme Court dismissed the case on technicalities before it was heard. Nike settled the case in California with Kasky for $1.5 million. The money went to the Fair Labor Association to monitor factories.

It seems clear that this was a missed opportunity for the U.S. Supreme Court to update the commercial speech doctrine to reflect current corporate communication practices. Very little commercial speech today simply proposes commercial transactions. Increasingly, advertisements do not even show specific products. Instead, corporations and organizations of all kinds rely on a variety of techniques and media to communicate images and emotions to create public impressions that may or may not be truthful or directly related to their products. The current commercial speech doctrine does not take the wide array of public relations practices into account. Public accountability suffers as a result. This case raises important questions about corporate accountability, but the questions have yet to be answered on a national scale.

FURTHER READING

Nike, Inc. v. Kasky, 539 U.S. 654 (2003).

REBECCA SELF

900 NUMBERS. Telephone numbers beginning with 900 in place of an area code provide callers with audio information and entertainment services ranging from stock market reports, medical services, surveys, chat lines and video game hints to psychic consultants and "adult" conversation. For these services, 900 number callers pay a charge per call or per time interval (in addition to the charge for the transmission of the call). These "*pay-per-call*" numbers were first established in 1980 by the American Broadcasting Company (ABC) for use during the U.S. presidential debates. In 1982, the National Aeronautics and Space

Administration (NASA) utilized a 900 number to provide citizens with information regarding the status of Space Shuttle flights. In 1987, 900 numbers became commercially available nationwide, and in the ensuing twenty years they have expanded into a global, multibillion-dollar enterprise.

The pay-per-call industry has developed its own jargon. *Activation* of a 900 number means that an *information provider* (IP)—the owner of the business who supplies the information and entertainment, or *program*, that the consumers will request—creates an account with a *service bureau*—a major telephone company (*telco*) that sells 900 number lines, processes incoming calls, and bills the caller. The telco tracks inbound consumer calls in terms of *daily call count* (number of calls) and *call count volume* (total minutes). The IP is remunerated for the *call count revenue* generated by consumer call count volume. Telcos offer *turnkey* 900 number enterprises for purchase by IPs, containing a complete setup with equipment and staffing.

900 number call charges can range from 50 cents per minute to $100 per call. Additional fees can be added based upon the length of the telephone call. Higher rates can range to $50 and more per minute during a call to a 900 number.

Improper disclosure to the caller regarding the cost and nature of calls account for a majority of consumer 900 number fraud complaints. Another fraudulent activity used by 900 number providers consists of switching a caller from a toll-free 800 number to a 900 pay-per-call number without the caller's knowledge or consent. Other fraudulent 900 number practices include, requesting the caller to dial a different 900 number in connection with the original call, thus incurring an additional charge, or, when the billing is per minute, delaying the caller on the line during a search for information or requiring the caller to listen to a long recorded sales pitch. 900 number providers are not required to identify anyone under eighteen years of age or ascertain whether the caller has authorization to use the telephone from which the call is made. Unscrupulous offers of credit repair, health aids, contests, dating services, sweepstake prize winnings, and awards contact are among the gimmicks utilized to entice consumers to dial 900 numbers. Contacting callers via fax, pager, or voice mail with an urgent message regarding a legal or family matter are methods used to entice callers to dial a 900 number.

The Federal Trade Commission (FTC) 900 Number Rule requires providers of 900 number audio information and entertainment to disclose certain information in 900 number services. Ads for 900 number calls must state the total cost of the call for flat fee or per-minute rates, the minimum charge, the length of the call, cost of transfer to other 900 numbers, and any other fees charged to the caller during the 900 number call. Printed ad information for 900 numbers may not be published in fine print and must contain audio disclosure information.

For 900 number calls with charges of more than two dollars, callers must hear a preamble message advising the cost of the call, a brief description of the service, and the name of the company providing the service. Callers must also be advised that anyone under the age of eighteen must have parental permission to continue the call. Callers are to be provided a three-second time frame after the preamble message to hang up without acquiring charges.

The Federal Communications Commission's regulations prohibit the disconnection of consumer regular local and long-distance phone services for nonpayment of 900 number charges. 900 number charges billed to a caller's local phone bill should include the date, time, the audio service provided, and the length of the call. Billing for 900 number charges must be listed separate from local and long-distance charges on the consumer's phone bill. Pay-per-call charges appearing on billing statements must include a toll-free or local number for the consumer to contact regarding the charges.

Not all 900 number providers are engaged in deceptive or fraudulent business activities. 900 numbers provide a vehicle of convenience for selling information and technical support services. The consumer who is unsuccessful in resolving 900 number billing charge disputes or has been subjected to a fraudulent 900 number scheme may contact the FCC, the FTC, their state's attorney general, or the Better Business Bureau.

FURTHER READING

Federal Communications Commission. "900 Number Pay-Per-Call and Other Information Services." Consumer and Governmental Affairs Bureau. Available at http://www.fcc.gov/cgb/consumerfacts/900Fact.html.

Federal Trade Commission. "900 Numbers: FTC Rule Helps Consumers." Federal Trade Commission, Available at http://www.ftc.gov/bcp/conline/pubs/tmarkg/nine.htm.

900 Profits. "900 Number Business Facts: About the 900 Business." 900 Profits. Available at http://900profits.com/900facts.html.

Open Encyclopedia. "900 Number." *Open Encyclopedia*. Available at http://open-encyclopedia.com/900_number.

The Better Business Bureau. "Calling '900' and '809' Telephone Numbers." The Better Business Bureau. Available at http://www.vegasbbb.org/release.html.

U.S. Code: Title 47, Section 228. "Regulation of Carrier Offering of Pay-Per-Call Services." Available at http://straylight.law.cornell.edu/uscode/47/228.html.

U.S. Postal Inspection Service. "900 Telephone Number Schemes." U.S. Postal Inspection Service. Available at http://www.usps.com/websites/depart/inspect/900.htm.

CHRISTINE ABEL NIX

NORTHERN PACIFIC RAILROAD STOCK RUN OF 1901. The Northern Pacific Railroad stock run of 1901, also known as the Northern Pacific Corner, was a week-long clash between two railroad tycoons: Edward Henry Harriman and James E. Hill. This epic battle was an attempt for both men to gain control of the Northern Pacific Railroad. The trading battle boosted the price of common stock from $101 a share all the way up to $1,000 a share, wreaking havoc throughout the stock market.

The Northern Pacific Railroad was created through an Act of Congress signed by President Abraham Lincoln on July 2, 1864. The railroad company was licensed to expand a railroad line westward from the Great Lakes. The railroad would begin at Lake Superior in either Minnesota or Wisconsin and end in the state of Oregon in or near Portland.

After several early American entrepreneurs had attempted to take over the Northern Pacific Railroad Company and take on the massive project of building the railroad to the west, the company found itself financially bankrupt in 1893. This bankruptcy was in large part a result of building numerous branch lines from the main artery of the railroad in an attempt to increase economic power.

However, in 1896, J. P. Morgan and Company, which had already attained fame for reorganizing several railroad lines and was currently in the process of reorganizing several eastern railroad systems (the Erie, the Reading, the Baltimore and Ohio), and James J. Hill, a railroad tycoon who had been extremely successful with the Great Northern Railway, acquired large interest in the company at a bargain price. Working together, Morgan and Hill became strong minority owners.

Edward Henry Harriman, who had an extensive history with various railroad companies including the Illinois Central and the Union Pacific, wanted to gain control of the Northern Pacific railroad line. Harriman and Hill had been bitter business rivals for many years. In the previous year Harriman had attempted to buy into the Burlington rail system through a purchase of a one-third interest from Hill, but Hill rejected the offer.

In 1901 Harriman, in an attempt to undermine his bitter rival, decided to turn his attention toward the Northern Pacific. He had been quietly purchasing shares of the company's stock throughout the past year and had decided to try for a takeover in 1901. In April of that year, Northern Pacific Railroad stocks were trading at $102 per share for common stock and $101 for preferred stock.

On Friday, May 3, Harriman purchased several thousand shares of the company's stock through Kuhn, Loeb & Company. At the end of the day he had accumulated over 370,000 shares of the company's common stock and almost 420,000 shares of the company's preferred stock. On May 4, Harriman ordered Kuhn, Loeb & Company to purchase 40,000 more shares of common stock, but his partner, Jacob Schiff of Kuhn, Loeb, canceled the order because he knew that, as a result of the large purchases on May 3, Harrison already owned a majority of all the company's stock and believed it was a waste of money to purchases more.

In a panic to prevent Harrington from seizing majority ownership, Morgan and Hill bought 150,000 shares of Northern Pacific's common stock on Monday, May 6, as soon as trading began. The stock price shot up to close at $130 a share that day. The following day, May 7, the price continued to rise to a market value just under $150 a share. The next day the price of the stock kept its rapid increasing pace and closed at $180.

As the price of the stock rose, numerous traders came to believe that the price would eventually fall back, so they sold it short—that is, they sold shares they did not own to their investors at a high price for later delivery, expecting to buy the shares and then deliver them after the price fell. Instead, the stock continued to soar. On May 9 the common stock of Northern Pacific hit record highs. Shares were being traded at $700 and actually peaked at $1,000 a share, a Wall Street record. The short sellers, stuck for these record prices, tried to raise the cash by frantically selling off their other stocks. Panic ran throughout the stock market, and numerous stocks went crashing downward, many being totally eliminated from market competition. U.S. Steel is reported to have fallen from $46 a share all the way down to $24 a share, practically cutting its trade price in half.

When the Northern Pacific stock run was over at the end of May 9, Harriman owned over 780,000 shares of the company's stock (preferred and common). Even though he owned a majority of the stock, he had failed to take control of the common stock by anywhere between 30,000 and 40,000 shares, which he would have held had Schiff followed through with Harriman's orders the preceding Saturday.

According to a recent reorganization of the company, company policy allowed the common stockholders to vote for the retiring the preferred stock annually at the start of the year for several years to come. As a majority holder of the stock, Harriman could dictate who would serve on the board of directors. However, he could not ensure that the preferred stock would not be retired. Therefore, a compromise between Harriman and Hill was made.

The compromise ensured that Harriman would have members serving on the board of directors, which included William Rockefeller, while Morgan and Hill would retain control of the company, and the two would settle all stockbroker dilemmas. To avoid future problems, Hill established a holding company, the Northern Securities Company, which oversaw Northern Pacific and other railroad lines that either Hill or Harriman controlled (including the Burlington). However, as a result of lawsuits by both the state of Minnesota and the federal government, the U.S. Supreme Court deemed the Northern Securities Company illegal under the Sherman Antitrust Act. The company was ordered to divest itself of stock in 1904.

FURTHER READING

Holbrook, Stewart H. *James J. Hill.* Random House of Canada Limited. New York: Alfred A. Knopf, 1967.

Mercer, Lloyd J. *E. H. Harriman: Master Railroader.* Twayne Publishers, Boston. G.K. Hall & Company, 1985.

Moody, John. *The Railroad Builders: A Chronicle of the Welding of the States.* New Haven: Glasgow, Brook & Co., 1919. Available at http://www.nubond.net/railroad/index.html.

GEORGEN GUERRERO

NURSING HOME FRAUD. Nursing homes offer a unique opportunity for fraud against insurance companies, Medicare and Medicaid. Many nursing homes have participated in "gaming" billing. Examples of gaming include unnecessary services, excessive prices, and fraudulent charges. Many private insurance companies have lawyers and investigators at their disposal to examine allegations of abuse and fraud, but Medicare and Medicaid provide an open door to fraud because of government bureaucracy and lack of oversight. Nearly 3 million people in nursing homes are covered by Medicare and Medicaid, and each year they pay about $50 billion for nursing care of all kinds. In order to understand the potential fraud in nursing homes, one has to understand how Medicare and Medicaid are paid to nursing home care.

Medicare Part A provides up to 100 days of coverage after hospitalization for stays in skilled nursing homes; after 20 days, the patient must make a daily copayment of $95. This is the fastest-growing part of the Medicare program, doubling about every five years in number of beneficiaries and cost.

Medicare Part B covers the medical supplies and services, whether or not they are in a nursing home, such as psychotherapy, lab services, and wound care. It pays 80 percent of the approved amount based on a fee schedule; the remaining 20 percent and the $100 deductible are paid by the individual. Payments from Medicare Part B are about $5 billion dollars.

Medicaid covers nursing home care for low-income families and individuals. Medicaid will provide for nursing home care only in Medicaid-certified facilities. Whereas Medicare will pay only for post-hospitalization skilled care, Medicaid pays for both skilled and long-term care. It also pays for intermediate care facilities. The costs for this program exceed about $40 billion a year.

Nursing home residents can be particularly vulnerable to fraud because they are often accessible and unprotected. Care for nursing home residents may be based on financial incentives rather than medical necessity. Some services can be reimbursed under more than one payment category, a situation that, of course, weakens oversight of expenditures and services. For example, investigations by the Department of Health and Human Services found that 32 percent of mental health services were unnecessary. They also found that Medicare beneficiaries were being billed for services that were never performed and supplies that were never distributed. Physicians decide which patients need supplies, but the suppliers determine the amount that is provided to the patient. One individual was charged $11,880 for wound filler when only $350 was necessary. Nursing homes have been offered incentives in exchange for allowing suppliers to provide products to patients in their facilities.

Hospice services have recently become a concern of federal investigators. They have found that as many as 20 percent of patients enrolled in hospice care are erroneously referred to the program. Also, some nursing home operators have control over the specific hospice they will permit to provide services to their residents. An exclusive arrangement with a nursing home to provide hospice services to the residents can net a substantial profit for the hospice provider. Sometimes, nursing home operators may request an illegal payoff to influence their decision to allow a particular hospice to provide services. Methods in which these payoffs are made include the hospice offering free goods, paying "room and board" payments to the nursing home that exceed the amount paid by Medicare, and the hospice referring patients to a specific nursing homes.

The U.S. Department of Health and Human Services (HHS) states that it is continuing to increase its investigations into the fraud that is rampant in nursing homes; however, there has been little progress. HHS believes that an increase in administrative awareness is not enough to solve the problem and that the answer lies in legislation. Changes in the payment methods and oversight of both the Medicare and Medicaid would likely decrease this fraud and increase the quality of care for millions of nursing home patients.

See also: Health Care Industry; Insurance Company Fraud

FURTHER READING

U.S. General Accounting Office. *Fraud and Abuse: Providers Target Medicare Patients in Nursing Facilities.* Washington, DC: General Accounting Office, 1996.

SHIYLOH L. DUNCAN

OCCUPATIONALLY RELATED DISEASES. Hazardous working conditions for laborers have been present since the existence of primitive societies. These occupational hazards can produce traumatic injuries (such as broken bones, burns, head injuries, and the loss of limbs) or occupationally related diseases, which may include physical deterioration and illness caused by repeated exposure to certain materials or processes over time. Throughout history, the health and safety of workers have been an issue of varying concern, but apparent increases in occupationally related diseases over the last century have resulted in more widespread awareness of potential health problems caused by conditions in the workplace. Research indicates that long-term exposure to small amounts of chemicals can cause nerve damage, increase the risks of cancer, and cause other diseases of the lungs, heart, skin, and other tissues. Repetitive movements required by some jobs may cause permanent physical ailments and disabilities. Even severe job-related stress may contribute to heart disease and other health disorders.

Now with the knowledge that certain kinds of employment can lead to dangerous physical ailments, workers have asked for government intervention to make workplaces safer and to provide compensation to employees for the perilous jobs that they do. Employers, arguing that their businesses cannot afford to change certain work practices and increase the monetary compensation available for their employees, have asked that the responsibility of maintaining work safety standards be strictly voluntary and that the government not get involved. To protect business interests and save expenses, some businesses unfortunately resort to illegally concealing known hazards from employees. The results of these criminal coverups can be tragic. In some exceptional circumstances, businesses may be criminally prosecuted. This, however, is rare, because intent is difficult to prove legally. Even when businesses are not overtly or knowingly breaking the law when it comes to maintaining worker safety standards, they may be found criminally negligent for exposing employees to certain workplace conditions.

Statistics indicate that occupationally related diseases have grown more problematic in recent decades. However, public policies designed to address these risks that workers face remain relatively limited, even when compared with policies dealing with injuries sustained while working. This lack of social policy pertaining to occupationally related diseases has been considered a troubling phenomenon by many, because recent statistics indicate that deaths resulting from occupational disease exceed 55,000 a year. Even so, the magnitude and prevalence of diseases acquired while working are most likely underestimated.

Background. Occupational hazards leading to disease have been documented since ancient times. Humans in early societies are believed to have contracted anthrax while skinning animals. Records also indicate that Roman slaves who were forced to mine were exposed to mercury fumes; that grinders in the sixteenth century contracted "grinders' disease" from inhaling silica; and that early printers, glass manufacturers, and those in the ceramics trade suffered lead poisoning. The Industrial Revolution brought increased work-related health hazards, since many new materials and occupational techniques for processing were implemented with no consideration of possible side-effects for employees.

In the 1970s, studies on the possible health risks posed by certain types of work environments emerged. Research lead by the U.S. Council on Environmental Quality found that approximately 700 new chemicals were introduced to the workplace to each year. Around the same time, the National Institute for Occupational Safety and Health (NIOSH) estimated that 880,000 workers were regularly exposed to various cancer-causing agents and other toxic substances during the course of the work day. Many of the illnesses caused by conditions at work were not previously recognized as occupationally related, since, unlike occupationally related traumatic injury, workers typically developed symptoms of disease only gradually after long-term exposure. Therefore, most efforts to decrease the danger of occupational hazards prior to the 1970s involved measures to prevent traumatic injury, such as installing guards on machines, implementing safety precautions, and providing helmets and other safety gear for workers. The first federal action to deal with a severe occupationally related disease was the Federal Coal Mine Safety and Health Act of 1969. This law set standards for coal dust in mines and provided federal compensation to miners afflicted with black lung disease. Shortly thereafter, Congress enacted the Occupational Safety and Health Act of 1970 (OSH Act), which covered a wide range of workplaces and allowed for the creation of the Occupational Safety and Health Administration (OSHA). OSHA was to be responsible for research related to workplace hazards, among other things.

Recent Findings. Current research allows us to know much more about occupationally related diseases and prevention measures. There is extensive international medical research indicating that chronic fatal diseases that occur later in life are caused by occupational exposures earlier in life. Among the first studies of this relationship were those on certain carcinogens, such as asbestos, arsenic, benzene, chromium, nickel, and petroleum. Researchers estimated that between 4 and 20 percent of all cancer deaths were due to occupational factors. More recently, medical research has shown that occupationally related diseases also include circulatory, chronic respiratory, renal, and neurological diseases. Specific cancers, such as lung, bladder, and leukemia have been the subject of more recent research implicating work conditions, as have new job-related diseases such as tuberculosis and hepatitis C. For example, studies on lung cancer caused by the workplace find that 31 percent of employees are exposed to arsenic, asbestos, beryllium, cadmium, chromium, diesel fumes, environmental tobacco smoke, nickel, radon, or silica.

Other types of problems can also arise from the kind of occupation one has. Those whose work involves repetitive movements, for example, may suffer various diseases. Administrative assistants who type as a regular responsibility of their jobs may eventually develop carpal tunnel syndrome, a disease that affects the joints and tendons in the hands and wrists, which may cause numbness and a loss of hand and arm function. Meat packers, computer operators, postal workers, bus drivers, and phone operators may also incur similar problems because of repetitive movements required by their jobs. Anyone with a desk job who sits for extensive periods of time may suffer circulatory, muscular, or spinal problems. Those whose work requires staring at a computer screen or printed documents for much of the day may suffer eye diseases.

Prevalence and Magnitude. In the United States the impact of occupationally related diseases is substantial. The NIOSH estimates that 3.6 million occupational illnesses and injuries are treated by hospital emergency rooms every year. In 2003 the Bureau of Labor Statistics (BLS) reported 294,500 occupationally related illnesses that year. The number of deaths attributable to occupationally related diseases varies, but recent estimates suggest that they exceed 55,000 per year.

It is so difficult to determine the exact number of illnesses and deaths caused by work-related factors because there is some difficulty linking illness to occupation. The problem is that there are many possible causal factors contributing to the development of various diseases, so the challenge is in establishing whether a particular disease was caused by an individual's job, hereditary influence, nutritional factors, or something else in one's life. For example, doctors have trouble differentiating non–occupationally related breathing problems from breathing problems caused by work conditions. Certain other symptoms, such as headaches, stomach pains, or dizziness, are extremely diffuse and may be the result of countless causes. Even the expected process of aging is associated with the onset of various diseases.

There is another challenge to those measuring the magnitude and prevalence of occupationally related diseases. Occupational risk factors and associated health problems contribute to various diseases, which means that we cannot conclude with certainty that workplace exposures may lead to any particular disease. Exposure to asbestos fibers, for example, may lead to asbestosis, cancer, or general breathing problems, but there is no method to predict which disease a person might suffer or whether the person will develop any of these diseases at all.

Legal Responses. The first laws designed to enhance the safety of workers passed in the mid-1800s. For the most part, these policies required employers to take only minimal precautions to safeguard their employees. At the beginning of the twentieth century, state-mandated workers' compensation programs were established in an attempt to settle disputes that had arisen between employers and employees concerning job related health problems. In the 1970s, the first federal occupational health program was enacted to reduce workers' exposure to hazardous materials. Legal consequences for those who endangered employees were increased in the 1980s, when some employers were criminally prosecuted for causing the injury or death of workers. Though successful prosecutions were still limited at this point, neglect of potential health threats presented by the workplace was for the first time considered a criminal act for employers. Today, the primary means of recourse for conditions that cause occupationally related diseases is through administrative regulation.

Costs. Costs related to occupationally related diseases are categorized as either direct or indirect. Direct costs include hospital and physician bills, medicine, insurance payments, rehabilitation, home or nursing home care, and medical supplies and equipment. Indirect costs include wages losses due to illness, household production losses, and employer productivity losses, which include recruiting and training replacements for ailing workers. Costs of occupationally related diseases vary according to several factors, including the type of illness acquired, the pre-existing health conditions of individuals, and the type of care or rehabilitation required. For example, asthma generally requires a great deal of outpatient care but relatively little inpatient care, resulting in higher initial costs but lower costs overall than some other diseases, such as cancer.

Occupationally related diseases are very costly to American society. Comprehensive estimates of the cost of occupationally related disease range between $128 billion and $155 billion per year and result in 49,000 to 74,000 deaths. This has a tremendous impact, as one may see by comparing this statistic to the 19,272 deaths caused by leukemia, 25,488 caused by homicide, 38,813 deaths caused by HIV/AIDS, 50,067 deaths from diabetes, and 143,769 deaths from strokes in 1992. In terms of financial impact, occupational diseases accounted for more than five times the cost of HIV/AIDS, three times the cost of Alzheimer's disease, 91 percent of the cost of cancer, and 82 percent of the cost of heart disease.

One means for receiving financial compensation for the losses incurred because of these diseases is made available to employees via workers' compensation lawsuits. Workers' compensation attorneys sue businesses on behalf of their ailing clients in order to compensate them for the financial burden caused by working for that company. Workers' compensation laws, approved by every state's legislature by 1949, provide that employees no longer need to prove in court that employers were negligent in allowing them to be exposed to hazardous conditions. Instead, businesses must have insurance to compensate diseased workers when their illnesses are work related. Unless an employee can prove that employers were aware of the health risk and intentionally exposed workers to that risk, torts will be unsuccessful. This means that the workers' compensation system is the exclusive remedy for occupationally diseased workers. However, this also means that workers with work-related diseases do not have to wait through the delays inherent in a civil trial to receive compensation. Instead, this "no fault" remedy ensures immediate compensation for some lost wages, medical expenses, and rehabilitation services.

Though there are now workers' compensation laws requiring employers to pay for a great portion of employee medical conditions arising from their occupational responsibilities, the resulting compensation does not adequately cover the expenses incurred by diseased employees. In 2002, employers paid $72.9 billion in workers' compensation premiums, but, considering the direct and indirect costs of occupationally related diseases, workers end up having to pay a good portion of the expenses themselves. Even when compensation claims are successful, however, a large share of the burden of occupationally related diseases is endured by the workers themselves. Workers' compensation systems were designed to provide only temporary relief until workers could return to their jobs, but even so, statistics indicate that typical workers receive only from one-half to two-thirds of their normal wages while recuperating. In addition, some workers attest that there are delays in obtaining payments, resulting from disputes with employers or administrative inefficiency. Frequently, employers contest the charges of their employees seeking compensation, because they believe the disease was not work-related or that it is not covered by relevant laws.

Although some workers are able to obtain large damage awards, most are unable to launch successful tort actions. It is also rare that the insurance companies are forced to pay for the future loss of wages of workers, even when the worker is so ill that he or she is never able to work again or dies as a result of the disease. Additionally, recent laws have been passed—such as one in California—that severely restrict the conditions under which employees may sue their companies and the amount that they may recover in damages.

Cultural Response. Cultural factors may play a very important role in recognizing the dimensions of occupationally related diseases. Health hazards incurred by employees in certain lines of work are acknowledged by the health and legal communities of most countries. However, it may be that culturally mediated values and expectations of governmental support may lead some to come forward with medical complaints, while others may suppress their symptoms or criticize others for making claims of occupationally related disease.

Some research concludes that those who argue that the causes of various illnesses are too easily ascribed to certain work conditions without having strong supporting evidence have opinions based on cultural beliefs and backgrounds. These arguments suggest that in some cultures frequent complaints such as back pain, general malaise, headaches, and any other series of symptoms associated with what has been termed "sick building syndrome" are primarily determined by psychological factors relating to happiness with one's job. Others argue that workers choose the job that they have as well as the hazards that accompany any particular kind of work. These arguments suggest that as long as workers are aware of the risks involved in their chosen occupations, they accept the job at their own peril and should not receive compensation from their employers for any diseases that result. As it was in the United States during the 1950s and 1960s, perhaps differing work ethics influence beliefs about whether people should complain about their employers, even if the complaints are medical in nature.

See also: Asbestos; Black Lung; Brown Lung Disease; OSHA

FURTHER READING

Epstein, Samuel S. *The Politics of Cancer.* Garden City, NY: Doubleday, Anchor Press, 1979.

Frank, Nancy. "Maiming and Killing: Occupational Health Crimes." *Annals of the American Academy of Political and Social Science* 525 (1993): 107–118.

Kogevinas, M. "The Importance of Cultural Factors in the Recognition of Occupational Disease." *Occupational and Environmental Medicine* 62 (2005): 286.

Leigh, J. Paul, and Robbins, John A. "Occupational Disease and Workers' Compensation: Coverage, Costs, and Consequences." *The Milbank Quarterly* 82 (2004): 689–721.

Schulte, Paul A. "Characterizing the Burden of Occupational Injury and Disease." *Journal of Occupational and Environmental Medicine* 47 (2005): 607–622.

Steenland, K., Burnett, C., Lalich, N., Ward, E., and Hurrell, J. "Dying for Work: The Magnitude of U.S. Mortality from Selected Causes of Death Associated with Occupation." *American Journal of Industrial Medicine* 43 (2003): 461–482.

Storey, Robert. "Activism and the Making of Occupational Health and Safety Law in Ontario (1960s–1980)." *Policy and Practice in Health and Safety* 3 (2005): 41–68.

U.S. Department of Health and Human Services, Public Health Service, Centers for Disease Control, National Institute for Occupational Safety and Health *Report on Occupational Safety and Health for FY 1985 under Public Law 91-596.* Washington, DC: NIOSH, 1986, p. 1.

KELLY WELCH

OSHA. Occupational safety and health legislation is not a topic commonly addressed in the criminological literature. No discussion of contemporary labor conditions in America is complete without an understanding of why and when occupational health and safety laws were created, what types and in what context these laws were developed, and what influences have helped shape the makers, breakers, and enforcers of occupational safety and health laws. Such an understanding also includes an appreciation of the coalescing economic, political, and social forces behind occupational safety and health legislation and the relationship between regulatory failures and state-corporate malfeasance.

Early History of U.S. Occupational Health and Safety Legislation. Although the American industrial revolution began in the late eighteenth century, the safety and health considerations of factory and other laborers were almost entirely ignored by governments for nearly one hundred years. Labor legislation in general came only after years of extreme labor abuses and intense struggle in states most populated by the major waves of European migration. Likewise, many of the earliest laws aimed at protecting the health and safety of workers were created in the most industrialized states, including Massachusetts, New York, New Jersey, Pennsylvania, Ohio, and Illinois.

Home to one of the nation's first industries, Massachusetts passed the first child labor law, created the first bureau of labor statistics, and in 1877 passed the first state factory inspection law in the country, allowing for government-paid factory inspectors. By 1890, twenty-one states had some type of worker health standard concerning accident prevention and workplace ventilation, and by 1920 thirty-five states had health and sanitation provisions, some of which required hazardous-dust and -fume removal for selected industries. Standards varied widely by state and were largely enforced by inspectors who had little or no scientific background or training.

Related to this history, workers' compensation laws, commonly regarded as the catalyst for industrial hazard prevention by employers, began to be introduced early in the twentieth century. Coverage began with civil employees, and by 1950 all states had enacted some form of workers' compensation. The fact that workers' compensation laws developed more rapidly than worker health and safety laws most likely reflected the privileging of business interests in being able to determine the conditions of the work environment. With workers' compensation legislation only, businesses were able to control what health and safety practices they wished to adopt in the workplace rather than being subject to the costlier and more burdensome state-mandated requirements.

By the middle of the twentieth century, industrial hygiene programs were being developed and legislated in most states. Industrial hygiene is the science of the study and control of occupational disease and other environmental factors affecting employee health. At the federal level, issues of occupational health during this time were mainly research topics rather than the focus of targeted legislation. Not until 1936 did the federal government finally become involved in occupational safety and health regulation with the passage of the Walsh-Healey Public Contracts Act. The Walsh-Healy Act allowed the Department of Labor to dictate certain safety standards for federal government contract work. A decade later, the Labor Management Relations Act (LMRA) contained a safety and health provision that allowed employees to walk off a job that was "reasonably believed" to be especially dangerous.

The year after the LMRA's passage, President Harry Truman initiated the first conference on industrial safety. The Eisenhower Administration continued this tradition, though no substantive legislative advancements were seen in worker health and safety legislation until the mid-1960s. The increasing costs of insurance claims and workers' compensation payments, coupled with lost production time, were believed to be sufficient incentives for most employers to provide safe workplaces. The rationale was simple: the safer the workplace, the more time employees would spend on the job and the greater the overall level of production.

Increased productivity and efficiency for industry and increased compensation for labor, however, did not necessarily translate into safer workplaces. Safety standards at the time were narrow, largely cosmetic, and poorly enforced by inspectors lacking the necessary professional training in such key fields as medicine, engineering, and chemistry. Moreover, workers' compensation payments by employers did not provide the expected deterrent effect.

From the 1960s to the Emergence of the OSH Act. The limited role of the government began to widen in the 1960s with the congressional enactment of a collection of acts that, as before, covered only a limited number of employees and industries. In 1965, however, the Public Health Service published the report *Protecting the Health of Eighty Million Workers* (most commonly known as the Frye Report). Although the specific recommendations of this report were not adopted, it drew the attention of health professionals to workplace safety and health issues that had not existed previously, and it would later inform successful legislation.

Following the release of the Frye Report, President Lyndon Johnson proposed an occupational safety and health program like none previously in place in the U.S. Despite the fact that by the late 1960s job-related accidents accounted for more than 14,000 annual deaths, 2.5 million disabilities, and an estimated 300,000 new cases of occupational disease, industry employers eschewed the program proposal and blocked the passage of Johnson's legislation, known as S.2864 and H.R. 14816.

In 1969, the 91st Congress took up the issue again, where a pair of bills was introduced in both the House and Senate. After much political debate, a compromise was struck between the more capital and labor friendly versions of the worker safety and health bills. On December 29, 1970, President Richard Nixon signed the Occupational Safety and Health (OSH) Act into law.

The OSH Act "assure[d] so far as possible every working man and woman in the nation safe and healthful working conditions" (OSHA 2003: 2). In addition to creating the Occupational Safety and Health Administration (OSHA), the OSH Act created the National Institute for Occupational Safety and Health (NIOSH) as its research branch under the Department of Health, Education, and Welfare (later Health and Human Services). NIOSH researches various occupational safety and health problems, provides technical assistance to OSHA, and recommends official standards to be considered by OSHA for policy adoption. The OSH Act also created the Occupational Safety and Health Review Commission (OSHRC), which reviews appeals and contested inspection, results by businesses.

Under the purview of the Act, the Assistant Secretary of Labor (also known as the OSHA Director) was granted authority to enact the following:

> Promulgate safety and health standards; conduct inspections and investigations, issue citations and propose penalties; set abatement fines for correcting unsafe or unhealthy

work conditions; require employers to keep records of job-related injuries or illnesses; petition the courts to restrain imminent danger situations; approve or reject state plans for administering and enforcing the Act; provide information and advice to employers and employees concerning compliance; and provide evaluative, consultive, and promotional programs to assist federal agencies in implementing job safety and health programs for federal employees. (OSHA 2003: 3)

OSHA: The First Decade. Although Nixon signed the OSH Act into law and effectively created OSHA and NIOSH, OSHA remained largely symbolic during its first few years. Immediately after OSHA's passage, the Nixon administration adopted the relatively lax 450 health standards used by the old Bureau of Labor Standards. The old labor standards were largely developed by private industry over the course of several decades, and most were created with little or no scientific evidence to support their adoption.

During OSHA's first three years, only three new health standards were adopted. Further, OSHA failed to use package regulations on fourteen suspected carcinogens, favoring instead the more limited approach of individually based regulations. Likewise, in enforcement, few inspectors were recruited to the new agency, and the relatively rare application of fines offered little deterrent value. In the early years, the average fine for violating a safety or health standard was less than $50, and the maximum fine for the most serious violations averaged only $625. Another problem in the early years was OSHA's small-business focus. By centering mostly on small businesses, OSHA antagonized a group that would later use the rallying call of "entrepreneurial freedom" to successfully stymie many OSHA initiatives. This antistate intervention, antiregulatory populism was later employed by the Reagan and both Bush administrations, which were generally inimical to state intervention in the workplace.

Following President Jimmy Carter's election, OSHA had mixed success. At the beginning of his term, Carter seemed committed to maintaining OSHA's presence by appointing Dr. Eula Bingham, who ran the agency from April 1977 until January 1981. Bingham issued rules on cancer policy, benzene, cotton dust, lead, employee access to exposure and medical records, chemical labeling (right to know), and hearing conservation. Bingham also challenged businesses for adopting opposition to OSHA regulations as a basic strategy.

Despite Bingham's best efforts, neither she nor subsequent administrators could alter the fact that OSHA was designed with a stronger directive than its resources would allow. By the late 1970s, priorities began to shift with the economic crisis, and Carter grew increasingly concerned about the burden that the OSH Act would place on businesses. More and more, regulation became dictated by "cost-benefit" analysis, which effectively limited the role of government when such action threatened the economic success of business. And, as in the past, final standard setting continued to progress at a glacial pace.

OSHA: The Deregulation Years. After Carter left office, the mild gains made by OSHA to protect workers were almost entirely lost. President Ronald Reagan's tenure in the White House lead to the slashing of any power that OSHA had left. Beginning under Reagan, the OSHA budget was cut, the number of inspectors fell, complaints from workers were discouraged, and a number of other actions resulted in an agency that was slow, moving toward voluntary compliance, and lacking in performance initiatives.

Reagan moved OSHA directly under the supervision of the Office of Management and Budget (OMB), which created elaborate and near-impossible hurdles to surmount in formulating new standards, while old standards were modified to provide policies more suitable to business interests.

Workers' Safety and Health under the Clinton Administration. Just as policy had shifted when first Carter and then Reagan took office, the election of President Bill Clinton seemed to offer a return to more labor-friendly policies, though little was done to stem the decline in OSHA during the early Clinton years. As a demonstration of this philosophical shift, in 1995, President Clinton and Vice-President Al Gore coauthored and published a booklet titled *The New OSHA: Reinventing Worker Safety and Health.* In this document, Clinton and Gore pointed out what they saw at the time as the two fundamental problems with OSHA: (1) the [economic] cost of occupational injuries and illnesses remained substantial ($110 billion a year), despite the fact that overall occupational injury and illness rates had declined since the 1970s; and (2) the public perception of OSHA remained one of an agency mired in red tape and nonspecific industry standards.

To remedy these problems, Clinton and Gore called for a three-pronged approach that included strong, targeted enforcement; clear regulations; and a focus on the most hazardous regions of industry. Unfortunately, the plan did not include a protocol for dramatically increasing funding and staffing, nor did it address the various deficiencies in standard setting, inspections, enforcement, and penalty collections. By shifting the measurement of OSHA's performance from the total number of inspections to a "results-oriented" measurement system, OSHA could focus on fewer, and (by its classification schema) more hazardous worksites. In short, the administration hoped that the results orientation of OSHA would provide the agency with more "bang for its buck" (Levenstein and Wooding 1997: 409).

By Clinton's second term, a majority Republican Congress was in place and would prove to be about as inimical to labor as either the Reagan or the first Bush administration. In 1997, Georgia Representative Charles W. Norwood, a Republican, was appointed Chair of the 1997 House Subcommittee on Workforce Protections. As Subcommittee Chair, Norwood oversaw all OSHA legislation including the OSHA Reform Act of 1997—a bill that unsuccessfully attempted to effectively abolish the agency.

OSHA in the Twenty-First Century. Since the creation of the OSH Act, U.S. employment has doubled, and it now stands at nearly 115 million workers at 7 million job sites. Each year almost 6000 Americans die from workplace injuries; as many as 50,000 workers die from illnesses in which workplace illnesses were a contributing factor; nearly 6 million employees suffer nonfatal workplace injuries; and the direct and indirect cost of occupational injuries and illnesses totals more than $170 billion (an increase of $60 billion in less than 10 years).

Although overall workplace fatalities and occupational injuries and illnesses have markedly decreased since OSHA's passage, critics maintain that this has more to do with the transformation of the American economy and OSHA's recordkeeping and data collection methods than with a dramatic increase in the agency's performance. In the late 1990s it was also estimated that in order for OSHA to inspect every workplace in the country (at the time, more than 6.5 million job sites), it would take just shy of nine decades. By 2006 there were 7 million job sites and even fewer OSHA inspectors than there had been a decade earlier. Of these 7 million job sites, according to former OSHA director John Henshaw, only 2 percent were being inspected each year.

Both Democrats and Republicans alike maintain that Clinton, in his last few years in office, put so much emphasis on the passage of the failed ergonomics standard that many other proposed rules were overlooked prior to his departure. In an unprecedented move, the incoming administration of President George W. Bush placed a temporary freeze on all pending rules passed toward the end of the Clinton administration. Following the President's initiative, Labor Secretary Elaine Chao instructed the entire Department to find items to eliminate. By the end of 2003, Bush had eliminated over half of the 44 rules pending from Clinton's last days in office. Moreover, between 2000 and 2004 OSHA eliminated almost five times as many standards as it had completed, most of which were considerably narrower than the older standards being eliminated.

Notably, one of the eliminated proposed standards, which had been under consideration since the Reagan administration, would have updated the lists of hundreds of industrial chemicals to which workers could be exposed. By rejecting the proposed standards, the new administration argued that it made more sense to regulate each substance, one at a time.

OSHA's Inspection, Enforcement, and Penalty Assessment Policies. OSHA is best known for its ability to cite employers for civil penalties due for violations of its workplace safety and health standards. As discussed previously, with its current number of investigators, OSHA in 2006 is able to investigate only some 2 percent of the seven million worksites in America. Thus, its investigations tend to center around large, unionized, high-risk industries and employment sites. Inspections can be planned or unplanned; in the latter case the employer is not legally granted advance notice of OSHA's inspection. According to OSHA, employers obtaining advance notice of an unplanned inspection can receive a criminal fine of up to $1,000, a six-month jail term, or both.

Given that the courts have generally granted businesses due process rights similar to or in excess of what is granted individual citizens, employers generally have the same protections that apply to state inspections, as well. In *Marshall v. Barlow's Inc.* (1978), the U.S. Supreme Court ruled that OSHA cannot enter any private premise for inspection purposes unless it first obtains either the employer's consent or a warrant issued by a court authorizing inspection. OSHA also must have probable cause for obtaining the warrant, though the courts have generally granted OSHA's request to conduct its health and safety investigations.

In terms of civil penalties, as of 2006 the maximum penalty per OSHA violation is $70,000 for a willful violation, and $7,000 for a willful, posting, serious, other than serious violation, or failure to abate a violation. A *willful violation* occurs when the employer intentionally and knowingly commits an offense or when the employer commits the offense with plain indifference to the law. A *serious violation* is a violation that creates a substantial probability that death or serious harm could result and the employer knows or should have known the hazard. The term *other than serious* refers to a violation that has a direct relationship to job safety and health but probably would not cause death or serious physical harm. A *posting violation* occurs when an employer fails to post OSHA-mandated signs. A *failure to abate a violation* refers to a situation in which an employer fails to correct a previously cited violation before the prescribed abatement date. Employers may appeal inspection results; however, employees may not contest citations, penalties, or lack of penalties imposed by OSHA.

Beyond the imposition of civil sanctions for workplace health and safety violations, OSHA also has criminal enforcement authority. Although OSHA cannot directly prosecute for violations, it can recommend and refer such requests to the Department of Justice (DOJ). However, in most cases, the OSHA Area Director refers any potential actions to the appropriate Regional Administrator, who will then determine with an OSHA Solicitor whether to push the referral toward the DOJ. OSHA does not refer the majority of even its most serious criminal violations to the DOJ, nor does the DOJ prosecute most of the criminal cases it receives from OSHA.

Criminal violations of safety and health laws include willful violations causing death to an employee, filing false statements to federal and state authorities, and disclosing the date of an upcoming inspection. A recent report by the *New York Times* found that from 1982 to 2002, OSHA investigated 1242 cases in which it concluded that worker deaths were caused by their employer's "willful" safety and health violations. Despite the fact that these were criminal violations, OSHA declined to refer cases to the DOJ in 93 percent of those cases. At least 70 of the employers who caused willful violations that resulted in employees' deaths were repeat offenders (many of whom had avoided prosecution for both the first and subsequent offenses). During this same 20-year period OSHA referred just 196 of its 1242 willful death cases to the DOJ. Although the DOJ declined to prosecute the majority of cases, it obtained 81 convictions (largely through pretrial settlements). Only 16 cases resulted in jail or prison sentences.

The DOJ maintains that this is largely because killing a worker is only a misdemeanor under federal law, punishable by six months in jail, which is far less than an individual would receive for a manslaughter conviction. Even a subsequent conviction for a willful violation that causes the death of an employee does not increase the penalty standard. Further, the DOJ maintains that, given the relatively vague language of the OSH Act, it is extremely difficult to meet the "beyond all reasonable doubt" burden required of criminal cases. Finally, DOJ claims that because very few OSHA compliance officers are trained to investigate criminal cases, they often unintentionally undermine evidence, which then cannot be used by federal prosecutors.

OSHA as Product of State-Corporate Malfeasance. The failings of OSHA are multifaceted and complex to understand. At the organizational level, OSHA is grossly underfunded and understaffed, and its Compliance Safety and Health Officers (CSHOs) face enormous pressures from industry, Congress, and even their own OSHA attorneys to do much with little. With a scarcity of various resources, OSHA routinely and improperly downgrades employer violations, which in turn, permits some companies to engage in chronic noncompliance. Moreover, when OSHA violates its own policies and procedures, only part of which includes the reclassification of citations and downgrading of penalties, many cases move outside the reach of criminal prosecution. Without the ability to criminally prosecute willful violations of the OSH Act, OSHA's enforcement capabilities become severely compromised, and any deterrent value associated with holding companies criminally liable is lost. Most importantly, noncompliance (whether on the part of OSHA or of business) creates an occupational environment in which injuries, illnesses, and fatalities are more likely to flourish.

Congress holds the responsibility of stewardship over the OSH Act. In 1995, the federal government spent only $3 per worker annually on occupational safety and health. It requires of OSHA an unusually protracted "risk benefit analysis" in finalizing standards, virtually all of which have prioritized the interests of business over the welfare of workers. Most recently, Congress in 2000 failed to pass the most sweeping ergonomic standard (which would have covered 6 million worksites) because of the undue economic burden it maintained would be borne by industry.

Inextricably linked to the structural and cultural climate of OSHA, as well as the decision-making rationales of government, is the key role that corporations and businesses play in controlling the occupational landscape in a capitalist political economy. Occupational diseases and injuries are the direct result of economic activity. Intense business opposition in the form of corporate Congressional lobbying, litigation, routine challenges of safety and health standards, and frequent appeals of regulatory citations are just some of the downward pressures that put worker safety and health at risk. With such agenda-laden pursuits at the organizational, governmental, and corporate levels, worker health and safety will rely more than ever on the public's awareness, education, mobilization, and directed efforts to demand transparency and accountability on the part of their employers and government to protect their well-being on the job.

See also: Industrial Accidents

FURTHER READING

Brill, H. "Government Breaks the Law: The Sabotaging of the Occupational Safety and Health Act." *Social Justice* 19 (1992): 63–81.

Byrum, L., Crus, P., Formica, M., Halprin, L., Heenan, M., Kauff, S., Leason, C., Lopez, M., Marrapese, M., McCadney, J., McMahon-Loyner, K., Miller, M., Murtha, F., O'Loughlin, Jr., J., Rath, M., Rodgers, W., Sapper, A., and Spracker, S. *Occupational Safety and Health Law Handbook.* Rockville, MD: Government Institutes, 2001.

Clinton, W. J., and Gore, A. *The New OSHA: Reinventing Worker Safety and Health.* Washington, DC: National Performance Review, 1995.

Levenstein, C., and Wooding, J. *Work, Health and Environment: Old Problems, New Solutions.* New York: Guilford Publications, 1997.

Mintz, B. *OSHA: History, Law and Politics.* Washington, DC: Bureau of National Affairs, 1984.

Nothstein, G. *The Law of Occupational Safety and Health.* New York: Free Press, 1981.

Rabinowitz, R. *Occupational Safety and Health Law.* Washington, DC: Bureau of National Affairs, 2002.

U.S. Department of Labor, Occupational Safety and Health Administration. *All about OSHA.* Washington, DC: U.S. Department of Labor, 2003.

U.S. Department of Labor, Occupational Safety and Health Administration. *Industrial Hygiene.* Washington, DC: U.S. Department of Labor, 1998.

Wooding, J., and Levenstein, C. *The Point of Production: Work Environment in Advanced Industrial Society.* New York: Guilford Publications, 1999.

DANIELLE MCGURRIN
JOSHUA FECTEAU

P

PAPER ENTREPRENEURIALISM. Paper entrepreneurialism is the idea that there are some investors who are primarily interested in short-term profit, rather than product development or building a relationship between a corporation and its host community. The main goal and criterion of success for these investors is immediate, or at least quick, financial profit, disregarding other criteria or parameters that would be oriented toward long-term planning and development or community and societal interests. Paper entrepreneurialism frequently takes the form of buying and selling of other companies or through investments in high-yield non-manufacturing areas. Such decisions are made without worker or community input. As such, paper entrepreneurialism, with its "artificial" premise, can be contrasted with "genuine" entrepreneurialism characterized by long-term profit, research, product development, quality improvement efforts, as well as working on creating and maintaining a constructive contribution to the community where a given corporation functions, or even to society in general in the case of larger, more influential corporations. In other words, speculative ventures can indeed be very successful in generating rapid growth; the problem is that the growth is on paper only, it is not growth in real economic terms. The term "paper entrepreneurialism" was coined by Robert Reich, who holds a Ph.D. in Economics from Harvard University, served as U.S. Secretary of Labor during President Clinton's first term, and is currently professor of public policy at Harvard's John F. Kennedy School of Government.

Paper entrepreneurialism is a central concept for understanding white-collar crime in contemporary society, "paper entrepreneurs" have been found increasingly in contemporary corporations. The period of the 1980s, with its series of major corporate takeovers, was crucial in establishing a trend of strengthening paper entrepreneurialism at the expense of genuine, traditional economic development. During the late 1970s and throughout the 1980s, corporate takeovers became an important new source of making money on Wall Street. Although there is some debate about whether the takeovers were ultimately good or bad for the national economy, there is no question that people such as the raiders, insiders, and brokers reaped profits that, from the larger societal standpoints, were excessive and disproportionate to the amount of work they had done. Critics of corporate takeovers and of other examples of paper entrepreneurialism—economic activities oriented exclusively toward capital gains, such as certain types of currency trading, loan swaps, land speculation, and futures trading—charge that in this kind of economic "activity" nothing is being produced but capital gains. In the late 1980s French economist and Nobel prize winner Maurice Allais called finance capitalism in the United States a "casino economy," as opposed to traditional, industrial capitalism in which profits are made not on paper but through actual production and sale of goods and services. Thus, Allais's concept of a casino economy is closely related to the concept of paper entrepreneurialism.

A leveraged buyout (LBO) is a very good example of paper entrepreneurialism. The $25 billion LBO of RJR Nabisco by Kohlberg Kravis Roberts & Co. in 1989 (chronicled in the book and film *Barbarians at the Gate*) is symbolic of Wall Street's decade of greed and the kind of selfish focus on short-term profit that is the essence of paper entrepreneurialism. An LBO occurs when a buyout firm gains control of a majority of the equity of a target company by using debt. A very common way of raising this money throughout the 1980s was by issuing so-called junk bonds—bonds that provide high yields but are inferior to investment-grade bonds in terms of default risk. Investment-grade bonds (securities that were rated AAA by major rating services such as Moody's or Standard and Poor) were virtually risk-free, but they barely yielded more than U.S. Treasury bonds. Entrepreneurs, such as Michael Milken, promoted the idea of subinvestment-grade, deep-discount bonds that would outperform higher-grade bond portfolios if acquired in sufficiently large quantities. During the 1980s buyout firms utilized unprecedented amounts of debt to acquire entire companies in one move. A target company's assets were frequently sold off to be able to pay off the debt that was accumulated to enable the LBO in the first place, while the target company's cash flow was frequently used as personal profit for buyout firm partners. Some LBOs may have fulfilled some positive role. In cases in which a company's true value is no longer reflected in its stock price because of poor management, a buyout may be the right remedy for the situation. The problem, however, is that most LBOs caused great economic hardships and disruptions, with buyout firm partners, bankers, and attorneys being virtually the only parties profiting from those deals. Many LBOs resulted in corporate bankruptcy. For example, the deal acquiring Federated Department Stores failed because the buyout company miscalculated the potential value of the transaction.

During the 1990s LBOs declined, primarily for two reasons: First, some fundamental parameters of financial markets severely restricted the use of LBOs. Since the junk bond market's demise in 1988, debt is significantly harder to acquire. Second, as a response to the pervasiveness of LBOs, companies developed a number of financial techniques such as the so-called poison pill, which provides protection especially against the most aggressive kind of LBO: a hostile takeover. A poison pill is a tactic intended to make a hostile LBO prohibitively expensive. For example, a company's stockholders may be offered shares of stock at a bargain price in the event that a single investor acquires a high percentage of the stock.

Despite the decline in LBOs in the late 1990s, paper entrepreneurialism continues today in other forms, such as loan scams and land speculation. Speculation is the practice of engaging in business with the goal of making quick profits from fluctuations in prices. This is contrasted with the practice of investing in a productive enterprise in order to share in its earnings. Typical of contemporary forms of speculation are investments in ventures involving abnormal risks along with the chance to earn unusually large profits, as well as the buying and selling of commodities and stocks and bonds with the object of taking advantage of rapid changes in price. Speculators fundamentally differ from long-term investors in that the latter seek to protect their principal as it yields a moderate return, but speculators sacrifice the safety of their principal in the hope of receiving a large, rapid return. Just as in other forms of paper entrepreneurialism, nothing is produced but the speculator's capital gains. Society does not benefit from this kind of "business."

With its focus on short-term profit serving only to enrich the speculators, at the expense of future-focused economic development, paper entrepreneurialism is frequently viewed as socially harmful because it disregards economic goals and strategies that would ultimately serve modern society and the communities that constitute society. There is increasing recognition in today's society that corporations are not just part of the world of business but also have a function in the larger society. That insight raises the issue of corporate social responsibility, which can be defined as the kind of corporate mentality and actions that acknowledge that there is more to running a business than just financial profit—corporations have a responsibility to contribute meaningfully to long-term community and societal development. As such, paper entrepreneurialism is the antonym of corporate social responsibility.

See also: Drexel Burnham Lambert; Junk Bonds

FURTHER READING

Friedrichs, David O. *Trusted Criminals: White Collar Crime in Contemporary Society.* Belmont, CA: Wadsworth, 1996.
Rosoff, Stephen M., Pontell, Henry N., and Tillman, Robert. *Profit Without Honor: White-Collar Crime and the Looting of America.* Upper Saddle River, NJ: Prentice Hall, 1998.
Shover, Neal, and Wright, John Paul (eds.). *Crimes of Privilege. Readings in White-Collar Crime.* New York, Oxford: Oxford University Press, 2001.

WOJCIECH CEBULAK

"PARKING" STOCK. The practice of "parking" stock in a brokerage account owned by another person or entity emerged in the 1980s as a tool for facilitating a hostile takeover of a company. Since then, parking stock in another's account continues as an illegitimate or illegal practice, from which the perpetrator gains wealth.

Stock is parked when it is acquired or held in order to conceal the identity of the true owner. Parking stock is an activity that often occurs for three reasons: (1) improving the appearance of market liquidity, (2) concealing an impending hostile takeover, and (3) generating higher commissions.

Market Liquidity. Liquidity, the number of shares traded daily, is important for the stock of thinly capitalized organizations. Increased liquidity stabilizes the stock's price, which is important to raising additional funds or meeting certain covenants imposed by lending banks. Certain stocks that are traded on the New York Stock Exchange and the NASDAQ use a *market maker*, an entity that helps to match buy and sell orders, in order to maintain stability of the stock's price. In the event there is an imbalance between the buying and selling of an organization's stock, the market maker buys and sells out of his or her own inventory to stabilize the supply and demand. In the case of an initial public offering (IPO), the investment bank that facilitated the organization's going public takes the role of a market maker until the stock's demand and supply have stabilized. All of these activities are legal and permissible, until stock parking takes place.

In 1986 Kureen & Cooper, a broker-dealer, found itself in the position as market maker for the stocks of two companies: Lopat and EAS. As part of its commission for underwriting the IPOs of these two companies, Kureen & Cooper received stock warrants that allowed it to buy a large amount of stock in each of the companies' shares at set prices after a set period of time. There was little demand for Lopat and EAS stock, so Kureen & Cooper was forced to buy the stock when a sell order was placed. In order to meet the minimum capital requirements set by the Securities and Exchange Commission (SEC), Kureen & Cooper was forced to sell the stock the same day it purchased it, which caused a decline in stock price. Since these declining stock prices jeopardized future commissions and profits, Kureen & Cooper parked stock in the accounts of both customers who were promised guaranteed profits and of unsuspecting customers. This form of sheltering stock ownership, in addition to some other forms of manipulation, permitted Kureen & Cooper to balance out its trading account each day, while creating an appearance of demand for the stocks of Lopat and EAS.

Hostile Takeover. An individual or company that is interested in taking over another company can do so through a friendly merger or aggressively as a hostile takeover. In a hostile takeover, the acquiring entity typically starts buying up the stock of the target company, usually without the knowledge of the target. During the acquisition of stock, there is a certain percent of ownership at which the acquirer must file reports announcing its intention of making an offer for all outstanding shares of stock. This offer is then voted on by the existing stockholders of the target company. Usually, when a hostile takeover is announced, management will activate the defenses of the organization in order to prevent the sale of the company. A greater percentage of ownership by the acquiring entity improves the chances that the acquisition will be approved. The percent of ownership that an acquiring entity must report is 5 percent of the outstanding shares of the target company. By parking a large block of stock with another individual or organization, the acquiring entity can almost double the percentage of the stock it controls beyond the point at which it would normally have to file if it were buying stock off the street in its own name. With a greater percentage ownership, the acquiring entity usually has a good chance of success in getting the acquisition approved.

Boyd Jeffries, of the Jeffries Group, Inc., accumulated 539,600 shares of Pacific Lumber stock, which he then sold to Charles Hurwitz. The sale of this parked stock presumably allowed Hurwitz to begin the hostile takeover of Pacific Lumber.

Jeffries eventually pleaded guilty and was sentenced to prison for parking stock for Ivan Boesky and Michael Milken. In addition, Milken also drew a ten-year sentence for parking stock.

Generating Commissions. Stockbrokers can use the technique of parking stock to increase their commissions. One way they can create commissions is by parking stock in fictitious or dormant accounts, creating an impression that there is an increasing demand and increasing stock prices. The broker then refers this stock to his or her clients, who then buy it, thereby generating commissions. A broker can also make commissions by trading funds in the account of his or her firm. By selling the firm's securities, by parking the stock in a fictitious or dormant account or improperly in active accounts, the broker can generate profits for the organization and pocket the sales commission.

See also: Boesky, Ivan; Drexel Burnham Lambert; Milken, Michael

FURTHER READING

Daly, Ned. "Ravaging the Redwood: Charles Hurwitz, Michael Milken and the Costs of Greed." *Multinational Monitor*, 2005. Available at http://multinationalmonitor.org/hyper/mm0994.html.

Federal Trade Commission. "Premerger Notification; Reporting and Waiting Period Requirements." 2005. Available at http://www.ftc.gov/os/2005/02/050223premergerfrn.pdf.

Findlaw. Docket Nos. 95-1123. 2005. Available at http://laws.findlaw.com/2nd/9511230.html.

"Headwaters Forest Fact Sheet." Jail Hurwitz, 2005. Available at http://www.jailhurwitz.com/headwaters_fact_sheet.htm.

Scranton, David F. "Managing Market Liquidity for an Institution's Stock." De Novo Banks, 2005. Available at http://www.denovobanks.com/strategies/story.asp?idstory=39.

Securities and Exchange Commission. Admin. Proc. File No. 3-8743. 2005. Availale at http://www.sec.gov/litigation/opinions/3437092.txt.

Securities and Exchange Commission. Litigation Release No. 15827. 2005. Available at http://www.sec.gov/litigation/litreleases/lr15827.txt.

SEC Forms. Wolf Popper LLC, 2005. Available at http://www.wolfpopper.com/wolfpopper/stockfraud/secforms.cfm.

WARREN WYLUPSKI

PESTICIDES. A pesticide is any substance used to combat animals or plants damaging to humans or to human enterprises such as agriculture. Pesticides are universally regulated within the United States. Misuse of pesticides, in violation of such regulations, can be a crime. Such misuse may also cause civil liability in a lawsuit. Pesticides may also be the cause of such criminal or civil liability because of dangerous substances and processes used in their manufacture. Pesticides also present some interesting ethical issues.

Pesticides are primarily regulated by the Federal Insecticide, Fungicide, and Rodenticide Act of 1972 (FIFRA). The manufacture and disposal of components and byproducts of pesticides may be regulated by other laws, such as the Resource Conservation and Recovery Act (RCRA) and the Toxic Substance Control Act (TSCA), and sites related to pesticide production can be regulated under "Superfund" (CERCLA); these regulations apply not just to pesticides but to any chemical manufacturing. However, FIFRA is the most important law in dealing with pesticides.

FIFRA establishes a registration process for all pesticides. Registration is based on the manufacturer's testing for effectiveness, dosage, and hazards of the pesticide. The FIFRA registration process creates a label for the pesticide container that instructs those using the pesticide ("applicators") in how to use it safely and effectively. The label is intended to protect these applicators, consumers of products that are exposed to pesticides, and the environment. The label carries the force of federal law.

The registration process also determines whether a pesticide will be "restricted." A restricted pesticide is not available to the general public. The decision to restrict a pesticide is made based on safety for groundwater, plants and animals away from the site where it is applied, and for people anywhere. A restricted pesticide may be used only by certified applicators. A certified applicator must be certified through one of the states' certification programs, which vary from state to state.

Misuse of pesticides most commonly consists of use inconsistent with the dosage or manner of application directed on the label or of omission of a required safety procedure. More serious violations involve the adulteration, unauthorized sale, or improperly recorded sale of a restricted pesticide. Sale or use of an unregistered pesticide is likewise misuse. The impact of misuse can be heavy fines for the perpetrator, and injury to people and property affected by the misuse. A serious example of the impacts of misuse involved two Mississippi exterminators who used an outdoor pesticide (methyl parathion) for indoor extermination of cockroaches over a period of two years. Several people, including two infants, suffered from the effects of pesticide poisoning. Homes, day care centers, churches, and other businesses were rendered unusable. The perpetrators were fined and imprisoned.

Most violations of FIFRA are dealt with through civil lawsuits, but deliberate violations are crimes. Someone who is in the business of selling or applying pesticides faces a maximum of $25,000 and a year in prison per violation. Private applicators, such as a private homeowner, face maximums of only $1000 and 30 days imprisonment per violation, and for producers it is $50,000 and 2 years, respectively.

Industrial and agricultural accidents can flow both from misuse and from manufacturing accidents. United Farm Workers claim that pesticide laws are not strong enough to protect agricultural workers, and such workers often bear the brunt of the effects of minor misuse. Certainly the most widely recognized example is the 1984 disaster at the pesticide plant run by Union Carbide in Bhopal, India, which killed more than 15,000 people. Warren Anderson, CEO of Union Carbide at the time of the explosion, faces criminal charges in India, but the United States has denied India's extradition request. Union Carbide is now owned by Dow Chemical, some of whose shareholders have requested through a November 2005 shareholder resolution that Dow address the potential liability to survivors of the Bhopal disaster; supporters of the resolution owned 4.5 million shares of stock worth over $190 million.

Other ethical issues from pesticide production and use involve actions that are in compliance with the existing laws but no less troubling. Under FIFRA, chlordane and heptachlor were banned as probable human carcinogens and because they accumulate in the food chain and are highly persistent in the environment. The U.S. Environmental Protection Agency (EPA) made an agreement with Velsicol Chemical Co. of Tennessee under which Velsicol would be able to continue to produce chlordane and heptachlor for shipment to other countries with lesser regulation. Both the ethics of shipping these pesticides overseas after they have been determined to be unsafe in the United States, and the prudence of allowing them into the food chain of produce that may ultimately be imported to the United States, have been severely criticized by environmentalists.

See also: Environmental White-Collar Crime; Seveso Dioxin Disaster; Union Carbide

FURTHER READING

Oliveira, Andrew, Schenck, Christopher, Cole, Christopher D., and Janes, Nicole L. "Environmental Crimes." *American Criminal Law Review* 42 (2005): 347–426.

U.S. Environmental Protection Agency. "Federal Insecticide, Fungicide, and Rodenticide Act." January 2006. U.S. EPA, Region 5. Available at http://www.epa.gov/region5/defs/html/fifra.htm.

Wikipedia, The Free Encyclopedia. "Federal Insecticide, Fungicide, and Rodenticide Act." 2006. Available at http://en.wikipedia.org/wiki/FIFRA.

Wikipedia, The Free Encyclopedia. "Pesticides." 2006. Available at http://en.wikipedia.org/wiki/ Pesticide.

SAMUEL V. S. SWINDELL

PHARMACEUTICAL COMPANIES. The theme of pharmaceutical companies, and the related issue of drugs for the Third World, proves that white-collar crime is not necessarily one act referable to one specific actor. In many cases white-collar crime is inherent to the legitimate system and makes it difficult to find the responsible actors.

In a strict juridical sense it is hard to define daily activities of pharmaceutical companies as criminal. The legal system and the organization of the pharmaceutical sector deliver a juridical framework that legitimizes harmful activities. The legal framework is unequally more directed to economic interests and less to social implications. Furthermore, companies, together with government, doctors, pharmacists, academic personnel, and social security services support and protect each other to protect their own interests. This protective legal framework and collusion can be referred to as the pharmaceutical complex. If we take the victim and his or her victimization as a point of view to define the criminological relevance, we easily could say that pharmaceutical activities in Third World countries are criminal. We may say that the sector is not criminal in its acts but in its consequences.

The relation between pharmaceutical companies and drugs for Third World countries is a topic that has determined the agenda of some nongovernmental organizations (NGOs) in recent years. The problem is related to different levels of the production chain of medicines. Some specific conflicts that illustrate this problematic relation are research and development, patent law and price fixing, clinical research in Third World countries, and offering medicines. More instances could be adduced.

Research and Development. Most pharmaceutical companies are not interested in doing research to improve the medical treatment of life threatening illnesses such as malaria, gonorrhea, or AIDS in the context of Third World countries. The reason is the limited economic profits related to the medical treatment. In the absence of a social security system, patients in Third World countries are unable to pay the same price as in Western countries. In Africa a tri-therapy (combination of antiretroviral medicines) for the treatment of AIDS costs as much as in the United States (between $10,000 and $15,000), but the annual GNP per capita ranges between a tenth and a third of this amount. Pharmaceutical companies pretend they are forced to lower the price of their medicines to a level beyond the profit level. That is the reason why companies prefer to develop new medicines for typical Western-cultural diseases, such as heart and vascular diseases and neurological illnesses.

223

This leads to an undermedicalization of Third World countries, with a high mortality rate for curable diseases, but also to overmedicalization of people in Western countries. As a solution to the life-threatening health problems of the population, some governments have started to develop copies of patent-protected medicines in case of emergency. This has created a new conflict between Western pharmaceutical companies and Third World countries.

Patent Law and Price Fixing. Since the World Trade Organization (WTO) introduced the TRIPs (Trade Related Aspects of Intellectual Property Rights) agreement in 1994, intellectual property rights have been related to international trading rights. Effectively, intellectual property rights have a global impact on the market now, whereas they had previously been related to local legal habits. Pharmaceutical companies that apply for patent protection of a new product receive a monopoly position worldwide for at least twenty years. The proceeds of that right must compensate the costly phase of research and development of new medicines. It is a supervised, but also protected, freedom to fix an artificial high price until the patent license is expired. Some Third World countries refuse to accept the consequences of the TRIPs agreement because it endangers public health. Because the price of new medicines under patent protection is so high, poor countries are isolated from the improvement of basic medical treatment. That is the reason why some governments have allowed production of copies of the protected medicine or accepted imports of cheap medicines. This violation of the TRIPs agreement was the immediate cause of a conflict between pharmaceutical companies on the one side and NGOs and governments of poorer countries on the other. The South African case is the best known example. The South African government, in its Medicines and Related Substances Control Amendment Act, accepted the production of copies and the import of cheap medicines in case of national emergency. In 1998 thirty-nine pharmaceutical companies charged the South African government before the High Court of South Africa in Pretoria of not respecting the TRIPs agreement. Because the pharmaceutical companies suspended the lawsuit for three years, the country was cut off from medicine supplies against AIDS. In 2001, at the start of the court procedure, the thirty-nine companies decided to drop the case under pressure of a social movement of patients and nongovernmental organizations worldwide. The conflict was resolved on the political level of the WTO. Developing countries and the least developed country members received, during a transitional period, a moratorium on the complete implementation of patent protection. Some countries are allowed during this period to produce generic products for export, only in the framework of humanitarian activities. Now that the protest has calmed down and NGOs have other priorities on the agenda, it is difficult to understand the real impact of the decisions taken by the WTO.

Clinical Research in Third World Countries. We find a third relationship between Third World countries and pharmaceutical companies in the research domain. Third World countries have some advantages over Western countries concerning research and development: research is cheap, there is a real need for medicines, and the population is "clean," meaning that, because of the undermedicalization, the effects of medicines can really be tested without interference from other medicines. Overmedicalization in Western countries makes it hard to find a clean research population. A negative side effect of these test cases is the limited duration of the project. Once the test is finished, the company leaves the country, leaving behind a patient whose cure is interrupted. As John Braithwaite also points out, risky medicines are tested on populations who do not have the means to respond when the medicine causes serious physical harm.

Offering Medicines. Public conflicts injure the image of companies and have economic implications. The conflict concerning the universal and unconditional application of the TRIPs–agreement, for example, caused a global social movement against the abuses of the pharmaceutical industry. One of the possibilities for a company to restore its image is to search for a way to turn the negative critique into a more positive idea about the social movement. To restore their image, companies started a charming offensive. Some companies offered medicines to specific Third World regions involving a large-scale publicity campaign. Although this looks like a generous gesture, a once-only offer lacks continuity, is limited to a small part of the population, and lacks quality control. Because of the limited period of time that the medicine is available, therapies that have been begun come to an abrupt end without being possible to complete the prescribed medicine course. This impedes the effects, while the patient develops immunity to these medical substances. Although the propaganda for these "humanitarian" actions may impress Western consumers, the offer helps only a small part of the population for only a short period of time. Finally, because of a lax control system for offered medicines, medicines that have been taken off the Western market are still available on the market of poorer countries, and medicines that are subject to a strict prescription regime in Western countries enjoy a more liberal regime in Third World countries.

The problem is not limited to Third World countries. All countries lacking a developed social security system or other social insurance system are confronted with the same problems. In Eastern Europe, for example, the population infected with HIV is dramatically increasing while the social security system is abominable. The relation between pharmaceutical companies and drugs for the Third World is dramatic because of the double irreconcilable function of the pharmaceutical industry, namely its economic importance as a private sector and its responsibility for public health.

See also: Dalkon Shield; DES; Infant Formula

FURTHER READING

Béraud, Claude. *Petite encyclopédie critique du médicament.* Paris: Les Editions de l'Atelier/Les Editions Ouvrières, 2002.

Braithwaite, John. *Corporate Crime in the Pharmaceutical Industry.* London: Routledge and Kegan Paul, 1983.

Braithwaite, John, and Drahos, Peter. *Global Business Regulation.* Cambridge, UK: Cambridge University Press, 2000.

Pignarre, Philippe. *Le grand secret de l'industrie pharmaceutique.* Paris: Edition la Découverte, 2003.

GUDRUN VANDE WALLE

PIPER ALPHA. Around 10 p.m. on July 6, 1988, a series of explosions tore through the Occidental Petroleum–owned *Piper Alpha* oil production platform in the Northern Sector of the British North Sea. One hundred sixty-seven persons were killed on *Piper Alpha*; sixty-one workers survived. Thirty bodies were never recovered from the North Sea after Occidental declined to pay for the excavation of the platform from the sea bed.

Subsequent accounts of events following the explosions indicate a high degree of management contribution to the events. Negligent emergency provision and undermaintained critical safety systems made a catastrophic situation worse: emergency lighting failed; there were hardly any flashlights available to the crew; all of the lifeboats were located in the same section of the platform, which also happened to be inaccessible; and no provision had been made for an alternative escape route to the sea. Most people on the platform gathered at the emergency muster point, the accommodation module, which was located above the gas compression module and therefore also happened to be one of the areas on the platform most exposed to fire and explosion. The accommodation module, constructed from wood and fiberglass, quickly began to burn. The water deluge system—the platform's main defense against fire—failed. When two life rafts were launched, they failed to inflate. The standby safety vessel, a converted fishing boat, had no medical supplies to treat survivors as they were pulled from the sea, and the *Tharos*, Occidental's state-of-the-art floating fire engine, could not muster sufficient water pressure to reach the flames.

Occidental's senior managers had been warned by their own consultants that the platform would not withstand prolonged exposure to high-intensity fire. It was a warning that they chose to ignore on the grounds that the company's assessment of the risk of such an incident occurring did not justify the expense of refitting the platform with high-grade fireproofing. The sequence of events that followed the initial explosions illustrate the strictly observed "production first" dictum of offshore management. Managements on platforms connected by the same pipeline chain, the *Tartan* and the *Claymore*, declined to shut down production and instead continued to feed the blaze with oil as they obediently awaited permission from senior management onshore for a costly closure of the pipeline. There was no prosecution of Occidental, a firm that already had a criminal record for killing one of its workers in September 1987.

Piper Alpha, rather than being understood as a one-off, unpredictable event, should be understood as the culmination of a generalized safety crisis in the industry. The origins of this crisis are in the failure of both the regulatory system and the operating oil companies' management regimes. It is worth highlighting three features of these. The origins of the crisis can be found in the political economy that ensured that the oil was to function as the motor of the neoliberal restructuring of the UK economy in the 1970s and 1980s. This had three principal effects. First, as W. G. Carson argued, the conditions within which British oil policy developed are best described as "the political economy of speed" whereby the speedy development of an industry—central to offsetting Britain's economic decline in the 1970s—came at great cost to the workers, measured in abnormally high rates of injury and death in the sector (eleven times the fatality rate in the construction industry and nearly nine times the rate in mining). A related effect was regulatory acceptance, the "institutionalization of tolerance" of this appalling toll, indicated by the legal anomalies, jurisdictional gaps, and low level of resources available to the regulatory regime.

Second, the particular features of the labor process in the offshore oil sector were a major contributory factor. The use of casualized and subcontracted labor was quickly established by the offshore drilling and operating companies in the early years of the industry. The legacy of this structure was that, over the years, the percentage of offshore workers employed as subcontractors has remained at between 80 and 90 percent. In the pre–*Piper Alpha* period, workers were usually employed on short-term contracts that often lasted no longer than a few weeks or months and contained few contractual rights. Trade union organization was virtually unheard of. Brutal management styles ensured that those who were found to have trade union sympathies, or those who vocally expressed concerns about safety, were routinely "NRBd" (told they were not required back). Eighty-three per cent of workers on board *Piper Alpha* on the night of the disaster were subcontracted. The marginalization of workers' expertise and knowledge of safety in the offshore management regime was to have catastrophic consequences. In the months preceding the disaster, management ignored a series of reports of gas leaks by workers on the *Piper Alpha*. On the day of the disaster, two workers had complained about a gas smell. Although one received permission by the platform safety officer to down tools, management had apparently declined to interfere with work routines and conduct an investigation.

Third, the contractual subordination of workers as a result of the offshore labor market structure had been exacerbated by a chain of events in the market that shook the industry in the mid-1980s. The collapse of the Organization of Petroleum Exporting Countries (OPEC) cartel quota system in 1985 (the average oil price per barrel plummeted from more than $30 in November 1985 to around $10 in April 1986) had a dramatic effect on the industry. In order to defend profit levels, oil companies slashed their operational budgets by between 30 and 40 percent across the board. The impact on the workforce was devastating. Wage levels fell dramatically, and 1986 saw up to 22,000 jobs lost in the industry. The operators' response to the oil price crash had far-reaching implications for workplace safety in the industry. Funding allocated to ensuring the regular maintenance of plant equipment suffered the same fate.

Today fatality and injury rates remain abnormally high in the industry, and despite the introduction of some limited improvements to hardware and a new regulatory regime following the official inquiry into the disaster, the workforce remains largely casualized and lacks trade union safety rights. In the sixteen years since *Piper Alpha* the workforce has remained under pressure as a result of successive cost-cutting exercises aimed at recuperating the costs resulting from *Piper Alpha*.

See also: Industrial Accidents

FURTHER READING

Carson, W. G. *The Other Price of Britain's Oil.* New Brunswick, NJ: Rutgers University Press, 1982.

Cullen, Lord. *The Public Inquiry into the* Piper Alpha *Disaster.* London: Her Majesty's Stationery Office, 1990.

Pate-Cornell, E. "Learning from the *Piper Alpha* Incident: a Post-Mortem Analysis of Technical and Organisational Factors." *Risk Analysis* 13.2 (1993): 60–78.

Woolfson, C., Foster, J., and Beck, M. *Paying for the* Piper: *Capital and Labour in Britain's Offshore Oil Industry.* London: Mansell, 1996.

Whyte, D. "Regulating Safety, Regulating Profit: Cost Cutting, Injury and Death in the North Sea after *Piper Alpha*." In R. Storey and E. Tucker, (eds.) *Working Disasters: the Politics of Recognition and Response.* Toronto: McGill/Queens University Press, 2005.

DAVE WHYTE

POLITICAL CORRUPTION. Political corruption is a phenomenon that transcends national borders. It can jeopardize democracies and the stability and security of societies as well as the legitimacy of public institutions. Political corruption has been broadly defined as the use of public power for personal gain. According to the World Bank, corruption constitutes the "missing link" between first- and second-generation economic reforms, because budget deviation and corrupt practices have an adverse effect on the delivery of services to the poorest people as well as on economic growth and the democratic stability of states.

Definition. It has been a challenge for academics and practitioners to define political corruption. By and large, political corruption has been defined in three different ways. First, several definitions focus on the public office. From this point of view, political corruption occurs when the acts of public servants in the conduct of their public duties deviate from certain norms. Second, political corruption can be defined using the theory of the market. Here, political corruption occurs when public officials use their power and influence to maximize the income from their offices, which are viewed as a place of business. Third, political corruption can be explained on the basis of the public-interest. This is the case when acts of political corruption go against the public interest.

The public-office definition and the market-oriented definition emphasize the concept of norms and legality, whereas the public interest–centered definition stresses the public benefit to society in general. Although these explanations provide a framework for understanding political corruption, there are several uncertainties. It is not clear which norms regulate the behavior of public officials, because there are a large number of regulations in each country, branch of government, and public office in general. Moreover, it is not noticeable that public offices participate in free market operations, because they are mostly regulatory agents of the market rather than service providers. In addition, there is often some ambiguity as to which public interests government officials are to preserve, because it has not been explicitly defined in norms and regulations.

Various international organizations responsible for fighting corruption have taken the public office–centered definition as the basis for their technical assistance orientation. In this respect, the World Bank defines corruption as the abuse of public office for private gain. Transparency International considers corruption as the misuse of entrusted power for private benefit. The UN's Global Programme against Corruption defines corruption as the abuse of power for private gain. Although the differences among these three definitions appear slight, they are nonetheless important. It should be noted that both the UN and Transparency International focus their definitions on the problems of both public and private corruption, whereas the World Bank centers its description exclusively on governmental offices.

Regarding the international legislation, it is worth mentioning that during the negotiation of the United Nations Convention against Corruption, which was adopted in October 2003, national representatives and field experts agreed not to define corruption in the convention, because the use of a single definition can produce legal, criminological, and political problems. Therefore, in the UN Convention, corruption is presented only in terms of offenders and offenses.

According to the UN Convention, offenders can be any public servants, whether elected or appointed to permanent or temporary offices, with paid or unpaid jobs, who hold a legislative, executive, judicial, or administrative office. In the convention eight transgressions are established as offenses: bribery, embezzlement, the trading of influence, abuses of functions,

Table 1 Political Corruption Offenses

Criminal Offense	Definition
1. Bribery of national or foreign public official	The *promise, offering or giving* as well as the *solicitation or acceptance*, directly or indirectly, of an undue advantage in order that the official act or refrain from acting in the exercise of duties
2. Embezzlement	Misappropriation or other diversion by a public official, for his or her own benefit or for the benefit of another person or entity, by virtue of position
3. Trading in influence	The *promise, offering or giving* as well as the *solicitation or acceptance*, directly or indirectly, of an undue advantage in order that the official provide an undue advantage for the original instigator of the act or for any other person
4. Abuse of functions	The performance of or failure to perform an act, in violation of laws, by a public official in the discharge of his or her functions, for the purpose of obtaining an undue advantage
5. Illicit enrichment	A significant increase in the assets of a public official that cannot be reasonably explained in relation to his or her lawful income
6. Laundering of proceeds of corruption	The conversion or transfer of property, knowing that such property is the proceeds of crime, for the purpose of concealing or disguising the illicit origin of the property or of helping any person who is involved in the commission of the predicate offense to evade the legal consequences of his or her action
7. Concealment	Persistence in the retention of property that results from the commission of any of the previous offenses, without having participated in such offenses
8. Obstruction of justice	The use of physical force, threats or intimidations or the promise, offering or giving of an undue advantage to induce false testimony or to interfere in the giving of testimony or the production of evidence in a proceeding in relation to the commission of any of the previous offenses

Source: Adapted from United Nations Convention against Corruption.

illicit enrichment, laundering of the proceeds of corruption, concealment, and obstruction of justice. Definitions of these forms appear in Table 1.

Political Corruption from Different Perspectives. Corruption has been studied by scholars from many disciplines. Among political scientists there is a discussion of the functionality and nonfunctionality of corruption in democracies. Among economists, the discussion about corruption has focused on its impacts on investment and economic growth and its presence as a result of institutional problems. Among criminologists, there is debate about whether political corruption constitutes a form of occupational crime or of organized-crime committed by state officials while carrying out their duties.

As regards political science, early theorists on corruption, led by Samuel Huntington, argued that corruption is functional for maintaining the political system. According to

Valdimer Key, corruption is necessary for politics. Jeanne Becquart considered corruption to have a redistributive effect and to be functional for direct participation in power. However, more recent political scientists consider corruption to be dysfunctional for democracy. For instance, according to Susan Rose-Ackerman, corrupt officials distort public sector choices to produce inefficient public policies. Donatella Della Porta and Alberto Vannucci argue that corruption reduces confidence in a government's capacity to address citizens' demands.

Regarding the economic perspective, Paulo Mauro has demonstrated that high levels of corruption are associated with lower levels of investment. Alberto Ades and Rafael Di Tella have suggested that in the presence of corruption, the positive impact of industrial investment is halved. Tanzi Vito and Hamid Davoodi have concluded that corruption makes public investment and economic growth unsustainable.

In the field of criminology, Marshall Clinard and Robert Quinney have suggested that political crime is a form of occupational crime, because politicians are at risk of committing these types of offenses. For these individuals, politics is a criminogenic occupation. In the same vein, David Nelken and Michael Levi have stated that corruption constitutes a tactical device to obtain power. Stephen Schafer has argued that politicians are convictional criminals because they are convinced of their correctness and they believe that there is nothing wrong with their behavior. William Chambliss has radicalized the debate by pointing out that public servants who commit crime while carrying out their duties should be considered state-organized criminals. This theory has not received much support among analysts, policy makers, and scholars because it cannot be proved that the *state* has criminal goals. On the contrary, it has been demonstrated by Edgardo Buscaglia and Jan van Dijk that the state is used by politicians and serious criminals looking for personal gain and protection while committing crime.

Curbing Corruption. The first efforts of the international community to curb corruption have focused on developing an international legal framework and providing technical assistance to the most affected countries. Usually the technical assistance provided focuses on creating an integrated strategy. International organizations such as the United Nations and Transparency International are agreed on the adoption of a *national integrity system*, which takes action to address the problem.

The national integrity system is based on strengthening public awareness and societal values to curb corruption. In addition, it requires actions to enhance public institutions such as the legislative, executive, and judicial branches of government, the audit office, the ombudsman, watchdog agencies, and the civil service. The participation of civil society, the media, the private sector, and international actors is focused on providing support for the implementation of programs in the aforementioned public agencies. Specific actions include the adoption of preventive measures, as well as actions focused on sanctioning.

As regards preventive actions, the aim of the national integrity system is to make the state work to serve the public, which implies that the state has to guarantee a good quality of life, promote sustainable development, and respect the rule of law. The recommendations proposed to achieve this aim are focused on two main areas of action: first, strengthening the judiciary by promoting its independence and efficiency; second, strengthening local government by adopting good governance practices and transparent decision-making mechanisms that should be open to citizen participation. These reforms should be accomplished by adopting reforms in the civil service, a code of conduct for public officials, and anti-corruption plans. Social preventive measures should be focused on increasing citizens' public awareness and promoting citizens' access to public information, investigative journalism, social control mechanisms, public complaints mechanisms, citizens', charters and service delivery surveys.

As regards actions focused on sanctioning, the United Nations recommendations involve: the promotion of financial investigation and the monitoring of assets, the introduction of electronic surveillance and integrity tests for public officials, the adoption of transnational instruments, the prevention of money laundering, the protection of whistleblowers, the extradition of those accused or convicted of a crime, the recovery of illegally obtained funds, and the promotion of international cooperation in the prosecution of cases.

See also: State-Corporate Crime

FURTHER READING

Becquart, Jeanne. "Paradoxes of Political Corruption: A French View." Pp. 191–210 in Arnold Heidenheimer, Victor Levine, and Michael Johnston (eds.). *Political Corruption: A Handbook.* Somerset, NJ: Transaction Publishers, 1990.

Buscaglia, Edgardo, and van Dijk, Jan. "Controlling Organized Crime and Corruption in the Public Sector." United Nations Office on Drugs and Crime, 2003. Available at http://www.unodc.org.

Clinard, Marshall, and Quinney, Richard. *Criminal Behavior Systems: A Typology.* New York: Holt, Rinehart and Winston, 1967.

Chambliss, William. "State-organized Crime." Pp. 299–326 in David Friedrichs (ed.). *State Crime: Defining, Delineating and Explaining State Crime. Volume I.* Aldershot, UK: Ashgate, 1998.

Hagan, Frank. *Political Crime: Ideology and Criminality.* Boston: Allyn & Bacon, 1997.

Nelken, David, and Levi, Michael. "The Corruption of Politics and the Politics of Corruption." Pp. 355–371 in David Friedrichs (ed.). *State Crime: Defining, Delineating and Explaining State Crime. Volume I.* Aldershot, UK: Ashgate, 1998.

Rose-Ackerman, Susan. *Corruption and Government. Causes, Consequences and Reform.* Cambridge, UK: Cambridge University Press, 1999.

Schafer, Stephen. *The Political Criminal: The Problem of Morality and Crime.* New York: Free Press, 1974.

United Nations Global Program against Corruption. *Anti-Corruption Tool Kit,* 3rd edition. Vienna: United Nations, 2004.

Vito, Tanzi, and Davoodi, Hamid. "Roads to Nowhere: How Corruption in Public Investment Hurts Growth." *International Monitory Fund, Economic Issues* 12 (1998).

NUBIA EVERTSSON

POLYCHLORINATED BIPHENYLS (PCBs). Initially discovered in 1865 and later synthesized in 1881, polychlorinated biphenyls (PCBs) are 209 chlorinated organic compounds that are synthesized as a mixture and therefore are commonly referred to as *congeners.* The mixture was widely used in electrical transformers, lighting ballasts, and industrial machinery as a lubricating and cooling fluid from 1927 through 1977.

Worker Health Risks. Adverse health effects posed by PCBs were first documented in 1933, when nearly 96 percent of the workers at the Swann Chemical Company contracted blackheads, acne, and other forms of chemically induced skin lesions. Other symptoms of exposure included loss of appetite, lack of energy, and sexual dysfunction. Later exposure by workers at the Halowax Corporation in 1936 resulted in severe liver damage. By 1965, the Monsanto Corporation had determined that dioxin, a contaminant frequently found in PCBs, was capable of causing cancer.

Environmental Hazards. Large quantities of PCBs were released into the environment from the early 1920s through the late 1970s in the course of product manufacturing and through accidental leaks, spills, and industrial fires. Once discharged, PCBs did not easily break down in soil or water and traveled great distances via the air and underground rivers (aquifers). The contaminants affixed themselves to organisms that birds, reptiles, and mammals would consume. The contaminants increased in concentration as they moved up the food chain—a process referred to as *bioaccumulation*. Ultimately, humans began consuming these high concentrations of PCBs and dioxins through contaminated sport fish (e.g., lake trout or bass) as well as through beef and dairy cattle that had been exposed to PCBs through feed and grazing pastures. Infants born to women who had consumed large quantities of contaminated fish and dairy exhibited behavioral problems such as a deficiency in motor skills and short-term memory loss.

In a 1968 case involving the residents of Kyushu, Japan, more than 1000 people became ill after eating a rice bran oil that was contaminated with PCBs. More than fifty deaths were attributed to this poisoning, and two out of twelve children were stillborn. By 1970, the Monsanto Corporation and Campbell's Soup had begun destroying pigs and chickens that had been feeding in areas where high levels of PCBs in soil were detected. The Agency for Toxic Substances and Disease Registry (ATSDR) and state and local public health agencies began alerting the public to the hazards posed by ingesting foodstuffs contaminated with PCBs.

In 1974, Congress passed the Safe Drinking Water Act in an effort to curtail ingestion of toxic substances, including PCBs. The U.S. Environmental Protection Agency (EPA) subsequently banned the use of PCBs in most industrial applications in 1979. However, substantial quantities of PCBs from used electrical equipment, faulty transformers, old lighting ballasts, and nonferrous wiring and insulation that had been disposed of in landfills continued to yield in excess of 74,000 pounds of PCBs during the six-year period from 1987 to 1993. Residual waste found at uncontrolled or abandoned hazardous waste sites continues to account for the majority of releases of PCBs into the environment.

Major Pollution Cases. While a myriad of cases involving the disposal of PCBs occurred from the early 1930s through the late 1970s, perhaps no single corporation is more associated with the discharge of PCBs than General Electric (GE). GE's production of electrical transformers and capacitors from the 1940s through the 1970s resulted in the substantial release of PCBs into major waterways such as the Hudson (New York) and Housatonic (Massachusetts) rivers. The Hudson River PCB plume spans nearly 200 miles, with an estimated 1.3 million pounds of contaminant alleged to have been released during the thirty years that plants operated in Hudson Falls and Fort Edward. Most of the contaminants settled into the river's bottom, adversely affecting both aquatic life and the $40 million per year commercial and recreational fishing industries along the Hudson. As part of a consent agreement between the U.S. Department of Justice, the EPA, and General Electric, GE has agreed to pay $78 million to the EPA as compensation for commercial response activities. General Electric will also undertake a major Hudson River dredging project in 2007.

Similarly, approximately 550 feet of sediment and 170 feet of soil located in and adjacent to the Housatonic River in Pittsfield, Massachusetts, were excavated in the 1990s as part of an agreement between GE and the EPA. General Electric also was held responsible for the removal of contaminated fill that it had given to the Town of Pittsfield for use as cover in playgrounds and residential neighborhoods. Some of this fill tested as high as 40,000 parts per million (ppm) of PCBs, well in excess of the EPA's legal safety standard of 2 ppm.

Much of the controversy surrounding General Electric's handling of the PCB contamination incidents in the Hudson Valley and Pittsfield stems from its efforts to downplay the product's risk to human health and the environment. As early as the 1930s, workers at General Electric, as well as some of its clientele, were complaining of chemical acne after being exposed to PCBs. In 1937, production managers at GE's Wireworks factory in York, Pennsylvania, began meeting with upper-level executives to discuss the outbreak of skin lesions and discomfort being experienced by employees at the facility. GE conducted confidential studies on the effects of PCB-in-oil exposure in 1938 and 1947 and found that exposure to these substances could damage target organs such as the liver and kidneys. Yet GE's most hotly debated action was the release of a 1999 internal research study that purportedly showed little correlation between exposure to PCBs and mortality. The study was touted by major industries such as Fox Valley Paper as evidence that the PCB scare had been overblown by the media and environmental watchdog organizations. However, it was later discovered that General Electric had not employed scientific rigor in its research, and the results were severely flawed. For example, the GE study had examined only airborne exposure to PCBs, not the more common routes of exposure: ingestion and absorption. The researchers had also preselected study participants—many of whom had worked for General Electric for less than a year. Lastly, the study failed to address those who had contracted—but not yet died from—cancer (i.e., it was a snapshot as opposed to a longitudinal study).

Much like other chemicals that became part of our daily lives during the twentieth century, PCBs were ultimately determined to be more dangerous than beneficial. The irresponsible behavior by the manufacturers and users of these substances, who ultimately did abandon their use though only after a period of intense public pressure and ensuing governmental regulation, is indicative of the wanton lack of regard of corporate America for the general health and welfare of its citizenry.

See also: Environmental White-Collar Crime

FURTHER READING

Agency for Toxic Substances and Disease Registry. "ToxFAQs for Polychlorinated Biphenyls (PCBs)." Available at http://www.astdr.cdc.gov/tfacts17.html. Accessed January 21, 2006.

Agency for Toxic Substances and Disease Registry. "Toxicological Profile for Polychlorinated Biphenyls (PCBs)." Available at http://www.atsdr.cdc.gov/toxprofiles/tp17.html. Accessed January 21, 2006.

Fox River Watch. "The GE Cancer Study Was Flawed." Available at http://www.foxriverwatch.com/general_electric_PCB-health_study.html. Accessed January 22, 2006.

Fox River Watch. "The History of PCBs: When Were Health Problems Detected?" Available at http://www.foxriverwatch.com/monsanto2a_pcb_pcbs.html. Accessed January 21, 2006.

Hudson River Sloop *Clearwater*. "Clearwater Presents the Hudson River PCB Story." Available at http://www.clearwater.org/pcbs/. Accessed January 22, 2006.

Public Interest Research Group. *"PIRG Make Polluters Pay!"* Available at http://www.pirg.org/ reports/ enviro/super25/page3.htm. Accessed January 22, 2006.

U.S. Environmental Protection Agency. "Consumer Factsheet on: Polychlorinated Biphenyls." Available at http://www.epa.gov/safewater/contaminants/dw_contamfs/pcbs.html. Accessed January 21, 2006.

U.S. Environmental Protection Agency. "General Electric to Remove Contaminated Soil and Sediments." Available at http://www.epa.gov/ne/ge/pressreleases/pr071097a.html. Accessed January 22, 2006.

U.S. Environmental Protection Agency. "Hudson River PCBs." Available at http://www.epa.gov/ region02/superfund/npl/0202229c.htm. Accessed January 22, 2006.

HANK J. BRIGHTMAN

PONZI, CHARLES (1882–1949). Charles Ponzi gave his name to a form of white-collar criminal behavior—the Ponzi scheme—that is reported time and time again in today's media. The ingredients of a Ponzi scheme are very simple. You have to get enough people interested in putting money into whatever investment you are promoting by promising them whirlwind profits. Then you pay off the initial investors with the funds that keep coming in as other people are dazzled by the amounts the first investors have received and clamor to get on the bandwagon. It is likely that those original investors will be so delighted with their profit that they will leave the money they have "earned" with you in order to reap even greater returns so that, for a time, a great deal of money will be coming in and not much will be going out. The difference between Ponzi schemes and pyramid frauds is that the latter rely on early entrants themselves recruiting subsequent participants in the deception. A Ponzi scheme depends upon human greed and demonstrates the truth of one of the oldest maxims in the financial world: If something is offered that flagrantly flies in the face of common sense, it very likely is nonsensical—and probably crooked.

Charles Ponzi was born Carlo K. Ponzi in Parma, Italy, in 1882 and emigrated to Boston when he was twenty years old. He spent the following fourteen years going from city to city, working intermittently as a dishwasher, waiter, store clerk, and interpreter. In 1907, back in Boston, he obtained a job answering foreign mail for a business firm. A letter from Spain included an international postage reply coupon. For Ponzi the coupon became a revelation. It had cost but one cent in Spain but could be traded in for six cents worth of postage in the United States. The key lay in an agreement entered into at the International Postal Congress in 1907 in Rome. To facilitate correspondence between richer relatives abroad and poorer family members in their home countries, the Congress had established a system of International Reply Coupons that could be purchased in one country and redeemed for postage stamps in another.

Ponzi had failed to appreciate that there was only a limited market for the coupons in the United States, that bureaucratic red tape would keep him from acquiring and disposing of the huge number of coupons that his scheme would require, and that considerable time delays in overseas transactions would tie up sums that he claimed (untruthfully) he planned to invest in the coupons.

Toward the end of 1919, Ponzi established the Securities Exchange Company, with but $150 of his own money. He promised in writing that in ninety days investors would be paid a fifty percent return on the money that they had put up. Then he hooked them by paying "dividends" in forty-five days at an interest rate that calculates out to 2400 percent annually. He accomplished this feat by using the new money to enrich the early investors.

Despite the appearance of great wealth, Ponzi was wildly in debt. In the eight months that he operated, he took in $9,582,000 but had outstanding notes totaling $14,374,000. Huge lines had formed outside his offices as people rushed to get in on the deal. The average customer bought $300 worth of Ponzi's elegant yellow certificates. Branch offices were created with agents who were paid 10 percent of the money they collected. It was estimated that during the half-year in 1920 that he conducted his business he took in one million dollars each week; all told, some 40,000 persons invested $15 million in Ponzi's scheme. He could have purchased almost two hundred thousand postal coupons with that sum; the records show that he had bought but two coupons. Moreover, three countries—France, Italy, and Romania—had withdrawn from the postal agreement and halted the sale of coupons not long after Ponzi began operating.

Ponzi, though only five feet four inches tall, presented a dapper public figure. He believed that an appearance of success was vital to promote his plan. He dressed elegantly, owned numerous trademark gold-handled canes, and bought a twenty-room mansion in suburban Lexington, outside Boston. Ponzi refused to discuss the details of what he might be doing with the money that had been given him and what his account books showed. Were he to do so, he told reporters, he was certain that the Du Ponts, the Vanderbilts, and the Astors—the big businessmen of the time—would steal his secret.

The beginning of the end came when the *Boston Post* raised questions about the legitimacy of Ponzi's business. Crowds stormed his offices, demanding their money back, but quieted down when he was able to pay them off. State officials then suspended trading in Ponzi stock, and their audit found that his company was bankrupt. Two days after that Ponzi admitted that he had served prison time in Canada on a forgery charge and later been incarcerated in the Atlanta federal prison for trying to smuggle five Italians from Canada into the United States.

Ponzi received a five-year sentence on a federal charge for his scam. When he was released on bail to appeal a Massachusetts conviction, he skipped off to Florida, assumed the name of Charles Burelli, and began to reenact the Ponzi script in land deals, marketing worthless swampland that he proclaimed to be prime property. Arrested, Ponzi served the next seven years in a Massachusetts prison and then was deported to Italy.

In Rome, he worked as an English translator until Benito Mussolini, the country's dictator, appointed him the head of the office in Rio de Janeiro for the Italian national airline. The airline became defunct during World War II, and in January 1949 Ponzi died in the charity ward of a Rio hospital.

Ponzi's name remains deeply embedded in the annals of financial skulduggery. When Kenneth Lay, the president of the Enron Company, which fiddled its books on a grand scale, came before a Congressional investigating committee in 1999, Senator Peter G. Fitzgerald, a Republican from Illinois, told him, "Mr. Lay, I've concluded that you're perhaps the most accomplished confidence man since Charles Ponzi. I'd say you were a carnival barker [persons who seek to entice customers into buying tickets for a sideshow], except that might not be fair to carnival barkers."

FURTHER READING

"Charles K. Ponzi Website." Available at http://www.mark-knutson.com. *Cunningham v. Brown*, United States Reports, Vol. 265, 1925, pp. 1–4.

Dunn, Donald H. *Ponzi: The Incredible Story of the King of Financial Cons*. New York: Broadway Books, 1993 [Original publication: New York: McGraw-Hill, 1975].

Russell, Francis. "Bubble, Bubble—No Toil, No Trouble." *American Heritage* 24.2 (1973): 74–80.

Streissguth, Thomas. *Hoaxers & Hustlers*. Minneapolis, MN: Oliver Press, 1994.

Wells, Joseph T. "Meet Mr. Ponzi: Charles Ponzi." Pp. 23–68 in *Frankensteins of Fraud: The 20th Century's Top Ten White-Collar Criminals*. Austin, TX: Obsidian, 2000.

GILBERT GEIS

POWER THEORY. Power theory is pertinent in the understanding of white-collar crime. The power theory has its roots in the two dominant perspectives in criminology for the explanation of deviant behavior—namely, the classical and positivist theories. The classical perspective is an offshoot of the Enlightenment theories of the eighteenth and nineteenth centuries. Its main argument is that crime is a consequence of egoistic and rational considerations and that punishment is in order to counteract the benefits derived from committing crime. The individual being punished and the general public are supposed to discover that crime does not pay. The premise of the classical theory's argument is that everyone is intelligent, educated, and properly socialized to know the difference between right and wrong. The reasoning that the individual possessed free-will and was rational and intelligent was a philosophical shift from the ancient regime where—Enlightenment theorists claimed—the individual's actions were believed to be determined by forces beyond his control. Offenders often adduced as a defense the belief that it was the demon that made them do it, and trial by ordeal was common with the goal of driving out the evil specters that inhabited the bodies of the offenders.

The positivist theories, on the other hand, argue that human behavior is determined by internal and external forces often beyond the control of the individual actor. Rather than punish law violators, the positivist theories recommend treatment and other rehabilitative programs to address the individual's problems. Following the medical model as postulated by the positivist theories, the individual is assumed to be sick and requiring treatment. The individual who commits crime is acting out of forces beyond his or her control. The individuals are perceived as victims of some biological, mental, psychological, or environmental conditions that predispose them to commit crime. The criminal justice response is to treat or resocialize the individuals concerned.

The positivist theory was the dominant paradigm for understanding criminal behavior at the time that Edwin Sutherland (1939) "discovered" white-collar crime. By this time, the social disorganization theories of the Chicago School had raised serious questions about the veracity of the positivist theories. The social disorganization theories attributed deviant behavior to the breakdown of societal institutions, thereby freeing people to engage in deviant behaviors. Deviance was no longer portrayed as behaviors in which only pathological people engage but as resulting from flaws in the social structure. The influence of the social disorganization theories might account for Sutherland's refutation of the psychological basis for understanding white-collar crime.

However, recent criminological theories point to the personality traits of white-collar offenders as important to the understanding of white-collar crime. David Friedrichs (2004: 196), citing other studies that examined in depth the personality traits of notorious white-collar offenders, noted common personality characteristics of white-collar offenders, such as obsession with power and control. According to these studies, white-collar offenders have little or no respect for laws and also have a tendency toward trampling upon other people's rights with impunity. Friedrichs describes white-collar criminals who meet these characteristics as narcissistic and as often having an overrated sense of self-importance and superiority.

Sutherland in 1939 defined white-collar crime as crime committed by persons of high social status in the course of legitimate occupation. White-collar crime encompasses crimes committed by individuals, businesses, corporations, and even states. David Simon (2002) appropriately refers to them as "elite deviants," because the actors often come from the highest strata of society. According to Simon (2002: 12), a major motivation for the elites in violating the laws regulating business or corporate activities is either "personal gain" or the advancement of the "power, profitability, or influence of the organizations involved."

There are two factors that account for why white-collar crime is widespread and pervasive in our society, and they include the economic difficulty and greed of white-collar offenders. Further support is given to white-collar crime by the criminogenic nature of corporate culture, and this is fueled by the prevailing values of power, materialism, individualism, and immediate gratification that characterize our society. White-collar crime is known to cause more injuries and deaths in our society than conventional crimes. White-collar crime is also considered to be the most pervading and amorphous of all crimes because of its potential to undermine social relations.

There is no unanimity on the relevance of personality traits in the explanation of white-collar crime. Friedrichs (2004: 195), citing studies by Coleman (2002), Punch (2000), and Snider (1993), identifies certain personality traits that are common among white-collar offenders. Such personality traits, according to the studies, include "risk taking and recklessness, ambitiousness and drive, and egocentricity and a hunger for power." Friedrichs further notes that these personality traits are also present in people who achieve success through legitimate means, suggesting that risk taking is not necessarily an undesirable attribute. However, these personality traits can become problematic and lead to excessive and illegal behavior when they are intermixed with paranoia and megalomania, notes Friedrichs. He further observes that these personality characteristics are common among overachievers. Such people hardly show contrition for any wrongdoing because of their penchant to view their actions as having some messianic purpose and their warped sense of self-importance.

It is common among white-collar offenders to rationalize their illegal conduct, according to Friedrichs (2004). Citing another study by Criddle (1987) that examined the personality traits of white-collar offenders, Friedrichs also found white-collar offenders to be clever people but to have a tendency to be aloof and easily frustrated, especially when things do not go their way. Another study that compared the personality traits of 350 incarcerated white-collar offenders with an equal number of corporate executives identified some consistent characteristics among the criminals, such as "greater tendencies toward irresponsibility, lack of dependability, and disregard for rules," states Friedrichs (2004: 195). Many white-collar offenders are driven by greed and an air of invincibility and poor judgment, according to another study by Ellin (2002). Other studies by Gottfredson and Hirschi (1990) and Wheeler (1992) identified excessive fear of failure and inability to defer gratification as important attributes in white-collar criminals. White-collar offenders also have difficulties in exercising self-control according to these studies. Low self–control, according to Gottfredson and Hirschi (1990), results from inadequate socialization, especially in the family domain sphere.

In conclusion, the power theory argues that most white-collar offenders tend to be overachievers, clever, and possess an incredible ability to manipulate others. Studies that examine the personality traits of white-collar offenders allege a pervasive tendency to disregard laws and as having no pang of conscience in violating other people's rights. These personality traits are encouraged by the prevailing culture of individualism, self-centeredness, competition, and winner-takes-all mentality in contemporary society.

FURTHER READING

Friedrichs, David O. *Trusted Criminals: White Collar Crime in Contemporary Society*, 2nd edition. Belmont, CA: Thomson/Wadsworth, 2004.
Simon, David R. *Elite Deviance*, 7th edition. Boston: Allyn and Bacon, 2002.

O. OKO ELECHI

PRICE FIXING. Price fixing is a general term that refers to an array of illegal behaviors committed by corporations, acting in collusion with one another, with the intent of maximizing profit margins. Its incidence is strikingly common, involving some of the nation's largest corporations, and its costs are enormous, resulting in billions of dollars lost by consumers every year.

Typically, price fixing concerns an explicit agreement among corporations in a particular industry not to undercut each other's prices. Such an action restrains trade and violates the principles of competition in a free, open market. Furthermore, it defrauds customers by creating unnaturally high prices. The corporations involved in the price fixing agreement form what is commonly referred to as a *cartel*. When a given industry is dominated by a cartel, an oligopoly—an industry with few sellers controlling over 50 percent of the market—is created; a similar concept is a monopoly—an industry with a single seller dominating the entire market. The objective of oligopolies is to increase the profits of all the sellers involved; price fixing is one such strategy used to accomplish this profit maximization.

Other than setting prices, however, price fixing can entail additional behaviors as well. For instance, price fixing also describes determining market shares, restricting production or sales, monitoring and enforcing agreements, and concealing the activities of the cartel.

Price fixing has a myriad of effects on market participants. Not only does it impact market revenues and costs of production, leading to the overcharging of consumers, but it also can result in a general social loss. That is, when a cartel fixes prices higher than they would have been without the cartel and restricts the manufacturing of the product, consumers withdraw from the market because of the increased costs and are compelled to use, if available, an inferior, non-cartelized product. Thus, the market loses the consumer, and the producers become highly inefficient, wasting labor and factory resources.

The true costs of price fixing are unknown, however. Although it is estimated that such activities cost consumers approximately $60 billion dollars annually, most incidents of price fixing never make it to trial, and concerning those that do, it is not always required that testimony be given concerning the economic impact of the situation. Surveys of large corporations across several industries, though, suggest that it is a fairly common phenomenon.

The presence or absence of cartels participating in price fixing agreements is dependent upon several factors. For instance, an industry with only a few firms increases the likelihood that a cartel will form, because the more firms that exist within an industry, the more difficult it is for cartel members to monitor and enforce collusion agreements. Specifically, it has been suggested that an industry with more than five firms is unlikely to transform into an oligopoly. Another factor influencing the formation of cartels is product homogeneity. If a product is made according to similar specifications by different firms, the price of the product will be nearly the same regardless of the product's manufacturer. In such situations, in order to increase profits, firms will collectively agree to charge more for the product than they would if they were operating in a truly free-enterprise system. Product homogeneity is more likely to be present in older industries, however. That is, new industries, which are still developing their technologies and producing heterogeneous products, are more likely to be operating at a competitive level than more mature industries. Restricted entry into a particular industry is another condition that facilitates the formation of cartels. When only a few firms have access to or can afford the technology to function in a given industry, less effort is required for managing and enforcing agreements, increasing the likelihood that collusion will occur.

Price fixing is illegal, and the primary legal tool against it in the United States is the Sherman Antitrust Act, passed in 1890. Historically, the concept of a *trust* was used to describe the outcome of a merger of several firms within an industry. Currently, a trust is synonymous with a cartel. The Department of Justice (DOJ) has sole responsibility for bringing about criminal, felony charges against any individual or firm that violates the Sherman Act. The Federal Trade Commission can also prosecute violators of the Sherman Act, but it can do so only under civil law. It should be noted, however, that the DOJ also has the option of civilly prosecuting Sherman Act violators; whether or not the DOJ seeks a criminal or civil prosecution, though, is greatly dependent upon the strength of the case, since the standard of proof is more stringent in criminal court—guilt beyond a reasonable doubt—than in civil court—the preponderance of evidence. State antitrust agencies, as well as private citizens, are also able to bring forth price-fixing allegations. All fifty states now have antitrust laws that prohibit unreasonable methods of competition.

In the past, the enforcement of antitrust laws was characterized by extreme laxness. After the creation of the Sherman Act, over seventy years went by before a businessperson was prosecuted specifically for price fixing and monopolization; furthermore, no one was sentenced to jail, for any antitrust violation, until twenty years after the legislation's passage. These shortcomings of enforcement can be attributed to a lack of official resources, particularly the small number of federal and state attorneys devoted to antitrust violations, and the perceived harmlessness of such actions. That is, until 1974, the contravening of the Sherman Act was deemed to be a misdemeanor offense.

A deluge of complaints by prosecutors and antitrust bar members and experts eventually led to the campaign spearheaded by Congress to increase penalties for Sherman Act violations. Antitrust offenses were eventually characterized as felonies, and fines against persons and firms were increased from $350,000 and $10 million, respectively, to $1 million and $100 million, respectively. Recent changes in federal sentencing guidelines, however, allow for prosecutors to seek fines higher than the statutory limit. For instance, in 1988 the courts ordered that Exxon pay $2.1 billion, Occidental $660 million, and Cities Service $600 million after each had been found guilty of price fixing.

One of the most notorious price-fixing cases in American history is known as the Electrical Conspiracy, wherein, during the mid-1940s and 1950s, General Electric and Westinghouse, along with twenty-nine other corporations, conspired to rig the sealed bidding of public agency contracts; this practice was used to ensure high prices, rotating the winners of the contracts in relation to their respective share of the market prior to the conspiracy. A more recent case, which demonstrates a current trend of global price-fixing enforcement, is that involving Archer Daniels Midland Co.—at one time, one of the country's most admired firms—and its collusion agreements in the international lysine market.

See also: Archer-Daniels-Midland (ADM); *Exxon Valdez*; Heavy Electrical Equipment Antitrust Cases of 1961

FURTHER READING

Bequai, August. *White Collar Crime: A 20th Century Crisis.* Lexington, MA: D.C. Health, 1978.
Connor, John M. *Global Price Fixing: Our Customers are the Enemy.* Norwell, MA: Kluwer Academic Publishers, 2001.
Kappeler, Victor E., Blumberg, Mark, and Potter, Gary W. *The Mythology of Crime and Criminal Justice,* 3rd edition. Prospect Heights, IL: Waveland Press, 2000.
O'Gara, John D. *Corporate Fraud: Case Studies in Detection and Prevention.* Hoboken, NJ: Wiley, 2004.
Simon, David R. *Elite Deviance,* 8th edition. Boston: Pearson/Allyn & Bacon, 2006.

DANIEL M. STEWART

PTL MINISTRY. See Bakker, Jim and Tammy Faye

R

RACKETEER INFLUENCED AND CORRUPT ORGANIZATIONS ACT (RICO).
For more than three decades the courts, prosecutors, plaintiffs' lawyers, and the civil and criminal defense bar have struggled with the extensive coverage of the Racketeer Influenced and Corrupt Organizations Act (RICO). Once violated, RICO provides a broad range or remedies designed to dismantle "root and branch" the criminal enterprise directing the racketeering activity. The RICO statute consists of eight sections, one of which, Section 1961, cites fifty-two predicate federal statutes, five generic references to federal labor and securities laws, and nine other state offenses. The Supreme Court has interpreted RICO numerous times since its inception in 1970 in both criminal and civil cases. RICO has undermined systematic criminal activity with a broad and flexible statutory scheme not only of organized crime families, but of other illegitimate as well as legitimate corporate activity. Because of RICO's considerable breadth, this article will focus on the main elements of RICO—enterprise and pattern—and how they have most recently been interpreted.

The RICO Act was set into motion by the 1968 President's Commission on Law Enforcement and Administration of Justice. The commission studied organized as well as white-collar crimes and determined that crime legislation prohibiting this type of crime had to achieve five goals. In 1970, RICO was enacted by Congress as Title IX of the Crime Control Act of 1970.

Before a prosecutor or a plaintiff can show a RICO violation, the prosecutor or plaintiff must first establish that a "lesser" crime, an act of racketeering, or what is also known as a *predicate act*, has been committed. A claim of RICO can be predicated on both federal and state statutes. For state crimes the Act dictates that a violation can be predicated on "any act or threat involving murder, kidnapping, gambling, arson, robbery, bribery, extortion . . . which is chargeable with state law and punishable by imprisonment for more than one year." Federal crimes that predicate RICO can generally be classified into categories including bribery, theft, murder, fraud, gambling, dealing in obscenity or narcotics, obstruction of justice, obstruction of state or local law enforcement, and interference with commerce. However, a defendant need not be criminally convicted before a civil plaintiff can sue under RICO. The statute requires only that the criminal acts are "chargeable" or "indictable" under state or federal law, not that the defendant has been charged or indicted.

Section 1962 of RICO, which is divided into four subsections, is most often employed by both prosecutors and plaintiffs. It states that it is unlawful for a person to use an enterprise to launder money generated by a pattern of racketeering activity and declares that a person cannot acquire or maintain interest in an enterprise through a pattern of racketeering activity. Section 1963 provides for criminal sanctions, while Sections 1964 through 1968 facilitate civil remedies as well as enforcement.

A RICO claim is among the most difficult violations to establish, in that one must prove a racketeering activity in addition to the presence of an enterprise and pattern. The consequences of violating RICO are disproportionately greater than the sum of committing just two predicate crimes. RICO penalties can include (1) a civil penalty of triple damages for victims of business or property injuries resulting from a RICO violation; (2) criminal fines up to twice the ill-gotten gain and imprisonment of up to 25 years; and (3) forfeiture of any interest acquired during commission of racketeering activity, any interest in property or contractual right obtained in a pattern of racketeering activity, and any proceeds derived from any proceeds obtained directly or indirectly from racketeering activity.

Enterprise. The element of *enterprise* establishes liability under Section 1962. Although RICO refers to defendants as "persons," a defendant can be either an individual of the corporation or the corporation itself, as long as the defendant is engaging in the unlawful pattern of criminal activity. Additionally, before RICO can be used, the existence of an "enterprise" must be proven, either as a legitimate or illegitimate entity. To violate RICO, this "person" must either directly or indirectly acquire an interest or control an "enterprise." Federal district and circuit courts have a substantial amount of power in determining what constitutes an enterprise. Courts have held that the numerous entities be illustrative not exhaustive, in that a "shifting definition of enterprise has been held necessary in view of the fluid nature of criminal associations." Furthermore, an enterprise can be a loosely assembled group and be referred to as "association-in-fact" enterprises under the RICO statute. Although these "association-in-fact" enterprises are not legal entities, they have a shared purpose and an identifiable structure and have an objective separate from the predicate acts themselves. Although the RICO enterprise itself frequently perpetrates the crime, more often than not it is a victim of the criminal act or merely a passive instrument. Just naming an entity as a RICO enterprise does not impose any liability on that entity; therefore banks, insurance agencies, and so forth that unknowingly facilitate criminal activities are often classified as RICO enterprises. Most courts have held that there is no need to make a distinction between an "enterprise" and a "person."

In 1981, *United States v. Turkette* held that the term "enterprise" constitutes that a plaintiff must establish the existence of an enterprise, legitimate or illegitimate, such as a corporation or a Mafia family. An enterprise is separate from the "pattern of racketeering element," however, and the prosecutor or plaintiff must always prove the existence of an enterprise and how it is connected to the pattern of racketeering activity. Yet in 2001 the Supreme Court ruled on a circuit court split and held that an employee of a corporation, even if a sole shareholder, is a legally distinct "person" associated with the "enterprise" of the corporation. Therefore, it is uniformly the law that the "person" and "enterprise" alleged under Section 1962(c) must be only legally, not necessarily actually, distinct.

Pattern. A RICO offense occurs when two or more predicate acts of "racketeering activity" occur; this constitutes a pattern. Section 1962 (a) is designed for those who manage or operate an enterprise's affairs through a pattern of racketeering activity, resulting in harm to the RICO plaintiff. Historically, RICO's pattern element followed a multiple-schemes test. which required not only that a RICO pattern of racketeering activity consist of multiple predicate acts but that the pattern comprise multiple "schemes." In *H. J. Inc. v. Northwestern Bell Telephone Company* (1989), the Supreme Court struck down this multiple-schemes test because it was too restrictive and could not encompass prosecutions of civil suits.

H. J. Inc. v. Northwestern Bell Telephone Company was an important case in that it significantly expanded the reach of the RICO Act to civil liability cases with regard to the racketeering pattern. In this case, customers of Northwestern Bell Telephone Company alleged that the company gave members of the Minnesota Public Utilities Commission numerous bribes with the objective of causing the commissioners to approve unfair and unreasonable rates. Plaintiffs sought an injunction and triple damages under the civil liability provisions of the RICO Act. The Court held that in order to prove a pattern of racketeering activity under RICO, "the plaintiff or prosecutor must show at least two racketeering predicates that are related and that amount to, or threaten the likelihood of, continued criminal activity, and although proof of multiple criminal schemes may be relevant to inquiry into continuity, it is not the only way to show continuity." In essence, the Court expanded upon the "continuity" and "relationship" requirements laid out in *Sedima, S.P.R.L. v. Imrex Co., Inc.* Although not noteworthy in regards to the relationship aspect, which generally is not hard to prove in showing a valid relationship among the acts in the pattern, the "continuity" requirement was significantly broadened. The Court's explanation for this requirement stated that "for a pattern of racketeering activity to exist the predicate offenses must themselves amount to, or otherwise constitute a threat of, continuing racketeering activity." The fundamental problem with the past multischeme test was that almost any pattern could be portrayed as either one scheme or multiple schemes, dependent upon the person who was determining the pattern.

Additionally, a two-category test was established by the *H.J., Inc.* Court to determine the threat of continuity as "open-ended" or "closed-ended." "Closed-ended" racketeering is established "by proving a series of related predicates extending over a substantial period of time." Even if the conduct has not extended over a "substantial period of time," it can still be shown to be sufficiently continuous to exhibit an "open-ended" threat of continuity. If the nature of the predicate acts themselves indicates that the activity is likely to continue, or if the acts are linked to an ongoing criminal enterprise, than the "open ended" requirement is met. In essence, the Court has left open a broad area in classifying the continuity concept, stating that "the precise methods by which relatedness and continuity or its threat may be proved, cannot be fixed in advance with such clarity that it will always be apparent whether in a particular case of 'pattern of racketeering activity' exists."

Currently, some circuit courts have been unwilling to abandon the multiple-schemes approach, as seen in *Midwest Grinding Co., Inc. v. Spitz*, decided in the Seventh Circuit Court in 1992, and more recently in *Western Associates Ltd. Partnership v. Market Square Associates*, decided in the D.C. Circuit Court in 2001. Both of these appellate courts allowed the petitioner to establish that the defendant had engaged in more than one racketeering scheme and injured more than one victim and thus apply the "multiple-scheme approach" to show a pattern.

Overall it is easier to sustain a civil burden of proof than a criminal one. A civil plaintiff need only convince a jury that the preponderance of evidence that the defendant committed acts of racketeering. A prosecutor, on the other hand, must establish that the acts of racketeering occurred beyond a reasonable doubt.

FURTHER READING

Title 18, U.S. Code, Sections 1963, 1964, 1965, 1966, 1967, and 1968.

Bryan, Kristen. "Racketeer Influenced and Corrupt Organizations." *American Criminal Law Review* 40 (2003): 987–1012.

Sawker, Laxmidas. "From the Mafia to Milking Cows: State RICO Act Expansion." *Arizona Law Review* 41 (1999): 1133–1168.

Sedima, S.P.R.L. v. Imrex Co., Inc., 105 S.Ct. 3275 (1985).

United States v. Turkette, 452 US 576 (1981).

Western Associates Ltd. Partnership v. Market Square Associates, 235 F.3d 629 (2001).

JILETTA L. KUBENA

RADICAL/CRITICAL THEORIES. The history of radical and critical criminology has gone through a number of stages, and each concept has been associated with well-known theorists.

Early Theorists/Theoretical Underpinnings. Radical and critical criminology can be traced back almost two centuries to the work of Karl Marx and Friedrich Engels.

Marx and Engels. Marx (1818–1883) is credited with developing a well-respected theory of class conflict. Engels (1820–1895) befriended Marx, and together they wrote several important articles. Both men suggested that conflict in society is a result of a scarcity of resources (such as property, wealth, power, and jobs). This creates inequalities among individuals and constituencies, which, in turn, leads to a struggle between those who possess these resources (owners of the means of production, also known as the capitalists) and those who do not (the working class or proletariat) (Marx and Engels, 1848/1988). According to Marx and Engels, law protects the property of the wealthy, promotes the ideological interests of the wealthy, and represses the working class. Marx (1853), in particular, "argued that both the . . . [amount] and the types of crime in modern society were produced by the fundamental conditions of bourgeois society." Marx argued that capitalist societies produce a conflict between those who own the means of production and those who do not. There were three important aspects of Marx and Engels' analysis of crime and capitalism. They were "criminalization as a violation of natural or human rights, crime and demoralization, and crime and primitive rebellion."

Marx and Engels

> saw crime . . . as an inevitable feature of existing social organization . . . because it is an expression of basic social and class inequalities. Working-class crime, especially, results from demoralization, and occasionally turns to primitive rebellion. The extent and the forms of crime, they suggest, should be understood in the context of the specific class relationships, state, and law associated with a given mode of production.

> Yet Marx and Engels did not explain crime simply by referring to economic factors, as many commentators wrongly claim. As noted, they clearly understood that crime involves a political process whereby the state criminalizes certain conduct and, by doing so, often reflects the interests not of society as a whole but of certain groups within. Crime, Marx and Engels sometimes suggested, was a form of rebellion against this process. This realization, however poorly articulated by Marx and Engels, was . . . [adopted] by criminologists in the 1970s and 1980s. (Beirne and Messerschmidt, 1991: 350)

Marx and Engels believed that the working class would be the "dynamite" for change in the political system.

Marx "also argued that the system of economic relationships effects the political, cultural, and religious institutions of society. Capitalistic societies are prone to develop laws, religions, and science—which protect the interests of capitalists" (Liska 1987: 174). Thus, class conflict leads to crime.

Dahrendorf. Ralf Dahrendorf, a British-German sociologist (1959) modified Marx's work and updated it to twentieth-century industrial society:

> Whereas Marx emphasized ownership of the means of production, Dahrendorf emphasizes power as the major social division; and whereas Marx argued that power is derived from ownership of the means of production, Dahrendorf argues that in contemporary industrial society power is frequently divorced from ownership of the means of production and is based on institutional authority. Dahrendorf focuses on the division between those who have and those who do not have authority to control behavior in institutional structures. Economic structures are important but not central. Additionally, Dahrendorf argues that authority in one institution (economic) does not necessarily overlap with authority relationships in other institutions (education, religion, government). (Liska 1987: 174)

Conflict Theorists. During the 1960s a handful of sociologists of crime developed conflict theory, of which there are several types. They range from conservative to radical perspectives, but all agree that conflict is a naturally occurring social phenomenon. Where they disagree is on its origin, its persistence, its ability to create change, and its contribution to criminal behavior.

Vold: Cultural Conflict. George B. Vold rooted his perspective in the Chicago School. He said that human interaction is constantly marked by conflict; the creation of laws, prosecution of criminals, and the interactions among participants in the criminal justice system are efforts by groups to gain control and advantage to support or protect their interests. Vold also suggested that the newly arrived immigrants are confronted with environments in which the norms are ambiguous, thus leading to cultural conflict (Vold 1958). In short, their norms clash with existing norms. For example, when a father from the "old country" shoots a boy for sleeping with his daughter, this may be interpreted as righting a wrong and perfectly normal back home but is considered totally inappropriate (and in fact illegal) in the United States.

Turk: Pluralistic Conflict. Austin T. Turk (1969) was one of the first persons to develop a general conflict theory of crime. He looked at the relationship between authorities (which have the power to control the public), and subjects (the powerless), in the context of institutions. Turk argued that conflict takes place based on the sophistication of the contending parties. He also suggested that repression takes place when there are noticeable cultural differences between authorities and citizens.

Radical Theorists. Dissatisfaction with the conflict explanations led a handful of theorists to elaborate a radical approach to the explanation of crime. This included Richard Quinney and William Chambliss (Bohm, 1982).

Quinney: Radical Criminology. Quinney, most appropriately labeled a neo-Marxist, argued that all crime in capitalist societies is considered a manifestation of class struggle, whereby people want wealth, power, money, status, and property. In countries dominated by a capitalist mode of production, a culture of competition arises. This is seen as normal and desirable and takes many forms, including criminality, evidenced in poor young men burglarizing residences, corporate executives overcharging consumers, and oppositional terrorist organizations bombing buildings with the hope of effecting social and political change (Quinney 1970).

Chambliss. Chambliss, a sociologist, conducted historical research on the relationship between economic interests and the origins and development of law. His study (1964) of the development of vagrancy laws is the best known. Chambliss pointed out that these laws exist in just about all states and tend to be used either to control "undesirables" or to provide a cheap and ready source of unskilled labor.

Critical Criminology Today. Over the past two decades, radical criminology has matured into a diverse body of work. These new theories are generally called critical criminology. Critical criminology has an emphasis on understanding crimes committed by the powerful and often includes white-collar, corporate, and political crime. A critical approach looks for deeper meanings in its analysis. Today, a variety of perspectives can be subsumed under this domain, including but not limited to postmodernism, left realism, feminism, and peacemaking.

Postmodernism is the intense analysis of symbols that are prevalent in culture. Such topics of investigation include the mass media and graffiti (Ferrell 1993, 1998; Ferrell and Sanders 1995). Content analysis is a favored research technique in postmodern studies.

Left realism, on the other hand, is the application of empirical analysis to problems affecting working-class or powerless people in society (e.g., Lea et al. 1986).

Feminism analyzes crime against women and the role of gender in crime causation (e.g., Adler 1975; Daly and Chesney-Lind 1988). Finally, peacemaking involves the use of victim-offender mediation (e.g., Pepinsky and Quinney 1991).

Although building blocks in the historical treatment of radical and critical criminology, and worthwhile reading for those attempting to understand recent trends in this area better, some of this work suffers from a variety of shortcomings (Ross 1998: Chapter 1). First, some of the work is overwritten and makes a questionable contribution to the advancement of radical and critical criminology. Second, there is an abundance of emotionally and ideologically loaded language, which detracts from the authors' ability to present a clear message to those in the policy community and in applied settings. Third, in an attempt to find cultural anchors, some authors make some minor errors. Fourth, with few exceptions, these works are heavily American-oriented. Most of the contributors are Americans and so are their examples. Fifth, the relevance of many assertions is not clearly explored. Sixth, some contributions are primarily typology-building exercises, the usefulness of which the authors fail to explore. Seventh, other pieces are inaccessible, have questionable relevance, incorporate undecipherable policy and applied applications, and suffer from unnecessary hyperbole. Eighth, some authors seem content to summarize other radical and critical scholars' works without reflecting on the literature's shortcomings. Ninth, authors can be criticized on a series of assumptions and overgeneralizations—in particular, faulty or unquestioned assumptions. Tenth, the reasons for case selection in case study comparisons are often not justified. Eleventh, many of the authors can too easily be charged with bias, since most are activists in the programs they are evaluating. None reviews why, for instance, any of their "radical" or "innovative" programs failed to work. Finally, some writers are prone to present redundant or repetitive and unoriginal laundry lists of problems with the criminal justice system. Many of the pieces review the all-too-familiar problems with the criminal justice system but offer (if not utopian and vague) untested methods to change the process. While the practical applications are the most useful, it is doubtful that all are successful.

Radical and critical criminology is too often dismissed by mainstream criminologists. Casual observers have a difficult time separating the message from the messenger. Central to its core, however, radical and critical criminology has sensitized us to the role of power in crime commission and to the notion that what constitutes power at any given time is subject to change.

Special attention should be given to the variety of radical and critical theories, including but not limited to Marxist, neo-Marxist, and conflict approaches (Ross 1998). Granted, many theories that have emanated from the radical/conflict tradition are parsimonious, have considerable explanatory power over other efforts, and are widely accepted among many criminologists, as evidenced by their inclusion in a large body of literature in political, white-collar, and state crime research (Ross 1998). However, there is considerable discomfort with their ability to be applied to practical policy concerns.

See also: Power Theory; Rational Choice Theory

FURTHER READING

Adler, Freda. *Sisters in Crime: The Rise of the New Female Criminal.* New York: McGraw Hill, 1975.

Beirne, P., and Messerschmidt, J. *Criminology.* Toronto: Harcourt Brace Jovanovich, 1991.

Bohm, Robert. M. "Radical Criminology: An Explication." *Criminology* 19.4 (1982): 565–589.

Chambliss, William. "A Sociological Analysis of the Law and Vagrancy." *Social Problems* 12 (1964): 67–77.

Dahrendorf, Ralf. *Class and Class Conflict in Industrial Society.* Stanford, CA: Stanford University Press, 1959.

Daley, Kathleen, and Chesney-Lind, Meda. 1988. "Feminism and Criminology." *Justice Quarterly* 5 (1988): 497–538.

Ferrell, Jeff. *Crimes of Style: Urban Graffiti and the Politics of Criminality.* Boston: Northeastern University Press, 1993.

Ferrell, J. "Stumbling toward a Critical Criminology (and into the Anarchy and Imagery of Postmodernism)." Pp. 63–76 in Jeffrey Ian Ross (ed.), *Cutting the Edge: Current Perspectives in Radical/Critical Criminology and Criminal Justice.* Westport, CT: Praeger Publishers, 1998.

Ferrell J., and Sanders, C. R. (eds.). *Cultural Criminology.* Boston: Northeastern University Press, 1995.

Lea, J., Jones, T., MacLean, B., and Young, J. *The Islington Crime Survey.* Aldershot, UK: Gower, 1986.

Liska, Allen. *Perspectives on Deviance.* Englewood Cliffs, NJ: Prentice Hall, 1987.

Marx, Karl, and Engels, Friedrich. *The Communist Manifesto*. 1848. (New York: Signet, 1988.)

Marx, Karl. *Theories of Surplus Value*. 3 vols. 1863. (New York: Prometheus Books, 2003.)

Pepinsky, Harold E., and Quinney, Richard (eds.). *Criminology as Peacemaking*. Bloomington: Indiana University Press, 1991.

Quinney, Richard. *The Social Reality of Crime*. Boston: Little, Brown, 1970.

Quinney, Richard. *Critique of Legal Order*. Boston: Little, Brown, 1974.

Quinney, Richard. *Class, State and Crime*. New York: Longman, 1980.

Ross, Jeffrey Ian (ed.). *Cutting the Edge: Current Perspectives in Radical/Critical Criminology and Criminal Justice*. Westport, CT: Praeger, 1998.

Turk, Austin. T. *Criminality and Legal Order*. Chicago: Rand McNally, 1969.

Vold, George. *Theoretical Criminology*. New York: Oxford University Press, 1958.

JEFFREY IAN ROSS

RATIONAL CHOICE THEORY. Rational Choice theory can be traced back to the writings of two of the most important enlightenment philosophers whose work was directly related to criminology: Cesare Beccaria and Jeremy Bentham.

Beccaria (1738–1794), an Italian philosopher and economist, wrote an influential essay titled *On Crimes and Punishments* (1764/1963). He believed that:

People are rational (i.e., they make cost benefit calculations).

Individuals are products of free will.

Criminal justice should operate on the principle of due process. (The government will ensure that a person's rights are protected in legal proceedings.)

The punishment should fit the crime.

Sanctions should be quick and certain and provide a measure of deterrence.

The punishment must be uniform among offenders.

Torture and capital punishment should be abolished and replaced by prison sentences.

In 1766, his approach was criticized because it appeared to be too rationalist. As a result, the Roman Catholic Church censored him. Nevertheless, Beccaria's ideas were incorporated into the new criminal codes of Western European countries and into the newly written U.S. Constitution and the Bill of Rights.

Bentham (1748–1823) was an English philosopher and statesman whose thinking was influenced by Beccaria. Among his many accomplishments was an influential book entitled *An Introduction to the Principles of Morals and Legislation* (1780). It argued that potential criminals consciously calculate the costs and benefits before committing a crime. If the potential costs outweigh the benefits, people will not break the law.

Bentham suggested that crime could be prevented through the proper development and judicious use of rewards and punishments. He advanced the idea and designed the panopticon, a large building in which, much as in the modern-day prisons that it inspired, a watcher at a central post can see into all the cells at any time. The design could be used for any facility that needs to keep people controlled: prisons to punish criminals, asylums to house the mentally insane, and hospitals to help those afflicted with terminal sickness.

Beccaria's and Bentham's proposals were mainly aimed at making punishment more humane and efficient. Their work should be interpreted as products of their time period. Beccaria and Bentham chose a limited number of reasonably acceptable options given the state of thought during this era. Their ideas were never intended to upset the existing power relations or structures. This is perhaps why much of their thinking resonates with contemporary conservatives, deterrence theory, and contemporary rational choice theorists.

Several keen observers noted that the deterrent factors of the criminal justice system that were believed to support the free-will explanation were not enough to stop many individuals from committing crimes. Thus thinkers of the day eventually suggested that something more elementary was behind criminal behavior.

During the 1970s the classical explanation to crime causation was reexamined. A number of developments aided this kind of thinking. One of them was Robert Martinson's classic and controversial essay "What Works" (1974), which concluded, after an exhaustive review of studies on rehabilitation, that little if any programs prevent prisoners from committing crime. Another was James Q. Wilson's book *Thinking about Crime* (1975), which argued that crime was hardly the function of poverty and that government social programs had minimal impact on the crime rate. What society needed instead were punishments and incarceration of known felons, particularly career criminals. This point of view was aided by a conservative shift in American politics and criminal justice policy in particular. Since this time, the draconian sentencing laws such as "three strikes, you're out" and mandatory minimum sentences have become the norm.

In this intellectual climate, many researchers developed more sophisticated rational choice explanations of criminality. Research utilizing these theories has been done with burglars (Cromwell, Olson, and Wester Avary, 1989), professional criminals (Tunnell, 1992), drug dealers (Jacobs and Miller, 1998; Knowles, 1999), robbers (Van Koppen and Jansen, 1999), and white-collar criminals (Shover and Hochstetler, 2006). This has led in due course to explanations and prevention strategies such as situational crime prevention, routine activities theory, and Crime Prevention Through Environmental Design (CPTED). Where rational choice theory runs into trouble is in explaining all types of violence.

See also: Power Theory

FURTHER READING

Beccaria, Cesare. *Essays on Crimes and Punishment.* 1764. (Translated with an introduction by H. Paolucci. New York: Macmillan, 1963.)

Bentham, Jeremy. *An Introduction to the Principles of Morals and Legislation.* 1780. (New York: Oxford University Press, 1996.)

Shover, Neal, and Hochstetler, Andrew. *Choosing White-Collar Crime.* New York: Cambridge University Press, 2006.

Tunnell, K. *Choosing Crime: The Criminal Calculus of Property Offenders.* Chicago: Nelson-Hall, 1992.

JEFFREY IAN ROSS

RELIGION AND WHITE-COLLAR CRIME. The economic losses from the various forms of white-collar crime cost society far more than all the "blue-collar" or street crime (e.g., robberies, burglaries, shoplifting) combined. For example, the losses from tax evasion alone run into the billions both in the United States and in other industrial societies. The

U.S. Internal Revenue Service (IRS) may lose as much as $64 billion in tax revenue annually from just one form of tax fraud: failure to report income from partnerships. Estimates of the amount of income lost to government as a result of tax cheating include 20 percent in the United States and 17 percent in Belgium. Britain's loss due to tax fraud amounts to a full 8 percent of its entire gross national product. A review of 18 relevant scientific investigations determined that, on average, 20 percent of American taxpayers acknowledge that they cheat on their taxes. Tax cheating is a serious problem that is fairly widespread.

However, most people do not engage in tax cheating and most other forms of white-collar crime. Why do some people hold positive attitudes toward the commission of tax fraud and other forms of white-collar crime, while most people do not? Why are some individuals more apt to engage in such behavior as tax cheating, bribery, and cheating on claiming government benefits? Criminological research on white-collar crime has often lagged behind research on street crime in testing hypotheses on these questions. Many forms of white-collar crimes are committed by organizations, not individuals, so new organizational theories may be required to explain the behaviors (Cressey 2001). However, other forms of white-collar crime, such as tax evasion, bribery, and cheating on government benefits, can be committed by individuals. Traditional explanations of crime such as social learning theory and social control theory can, therefore, be applied to these individualistic forms of white-collar crime (Barnett 2000).

Many traditional criminological theories can be used to explain an inverse relationship between religion and crime. From the standpoint of a social learning theory of criminal attitudes and behavior, religion decreases the risk of crime through promoting negative definitions of criminal behavior. Literally all of the world's religions preach against theft (e.g., "thou shalt not steal"). White-collar crimes often represent the unlawful taking or withholding of monies and property. Persons who have been highly exposed to religious teachings would be anticipated to have internalized more negative views of white-collar crime than their counterparts. Tax fraud, in particular, is often condemned by religion. In Christian scripture, for example, the obligations to pay taxes is discussed in all of the Gospels and in the Letter to the Romans.

From the standpoint of social control theory, religious involvement may strengthen religious beliefs against theft. Bonds to religious beliefs may give individuals a stake in conformity. If they do deviate, and are caught, they may be faced with embarrassment in the religious community. These and other explanations of religion's impact on crime have not been systematically applied, very often, to the case of white-collar crime. Of sixty studies reviewed in a recent exhaustive meta-analysis of research on religion and crime, only five had any information on religion as a deterrent to white-collar crime (Baier and White 2001).

Two studies based in Oklahoma City determined that religious attendance lowers the intention to commit tax fraud. Further, the importance that an individual gives to religion, or "religious salience," was found to deter intentions to cheat on taxes (Grasmick et al. 1991). Two studies of Catholics illustrated that social bonds to the parish tend to lower reports of willingness to engage in tax fraud in the future. However, there has been no rigorous study on nations other than the United States. Further, all of the five studies failed to control for factors that may contaminate the religion–tax fraud relationship, such as financial dissatisfaction and basic confidence or perceived legitimacy of the government. Finally, forms of white-collar crime other than tax evasion have been neglected in the literature on religion and white-collar crime, and most dimensions of religiosity have been neglected.

The aspects of religiosity that are most apt to discourage criminalistic attitudes and behavior are still somewhat ambiguous. There are thirteen major dimensions of religion: beliefs, affiliation, organizational religiosity (e.g., attendance), nonorganizational religiosity (e.g., meditation), subjective identification, commitment/motivation, quest, experience, religious well-being/satisfaction, religious coping mechanisms (e.g., prayer), religious knowledge, and consequential religiosity (Koenig et al. 2001: 20–23). Most of these dimensions have received very little attention in the criminological literature. The limited work on white-collar crime has focused on attendance, affiliation, and subjective identification. Most studies use church attendance, often as an index of exposure to religious teachings against theft.

Recent research on religion and attitudes towards white collar crime has addressed several of the gaps in past research. Do attitudes predict behavior? Attitudes towards the acceptability of tax fraud have been found to be consistently predictive of actual tax fraud behavior (e.g., Varma and Doob 1998). That is, the stronger the attitudes condoning tax fraud, the greater the likelihood that the individual will actually cheat on his or her taxes. In one study of thirteen predictors of the intention to cheat on taxes in the future, the most important predictor was the degree of tax fraud acceptability (other than the number of times a person committed tax fraud in the past five years) (Petee et al. 1994). A strong association between tax fraud attitudes and behavior has been found to be the case in Canada, the Netherlands, the United States, and a host of other industrial nations.

This author's team (Stack and Kposowa 2004) has presented the most systematic cross-national data and analysis on religion and attitudes toward white-collar crime. The data are from the World Values Surveys (WVS), which are based on national representative samples of the adult population. Data are discussed herein for four of the world's most advanced industrial societies: Britain, France, Germany, and the United States. The results illustrate the relationship between two aspects of religion (attendance or organizational religiosity, affiliation vs. no affiliation) and the degree of approval (rated as 1 to 10 from always wrong to always right). Three white-collar crimes are analyzed: cheating on government benefits, accepting a bribe in the course of one's business, and tax evasion (Barnett 2000).

First, an index of religious participation—church attendance—is linked to white-collar crime. For example, in Germany, 57 percent of weekly church attendees say that tax fraud is always wrong, compared to 37 percent of persons who go to church less frequently. The same pattern holds for other industrial nations. Second, we would expect that persons with religious affiliations, ties to organized religion, would be less approving of white-collar crime than persons who are not members of any organized religion. Persons with religious ties would be more apt to hold negative definition of white-collar crime than individuals without religious affiliations. The latter group of religious "nones" could be expected to be relatively lacking in religious socialization to negative definitions of theft (e.g., "thou shalt not steal"). There was a strong tendency for religious affiliates to be more disapproving of white-collar crime than the religious nones in all three nations. For example, in Germany, 43 percent of those with an affiliation find tax fraud to be always wrong, compared to only 27 percent of the nonaffiliated. However, regular exposure to religious teaching has generally been found to be a stronger predictor of attitudes toward white-collar crime and behavior than having a religious affiliation.

Next, it is necessary to weigh the importance of religion compared to other socioeconomic variables. Economic strain, a gap between actual and desired economic outcomes, or simply financial dissatisfaction is often a good predictor of positive definitions of deviance. For example, analyses of the WVS data have shown that the greater the financial dissatisfaction reported by the individual, the greater their approval of tax fraud. From social bonds theory, persons who are married may be more conservative in their attitudes towards theft. One may lose some of the love and respect of a spouse if he or she catches you cheating on income taxes or accepting bribes and so on. Further, persons who have confidence in their government may find it hypocritical to cheat on the government that they personally like. In terms of demographics, both women and older persons tend to report more negative definitions of theft. The question is, in short, how does religion fare compared to these powerful predictors in its capability to predict the acceptability of white-collar crime?

A multivariate analysis was undertaken to sort out the impact of religiosity on white-collar crime and to weight its importance relative to the other predictors of white-collar crime. For benefit fraud, the greater the church attendance, the lower the approval of white-collar crime. However, financial dissatisfaction was slightly more strongly related to white-collar crime than this aspect of religion.

For the case of bribery, the greater the church attendance, the lower the acceptability of taking bribes. Church attendance was substantially more important in explaining variation in attitudes toward bribery than financial dissatisfaction was. Finally, controlling for the other variables, church attendance was the single most important variable explaining variation in the approval of tax fraud. In the case of this form of white-collar crime, religiosity was over three times as important as financial dissatisfaction in explaining differences of opinion on tax fraud.

Religion is typically one of the top two predictors of attitudes toward tax fraud, bribery, and cheating the government on benefits. It is generally more important than financial dissatisfaction (economic strain). It is also more important than the degree of confidence in government. Only age tends to be somewhat more important than religion in predicting all three indicators of white-collar crime. However, unlike age, church attendance may be more amenable to change over time. It is also noteworthy that religion is predictive of attitudes toward crime in all four nations.

Less-researched dimensions of religiosity are also related to dimensions of white-collar crime: bribes, benefit fraud, and tax evasion. Religious salience (reporting "I am a religious person") was about as importance as attendance in predicting negative definitions of crime. An index of religious coping ("Religion gives me strength and comfort") was also about as important as attendance. The sheer number of reported religious beliefs (in God, devil, afterlife, etc.) tended to be the best predictor of crime attitudes. The number of beliefs can be taken as an index of religious integration—the degree to which the individual subordinates himself or herself to religion. Persons high on this dimension may be the most respectful of authority and rules. This orientation may generalize to holding negative definitions of violation of society's laws.

Cressey (2001) reported that the testing of criminological theory in the area of white-collar crime is in a relatively impoverished state. Religion has been neglected in theoretical discussions of white-collar crime. However, the few available relevant studies often find a strong inverse association between religion and white-collar crime. However, exactly how religion deters white-collar crime remains unclear. Determining which dimensions of religion are most important in explaining variability in crime will require substantial research.

FURTHER READING

Barnett, Cynthia. *The Measurement of White Collar Crime Using UCR Data.* Washington, DC: Department of Justice, 2000.

Cressey, Donald. "The Poverty of Theory in Corporate Crime Research." Pp. 175–193 in Neal Shover and John Paul Wright (eds.), *Crimes of Privilege: Readings in White Collar Crime.* New York: Oxford University Press, 2001.

Grasmick, Harold G., Bursik, Robert J. Jr., and Cochran, John. "Render Unto Caesar What is Caesar's: Religiosity and Taxpayers' Inclinations to Cheat." *The Sociological Quarterly* 32 (1991): 251–266.

Petee, Thomas A., Milner, Trudie F., and Welch, Michael R. "Levels of Social Integration in Group Contexts and the Effects of Informal Sanction Threat on Deviance," *Criminology* 32(1994): 85–106.

Stack, Steven, and Kposowa, Augustine. "The Effect of Moral Communities on Tax Fraud." Paper presented at the annual meeting of the Society for the Study of Social Problems, San Francisco, August 2004.

Varma, Kimberly, and Doob, Anthony. "Deterring Economic Crimes: The Case of Tax Evasion." *Canadian Journal of Criminology* 40 (1998): 165–184.

STEVEN STACK

ROUTINE ACTIVITIES AND WHITE-COLLAR CRIME. Routine activities theory is a rational choice perspective of crime, developed in 1979 by Lawrence E. Cohen and Marcus Felson, and argues that routine activities of everyday life bring together three key concepts of a crime: motivated offenders, suitable targets, and the absence of capable guardians or protectors of property. These key concepts converge at a common space and time. Routine activities theory is particularly relevant to white-collar crime because the occupational setting often provides a common space and time for the convergence of the key concepts.

A basic tenet of the theory is that through engaging in routine activities, a potential offender or a potential victim is exposed to the opportunity to offend or to become a victim of criminal behavior. *Routine activities* are recurrent and prevalent activities that provide for basic needs of an individual or the population in general. However, routine activities may include activities that provide more than the basic needs of the population or an individual. The defining factor is that the activity is prevalent and part of everyday life. They may occur at home, in jobs away from home, and in other activities away from home. Examples of routine activities would include activities associated with going to work, obtaining food and shelter, sexual outlet, leisure, social interaction, learning, and childrearing. Generally, white-collar crime occurs in a legitimate occupational context. The routine activity of performing legitimate occupational duties places an offender in an opportunistic situation for illegal behavior. Additionally, the routine activities of business organizations in producing or providing goods and services to customers or clients expose the organization and its customers or clients to the opportunity of engaging in or becoming the victim of illegal behavior.

The first of the three converging concepts of crime is a motivated offender. The theory subscribes to the rational choice perspective in regards to motivation to engage in criminal behavior. In other words, the theory assumes that the offender possesses the inclination or free will to commit a criminal act. The offender is inclined or motivated to commit the criminal act in order to obtain some type of benefit, such as property, money, or sexual outlet. In relation to white-collar crime, the most common desired benefit would be money or property. White-collar criminals may be motivated not only by the desire to obtain more money or property but also by the motivation to keep what they have already obtained. The corporate executive may have obtained a certain socioeconomic status and finds that status may be in jeopardy; therefore, the executive may be motivated to engage in illegal activity in order to maintain the achieved status. Additionally, for the executives of a corporation, the motivation may be to increase the corporation's profit margin or create the appearance of a more profitable business than what truly exists. Doing this enhances not only the image of the corporation but also the images of those managing the corporation. Falsely inflating the value of the corporation can increase the personal financial gain of the executives.

The second key concept outlined in the routine activities theory is that of a suitable target. Factors such as value, physical visibility, access, ease of removal of property, and physical capacity of personal victims to resist are considered when determining target suitability. Inherent to human nature is the desire to expend the least amount of effort and time to accomplish something. Therefore, in evaluating target suitability, an offender also takes into account the effort and time a particular target will require in order to be victimized. Another consideration on target suitability is the risk factor of the potential target. Occupational structure often places the white-collar criminal in close proximity to suitable targets. The offender may be employed in a position of trust that provides access to property, including money, of the employer or the employer's customers or clients. In terms of the corporation or corporation management being the white-collar criminal, the routine activity of conducting the legitimate business of the corporation places it in a position of obtaining suitable targets in the form of customers, the public in general, other businesses, or the government. Those dealing with a corporation are usually vulnerable to a corrupt corporation, because they are in a position where they must rely on the good faith of the corporation and often have very little control over the corporation.

The final concept of routine activities theory is that of the absence of capable guardians or protectors of the potential victim of the criminal behavior. In the examination of street crime, this concept analyzes the physical barriers that serve to protect the potential victim. In a property crime, these guardians can take the form of an alarm system, locks, or a person being present on or near the property. In an assault, capable guardians could take the form of others nearby who could come to the aid of the victim, or the physical size and capabilities of the victim. The occupational structure often creates opportunities in which an offender is exposed to potential victims who lack protection from capable guardians. Employees are routinely given access to the assets of their employers and the customers or clients of their employer. There may be guardians in place to protect these assets, but the offender may develop methods to overcome or circumvent these guardians. Additionally, the offender may be in a position of trust in which there are few, if any, guardians of the targeted assets.

An example of the application of routine activities theory to white-collar crime may provide a better understanding of the concepts. The crime of identity theft has recently received a great deal of attention. In conducting the routine activities of a bank in providing services to its customers, employees of the bank are exposed to sensitive information regarding their customers. Such information could include bank account information, social security numbers, credit card numbers, and other personal identifying information. A teller, motivated by the need to obtain money to pay bills, or even a bank officer, motivated by the desire to maintain a certain standard of living, examines the suitability of potential targets of their motivation to obtain money. Although there are capable guardians in place to protect the customer's money on deposit with the bank, there are few guardians to protect the identifying information of customers. In order to perform their duties adequately, the bank employees have access to this information. Obtaining identifying information on customers does not directly benefit the offender employees, but the information can be used by the offender to obtain goods and services and even credit, in the name of and based on the good credit of the customer. Additionally, this information can be sold to others who will use the information in an illegal manner. The offender has identified a suitable target because of the ease of access, the value of the information, and the low risk of being detected, especially if the information is sold to another person, who then misuses the information. The three key concepts of a motivated offender, a suitable target, and an absence of capable guardians have converged at a common space and time during the routine activities of the bank employee and the routine activities of the bank business to provide for the opportunity of the commission of the white-collar crime of identity theft.

See also: Identity Theft; Power Theory; Rational Choice Theory

FURTHER READING

Cohen, Lawrence, and Felson, Marcus. "Social Change and Crime Rate Trends: A Routine Activity Approach." *American Sociological Review* 44:4 (August, 1979): 588–608.

Felson, Marcus. "Routine Activities and Crime Prevention in the Developing Metropolis." *Criminology* 25:4 (1987): 911–31.

Felson, Marcus. *Crime and Everyday Life: Insights and Implications for Society.* Thousand Oaks, CA: Pine Forge Press, 1994.

Friedrichs, David O. *Trusted Criminals,* 2nd edition. Belmont, CA: Wadsworth, 2004.

Piquero, Nicole, and Benson, Michael. "White-Collar Crime and Criminal Careers: Specifying a Trajectory of Punctuated Situational Offending." *Journal of Contemporary Criminal Justice* 20 (2004): 148–165.

KEN W. BALUSEK

S

SALT LAKE CITY OLYMPICS BRIBERY. The five year investigation and federal case involving the Salt Lake City Olympic bribery scandal exposed a history of questionable business practices engaged in by the Salt Lake City bid and organizing committee, the United States Olympic Committee (USOC), and the International Olympic Committee (IOC). The case also demonstrates that the age-old white-collar/corporate crime justification, "just following normal business practice," is as common and effective as ever.

The scandal involving the decision to hold the 2002 Winter Olympics in Salt Lake City dates back to the early 1990s. In 1990, Thomas K. Welch and David R. Johnson, the president and vice president, respectively, of the Salt Lake City Olympic bid committee, allegedly began depositing money into a Mexican bank account belonging to Alfred LaMont, international relations director for the USOC, in return for his assistance in making contacts within the IOC. Despite efforts to retain one of the IOC members as a "consultant" and provide an immigration visa for the son of another, the Salt Lake City bid committee lost the campaign for the 1998 Winter Games to Nagano, Japan. Discouraged, Welch and Johnson returned to the United States. They publicly claimed that the Japanese had bought the election and vowed, in the future, to pay special attention to certain influential individuals, using the knowledge that "saltwater taffy and jars of honey" were no longer sufficient gifts to win the loyalties of IOC members (Foy 2003).

From that point on, the Salt Lake City bid committee took more extreme measures to secure Salt Lake as the site of the 2002 Winter Games. The committee allegedly bestowed over $1 million in cash, gifts, and favors to various members of the IOC, with a large portion of the funds coming from an account designed to provide humanitarian aid to impoverished foreign athletes. In a memo written by Welch and Johnson, now known as the "Geld Report," the two evidently made pointed notes regarding members of the IOC. The names of loyal supporters on the committee were tagged with the word "geld" (the German word for "money"), and other names were followed by notations such as "husband needs a job" and "son, 17, needs a future, equipment, geld" (Mackay 2003). Accordingly, a former Finnish committee member's husband was paid $35,000 by the bid committee for producing a study on forestry that was apparently never read; visas and educational opportunities were obtained for other IOC family members; and a wide range of additional favors and gifts were provided by the Salt Lake bid committee, including ski vacations, trips to Paris, shopping sprees, a cancer treatment, purebred dogs, collector guns, Rolex watches, jobs at Salt Lake City Hall and First Security Bank, and even envelopes full of cash. The "generosity" was exposed in November 1998, when the bid committee provided the daughter of one delegate with a scholarship to American University in Washington.

As a result of the alleged bribery, six members of the IOC were expelled, four resigned, and fifteen counts of conspiracy and fraud were levied against Welch and Johnson. District Judge David Sam originally dismissed the case in 2001, arguing that it was founded on an obscure Utah commercial bribery law and sparing Salt Lake City the embarrassment of a major court case coinciding with the 2002 Games. The U.S. Court of Appeals reversed the decision, however, on the grounds that the U.S. government had a vested interest in denouncing any corruption involved in the Olympic bid process. The case went to trial in October 2003.

The defense presented the precise documentation of all payments and gifts to the IOC as evidence that Welch and Johnson were not engaging in covert bribery but rather following normal Olympic business practices. Furthermore, the defense argued that the two were only part of a larger network of influential Utah residents and politicians as well as high-ranking government and Olympic committee members involved in the bid campaign and were being used as scapegoats.

Before the jury could decide the case, Judge Sam granted the defendants' motion for acquittal, citing a lack of criminal intent on the part of Welch and Johnson. He ruled that there was insufficient evidence to sustain a conviction on any of the fifteen counts against the two men.

Despite the case being thrown out, the Justice Department maintains that future misconduct by United States bid cities will not be tolerated. Members of the IOC do not believe that the case will have any impact on future United States Olympic bids.

FURTHER READING

Foy, Paul. "Prosecutors Open Case against Olympic Bid Leaders, Citing 'Campaign of Bribery.'" The Associated Press (October 31, 2003).

Gorrell, Mike. "How the Games Were Won: Generosity or Bribery?" *The Salt Lake Tribune* (October 26, 2003): A20.

Hemphill, Lex. "Acquittals End Bid Scandal That Dogged Winter Games." *The New York Times* (December 6, 2003): D5.

Mackay, Duncan. "Olympic Bribery Scandal Refuses to Lie Down." *Guardian Unlimited* (April 24, 2003). Available at http://www.guardian.co.uk.

Sullivan, Robert. "How the Olympics Were Bought." *Time* (January 25, 1999): 38–43.

LYNN LANGTON

SELF-CONTROL THEORY. In 1990 Michael Gottfredson and Travis Hirschi wrote *A General Theory of Crime*, which characterized criminal offenders as lacking self-control. They contended that a wide range of crimes could be explained by lack of self control, especially in circumstances of increased opportunities. The underlying assumption of self-control theory is that all humans are motivated to break rules and make choices of whether to commit deviant or illegal actions. These choices are dependent on how the individual has been socialized to suppress or restrain criminal actions. Therefore, most people do not choose to engage in criminal activity because they have been effectively socialized by parents or other sources to manage their behavior. This theory accepts both the classical school of thought (that crime is a consequence of unrestrained human behavior that seeks immediate pleasure and seeks to avoid immediate pain), and specific facets of modern positivism (that the roles families play can and do have an effect on an individual's later criminality). Individuals that engage in such activities have low self-control, with "here and now" orientations. According to Gottfredson and Hirschi, this lack of self-control is a result of three conditions that were not met in an offender's childhood: (1) behavior was not monitored during childhood; (2) it was not recognized when the child acted out in a deviant manner; and (3) deviant behavior was not adequately punished. Gottfredson and Hirschi also contend that all crimes share certain characteristics, such as they are easy, provide immediate gratification of desires, require little skill or planning, and offer few long-term benefits or monetary gains.

Whereas most scholars conceptualize white-collar crime as separate theoretical entities from non-white-collar crime, Gottfredson and Hirschi assert that white-collar offenders are not distinct from their non-white-collar crime offender counterparts. Furthermore, both types of offenders are likely to have prior criminal records and poor social adjustment. Relying on FBI Crime Report data, Gottfredson and Hirschi deduct that white-collar crime is not distinct because it shares other crimes' characteristics: a spontaneity and quickness that requires no specialized knowledge and limited profits. However, their study examined only embezzlement, fraud, and forgery, which were primarily low-level crimes committed by poor individuals.

While some support has been found for self-control theory in terms of white-collar crime, it has been criticized in numerous ways since its inception. One of its primary criticisms is the exclusion of corporate and business offenses. Furthermore, scholars have concluded that white-collar crime is not as uncommon as Gottfredson and Hirschi assert. In fact, most white-collar crime studies indicate that it is at least as common as, or more common than, conventional street crime. In 1996 Reed and Yeager noted that white-collar offenses, especially corporate and organizational crimes, are not necessarily quick and spontaneous acts. They are usually offenses that involve long-term and extensive schemes. Corporate and organizational crimes do not frequently result in immediate self-gratification or rewards. For example, long-term price gouging, which is used to meet or exceed corporate interests and goals, is often a pursuit that occurs over a significant period of time.

A study conducted by Benson and Moore in 1992 examined the theory by empirically comparing federal white-collar offenders with persons convicted of narcotics violations, bank robbery, and postal forgery. Their results suggested that white-collar offenders were four times more likely to have been previously arrested for a white-collar crime than non-white-collar criminals. This is contradictory to Gottfredson and Hirschi's versatility contention, in which white-collar offenders are no more likely to be specialized than their non-white-collar crime offender counterparts and are not any more likely to gain significant profit. One of the most recent examples that contradicts Gottfredson and Hirschi's assumptions is that of Andrew Fastow, an Enron executive, whose extensive knowledge of the stock market was used to manipulate secondary companies to gain substantial monetary profits for himself and other top-level Enron executives.

Further criticisms have included that self-control theory is too broad, in that it can be applied to all human behavior, but not to specific criminal acts. It has also failed to account for the organizational behavior that can shape perceptions of self-interest, motives, and opportunities for criminal behavior. Other criticism have included the theory's exclusion of why corporate managers jeopardize their self-interest by committing acts of deviance and why white-collar offenders do not commit other, more conventional crimes.

Studies that have looked to corroborate the theory have found some support. A 1990 study, conducted by Weisburd, Chayet, and Waring, tested the theory on a group of federal white-collar offenders who were imprisoned for a range of crimes that included antitrust offenses, false claims and statements, IRS fraud, securities and exchange fraud, postal and wire fraud, credit and lending institution fraud, bank embezzlement, IRS fraud, and bribery. Their results indicated that 43 percent had been arrested before and that 34 percent had prior convictions. Findings also indicated that even after excluding individuals who did not hold elite positions or were in possession of significant assets at the time of their offense, arrests rates were 25 percent. Gottfredson and Hirschi have responded to criticisms of self-control theory and maintain their support of its use in explaining white-collar crime. However, current studies continue to indicate only moderate support for self-control theory in explaining white-collar criminality.

FURTHER READING

Alalehto, T. "Economic Crime: Does Personality Matter." *International Journal of Offender Therapy and Comparative Criminology* 47 (2003): 335–355.

Benson, M., and Moore, E. "Are White-Collar and Common Offenders the Same? An Empirical and Theoretical Critique of a Recently Proposed General Theory of Crime." *Journal of Research in Crime and Delinquency* 29 (1992): 251–272.

Curren, D. J., and Renzetti, C. M. *Theories of Crime*, 2nd edition. Boston: Allyn & Bacon, 2001.

Gottfredson, M., and Hirschi, T. *A General Theory of Crime*. Stanford, CA: Stanford University Press, 1990.

Lanier, M. M., and Henry, S. *Essential Criminology*, 2nd edition. Boulder, CO: Westview Press, 2004.

Reed, G., and Yeager, P. "Organizational Offending and Neoclassical Criminology: Challenging the Reach of a General Theory of Crime." *Criminology* 34 (1996): 357–382.

Weisburd, D., Chayet, E. F., and Waring, E. J. "White-Collar Crime and Criminal Careers: Some Preliminary Findings." *Crime and Delinquency* 36 (1990): 342–355.

JILETTA L. KUBENA

SEVESO DIOXIN DISASTER. The Seveso dioxin disaster was a major industrial accident that, besides having public health implications, has had an impact on Italian torts law as well as on the European legal framework for managing industrial accidents. It represents an example of how policies may lead to (1) an inadequate management of the aftermath of industrial accidents, (2) a lengthy legal process to compensate industrial accident victims, and (2) the impossibility of holding corporations criminally liable for managerial choices that are then implemented by their employees. On the other hand, the Seveso disaster is an example of how policymakers can use human tragedies as opportunities to implement better policies, which in the specific case reformed the rules on the liability for nonpecuniary damages and on the management of dangerous industrial activities.

On July 10, 1976, a safety valve broke down at ICMESA, a Swiss-owned chemical plant located in Seveso, a small town 10 miles north of Milan, Italy. The plant manufactured phenol 2, 4, 5-trichlorophenol (TCP), an intermediate in the production of an herbicide. A by-product of this process is the highly toxic substance dioxin. As a consequence of the failure of the safety valve, over 60 pounds of dioxin were released into the environment, exposing approximately 37,000 people to this highly toxic substance. With some delay (substantially due to ICMESA efforts to cover up the accident), Italian authorities acknowledged that the Seveso population was exposed to dangerously high levels of dioxin and evacuated the area. Although there were no human casualties, animals died, homes had to be demolished as part of the cleanup operation, and hundreds of residents, who had experienced eye, throat irritations, burnlike sores on the exposed skin, headaches, dizziness and diarrhea, were forced to leave Seveso. Because of the substantial extent of the population's exposure to dioxin, which causes birth defects among other harms, Italian public authorities were also persuaded to lift temporarily the law banning abortion, thus allowing several pregnant women terminate pregnancies voluntary. Because of the lift on the abortion ban, scientific investigators were prevented from carefully assessing the level of birth defects that followed the disaster.

Criminal investigations followed the release of the dioxin cloud, concluding that the flow of refrigerating water that cooled off the TCP vessel had been inadvertently stopped by an ICEMSA employee, thus creating excessive pressure in the system, which later caused the failure of the safety valve. At trial, the prosecutors showed that the employee's negligence was made possible by ICMESA management failure to put in place safety measures that would have prevented the accident from happening. Consequently, on May 23, 1983, five ICMESA managers were convicted for "negligently causing . . . a disaster" (Italian Criminal Code, Sect. 449) and for omitting to put safety measures in place (Italian Criminal Code, Sect. 451). By contrast, no managers of the Swiss parent corporation were convicted. Under Italian criminal law provisions that were in place at the time of the trial, executives of a parent company could be held criminally liable only if, under the internal policies, plant managers did not have knowledge and authority to implement safety measures to prevent industrial accidents from happening. With the Court having conclude that plant managers were in the position to implement a safety program that would have prevented the accident from taking place, criminal liability did not extend to the managers of the parent company. However, in the aftermath of the criminal trial, the parent corporation reached an agreement to compensate all pecuniary damages arising out of the dioxin leak to all victims and, later on, to a number of local municipalities and to the Italian Government. Because of the "one-time" and "indivisible nature" of the accident, the settlement negotiations on behalf of the municipalities were led by the Office of the Prime Minister. Under the agreement, the parent company paid over $10 billion in cleanup costs and compensation to those who suffered physical injuries as a result of the incident.

However, nonpecuniary damages, which can be awarded if the wrongdoer is found criminally liable for same actions that caused the injury, were left outside the scope of the settlement. Indeed, epidemiologic studies had shown that a significant increase in cancer incidence and mortality from certain cancers and cardiovascular diseases has been reported in the contaminated area. Therefore, many Seveso residents exposed to the toxic cloud filed civil claims to recover pain and suffering cause by the anxiety of getting impaired as a consequence of dioxin exposure. On February 24, 2002, the highest Italian court awarded damages to a plaintiff who had suffered emotional distress. This legal opinion expanded the scope of recoverable conditions under Italian tort law by considering eligible for compensation of nonpecuniary damages also awarding victims who suffer no physical injuries. As consequence, possibly over 10,000 Seveso residents will likely file similar lawsuits in the next few years, as a legal representative of the Association of Dioxin Victims announced to the press.

The Seveso disaster also pushed European policymakers to implement a set of innovative public policies for managing dangerous industrial activities. Most notably, the EU Parliament enacted two directives, the Seveso I Directive (82/501/EEC), and its later version, the Seveso II Directive (96/82/EC), both requiring manufacturers to identify potential danger areas in the manufacturing process and to take all necessary measures to prevent major accidents in order to (1) prevent major accidents resulting from their industrial activities and (2) limit the consequences for both people and the environment of accidents that might take place.

See also: Chemical Crimes; Environmental White-Collar Crime; Industrial Accidents; Union Carbide

FURTHER READING

Bertazzi, P. A., Consonni, Dario, Bachetti, Silvia, Rubagotti, Maurizia, Baccarelli, Andrea, Zocchetti, Carlo, and Pesatori, Angela C. "Health Effects of Dioxin Exposure: A 20-Year Mortality Study." *American Journal of Epidemiology* 153 (2001): 1031–1044.

De Marchi, B., Funtowicz, S., and Ravetz, J. "Seveso: A Paradoxical Classic Disaster." In J. K. Mitchell (ed.), *The Long Road to Recovery: Community Responses to Industrial Disaster.* Tokyo: The United Nations University Press, 1997.

Hay, A. "Toxic Cloud over Seveso." *Nature* 263 (1976): 636–638.

Sambeth, Jörg. *Zwischenfall in Seveso.* Zürich: Unionsverlag, 2004.

ANDREA BOGGIO

SILKWOOD, KAREN. See Kerr-McGee

SILVER VALLEY MINING POLLUTION. Over a hundred years of mining (since the 1880s) have extracted an estimated $5.8 billion worth of metals such as silver and zinc from the Silver Valley of Idaho, bringing prosperity to mining company shareholders and mansions and office buildings to Spokane, Washington. In addition, the metals helped build the country's industrial infrastructure and supported war efforts. A byproduct of the mining companies' production, however, has been a legacy of physical harm, economic burden, and strain on the social fabric of communities in the region. This case provides a useful illustration of the difficulties of ameliorating the effects of environmental white collar crime.

An estimated 100 million tons of mine sediments, including arsenic, cadmium, and zinc, as well as approximately 30,000 tons of lead released into the air from smelter stacks, have polluted an area roughly the size of Rhode Island. Heavy metals such as lead entered the

261

bloodstreams of many of the local residents through contaminated soil, water, and air. In 1973, Gulf Resources ran the Bunker Hill lead smelter in the heart of the Silver Valley. The smelter was equipped with a baghouse—a huge air filter—to scrub lead from the smelter emissions, but the baghouse had been damaged in a fire. The smelter was operated for six months in that condition, raining 1,500 tons of lead oxide on the nearby towns. The fog of lead in the air was thick enough to require drivers to use their headlights while driving during the day. The children experienced lead levels in their blood over six to ten times the federal level of concern. The children were at risk for neurological damage, including lowered IQs and other symptoms of heavy metal poisoning, such as attention deficit disorders. Testing shows that lead levels in the blood of children have decreased from the 1970s, but they are still exposed to lead in their homes and schoolyards in quantities above the level deemed safe by the EPA. The Silver Valley now has the highest cancer rate in Idaho.

The mining contaminants also poisoned the animals and plants in the region. Farmers lost their livestock. Eighty-eight percent of the bird species in the region are at risk of heavy metal poisoning. Lead paralyzes the throats of migrating tundra swans and mergansers, causing them to suffocate. Sixty-seven percent of the mammal species and most of the fish are also threatened. Several of the rivers and creeks that run through the Silver Valley are devoid of aquatic life. In addition, for many years after the smelter was dismantled, the vegetation in the surrounding area was stunted, resembling forests of bonsai trees.

In addition to the physical costs, the legacy of mining also includes severe economic costs that have been "externalized" to the general public. It has been estimated that it would require over $1.4 billion to clean up the contaminated soil and water in the region. The U.S. Environmental Protection Agency's Superfund program intends to spend $359 million over 30 years on ecological cleanup. The EPA has already spent over $200 million on efforts to clean a 21-square-mile area named Bunker Hill in which smelting and mining concentrated much of the heavy metals. A large portion of the money has been spent disposing of contaminated topsoil in residential yards. Approximately $100 million are expected to be spent addressing the human health effects of heavy-metal exposure.

There are also less direct economic costs associated with the mining pollution. The contamination is one of the factors depressing the local real estate market. Lawsuits have been filed against homeowners who failed to disclose the lead contamination of their yards and houses to new buyers.

Some members of the business community in the Silver Valley fear that the stigma of a Superfund site in their area threatens the prosperity of the local recreation and tourism industry. These economic concerns also add stress to the social fabric of the region. There are now two deeply divided factions in the Silver Valley. One side argues that the dangers from the contamination are exaggerated, that the cleanup hurts economic development, and that the EPA should leave the area immediately. In fact, some blame the EPA for the loss of mining jobs in the region. Hostility toward the EPA is evident in the region. Many homes display signs exhorting the agency to leave. A columnist for a local press advocated that residents should be required to arm themselves in order to defend against federal agents accessing private property for cleanup efforts. The other faction counters that the EPA has not yet done enough to decontaminate the area and the heavy metals still pose long-term hazards. Winds blow contaminated topsoil onto newly-cleaned yards, and rainstorms deposit new loads of heavy metals into the waterways. There are concerns that not enough is being done to monitor and treat the health threats posed by the heavy metals. Some of the local cleanup advocates charge that they have been subject to serious harassment by the anti-EPA faction.

The mining pollution has also been a source of conflict between many of the local residents and a Native American tribe that owns part of Lake Coeur d'Alene. The Coeur d'Alene Tribe wants an effective plan to monitor and manage the estimated 77 million tons of heavy metals that line the bottom of the lake. If the heavy metals migrate from the bottom of the lake, they will threaten the fish and plants that are important parts of the tribe's heritage. Again, many local business leaders, in an effort to avoid negative publicity, want the lake de-listed as a Superfund site, which would mean Superfund resources would no longer be available to address the lake's contamination. The controversy has also created conflict with the state of Washington. Polluted water that flows out of Lake Coeur d'Alene travels downstream and deposits heavy metals in the soil along rivers in Washington.

The case also illustrates the difficulties of controlling actions of corporations such as the mining firms and holding them accountable for the byproducts of their activities. In 1977 a political ally of Gulf Resources amended the Clean Air Act to allow the corporation to build higher smelter stacks in order to disperse lead over a greater area rather than reduce emissions. When mining corporations were sued to recover some of the cleanup costs in 1986, the amount awarded was only, $4.5 million, a small fraction of the required costs. Gulf Resources shifted many of its assets overseas and declared bankruptcy, which transferred the burden of cleanup to the Superfund program.

See also: Environmental White-Collar Crime

FURTHER READING

Barnett, Harold C. *Toxic Debts*. Chapel Hill: University of North Carolina Press, 1994.
Dorn Steele, Karen. "EPA Cleanup Plan Spreads into Basin." *The Spokesman Review* (October 21, 2001). Available at http://www.spokesmanreview.com.
Dorn Steele, Karen. "Mining Enriched Region, Left Big Mess." *The Spokesman Review* (July 21, 2002). Available at http://www.spokesmanreview.com.
U.S. Environmental Protection Agency. "Second Five Year Review." June 1, 2005. Available at http://yosemite.epa.gov/r10/cleanup.nsf/sites/cda.

GARY E. REED

SOUTH SEA BUBBLE. The "South Sea Bubble" was a stock scandal that shook the English business world in the mid-eighteenth century. Government officials, members of Parliament, and private citizens, including two of the king's mistresses, were bribed to promote the sale of shares in the South Sea Company on the newly emergent London stock exchange.

The price of the stock was pushed to extremely high levels by market manipulations carried out by company directors. A Parliament inquiry, launched when the stock collapsed, discovered that there were no laws against what had been done. Nonetheless, the investigative commission determined the financial worth of wrongdoers and fined them in terms of how much they owned and how much of a part they had played in bilking the public.

The South Sea Company. The South Sea Company had been chartered in 1711 in concert with the newly developed approach in England of launching business ventures by soliciting a large number of investors in a joint-stock corporation, the forerunner of today's stock market. The company declared two goals: first, to ease the backbreaking burden of a £10 million national debt by transferring the sums owed by the government into holdings in the company; and second, to reap heady profits from trade in the "South Seas," by which was meant the coast of South America. The trading area was heralded as rich with readily acquired precious minerals and receptive to importing slaves. The Scheme (as it was called) was wildly improbable from the start, since Spain controlled the South American ports and had no intention of allowing other nations to intrude on its monopoly.

A fierce speculative fever, fueled by bribes and artfully planted misinformation, sent the stock on a roller-coaster price ride that lasted almost a decade. The buyers had no previous experience in stock shenanigans with which to judge the maneuvers of the South Sea Company. Widows of wealthy men, in particular, who had been sequestered from financial matters, were prominent among the frenzied purchasers seeking easy riches. The company required a down payment of only 10 percent of the purchase price and conveyed the idea that quick profits could more than meet the deadline for the payment of the remaining 90 percent of the cost of the stock. On its initial offering in October 1711, the stock was quoted at between £73 and £76. By mid-July 1720 it had risen to almost £1,000.

A considerable number of companies came into being in the effort to copy the South Sea Company's success. Some of these companies were asking for funds to accomplish some notably peculiar goals, including a perpetual-motion machine. More straightforward was a promoter who asked for investments in a company whose goal he said he would announce six months later; first-day investments were heavy, and immediately afterward he disappeared with the loot, never to be located. The South Sea Company sought to protect its fortunes by getting Parliament to outlaw new corporate groups, who were seen as competitors draining off money that could have gone into South Sea coffers. The plan backfired, however, because holders of South Sea shares cashed them into meet the subsequent demands for capital by the other companies in which they also had invested.

When the South Sea bubble burst, the treasurer, Robert Knight, absconded to the Duchy of Brabant (now part of the Netherlands and Belgium), taking records of the bribery conspiracy with him. An intense manhunt finally captured him, but Brabant authorities invoked an ancient law that specified that persons within their territory could be tried only by their courts. Knight was never charged with a crime, and the some of the important details of the scandal never came to light.

Punishing the Predators. The Parliamentary inquiry found that 122 members of the House of Lords and 462 members of the House of Commons had invested in the Scheme and that between forty and fifty had been bribed to support it. Robert Molesworth, a parliamentarian who had lost a considerable amount of money on South Sea stock, argued, unsuccessfully, that the company directors should be deemed guilty of parricide—the killing of a father—because they had in effect strangled their fatherland. If found guilty, he declared, they should be given the penalty decreed in ancient Rome for that offense: being sewn up in sacks with a monkey and a snake and cast into a river. Some persons implicated in the bribery resorted to manipulation. Lord Stanford successfully lobbied other members of Parliament either to support him or to abstain from voting on his fate. A handful of wrongdoers, including the chancellor of the exchequer, were expelled from Parliament and imprisoned in the Tower of London. Sir John Blunt, the director of the Company, was said to have £183,000, and the authorities confiscated all but £5,000 of that amount. On Blunt's death some time later, it was found that he had secreted or subsequently earned enough money to leave a sizable inheritance to his seventeen children.

Edward Gibbon, the famed historian of the Roman Empire, in his autobiography protested against the South Sea Company penalties that saw his grandfather severely fined. Gibbon claimed, with some justice, that the courtwas improvising law as it went along rather than acting in regard to existing statutes.

Of particular importance was the fact that the South Sea scandal led the British Parliament to pass the Bubble Act, which was not repealed until 1825 (almost a century later), to check the inauguration of corporate forms. The Act led to the neglect for decades of attention to the question of how best to structure and control the corporate form, which inevitably would come to dominate world of finance. This neglect also inhibited the growth of corporations in the American colonies.

FURTHER READING

Balen, Malcolm. *The Secret History of the South Sea Bubble: The World's First Great Financial Scandal.* New York: Fourth Estate, 2003.

Carswell, John. *The South Sea Bubble.* Stroud, UK: Alan Sutton, 2001.

Cowles, Virginia. *The Great Swindle: The Story of the South Sea Bubble.* New York: Harper, 1960.

Dale, Richard. *The First Crash: Lessons from the South Sea Bubble.* Princeton, NJ: Princeton University Press, 2004.

Erleigh, Gerald R. *The South Sea Bubble.* New York: Putnam's, 1933.

Langdon-Davies, John. *The South Sea Bubble: A Collection of Contemporary Documents.* London: Cape, 1965.

Mackay, Charles. "The South Sea Bubble." Pp. 45–84 in *Memoirs of Extraordinary Popular Delusions and the Madness of Crowds.* London: George Routledge,1869.

GILBERT GEIS

STANDARD OIL. The Standard Oil Company was a large oil-producing and oil-transporting organization that created, refined, and marketed a large share of the oil industry's products in the United States throughout the latter half of the nineteenth century and during the early years of the twentieth. The company began in Cleveland, Ohio, with John D. Rockefeller as its president. Standard Oil was successful in acquiring most of its competition throughout the Midwest and Northeast during its early years of operation, and by the late nineteenth century,

Rockefeller and his associates oversaw the operation of several smaller companies branded with the Standard name across many states. However, in the late-1880s, state laws were enacted that served to restrict the scale of large companies and prevent the development of monopolistic enterprises. In response, Standard combined its companies under one group of trustees, but the Sherman Anti-Trust Act of 1890 and the antitrust laws passed shortly thereafter eventually led Standard to separate into over thirty separate companies, each with a separate board of directors. These companies formed what have become the nucleus of today's oil industry, including, but not limited to, ExxonMobil, Conoco-Phillips, Chevron, and British Petroleum (BP) of North America.

The American oil industry had its beginnings in Titusville, a city in Western Pennsylvania, in 1859. These oil fields provided for the first broad-scale oil production and refining in the United States. At the time, oil was predominantly used to produce kerosene, used in homes as fuel for lamps before the development of electric lighting. Samuel Andrews, a British chemist, had developed and implemented an exceptional method of producing kerosene from crude oil and was seeking investors to build and operate an oil refinery. At this time, Rockefeller partnered with Andrews to open the first oil refinery in Cleveland during the mid-1860s.

During the late-1860s and early-1870s, Cleveland, along with various areas in the Northeast, served as centers for oil refining in the United States. In 1867, Rockefeller and Andrews absorbed a refinery operated by Rockefeller's brother William and another oil company managed by Henry Morrison Flagler. The resulting company was branded Standard Oil of Ohio and was headquartered in Cleveland. The company owned several refineries, a fleet of oil tank railroad cars, warehouses in Pennsylvania located near oil fields, warehouses in New York state, an oil barrel-making plant, and a portion of forest land to supply the barrel-making plant with lumber. Three shipping railways served Cleveland, a port city on Lake Erie, thus facilitating accessibility to the oil fields of western Pennsylvania. Because of Standard's geographic location and dominance in the industry, Rockefeller negotiated low shipping rates from the rail companies transporting the barrels of oil. In turn, Standard became the most dominant oil company in the United States, as it could provided the lowest prices for oil products. For example, the price of Standard's oil fell dramatically from $20 a barrel in 1859 to $4 a barrel in 1870. By the late nineteenth century, smaller oil companies, however well managed and with high-quality products, were unable to compete with Standard Oil's products. Standard began to absorb these smaller companies, and by the early-1880s Rockefeller and his associates accounted for and controlled between 90 and 95 percent of all oil refined in the United States.

Because of Standard Oil's immense presence in the American oil market at the end of the nineteenth century, many commentators began to question Rockefeller's tactics, claiming that because Standard controlled so much of the industry, the company constituted a monopoly. Because of its access to resources and wide expanse, the company was able to absorb the competition by cutting prices, which in turn led these competitors to file bankruptcy, thus enabling Rockefeller to purchase their companies. Others have claimed that railroad operators, working under Rockefeller's influence, could charge large fees to ship products from other oil companies, which further helped Standard to absorb the competition. Critics of those who spoke out against Standard Oil's practices argue that although Standard was in fact a monopoly, it was an efficient monopoly, earning its place in the market because it was most successful by legitimate business means, not means coercive and harmful to the consumer and environment.

Debate concerning the status of Standard Oil as a monopoly notwithstanding, state laws enacted in the late nineteenth century served to limit the size and extent of companies such as Standard, and Rockefeller and his associates reorganized their large company so that they would not lose control of the large corporation that they had built and managed for over twenty years. In 1882, individual oil companies acquired by Rockefeller came under the management of a single group of trustees, allowing Rockefeller overall corporate control, and opportunity for the different oil companies branded with the Standard name to invest in each other. This form of corporate organization, viewed positively upon the observance of the success of Standard's use of the method, led other large corporations to begin implementation of the principles of corporate trust organization practiced by Standard's geographically disparate companies.

Nevertheless, during this time, federal and state governments were seeking to stop the development of the trust arrangement of corporate organization, through the use of antitrust laws. The United States Congress passed the Sherman Anti-Trust Act in 1890, which was signed by President Benjamin Harrison and named for the author of the Act, Senator John Sherman of Ohio. The Act was passed in response to the perception that the trust arrangement contributed to and perpetuated monopoly capitalism. Yet the Act was not used with regularity in the courts for more than two decades. In 1911, the U.S. Supreme Court upheld a lower court finding that Standard Oil was in fact in violation of the Act, and the company was ordered to separate into over thirty separate companies, each with a separate board of directors. Currently and historically, violations of the Act have not been prosecuted criminally but adjudicated in civil court, where economic harm and benefit of the company in question is examined, specifically in relation to the company's relationship with, and service provision to, consumers.

The result of the dissolution of the Standard Oil Trust was the formation of the "Seven Sisters" oil conglomerate, of which several companies today form a large nucleus of the United States oil industry. The current surviving members of the Seven Sisters, descendants of the original Standard companies, include Standard Oil of New Jersey and Standard Oil of New York (both currently part of ExxonMobil) and Standard Oil of California (now known as Chevron). Other large companies, currently operating on a broad-scale in the United States, that at one time were part of the Standard Oil Trust but were not comprised in the Seven Sisters include Standard Oil of Ohio and Standard Oil of Indiana (both currently part of BP of North America) and the Continental Oil Company (currently part of Conoco-Phillips). In 1984, Chevron merged with the Gulf Oil Corporation to form, at that time, the largest corporate merger in global history. Because Gulf Oil was the eighth largest manufacturing company in the United States during the mid-twentieth century and was once part of the Seven Sisters enterprise, many service stations and a refinery in the Eastern United States were sold, and many of its worldwide subsidiaries were divested to satisfy antitrust requirements.

See also: *Exxon Valdez*; Halliburton; Kerr-McGee; Political Corruption; Power Theory; Price Fixing

FURTHER READING

Hidy, Ralph W., and Muriel E. Hidy. *Pioneering in Big Business, 1882–1911: History of Standard Oil Company (New Jersey)*. New York: Harper and Brothers, 1955.
Tarbell, Ida M. *The History of the Standard Oil Company*. New York: Harper & Row, 1904.

Thorelli, Hans B. *The Federal Anti-Trust Policy: Origination of an American Tradition*. Baltimore: The Johns Hopkins Press, 1955.

COURTNEY A. WAID

STATE-CORPORATE CRIME. The concept of state-corporate crime grew out of the recognition that some organizational crimes are the collective product of the interaction between a business corporation and a state agency engaged in a joint endeavor. A case study of the space shuttle *Challenger* disaster by Ronald C. Kramer and Raymond J. Michalowski (1990) prompted the development of the term. The fact that organizations (NASA and Morton Thiokol) from two different sectors of society had acted together in that case to produce a serious social harm suggested that a more general conceptualization of deviant organizational relationships between business corporations and government agencies was needed. State-corporate crime has been formally defined as the illegal or socially injurious actions that occur when one or more institutions of political governance pursue a goal in direct cooperation with one or more institutions of economic production and distribution. Since the topic was first introduced, a substantial number of case studies have been carried out that utilize the concept.

In their original paper, on the topic Kramer and Michalowski (1990) noted that the study of corporate crime to that point had resulted in an important insight and an important oversight. The insight, due in part to the earlier distinction between occupational and corporate crime, was that corporate crime is actually a form of organizational deviance. Insofar as corporations are formal organizations, the study of corporate crime can and should incorporate the theoretical and substantive insights of organizational research. The oversight was the failure to recognize that since the modern corporation emerged as the basic unit of economic activity within private production systems in the late nineteenth century, corporations and governments have been functionally interdependent. The modern corporation in the United States could not have developed, nor could it currently function, without the legal, economic, and political infrastructure provided by government. Governments in private-production systems, in turn, depend upon corporations to supply necessary goods and services and to provide the economic base in the form of individual salaries and corporate profits upon which governments must depend for their revenues.

Kramer and Michalowski went on to note that the structural relations between corporate and governmental organizations had been relatively peripheral to the study of corporate crime despite their ubiquity. Instead, two nearly independent bodies of research had developed. Theory and research in the area of corporate crime had concentrated primarily on organizational deviance within private business corporations. Paralleling that work but seldom intersecting with it, others had examined crimes and malfeasance by governments. Kramer and Michalowski suggested that many forms of organizational deviance are generated at the interstices of corporations and government. They used the term *state-corporate crime* to denote these forms of organizational deviance.

Although the concept of state-corporate crime could be applied to illegal or socially injurious actions in societies ranging from private-production systems to centrally planned political economies, most of the research to date has focused on state-corporate crimes within the private-production system of U.S. capitalism. State-corporate crimes within a capitalist economy involve the active participation of two or more organizations, at least one of which is in the civil sector and one of which is in the state sector.

The deviant interorganizational relationships that serve as the basis for state-corporate crime can take several forms. Kramer's (1992) analysis of the space shuttle *Challenger* explosion, and David Kauzlarich and Kramer's (1993) study of the relationship between the U.S. government and weapons manufacturers in the nuclear weapons production process, both emphasize the central and direct role of the state in initiating a cooperative activity involving both government and business that leads to a deviant outcome. Judy Aulette and Michalowski's (1993) examination of the fire at the Imperial Food Products chicken processing plant in Hamlet, North Carolina, and Rick Matthews and Kauzlarich's (2000) analysis of the crash of ValuJet 592 suggest a different kind of relationship, one where government omissions permit corporations to pursue illegal and potentially harmful courses of action that, in a general way, facilitate the fulfillment of certain state policies.

Assessing this work, Kramer et al. (2002) note that state-corporate crime takes two distinct forms. One is *state-initiated corporate crime*, and the other is *state-facilitated corporate crime*. State-initiated corporate crime occurs when corporations, employed by the government, engage in organizational deviance at the direction of, or with the tacit approval of, the government. State-facilitated corporate crime occurs when government regulatory institutions fail to restrain deviant business activities, either because of direct collusion between business and government or because they adhere to shared goals whose attainment would be hampered by aggressive regulation.

As a sensitizing concept the term "state-corporate crime" has three useful characteristics. First, it directs attention toward the way in which deviant organizational outcomes are not discrete acts but rather the product of the relationships between different social institutions. Second, by focusing on the relational character of the state, the concept of state-corporate crime foregrounds the ways in which horizontal relationships between economic and political institutions contain powerful potentials for the production of socially injurious actions. This relational approach provides a more nuanced understanding of the processes leading to deviant organizational outcomes than do approaches that treat either businesses or government as closed systems. Third, the relational character of state-corporate crime also directs us to consider the vertical relationships between different levels of organizational action: the individual, the institutional, and the political-economic.

See also: Imperial Food Plant Fire; NASA; ValuJet Flight 592

FURTHER READING

Aulette, Judy Root, and Michalowski, Raymond. "Fire in Hamlet: A Case Study of a State-Corporate Crime." Pp.171–206 in Kenneth D. Tunnell (ed.), *Political Crime in Contemporary America: A Critical Approach.* New York: Garland, 1993.

Kauzlarich, David, and Kramer, Ronald C. "State-Corporate Crime in the US Nuclear Weapons Production Complex." *Journal of Human Justice* 5.1 (1993, Autumn): 4–28.

Kramer, Ronald C. "The Space Shuttle *Challenger* Explosion: A Case Study of State-Corporate Crime." Pp. 212–241 in Kip Schlegel and David Weisburd (eds.), *White Collar Crime Reconsidered.* Boston: Northeastern University Press, 1992.

Kramer, Ronald C., and Michalowski, Raymond. "State Corporate Crime." Paper presented to the American Society of Criminology, Baltimore, November 1990.

Kramer, Ronald C., Michalowski, Raymond J., and Kauzlarich, David. "The Origins and Development of the Concept and Theory of State-Corporate Crime." *Crime and Delinquency* 48.2 (April, 2002): 263–282.

Matthews, Rick A., and Kauzlarich, David. "The Crash of ValuJet Flight 592: A Case Study in State-Corporate Crime." *Sociological Focus* 3.3 (August, 2000): 281–298.

Michalowski, Raymond J., and Kramer, Ronald C. *State-Corporate Crime: Wrongdoing at the Intersection of Business and Government.* Piscataway, NJ: Rutgers University Press, 2006.

RONALD C. KRAMER

STEWART, MARTHA (1941–). Martha Stewart: those two words represent a brand name, a media conglomerate, and a woman. Prior to 2002, Martha Stewart the woman was known as stockbroker gone domestic diva—a meticulous, business-minded media mogul who could cook, sew, scrub, and decorate. In early 2002, her publicly traded conglomerate, Martha Stewart Living Omnimedia Inc., had four major branches: publishing (magazines and books), television production, merchandising, and direct (Internet and catalog) sales.

Events of and following December 27, 2001, surely haunt the goddess of good things. In the media, she's gone from domestic diva to convicted felon to makeover maven.

According to court documents, on the morning of December 27, 2001, Martha Stewart's broker, Peter Bacanovic, was on vacation. Stewart's assistant nonetheless took a message from him that ImClone stock was dropping. Stewart called his office. Bacanovic's assistant, Douglas Faneuil, reported that ImClone's President and CEO, Samuel Waksal, was unloading all of his own company's stock. Sharing this information was an illegal process called piggybacking: brokers are not to use their knowledge of one client to the benefit of another. As a former stockbroker herself, Stewart knew that. She nonetheless sold her 3928 shares of ImClone stock, avoiding losses of between $45,000 and $51,000.

On December 28, the FDA rejected ImClone's application for a colorectal cancer drug called Erbitux. ImClone's stock dropped 18 percent that day. Stewart was neither tried nor convicted of insider trading. Instead she was indicted, tried, and found guilty on charges of conspiracy, obstructing justice, and giving false statements. It wasn't the piggybacking or stock sale that landed Martha Stewart in jail—it was what happened next.

In 2002, after learning of a federal investigation into the sale of ImClone stock, Stewart and Bacanovic reportedly lied, schemed, and concealed the truth about their dealings. Specifically, Stewart and Bacanovic created a story that they had agreed in the fall of 2001 that Stewart would sell her ImClone stocks should they drop to $60 per share. Both Stewart and Bacanovic told federal authorities of this "decision"; Bacanovic falsified notes after the fact to make the agreement appear legitimate. Stewart altered the December 27, 2001, log of the phone message from Bacanovic but later had her assistant return it to its original wording. Later Stewart told authorities she didn't know whether there was a record of that message! Both parties also reported having spoken to each other of this prior agreement on December 27, even though Bacanovic was on vacation and never actually spoke to Stewart that day.

On March 5, 2004, a jury of eight women and four men found Martha Stewart, then 62 years old, guilty of four counts: one count of conspiracy to obstruct justice, make false statements, and commit perjury; two charges of false statements, and one count of obstruction of justice. Another charge claiming that Stewart had publicly lied about her involvement to preserve the stock value of her own company was thrown out. Martha Stewart was sentenced by Judge Miriam Goldman Cedarbaum to the lowest possible term: five months in federal prison and a $30,000 fine, five months of home confinement, and two years of supervised probation.

Stewart served her five months in an Alderson, West Viginia, prison from October 2004 to March 2005. Peter Bacanovic was similarly sentenced to five months in jail, five months of home arrest, and two years supervised probation. Sam Waksal is serving seven years in federal prison. He and his father, Jack Waksal, paid approximately six million dollars in disgorgement and civil penalties for illegal trades in ImClone securities.

In an ironic twist of fate, Erbitux, the ImClone drug declined by the FDA in December 2001, was approved before Martha Stewart was convicted.

Critics charge that Stewart has been treated unfairly by media and the public. Consider other recent scandals with lesser known, male CEOs. Dennis Kozlowski and Mark Swartz were charged with stealing $600 million from Tyco. John Rigas and his sons were charged with pocketing millions of dollars of Aldelphia profit. The collapse of Enron and WorldCom has cost billions of dollars of losses for investors and thousands of jobs. Ex-Enron CEO Jeff Skilling and World Com's former CEO, Bernard Ebbers, have both been indicted on charges related to the downfall of those companies. In comparison, Martha Stewart's crimes were inconsequential in human and financial costs—they certainly didn't warrant under any logical decision-making criteria more air time or public concern than these other white-collar crimes. Yet, both in print copy and in air time, the media have granted far more energy to Stewart than to crimes of far more significant public consequences. For most Americans, other, more damaging white-collar crimes have hardly entered the public consciousness. The claim that Stewart was treated differently at least as a result of her previous public image, if not because she is a powerful woman, seem to have merit.

In the end, though, Stewart's case may prove the adage that "any press is good press." When Stewart was released from Alderson on March 4, 2005, she had lost weight and had a team of image makers guiding her every move. They were crafting a kinder, gentler Martha for the public. Stewart asked paparazzi and reporters outside her home whether they'd like breakfast; she wore a shawl knitted by a fellow inmate; she called for greater public investment in fair treatment and rehabilitation programs for federal inmates. Reality television guru Mark Burnett approached Stewart to star in a spin-off of *The Apprentice*. She has launched a new daytime talk show. Stewart's company's stock soared while she was in prison, from $8.70 per share after her conviction to $37 by the time she was released from prison. In appears that for Martha Stewart, in some ways, being a convicted felon may turn out to be a good thing.

FURTHER READING

"Martha Stewart." Times Topics. *The New York Times*. Available at http://topics.nytimes.com/top/reference/timestopics/people/s/martha_stewart/. Accessed September 27, 2006.

REBECCA SELF

STRAIN THEORY AND WHITE-COLLAR CRIME. As the theory of "anomie" remains a popular explanation as to why crime occurs, a related theory of "strain" is a common motivation cited as to why corporate and white-collar crime happens. Strain theory asserts that crime results from conditions and periods where there is pressure to attain a goal or outcome, such as maximizing material gain, that is rendered unattainable because the means of achieving this goal are blocked or unavailable. This theory is commonly employed and tested to explain financial crimes, but it also holds considerable explanatory power in relation to other types of white-collar crimes. Several studies in the area of corporate and white-collar crime have examined the relationships between criminality and pressures to attain a goal (such as profit) in the absence of legitimate means to achieve it. Strain theory and variants of this theorization are have proven very useful, if not controversial, in the explanation of most types of white-collar and corporate crime.

Most theories of white-collar crime attempt to answer "why" such acts occur; the most commonly reason cited is that it is in the culprit's best interest to do so. Strain theory is a version of this explanation that its forerunner, Robert Merton (1957), used to explain differences in crime rates in the United States. Like Edwin Sutherland's theory of differential association, strain theory has been used to explain all types of crime, making it useful to the study of white-collar crime, although Merton originally developed it mainly to explain property crimes that are attributable to lower-class groups. Strain theory involves the interplay between two sociological concepts: One is the culturally determined *goals* of a society and the other is structurally available *means* to achieve these goals. Merton's theory became known as "strain theory" because he thought crime was rooted in a disjunction or disconnect from the stated goals of the social structure and the culturally acceptable means to achieve them. When there is no legitimate means to realize a stated goal, a society or group could be said to be experiencing "strain." In a society or subculture that is experiencing strain, crime would be more likely as a deviant, individual innovation to accomplish the given goals of the group. He used the term "anomie" or "anomic" to describe such conditions where there were pressures, but not existing means, to achieve these goals. This conception of anomie is different than classical social theorist Emile Durkheim's notion of anomie as a state of normlessness or a loss of social regulation. For Merton and strain theorists, crime is the result of a deviant adaptation to an environment where these anomic conditions existed. For strain theorists, crime and deviant behavior stem from very conventional motives by embracing and not rejecting the goals of a society.

Merton's original formulation of strain theory has undergone numerous revisions and received a great number of criticisms in its application to crime. These criticisms are mostly due to the fact that not all individuals in a society or group might share the same goals of the society as a whole and that his original framework focused on the crimes of the lower classes, while research has clearly demonstrated that many costly crimes are committed by those of higher status who do not experience the same type of "strain" Merton discusses. Contemporaries such as Box (1983) have argued that although these criticisms are valid, they lose their strength once his theory is modified to include variations in status and the conditions that are fostered within a corporate environment. Reorienting the understanding of stain theory *not* as an explanation of individual behavior but on the structural or status positioning of individuals, Box sees the modern corporation's goal-seeking structure of profit maximization, combined with uncertain economic conditions, as making a corporation inherently criminogenic.

As business professionals and corporations are routinely faced with economic contractions, an uncertain environment, and pressures to cut costs, these individuals may seek out alternative means of making money such as avoidance, evasion, or blatant violations of ethics or laws. The application of a neo-Mertonian theory of institutional strain is one that focuses not on the individual but on the overarching social processes and structures under which white-collar and corporate violations take place. In a similar vein, Messner and Rosenfeld (2000) in their book *Crime and the American Dream* have argued that the social structure of the United States involves the institutional dominance of corporations and cultural values that place emphasis on material gain, individual achievement, competition not cooperation, and the fetishism of money. The institutional structure that places disproportionate emphasis on "getting ahead" and acquiring wealth over the legitimate means to achieve them is a source of crime in the United States. The American Dream itself, coupled with failure rates of business and unemployment, has been cited as a source of strain and white-collar crime in the United States. Furthermore, the means of achieving this dream is simply not available to a large proportion of people in the United States.

While Merton's theory has had mixed results in relation to other forms of crime, it has proven quite formidable when applied to corporate and white-collar crime. In many ways, the modern corporation is an ideal structure to test the conceptual notions identified in strain theory—after all, the primary goal of a business or corporation is to accumulate capital. More specifically, the principal function of a corporation is to maximize profits and minimize costs. In line with Max Weber's thesis of bureaucratic organizations, corporations and the personalities they foster are rational, goal-directed hierarchies that seek to maximize profits. These goals are expected to be internalized and embraced by those who manage and work within the corporation. If, for some reason—be it a cyclical downturn in the general economy, financial mismanagement or some other inability to acquire wealth legitimately—the goals become unattainable, an organization could be said to be experiencing strain and therefore be "anomic." Under these conditions, and the ensuing pressures to attain profits or material success, crime or deviance may become an attractive solution to mitigate the pressures exerted on the firm or individual to make money or maximize the profits of the firm.

The usefulness of strain theory is evident in both case studies of white-collar criminality and large sample, comprehensive studies of variations in levels of offending patterns by corporations. Recent, high-profile accounts of securities fraud and accounting scandals suggest that contradictions in the market and other pressures on profits led the executives of firms such as Enron, Tyco, and WorldCom to begin using illegal and fraudulent accounting techniques to hide the fact that their firms were losing money, while enriching themselves. Furthermore, these companies operated in an industrial environment where "innovative" means were encouraged as a way to make money. During some of the savings and loan scandals in the 1980s, at savings and loans that could not make money legitimately, managers and executives began plundering the companies and intentionally writing bad loans. In the 1970s, Ford Motor Company, faced with a defective automobile that incinerated people, studied the impact on its bottom line and intentionally refused to fix the defect afterward. These decisions took place during a time when Ford was experiencing considerable strain to make smaller and cheaper cars as imports had begun to erode Ford's market share and profit margins.

The inability to acquire profits legitimately is an obvious motive for an individual or business to commit a crime. White-collar criminologists have theorized that the organizational and normative conditions present in a company experiencing financial troubles or other types of organizational strain can cause a greater likelihood of criminal outcomes. Pressure on profit margins is a clear measure of financial strain and indicative of blocked means. Although theories embracing the social strain theoretical framework to explain white-collar crime suggest a relationship between the profit goal and crime, the direction of this relationship is unclear. Most research suggests that strain theory lends itself to being empirically tested by examining the legal and illegal behaviors within and among corporations that face periods of financial strain, such as low profitability or contracting markets. This theorization is complicated by the fact that, if deviance is related to cost-cutting and profit-maximizing behaviors, it is equally plausible that corporations that break the law are more profitable. Although many studies of corporate and white-collar crime look at some form of financial performance, it may be that illegality *is not* related to financial performance or goals at all. That is, all firms and managers receive pressure to achieve financial goals, regardless of profit or sales levels. All firms may experience a general pressure, spread across all firms, to violate laws. The fact remains that the drive to get and maintain material wealth is a factor in decisions made by white-collar criminals. Strain theory is a conception of this motive that is well equipped to explain how and why these decisions are made.

See also: Ford Pinto; Iacocca, Lee

FURTHER READING

Box, S. *Power, Crime and Mystification*. London: Tavistock, 1983.
Merton, R. K. *Social Theory and Social Structure*. Glencoe, IL: The Free Press, 1957.
Messner, S. F., and Rosenfeld, R. *Crime and the American Dream*. 3rd edition. Belmont, CA: Wadsworth Publishing, 2000.

BRIAN WOLF

SWAGGART, JIMMY (1935–). Jimmy Swaggart was born in Farriday, Louisiana, on March 15, 1935. A cousin to rock and roll legend Jerry Lee Lewis and country music star Mickey Gilley, Swaggart became a gospel singer and, in 1958, an Assemblies of God minister. In the 1960s he became known for his gospel albums and developed a following on the revival circuit. In 1969, Swaggart started the radio program "The Camp Meeting Hour." During the 1970s, Swaggart expanded into the world of television and became a popular televangelist.

In the 1980s Swaggart reached his peak of popularity. Over 200 stations broadcast "The Jimmy Swaggart Telecast" into two million households every week. At the time, Jimmy Swaggart Ministries was based in Baton Rouge, Louisiana, and drew in approximately $100 million a year. The ministry expanded to include a local congregation of more than 4000 members as well as the Jimmy Swaggart Bible College.

In 1986 Swaggart publicly denounced New Orleans preacher Marvin Gorman for engaging in extramarital affairs. Gorman was defrocked as a result, sued, received a judgment against Swaggart for defamation, and was awarded damages in the amount of $10 million in 1991.

In 1987 Swaggart publicly denounced PTL minister Jim Bakker's sexual incident with Jessica Hahn, an incident that was one of the causes that eventually led to the downfall of Bakker's PTL Ministry. It was widely rumored that Swaggart intended a hostile takeover of PTL in cooperation with the Assemblies of God and the *Charlotte Observer*. Bakker had previously pulled Swaggart's half-hour show from its slot on PTL's network.

In 1988, a year after publicly denouncing Bakker's transgressions, Swaggart was forced to publicly confess to his own. In 1987 Swaggart was photographed with prostitute Debra Murphree by an associate of Gorman outside the Texas Hotel in Metairie, Louisiana. Speaking tearfully from his television pulpit, Swaggart begged his audience for forgiveness. He was disciplined by the Assemblies of God leadership and banned from preaching for three months. In addition, a two-year ban was imposed on Swaggart's television ministry. Swaggart refused to abide by the prohibition against televangelism and was defrocked by the Assemblies of God after he resigned from the denomination. Subsequently, allegations of other instances of extramarital sexual conduct by Swaggart emerged. In October 1991, police in Indio, California, arrested Swaggart in a red-light district for driving on the wrong side of the road. Swaggart's passenger was prostitute Rosemary Garcia.

Although his personal ethics have come into question, Swaggart has never been charged with a white-collar crime. As a result of his personal indiscretions, Swaggart's ministry lost much of its national audience; however, the ministry is still in operation today. The Jimmy Swaggart Telecast is presently airing in over fifty countries of the world, in addition to the United States and Canada. Currently, the Swaggart Ministry includes over sixty radio stations, which air 24 hours a day. Swaggart is one of the best-selling gospel music artists of all-time, with total sales in excess of fifty million copies worldwide.

See also: Bakker, Jim and Tammy Faye

FURTHER READING

"Jimmy Swaggart." Wikipedia, The Free Encyclopedia. Available at http://en.wikipedia.org/wiki/Jimmy_Swaggart. Accessed August 24, 2006.

Lundy, H. *Let Us Prey: The Public Trial of Jimmy Swaggart*. Columbus, MS: Genesis Press, 1999.

Seaman, A. R. *Swaggart: the Unauthorized Biography of an American Evangelist*. New York: Continuum, 1999.

Shepard, C. E. *Forgiven: The Rise and Fall of Jim Bakker and the PTL Ministry*. New York: Atlantic Monthly Press, 1989.

KATHERINE M. BROWN

SWISS BANKS. During the mid-1990s, several lawsuits were filed against Swiss banks on behalf of Holocaust survivors. These suits alleged that the banks were illegally holding millions of dollars in assets that belonged to Holocaust victims and should have been returned to the heirs of the deceased after the war.

During this same time, Assistant Secretary of State Stuart Eizenstat was leading a commission composed of eleven U.S. agencies that were given the charge to investigate the connections between the Swiss banks and the Third Reich. In August 1998, the Swiss banks settled the suit, agreeing to pay $1.25 billion to the survivors. These lawsuits, coupled with the investigation by the Eizenstat commission, led to a flurry of research by journalists and historians alike. Several findings called into question Switzerland's official claim of neutrality during World War II.

During World War II, the official currency of Germany, the reichsmark, was not accepted by several countries, making it difficult for Germany to purchase goods and services needed to conduct the war. One way of getting around this problem was to use gold and then to sell the gold to obtain a currency that could be used (i.e., Swiss francs). According to the Eizenstat report, Germany transferred some $400 million worth of gold (about $3.9 billion in today's dollars) to Swiss banks between 1939 and 1945. The Swiss National Bank bought about $267 million of the gold ($2.7 billion in today's dollars), while the rest of the gold went directly into accounts of banks in other countries from which Germany was buying goods or services. Some of this gold was plundered from the banks of occupied territories, and some of it was stolen directly from Jewish victims (either seizing gold assets or, in other instances, removing gold from teeth). In this way, the Swiss National Bank both knowingly aided the Third Reich and profited from the war. The bank also prolonged Germany's war efforts by providing much needed resources.

In addition, after the war Swiss banks continued to hold millions of dollars that Jews had deposited before and during the war, expecting to reclaim the money later. Many of the depositors, however, died in the Holocaust. When surviving family members attempted to withdraw the money, they were often met with bureaucratic responses from Swiss banking officials. Often the banks demanded an official death certificate—a document the SS death squads and camp administrators did not bother to issue. In other instances, bank officials asked for documentation that survivors were unlikely to have (i.e., bank statements, deposit slips, etc.). This left many survivors unable to reclaim family assets and left the Swiss banks with millions of dollars in dormant accounts (by some conservative estimates, there were over 6000 of these accounts). In contrast, some banks in other countries were much more understanding in returning assets to survivors, waiving requirements such as death certificates.

While helping Germany finance the war, Swiss banks were also found to have held assets for high-ranking members of the Nazi party, a significant amount of which was stolen from Jewish victims. Finally, they were accused of financing intelligence programs run by the Nazis.

Although Switzerland was neutral in the war, in that its military did not become involved, it is clear that in other important ways it was not impartial. In addition to the activities of Swiss banks, some Swiss industries manufactured goods for the Germans. Also, Switzerland was not a safe haven for Jews seeking asylum, as they—like the United States and Canada—passed immigration laws limiting the number of immigrants. Finally, the Swiss corporations continued to conduct trade with Germany and the other Axis powers.

The fact that Swiss banks were involved in helping finance the war efforts of Nazi Germany was well known to members of the U.S. government during World War II. In 1943, for example, the United States, along with eighteen other countries, sent a notice to the

Swiss banks asking them to discontinue these practices. The banks, however, continued their involvement.

Although it is relatively easy to target the Swiss banks for their complicity in the Holocaust, it is important to remember that the Swiss were not the only ones doing business with the Germans. For example, the U.S-based banks of J. P. Morgan and Chase each had branches in Paris, France, that continued to conduct business with German industries. Their defense—typical of other companies—was that they had lost control over their operations. However, in 2001 J. P. Morgan settled a lawsuit for $2.75 million, and in 2002 it merged with Chase Manhattan, which had earlier settled as a party in the Drai Commission's settlement in 2001. Other businesses found to have been involved in the German war effort include many German companies, such as IG Farben, Daimler, Volkswagen, and Krupp; and as many as 300 U.S.-based corporations, such as Ford, General Motors, IBM, and Kodak, are also accused of profiting from their involvement with the Third Reich.

See also: Corporate Crime; Corporate War Crimes

FURTHER READING

Bazyler, Michael. *Holocaust Justice: The Battle for Restitution in America's Courts.* New York: New York University Press, 2003.

Eizenstat, Stuart E. *Imperfect Justice: Looted Assets, Slave Labor, and the Unfinished Business of WWII.* New York: Public Affairs, 2003.

LeBor, Adam. *Hitler's Secret Bankers: The Myth of Swiss Neutrality during the Holocaust.* Secaucus, NJ: Carol Publishing Group, 1999.

Rickman, Gregg. *Swiss Banks, Jewish Souls.* New Brunswick, NJ: Transaction Publishers, 1999.

RICK A. MATTHEWS

T

TEAPOT DOME. In 1929, Albert B. Fall, U.S. Secretary of the Interior under President Warren G. Harding, was convicted of accepting bribes for the leasing of two naval oil reserves: Naval Petroleum Reserve 1, located at Elk Hills, California, and Naval Petroleum Reserve 3, located at Teapot Dome, Wyoming. Fall's position gave him control of the oil reserves, and he began to lease out those reserves privately. An investigation of the Teapot Dome scandal revealed numerous dealings typical of white-collar crime, including hush money, unsecured loans, secret meetings, and recovered suitcases full of bonds and cash. The investigation ended with the exposure of corruption within the federal government, and the Teapot Dome scandal caused the Navy to question its policies regarding naval oil reserves.

Background. At the beginning of the twentieth century, the U.S. Navy decided to change its fuel source from coal to oil. At this time, the Navy was consuming the largest amount of fuel in the world, causing conservationists to question how long the fuel supply would last. Debate and concern continued, and in 1912 President Taft created one of the first naval oil reserves by withdrawing Naval Petroleum Reserve 1, Elk Hills, from public lands in California. Later, in 1915, President Wilson created Naval Petroleum Reserve 3 at Teapot Dome, Wyoming.

The Scandal. After Harding was elected president in 1920, he appointed Fall as his Secretary of the Interior. Before his appointment, Fall represented New Mexico as a Republican senator and was known to be an anticonservationist. He also owned a ranch in New Mexico and was struggling with financial problems.

One of the first tasks Fall undertook in his new post was convincing President Harding in 1921 to sign over control of the Elk Hills and Teapot Dome oil reserves from the Department of the Navy to the Department of the Interior. His next act was to begin privately leasing out the oil reserves to two companies. Fall did this without any bids from other competitors and without the awareness of the general public or Congress.

On April 7, 1922, Fall leased part of Naval Petroleum Reserve 3 oil reserve at Teapot Dome, Wyoming, to Edward L. Doheny's Pan-American Petroleum and Transport Company. Later that same year, on December 11, Fall leased all of the other oil reserve, Naval Petroleum Reserve 1 at Elk Hills, California, to Harry F. Sinclair's company, Mammoth Oil Company.

The Investigation. On April 15, 1922, Wyoming's Democratic senator John B. Kendrick motioned for the Senate to gather information regarding the leasing of the Teapot Dome oil reserve. Kendrick had been asked by oilmen from the area to look into the matter because they had heard rumors that Teapot Dome had been secretly leased. The senator had questioned individuals at both the Navy Department and the Department of Interior but had received no valuable information. After a unanimous decision was made by the Senate, an official investigation began on April 29, 1922.

Not long after the Senate had passed Kendrick's motion, a spokesman from the Department of the Interior came forward and stated that the oil reserve at Teapot Dome had been secretly leased, beginning a Congressional hearing. During the first week of the hearing, Fall testified that he had leased the oil reserve at Teapot Dome to Doheny because wells that were being built on land surrounding the reserve were exhausting the oil from the reserve. For this reason, Fall believed it was essential to lease the land and begin drilling. He told congressmen that asking for bids would not have produced the price he believed he could get by privately leasing the reserve. Fall also admitted he had secretly leased the Elk Hills reserve in California, stating that he thought publicity of his dealings would upset other nations, particularly Japan, because there were tensions in the Pacific.

The hearing committee seemed to accept this explanation and was beginning to think that it had hit a dead end when it learned that Fall was no longer in financial trouble. The committee was given evidence that Fall had been ten years behind on his taxes, which had suddenly been paid off. The committee was also told by Carl Magee, Fall's neighbor and political opponent, that Fall had been making expensive improvements to his New Mexico ranch. Fall told the committee that he had been loaned $100,000 by Ned McLean, his friend and the publisher of the *Washington Post*. Fall's statement was true; however, the checks that were written out to Fall had been returned to McLean uncashed.

This new evidence caused the hearing committee to question how Fall had managed to pay off his taxes and improve his ranch. A few months later, Fall resigned from his position as Secretary of the Interior. The investigation continued, and it was revealed that both Doheny and Sinclair had given Fall large amounts of money that were said to be "loans." Fall had received $100,000 in cash from Doheny and over $300,000 as a combination of cash and government bonds.

After the information and evidence were collected, the investigation ended, resulting in criminal prosecutions. Fall was found guilty of accepting bribes from Doheny and Sinclair, fined $100,000, and sentenced to a year of imprisonment. Doheny and Sinclair were found not guilty of bribery and were set free; however, Sinclair was later imprisoned for hiring detectives to follow jury members and for contempt of the Senate. The last ruling in this case came in 1927, when the Supreme Court handed down the decision that the oil reserves were to be returned to the federal government.

FURTHER READING

Essential Documents in American History, Essential Documents, 1492-Present: 5–6. Retrieved February 18, 2005 from Academic Search Premier database.

Haydock, Michael D. "American First!" *American History* 34.1 (1999): 16–26.

Jacobson, Louis. "Infamous Teapot Dome Percolates New Ideas." *National Journal* 34.37 (2002): 2642–44.

Schwarz, Frederic D. "1922." *American Heritage* 48.2 (1997): 105–07.

Schwarz, Frederic D. "1923." *American Heritage* 49.6 (1998): 117–18.

Shulman, Peter A. "Science Can Never Demobilize: The United States Navy and Petroleum Geology, 1898–1924." *History and Technology* 19.4 (2003): 365–85.

"Teapot Dome: Joint Resolution of Congress on Cancellation of Oil Leases." (1924).

MARY BETH SARVER

TECHNIQUES OF NEUTRALIZATION AND WHITE-COLLAR CRIME. The *techniques of neutralization* are linguistic devices, such as rationalizations, excuses, and justifications, that serve to decrease the dissonance that may occur when a person committed to conventional behavior and laws engages in deviance or lawbreaking. The techniques allow an actor to maintain a positive and conventional identity despite his disputed behavior. The techniques of neutralization are particularly relevant for cases of white-collar crime because white-collar offenders are likely to see themselves as law-abiding citizens and not as conventional criminals.

The study of the techniques for neutralizing white-collar crime has evolved since the time that several social scientists became interested in the ways in which actors explain their behaviors. In 1940, C. Wright Mills discussed the "vocabularies of motive" people use to provide reasons for their actions. People learn the acceptable motives for actions, and if they anticipate that they cannot provide an adequate motive, such knowledge may constrain their behavior.

Edwin Sutherland argued in 1947 that persons who learn motives, drives, and rationalizations that are favorable to lawbreaking are more likely to violate the law. Donald Cressey's 1953 study of convicted embezzlers was an important attempt to examine the rationalizations used by white-collar criminals. Yet one of the most cited works on this topic is Sykes and Matza's 1957 article on the techniques of neutralization and delinquency.

Sykes and Matza analyzed the techniques juvenile delinquents use to neutralize the guilt they feel when violating important normative standards. The linguistic techniques allow juveniles to commit deviant acts yet avoid defining themselves as criminal or delinquent. The techniques of neutralization are primarily either excuses or justifications. Excuses imply that the behavior in question is wrong or inappropriate but the actor is not fully responsible. Justifications, on the other hand, signify that the actor is responsible for the behavior but the behavior is appropriate or proper. The techniques of neutralization are also useful for explaining white-collar crime because most white-collar actors have a stake in maintaining definitions of themselves as being in compliance with normative standards, rather than seeing themselves as deviants or criminals. The techniques of neutralization may create the opportunity for a white-collar employee to consider and engage in behaviors that are incongruous with his self-image.

Each of the five techniques of neutralization described by Sykes and Matza is applicable to white-collar crime. The first technique is to deny responsibility for the negative action. For years, Buffalo Mining, owned by Pittston Mining Corporation, stored mining waste in the Buffalo Creek dam above the town of Saunders, West Virginia. Pittston Mining was warned that the dam wasunsafe, that the company was violating federal safety standards, and that the dam showed signs of erosion. In 1972, after heavy rains, the dam collapsed and washed away the town, killing 125 residents and leaving 4000 homeless. Executives at Pittston Mining denied responsibility for the damage by claiming the collapse of the dam was "an act of God." They successfully avoided criminal indictment and reached a $13.5 million civil settlement.

The second technique of neutralization is to deny that the behavior caused harm. In 1961, executives from General Electric Corporation and Westinghouse Corporation were sentenced to up to thirty days in jail and fines for violating the Sherman Act of 1890. The companies had conspired for decades to violate the spirit of the free market; they refused to compete against each other and fixed the prices of heavy electrical equipment. Buyers estimated that they had overpaid at least $160 million due to the conspiracy. The executives attempted to neutralize their guilt by claiming the price-fixing, while illegal, was not criminal because it caused no harm. They argued that they did not attempt to hurt customers; in fact, they tried to reduce the volatility of the market by agreeing upon prices. In addition, the heavy electrical equipment executives claimed they did not charge excessive prices, but rather that customers were charged fair amounts.

The third technique of neutralization is to deny there was a victim of the act. Guilt may be reduced by denying that a real or innocent person was harmed by an action. During the Holocaust, the Nazis employed this technique of neutralization to decrease the guilt and doubts associated with the murder of an estimated 5 million to 6 million Jews. German propaganda denied Jews were victims by portraying them as evil, nonhuman, and criminal; therefore, the Nazis argued, the Jews deserved destruction. Jews were depicted as an evil danger plotting to destroy Germany and conspiring to dominate the world. Propaganda was designed to characterize Jews as subhuman. They were described as vermin and lice; therefore, killing them was presented as an act of hygiene, rather than the murder of innocent humans. The Jews were also depicted in propaganda as having a criminal heredity that included the alleged torture of Christian children. This technique was furthered by a campaign to blame all cases of missing children on Jews.

The fourth technique of neutralization is to condemn the condemners. This mechanism serves to deflect blame from one's actions and, instead, focuses attention on the motives and actions of one's critics. Doctors sanctioned for Medicaid fraud attempted to neutralize their guilt by arguing that the behavior of system officials was much worse than the doctors' transgressions. Doctors claimed the Medicaid system invited cheating through its arbitrary, irrational, and often-changed decisions. They reasoned that cheating the system was more rational than trying to comply with the capricious rules of unjust system administrators; therefore, the doctors argued, it was not fair to punish them.

The fifth technique of neutralization is to appeal to a higher loyalty. Law violators may justify breaking the law by claiming they were conforming to other normative standards that conflicted with the law. The Reagan administration used this technique to justify its actions in the Iran-Contra affair. The administration arranged the sale of weapons to Iran and used the funds to arm the Nicaraguan Contras. This was done to help the Contras overthrow Nicaragua's Sandinista government. In supplying arms to the Contras, the administration violated the Boland Amendment, which expressly prohibited military aid to the Contras. Reagan administration officials justified this violation by claiming their actions served a higher purpose than the law. They argued that their actions were helping to spread democracy in the region and that they had acted to protect human life.

See also: Buffalo Creek Flood; Heavy Electrical Equipment Antitrust Cases of 1961; Iran-Contra

FURTHER READING

Benson, Michael L. "Denying the Guilty Mind: Accounting for Involvement in White-Collar Crime." *Criminology* 23 (1985): 583–608.

Box, Steven. *Power, Crime and Mystification.* London: Tavistock, 1983.

Cressey, Donald R. *Other People's Money.* Glencoe, IL: Free Press, 1953.

Geis, Gil. "The Heavy Electrical Equipment Antitrust Cases: Price-Fixing Techniques and Rationalizations." iIn David Ermann and Richard Lundman, (eds.), *Corporate and Governmental Deviance,* 6th edition. Oxford: Oxford University Press, 2002.

Jesilow, Paul, Pontell, Henry, and Geis, Gil. *Prescription for Profit: How Doctors Defraud Medicaid.* Berkeley: University of California Press, 1993.

Sykes, Gresham, and Matza, David. "Techniques of Neutralization: A Theory of Delinquency." *American Sociological Review* 22 (1957): 664–70.

GARY E. REED

THREE-MILE ISLAND. The worst nuclear accident in the history of the United States occurred at the Three-Mile Island (TMI) nuclear power plant in March 1979. The plant, located approximately ten miles south of Harrisburg, Pennsylvania, on the Susquahanna River, came dangerously close to a nuclear meltdown that would have had devastating results. Now, more than twenty-five years later, the incident, the cleanup, and the long-term effects are still the subject of scrutiny and debate.

The Accident. The TMI nuclear power plant began operations in September 1974, and for several years the Unit 1 reactor successfully supplied electricity for the area. Problems began at TMI, however, when the Unit 2 reactor came on line in December 1978. The second reactor was over budget, behind schedule, and hastily opened for operation. Less than a month into operation, the new reactor had to be shut down for two weeks because of leaks in the piping and pump system. Unit 2 was reopened, and only ninety days after it first began running, the aforementioned disaster began around four o'clock in the morning of Wednesday, March 28, 1979.

To this day, the Nuclear Regulatory Commission (NRC) is not certain why the valves and pumps in the TMI Unit 2 reactor first began to fail. From the initial point of failure, though, the problems quickly escalated out of control. First, the secondary loop feedwater pumps, responsible for supplying the water that would pick up heat from the primary nuclear sector of the plant and emerge as nonradioactive steam, shut down. Without water pushing through the secondary loop, the heat being generated in the radioactive core had no way of escaping. The temperature and pressure in the primary loop quickly began to rise. A pressure relief valve inside the reactor opened to release the radioactive steam from the primary loop into a holding tank and alleviate the building pressure within the core. Although the valve was supposed to close as soon as the pressure decreased inside the reactor, it became stuck in an open position.

The pressure in the reactor then began dropping as water and steam drained off the core through the open release valve. In response, several of the reactor's emergency feedwater pumps began operating automatically to ensure that there was enough water in the steam generators to cool the core. However, the cutoff valves connecting the backup pumps to the rest of the system had been closed days before during routine tests, and operators had neglected to reopen them. Thus, even though the emergency pumps were running, no water could reach the cooling steam generators. Although the panel in the control room had two lights alerting operators that the valves were closed, one was covered up by a dangling maintenance tag, and the other went unnoticed. In fact, it took eight minutes for plant operators to realize that the valves were shut.

About fourteen seconds into the accident, the two control room operators did notice that the emergency feedwater pumps were running and also that an indicator light was showing the initial pressure relief valve had closed as it should have. Because the light was on erroneously, operators were unaware that the valve was standing ajar, allowing water and steam to escape. A Loss-of-Coolant Accident (LOCA) developed as over 32,000 gallons of water needed to cool the reactor core rushed out of the release valve during the two hours and twenty-two minutes it was left standing open.

Plant operators saw that the water level was continuing to drop within the pressurizer and turned on another backup pump. The water level immediately began rising, but the pressure inside the reactor continued to fall. About two minutes into the accident, the steam generators boiled dry because none of the emergency water could reach them through the still closed cutoff valve. This situation caused another substantial decrease in the pressure, which triggered two more high-powered emergency pumps to activate. Concerned that the water level might get too high, the control-room operators shut down the backup pumps after two and a half minutes, not noticing that the pressure was still falling and that the temperature remained high despite the addition of coolant water. Not only was water still escaping through the open release valve, the temperature inside the reactor was hot enough that water was also quickly boiling off the core.

Although there were several indications that a LOCA was occurring, operators were concerned at this point with the radioactive water that had leaked through the open release valve and covered the floor of the containment and auxiliary buildings. Levels of radiation were continuing to rise within the plant, and plant staff, following protocol, declared a "site emergency" just before seven o'clock in the morning.

An even bigger problem, however, was that so much water had drained out of the reactor's core that the fuel rods were exposed. The rods warmed to 4300 degrees, dangerously close to the 5200 degree meltdown point. It took almost sixteen hours for plant operators to recognize and correct the problems with the valves and pumps and stabilize the temperature and pressure inside the nuclear reactor. By this time, though, a hydrogen bubble had formed above the nuclear reactor core. Now the real threat was that the bubble would block the flow of water to the core and cause an explosion if the hydrogen were to mix with the oxygen in the water and catch fire.

Five days after the chain of events began, engineers from the Nuclear Regulatory Commission (NRC) announced they had shrunk the hydrogen bubble and that the threat of a hydrogen fire had been miscalculated. It was another month before the Unit 2 reactor could be shut down completely. Three years later, the full extent of the damage was revealed when a robotic camera provided pictures of the core. Fifty percent of the core had been entirely destroyed, and approximately twenty tons of molten uranium had settled on the bottom of the reactor room.

Placing the Blame. A report commissioned by President Jimmy Carter following the incident suggests that the standards surrounding nuclear power, particularly at TMI, had become grievously relaxed, and the associated dangers were not being taken seriously. For starters, the training provided by Metropolitan Edison, the plant's parent company, did not adequately prepare control room operators to deal with a problem such as the one they had encountered on March 28. Had operators been properly trained to understand the various signals they were receiving, they would not have shut off the emergency water pumps, and the incident could have remained relatively minor. Furthermore, the pressure relief valve that failed to close during the TMI accident had malfunctioned eleven times before at other power plants. Thus, the NRC was also at fault for not requiring the replacement of a valve known to be defective. Finally, the report also placed some of the blame on human error for neglecting to open the hand-operated valves that would have allowed the emergency water system to save the plant. Overall, investigators into the incident found that the equipment, attitudes, and operating training practices at TMI made an accident virtually inevitable.

In addition to the questionable environment surrounding the plant prior to the accident, the way the public was handled throughout the course of the crisis also raised some controversy. Fearing a public-relations nightmare, plant officials and operators were reluctant to notify residents that a problem had occurred within the plant. A study conducted after the incident revealed that 24 percent of sampled residents living within a fifteen-mile radius of TMI were not aware that anything was amiss at the plant until nearly two days after the accident had occurred.

Citizens who saw media reports of the accident came to believe that they had been intentionally misled by the NRC and Metropolitan Edison. In briefings with the media and with state government officials, spokespersons from Metropolitan Edison continually downplayed the accident, providing incomplete and inaccurate information. This made matters worse for nearby residents, whose fear and confusion only increased as the media was left to speculate on worst-case scenarios. Furthermore, government officials were not able to accurately assess the gravity of the plant's condition because TMI managers continued to give the impression that the situation was more stable and under better control than they apparently knew it to be.

After being told for two days that the plant was stable and under control, residents received word on Friday March 30, that the incident had not been contained. Many residents were learning not only that there had been an accident at TMI but also that a hydrogen bubble had formed inside the reactor's core and was threatening an explosion. To relieve some of the pressure building up inside the reactor, a burst of radiation had to be released into the air. The governor advised that pregnant women and children should evacuate the area. However, 150,000 additional residents also chose to leave the area rather than wait to find out whether the reactor would detonate.

The Aftermath. When area residents felt safe enough to return to their homes, they still had to face concerns that the amount of radiation released from the plant was greater and more damaging than officials had disclosed. Approximately 40,000 gallons of contaminated wastewater had been dumped into the Susquahanna River during the accident, bursts of radiation had been released into the air, and residents had to trust that these levels of radiation had not exposed them to harmful short- and long-term effects. Unfortunately, research on these health effects was rather contradictory.

Studies of short-term effects revealed that a number of residents suffered from post-traumatic stress disorder following the accident. Residents also reported stress-related illnesses such as insomnia, headaches, sweating spells, loss of appetite, stomach troubles, hair loss, and skin rashes. A 1982 study conducted by a former secretary of health in Pennsylvania identified a brief but substantial increase in the neonatal mortality rate in a ten-mile radius of TMI in the months following the incident. Other short-term studies, however, showed less substantial health problems resulting from the accident. Researchers found no significant increase in the number of doctor visits or medical procedures needed in the months following the incident, suggesting that most resulting health troubles were not serious enough to warrant medical attention.

The long-term health effects of the TMI accident are as heavily contested as the short-term effects. In 1997, researchers at the School of Public Health at the University of North Carolina, Chapel Hill, concluded that the rates of lung cancer and leukemia were between two and ten times higher for residents who had lived in the ten-mile area downwind of TMI between 1979 and 1985. At the same time, though, a study conducted by Columbia University and the National Cancer Institute examined the long-term effects of the accident and concluded that there were no public health hazards attributable to the incident. A reanalysis of the Columbia University data found a relationship of heightened cancer rates across increasing levels of radiation exposure. Finally, the most recent long-term study tracked a cohort of TMI residents for the twenty years following the incident and found no consistent evidence that the radioactivity released during the accident has had a significant effect on the overall mortality of area residents. The research did reveal, however, a slightly elevated level in cancer mortality and overall mortality in the TMI area since 1979.

There have also been ongoing legal and financial ramifications of the TMI near-meltdown. In 1983, federal prosecutors filed eleven felony charges against Metropolitan Edison after investigations into the 1979 incident found that TMI employees had been falsifying reactor leak data in order to allow the continued operation of Unit 2. Metropolitan Edison pleaded guilty to one count of violating the Atomic Energy Act and no contest to six other charges. General Public Utilities Corporation, the plant's parent electric company, settled lawsuits with residents tallying $25 million. An additional 2000 claims were still pending against the company until 2002, when the U.S. Third Circuit Court of Appeals dismissed all further appeals due to the lack of definitive evidence of health consequences directly stemming from the accident. The electric company took an additional financial loss when the one functioning unit of TMI was sold for $100 million, one-seventh of its estimated market value.

The incident has also had negative and positive impacts on the nuclear power industry as a whole. Since the accident, not one nuclear power plant has been constructed in the United States, and sixty others have been abandoned or shut down. For those plants continuing operations, though, adherence to regulatory standards has been substantially improved. Emergency preparedness programs and other training programs have been revamped. Plant-design and equipment requirements have been upgraded and strengthened. NRC inspection programs have been expanded, and the industry now has its own "policing" agency, known as the Institute of Nuclear Power Operations (INPO).

Post-TMI, the nation shied away from the use of nuclear power for many years, viewing it as an expensive and potentially hazardous alternative to coal and hydroelectric power. However, with the Bush administration's renewed interest in and support of nuclear power, the industry may make a comeback.

See also: Environmental White-Collar Crime

FURTHER READING

Brunn, Stanley D., Johnson, James H., and Zeigler, Donald J. *Final Report on a Social Survey of Three Mile Island Area Residents.* East Lansing: Michigan State University, 1979.

Hampton, Wilborn. *Meltdown: A Race against Nuclear Disaster at Three-Mile Island: A Reporter's Story.* Cambridge, MA: Candlewick Press, 2001.

Hu, The-wei. *Health-related Economic Cost of the Three Mile Island Accident.* State College, PA: Pennsylvania State University, 1980.

Sills, David L., Wolf, C. P., and Shelanski, Vivian B. *Accident at Three Mile Island: The Human Dimension.* Boulder, CO: Westview Press, 1982.

Talbott, Evelyn O., Youk, Ada O., McHugh-Pemu, Kathlee, and Zborowski, Jeanne V. "Long-Term Follow-up of the Residents of the Three Mile Island Accident Area: 1979–1998." *Environmental Health Perspectives* (2003).

LYNN LANGTON

TRAIL SMELTER. The *Trail Smelter* verdict has often been called the foundation of international environmental law. One of only a handful of international environmental law decisions, the *Trail Smelter* arbitration grew out of an early twentieth-century dispute between the United States and Canada over transboundary air pollution. The pollution was generated by one of Canada's most influential corporations—Consolidated Mining and Smelting—at its facility located in Trail, British Columbia, eleven miles from the United States–Canada.

At the beginning of the twentieth century, Consolidated's Trail smelter was the largest zinc and lead smelter in the world. The processes Consolidated used to refine raw ore released large quantities of sulfur dioxide into the atmosphere. By 1930, sulfur dioxide emissions had reached 700 tons per day—more than double the rate in 1924. These sulfurous fumes devastated the Canadian countryside. Farmers complained that the smelter's fumes caused irreparable damage to their crops, livestock, orchards, and timber. After paying compensation to resolve a series of disputes with local Canadian farmers in the 1920s, Consolidated built a 409-foot smokestack at its Trail facility in 1926. This giant smokestack was intended to minimize local environmental damage. In taking this tack, Consolidated adopted what was to be a dominant paradigm in pollution control until the 1970s—"the solution to pollution is dilution." The new smokestack greatly cut down on local Canadian complaints about fumes. Unfortunately, it did so by funneling the smelter's fumes higher into the wind stream, thereby moving the locus of harm to the other side of the United States–Canada border.

Within months, farmers in Washington state were complaining that sulfur fumes from the Trail smelter were crossing the border and causing property and environmental damage to their farms. Because an international border ran through the middle of this otherwise ordinary nuisance dispute, existing law prevented these injured Washington farmers from obtaining adequate recourse in either American or Canadian courts. When they failed to obtain satisfaction directly from Consolidated Mining and Smelting, the farmers petitioned the relatively sympathetic Roosevelt administration (Teddy, not Franklin) to intervene on their behalf. Canada took up the defense of its corporate citizen.

From this relatively mundane beginning as a simple tort issue, the *Trail Smelter* dispute morphed into an international incident. Almost a decade of diplomatic wrangling ensued. On August 7, 1928, the governments of the United States and Canada jointly agreed to refer the dispute to the International Joint Commission. After more than two years of deliberation, the International Joint Commission issued a decision on February 28, 1931, ordering Canada to pay the United States $350,000 as compensation for damages.

Nonetheless, environmental conditions continued to deteriorate as the Trail smelter's industrial production increased. By February 1933, the United States government was again complaining to the Canadian government about pollution from the smelter. Finally, on April 15, 1935, both nations signed a convention agreeing to arbitrate the dispute. Article III of this convention directed a tribunal to resolve a series of questions: whether the Trail smelter caused damage in the state of Washington; if so, whether and how it should be required to refrain from doing so in the future; and what damages, if any, Canada should pay the United States. Each state appointed one of its nationals to the tribunal: Robert A. E. Greenshields for Canada and Charles Warren for the United States. The two national arbiters then named a third arbiter, Jan Frans Hostie of Belgium, who served as the tribunal's chair.

This panel, which came to be known as the *Trail Smelter* Tribunal, issued a preliminary opinion on April 16, 1938, directing Canada to pay an additional $78,000 in damages and implementing an interim sulfur emissions monitoring regime. On March 11, 1941, the tribunal issued its final decision, requiring Canada to impose $20 million worth of operational modifications on the smelter in order to eliminate or greatly reduce sulfur emissions. In this final decision, the *Trail Smelter* Tribunal definitively articulated a standard for state responsibility for pollution. Known as the *Trail Smelter* principles, the tribunal announced: (1) that "no state has the right to use or permit the use of its territory in such a manner as to cause injury by fumes in or to the territory of another" (generally summarized as imposing a state duty to prevent transboundary harm); and (2) that a polluting state has a duty to pay compensation for transboundary harm it causes (often referred to as the "polluter pays" principle.) These *Trail Smelter* principles have become a cornerstone of international environmental law. A host of environmental treaties trace their origins more or less directly back to *Trail Smelter*. The *Trail Smelter* principles have also found their way into opinions issued by the International Court of Justice and into a multitude of projects undertaken by the International Law Commission.

The *Trail Smelter* arbitration was shaped by its historical circumstances and by the intricate diplomatic dance between the United States and Canada. The tribunal had to strike a balance between Canadian smelting and American farming—at least arguably equally viable economic activities. Moreover, both parties were keenly aware that prevailing wind conditions elsewhere blew industrial fumes from facilities in the United States across the Canadian border. Thus, the United States government found itself negotiating a delicate line—with its concern for vindicating the injury suffered by Washington-based farmers tempered by a reluctance to create a precedent that American industry located elsewhere in the country might find unduly burdensome.

This conflict of interest has led critics to question *Trail Smelter's* legacy on a number of grounds. First, the tribunal ultimately adopted a fairly limited *ex post* remedy—opting to limit the negative effects borne by Washington farmers rather than require the smelter to eliminate those effects proactively. Second, the tribunal limited the state duty to prevent transboundary harm to those situations in which injury is established by clear and convincing evidence—thus excluding the vast majority of harms from its scope. Finally, the tribunal's assumption that Canada could exert substantial control over all industry operating within its territory rings hollow in the age of the multinational corporation.

The Trail smelter is currently owned and operated by Teck Cominco Metals, Ltd. A museum on the smelter grounds is dedicated to the historic *Trail Smelter* arbitration. Canada and the United States are engaged in ongoing litigation over the cleanup of pollution in Lake Roosevelt and the Columbia River attributable to the Trail smelter's slag disposal and wastewater discharge practices.

See also: Environmental White-Collar Crime

FURTHER READING

Bratspies, Rebecca M., and Miller, Russell A. (eds.). *Transboundary Harm in International Law: Lessons from the Trail Smelter Arbitration.* New York: Cambridge University Press, 2006.

Kiss, Alexandre, and Shelton, Dinah. *International Environmental Law.* New York: Transnational, 1991.

Sand, Phillipe. *Principles of International Environmental Law*, 2nd edition. London: Cambridge University Press, 2005.

Wirth, John D., *Smelter Smoke in North America.* Lawrence: University Press of Kansas, 2000.

REBECCA M. BRATSPIES

U

UNION CARBIDE. In Bhopal, India, a chemical plant operated by Union Carbide of India Limited (UCIL), a subsidiary of Union Carbide Corporation (UCC), used highly toxic chemicals, including methyl iso cyanate (MIC), to produce pesticides. On the night of Sunday, December 2, 1984, water entered an MIC storage tank, setting in process an exothermic reaction. Soon a cocktail of poisonous gases, vapors, and liquids, including up to forty tons of MIC, was spewed into the atmosphere.

The Indian government initially put the number of acute deaths at 1700, a figure subsequently revised to 3329. Twenty years after the leak, in 2004, Amnesty International estimated that there had been over 7000 such deaths, and that 15,000 people had since died from longer-term effects. About 100,000 "survivors" will never work again. These "human" effects do not begin to account for the environmental damage caused by the leak. Dow Chemical, the world's largest chemical company, effectively took over UCC in 2001 but refuses to accept any responsibility for "cleaning up" the affected surroundings.

Union Carbide worked hard at influencing both public opinion and the legal process through a series of spurious arguments about the incident, the nature of the Indian company, conditions at the Bhopal plant, and treatment of its employees. These arguments included claims that: (1) safety standards at the Bhopal plant were identical to standards at the UCC plant in Institute, West Virginia; (2) the Bhopal plant had an excellent safety record, and the plant's standard operating procedures—UCC's responsibility—were basically sound; (3) the production of MIC in India, the location of the plant, and the quality of the materials used were all the responsibility of UCIL and the Indian state; (4) UCIL was an independent company responsible for its own affairs; (5) India's "cultural backwardness" was responsible for the plant's poor maintenance and management, poor planning procedures, and inadequate enforcement of safety regulations; and (6) the accident was caused by sabotage, first blamed on Sikh extremists and then on an errant tea-boy. Such arguments are classic strategies in naming an event an "industrial accident."

When the leak occurred, key safety features were either inoperable or inadequate to their task: the vent gas scrubber was turned off, the flare tower was inoperative, and hoses that might have doused the gas had insufficient water pressure to reach the stack from which it was escaping. Further, although the storage tanks should have been refrigerated, the refrigeration unit had been turned off to save $50 per week. Serious questions regarding the plant design itself should also be addressed. For example, plant instrumentation was inadequate to monitor normal plant processes. The refrigeration plant at Bhopal, even when it was working, was not powerful enough to cool all the MIC stored there, and the vent gas scrubber and flare tower were only designed to deal with limited types of emissions.

In these respects, Bhopal was demonstrably inadequate and inferior to the West Virginia plant. Nevertheless, even with this inferior technology, far fewer people would have died if: (1) the plant had not been sited near shantytowns; (2) there had been adequate risk assessment, modeling, and monitoring of discharges, and emergency planning and management; (3) plant personnel, local medical services, and the state and national government had known more about the nature and effects of the deadly gaseous emissions (in the immediate aftermath of the leak, UCC refused to divulge any information about the chemical content of the leaked substances, making it very difficult to properly treat victims).

Further, UCC clearly owned and controlled UCIL; UCC owned 50.9 percent of UCIL and exercised significant control over it. UCIL's production and marketing strategies were dictated by the corporate strategies of UCC. UCC had dictated which chemicals were produced and how they were stored, UCC had monitored safety procedures, and UCIL had been forced to rely upon UCC for technological assistance and updates. Indeed, UCIL's production of the pesticides Temik and Sevin took place under commodified conditions: they were to be produced and sold in such a way that subdivisions of the company showed a normal profitable return on investment. It is questionable whether it was possible for UCIL to do so safely. Following two decades of huge growth, the pesticides market in India had become extremely competitive by the end of the 1970s. By the beginning of the 1980s, pesticide demand in India had all but collapsed. Thus the industry became characterized by harsher and increasing levels of competition.

UCC seems to have been responsible for both the acts of commission and omission that created the Bhopal disaster. The contentions made by UCC in its publicity and its legal arguments concerning the Bhopal disaster do not stand up to scrutiny.

On visiting Bhopal in the aftermath of the leak, Warren Anderson, UCC's chief executive officer, was arrested. He was released days later, never to return to India. Although in December 1991, the chief magistrate in Bhopal ordered Anderson and the company to appear in court on charges of culpable homicide, neither appeared, and both are listed as "proclaimed absconders." Overwhelmingly, legal activity has centered on civil suits for compensation—and, following a flurry of such suits, the Indian government assumed legal powers to secure damages in March 1985, on behalf of victims who were not consulted. The initial sum demanded by the Indian government was $3.3 billion; in 1989, UCC and the Indian government reached an out-of-court settlement of $470 million. This judgment rendered UCC immune from all litigation, including criminal charges. The money was to compensate the families of the 3329 dead and the 20,000 seriously injured who were officially recognized as such by the Indian government.

But the money has still not been fully distributed. Union Carbide, now owned by Dow Chemical, paid out £250 million in compensation to residents in 1989, but only a part of that sum has been distributed. Successful claims have resulted in minimal payments, which began only in 1992. In July 2004, India's Supreme Court ordered the government to distribute money held in the bank, currently worth £174 million, to the 566,876 Bhopal survivors and relatives whose claims have been successfully lodged. As late as September 2004, around $330 million continued to be held by the Reserve Bank of India.

See also: Environmental White-Collar Crime; *Herald of Free Enterprise*; Industrial Accidents; *Piper Alpha*; Seveso Dioxin Disaster

FURTHER READING

Amnesty International. "Clouds of Injustice. Bhopal Disaster Twenty Tears On." 2004. Available at http://web.amnesty.org/wire/December2004/Bhopal. Accessed August 11, 2006.

Cassells, Jamie. *The Uncertain Promise of Law: Lessons from Bhopal.* Toronto: University of Toronto Press, 1993.

Everest, Larry. *Behind the Poison Cloud.* Chicago: Banner Press, 1985.

Pearce, Frank, and Tombs, Steve. *Toxic Capitalism: Corporate Crime and the Chemical Industry.* Aldershot, UK: Ashgate, 1998.

Shrivastava, Paul. *Bhopal: Anatomy of a Crisis.* London: Paul Chapman, 1992.

STEVE TOMBS

V

VALUJET FLIGHT 592. On May 11, 1996, ValuJet flight 592 crashed in the Florida Everglades, killing all 105 passengers and 5 crew members. At first, the crash was viewed as an accident that was caused by a fire in the cargo compartment. Subsequent investigations, however, demonstrated patterns of negligence and noncompliance with regulatory laws concerning the handling, transportation, and disposal of explosive materials among several key actors, including the airline ValuJet, a maintenance company called SabreTech, and the Federal Aviation Administration (FAA).

ValuJet was in its fourth year of existence when flight 592 crashed. In this brief time, the company had grown from a fleet of two aircraft to fifty. ValuJet, as the name implied, marketed itself as a cheaper alternative to the major airlines and offered flights for as low as $39. In order to offer such cheap flights and yet be profitable, ValuJet employed a number of cost-reducing policies, such as paying pilots based on the number of flights flown (they earned about half as much as other pilots), paying hostesses and other employees wages significantly below the industry average, and perhaps most significantly, outsourcing its maintenance to the lowest bidder. The large increase in airplanes owned by ValuJet was accomplished by purchasing older planes in need of repair and then outsourcing the repairs to maintenance companies. In all, ValuJet outsourced maintenance work to twenty-one companies, including the Miami-based SabreTech.

In January 1996, ValuJet purchased three older aircraft and sent them to SabreTech. SabreTech was contracted to perform maintenance tasks on each aircraft, including inspection of the oxygen generators, cylindrical canisters that provide oxygen in case of an emergency, such as loss of cabin air pressure. A mask and tube are connected to the generator, which allows passengers to breathe. Oxygen is generated by an intense chemical reaction, which produces heat as a by-product. Because the generators are mounted behind heat-resistant shields, both passengers and the aircraft are protected from harm. SabreTech discovered that the oxygen generators on two of the planes were past their expiration date and needed to be replaced.

SabreTech was hired by ValuJet to replace the generators, and a return date for each plane was established. The contract stipulated a $2500-per-day credit to ValuJet for every day either aircraft was late. SabreTech mechanics reported that there was considerable pressure on them to complete the task on time, and crews worked twelve hours a day, seven days a week.

SabreTech employees did not follow FAA guidelines for the safe removal, storage, and disposal of oxygen generators. Nobody at SabreTech was familiar with the guidelines, nor had anyone ever before removed and replaced oxygen generators. The accounts of mechanics and supervisors differ, but some mechanics reportedly asked superiors about whether the oxygen generators were dangerous and whether specific safety precautions were supposed to be taken. According to the mechanics, they were not given specific guidelines or procedures, nor were they told to take any precautionary measures.

After the oxygen generators were removed from the aircraft, they were placed in five cardboard boxes and marked "aircraft parts." These boxes were taken to a ValuJet loading dock and were eventually loaded into the cargo hold of flight 592 (from Miami to Atlanta).

An analysis of the crash by the National Transportation Safety Board (NTSB) revealed that the improperly packaged oxygen generators were the cause of the fire that caused flight 592 to crash (NTSB 1997). This fire likely started when one of the improperly stored canisters' ignition pins was activated from being jostled in the cargo hold during takeoff. Flight 592 crashed within fifteen minutes of takeoff, before the pilots could even turn the plane around and head back to Miami.

FAA guidelines about the handling, storage, and presentation of incendiary devices are clear. These canisters should never have been placed in the cargo hold of a commercial aircraft marked as "aircraft parts." Such an action was akin to placing a ticking bomb on the plane, and it resulted in the deaths of 110 people. At the same time, the subsequent NTSB investigation revealed that the FAA had been negligent in overseeing both the growth of ValuJet and its many safety violations. ValuJet had an accident rate that was fourteen times higher than those of the major airlines and a serious accident rate that was thirty-two times higher. However, the FAA chose not to shut down ValuJet until after flight 592 crashed. Finally, ValuJet was found to be complicit in the crime in that it had outsourced its maintenance responsibilities to the lowest possible bidder without regard to either the bidder's competence in completing the work properly or its ability to do it safely. FAA regulations require that all airlines outsourcing maintenance must oversee subcontracted companies to ensure that all work is being completed in accordance with FAA guidelines.

See also: Corporate Crime; State-Corporate Crime

FURTHER READING

Matthews, Rick A., and Kauzlarich, David. "The Crash of ValuJet Flight 592: A Case Study in State–Corporate Crime." *Sociological Focus* 33.2 (2000): 281–98.
National Transportation Safety Board. *Aircraft Accident Report: In-Flight Fire and Impact with Terrain, ValuJet Airlines Flight 592.* Washington, DC: GPO, 1997.

RICK A. MATTHEWS
DAVID KAUZLARICH

VICTIMIZATION. Relatively little is known about victimization of white-collar crime. While white-collar crime victimization is a prevalent phenomenon, the majority of victimizations go unreported because of embarrassment and lack of confidence in the justice system.

Research has suggested, however, that victims of white-collar crime experience the same harmful effects as victims of violent street crime. Studies examining its occurrence have generally focused on financial victimizations commonly referred to as fraud. Research has found that age, education, risk taking, prior victimizations, and victim facilitation are all significantly related to fraud victimization.

The first national estimate of the incidence and prevalence of personal fraud was conducted by Titus et al. (1995). They found a 58 percent lifetime victimization rate (both successful and attempted) among their sample of 1246 respondents from a national telephone survey. Thirty-one percent of the sample reported being the targets of fraud attempts in the past year, and 48 percent of those attempts were successful. Subsequent studies have found similar victimization rates.

It has been traditionally thought that the elderly are the most at risk for white-collar crime victimization; however, studies have found that younger people tend to be more at risk for victimization. Younger people socialize more, which is a factor relating to victimization, and they tend to be more open to financial risk taking than older people. Thus they are more likely to listen to the perpetrators of fraud and become involved in fraudulent schemes. In fact, Van Wyk and Benson (1997) found that the effect of age is about two and a half times greater than the effect of risk taking. Education is also a factor in predicting the risk of white-collar crime victimization; people with high-school diplomas or bachelor's degrees are more at risk for white-collar fraud victimization than people without high-school diplomas or those with graduate degrees.

Another important characteristic leading to fraud victimization is the victim's own facilitation. Victims tend to take steps that lead to the initial contact with the offender, they willingly provide pertinent information about themselves, and they willingly give the offender money. These actions create a sense of trust between the victim and the offender, enabling the offender to carry out the scam with little complication. Similarly, past victimization is significantly related to future victimization; often victims are added to "mooch" lists that are shared among other con artists. The most popular scams of this form are fraud recovery scams in which con artists offer to help victims recover their lost funds for a certain percentage of the amount of the original losses.

Fraud affects one-third of the American population; however, the official reporting of white-collar crime victimization is significantly lower than that of conventional crime reporting. Yet victims of white-collar crime experience substantial negative effects, such as financial loss, blows to self-esteem and social reputation, physical and mental health problems, and embarrassment. These negative experiences are comparable in intensity to the experiences of those who are victimized by violent street crimes. It has even been suggested that victims of white-collar crime fare worse than victims of violent street crime in terms of self-blaming and financial losses. In terms of recuperation, social support is an important factor for the recovery of violent street-crime victims, yet that same factor puts white-collar crime victims at a greater risk for future victimizations and offers no protection from depressive disorders. Interestingly, some fraud victimizations have been equated to rape victimizations. Victims of both crime types experience neglect and are subjected to a double standard. Both types of crime may involve victim facilitation, so that questions of guilt and responsibility are the burden of the victim. Finally, both crime types are rarely reported.

Approximately two-thirds of white-collar crime victimizations go unreported. Many victims of financial crimes feel as if they are treated like second-class victims in the legal system. Many victims do not know where to report their victimization, nor they do not believe anything will be done. When victimizations are reported, the crimes are often treated as civil matters rather than criminal matters. Victims also rarely receive restitution; they are therefore unwilling to waste more money and time. Another reason given for not reporting a victimization is that many victims are too embarrassed to admit what happened to them; they feel stupid or ashamed. The same is true when corporations become victims of white-collar crimes, they are embarrassed and they do not want to waste their time and money rectifying the situation. Perhaps the one factor that has the most effect on the likelihood of reporting white-collar victimization is the amount of money lost in the transaction; as the dollar amount lost increases, the likelihood of reporting the crime increases.

FURTHER READING

Levi, M. "White-Collar Crime Victimization." Pp. 67–74 in Neal Shover, John Paul Wright (eds.), *Crimes of Privilege: Readings in White-collar Crime.* New York: Oxford University Press, 1992.

Schichor, D., Sechrest, D., and Doocy, J. "Victims of Investment Fraud." Pp. 87–96 in *Contemporary Issues in Crime & Criminal Justice: Essays in Honor of Gilbert Geis.* Upper Saddle River, NJ: Prentice Hall, 2000.

Titus, R. M., Heinzelman, F., and Boyle, J M. "Victimization of Persons by Fraud." *Crime and Delinquency* 41 (1995): 54–72.

Van Wyk, J., and Benson, M. "Fraud Victimization: Risky Business Just Bad Luck?" *American Journal of Criminal Justice* 21 (1997): 163–79.

Van Wyk, J., and Mason, K. "Investigating Vulnerability and Reporting Behavior for Consumer Fraud Victimization." *Journal of Contemporary Criminal Justice* 17 (2001): 328–345.

ANDREA SCHOEPFER

VICTORIA INSURANCE COMPANY. In the late 1980s, policy makers, who were just becoming aware of the debacle that was taking place in the savings and loan industry, were worried that the insurance industry might be facing a similar crisis. On April 24, 1991, the Senate Permanent Subcommittee on Investigations opened hearings that focused on the operations of a network of insurance companies operated by Alan Teale, a British citizen and a former Lloyd's of London broker. What the committee and its investigators found can best be described as a series of Chinese boxes, in which one set of fraudulent organizations and scams revealed the existence of another set, which led to another set, and so on. One of those boxes was a Georgia-based company: Victoria Insurance. Victoria was only in business for eighteen months, but when regulators shut it down in 1988, the firm had $20 million in unpaid claims and only $691,000 in assets. The short history of Victoria reveals how easy it was in the late 1980s to start an insurance company with little or no real assets, take in huge amounts of money in premiums, move that money overseas, and then shut down the whole operation, leaving the policyholders with worthless claims.

After its application for an insurance license was turned down in Delaware in 1986, Victoria's principals, including Teale, made a similar request in Georgia. The application, which normally took from two to six months to review, was approved in only four weeks, no doubt helped along by the fact that one of the company's directors was a former Georgia insurance commissioner. In order to obtain its Georgia license, Victoria was required to put $1.5 million in a bank account before it could start business. The funds came from a group that operated under the name Arab American Trust Fund (AATF), which, according to regulators, was controlled by the Kuwaiti royal family (although representatives of the royal family later denied this). Within three weeks of establishing the account, $1.2 million was transferred to accounts in London. As a result, the company was technically insolvent from its very beginning.

Victoria specialized in "high-risk" liability and casualty policies. Among its most popular programs were disability policies sold to professional athletes. Operating through an insurance wholesaler in New York and a series of brokers across the country, Victoria issued over 200 policies to professional athletes in the United States and around the world. Among the professional football players who purchased policies in the United States were Kenny Flowers, a running back for the Atlanta Falcons; Jim Kelly, a quarterback for the Buffalo Bills; John Elway, a quarterback for the Denver Broncos; Brian Bosworth of the Seattle Seahawks; and Bo Jackson of the Los Angeles Raiders. All of these players paid between $60,000 and $115,000 for policies from Victoria, which was to pay them as much as $3 million if they sustained a career-ending injury. Many of these athletes, fortunately, never needed to file a claim against their policies. Others who did experience serious injuries were not so lucky.

With their high salaries and entourages of agents and publicists, professional athletes may not at first appear to be hapless victims. In the mid-1980s, however, many athletes were not paid the astronomical sums that professional athletes receive today. If their careers ended suddenly, they could find themselves in desperate financial straits.

One of the athletes victimized by Victoria was Kenneth Flowers. In April 1987, during his senior year in college, Flowers was drafted to play football for the Atlanta Falcons. That summer his agent advised him to purchase a disability insurance policy from Victoria as a measure of protection in the event of an injury. Flowers took that advice and sent a check for $7380 to Whittier and Associates for a policy that would have paid him $230,000 if he sustained an injury. In August 1988, in a preseason exhibition game, Flowers, a running back, sustained a serious injury that resulted in surgery that involved inserting seven screws into his knee. He was out for the entire 1988 season and was eventually released by the Falcons. He then filed a claim with Victoria, but he never received any payment. In 1991, Flowers was working at a private hospital near Atlanta where he was paid $6.35 an hour.

In the summer of 1988, Georgia regulators conducted a routine examination of Victoria's books. According to those books, the company had assets of $20 million, including $16 million in U.S. zero-coupon bonds. The problem was that these assets were not located in Georgia, as required by state law, but instead were purportedly held on deposit with a firm known as Goldman Dollar Securities in Paris, France (no relation to Goldman-Sachs in the United States). When the regulators demanded that those assets be moved to the United States, Victoria's operators stalled. Later it was discovered that there was no Goldman Dollar Securities and the address given was for a "mail drop" in Paris.

The Victoria story ended with regulators trying to clean up the mess, congressional committee members shaking their heads, and professional athletes left holding the bag. But it was not the end of the story for many of the people behind Victoria; several of them, including the infamous Alan Teale, went on to illustrious careers in insurance fraud.

See also: Insurance Industry Fraud

FURTHER READING

Tillman, Robert. *Global Pirates: Fraud in the Offshore Insurance Industry.* Boston: Northeastern University Press, 1998.

ROBERT H. TILLMAN

W

WALLACH, E. ROBERT (1934–). E. Robert Wallach, currently an attorney in California, was one of the key players in the Wedtech Corporation scandal. He was convicted on charges of conspiracy and fraud in 1989 for using his influence on one of President Reagan's administrators, Attorney General Edwin Meese III, to help Wedtech win defense contracts through the government without bids. Wallach's conviction was eventually overturned on the grounds of false testimony given by a key witness.

The Wedtech firm was participating, at the time, in a government program run by the Small Business Administration (SBA) that was designed to award no-bid defense contracts to small businesses that were at least 51 percent owned by members of minority groups. Wedtech owner John Mariotta was of Puerto Rican descent and met the requirements for the program, but he and co-owner Fred Neuberger owned equal parts of the corporation. In order for Wedtech to gain support from the Small Business Administration, the owners forged papers stating that Mariotta owned 75 percent of the company.

In 1981, Mariotta and Neuberger retained the services of Wallach, who was a friend and personal attorney to Meese in Washington. Wedtech paid Wallach over $1 million to use his influence on Meese to help the firm obtain contracts that eventually totaled over $250 million. Beginning in 1981, Wallach sent six letters to the attorney general lying about the true ownership of Wedtech and asking that Meese use his influence in Washington to promote the company and to arrange meetings with the Department of Defense, which resulted in a $32 million contract between Wedtech and the U.S. Army.

At this point in 1985, Wallach brought financial consultants W. Franklyn Chinn and R. Kent London into the scandal. Chinn and London were responsible for helping Wedtech sell its stock in exchange for payments totaling $240,000. Both men were charged and indicted for accepting bribes and kickbacks from two Wedtech employees: Mario Moreno and Anthony Guariglia.

The lying and deceit eventually caught the attention of investigators, including United States Attorney Rudolph Giuliani, and twenty individuals were charged and indicted for crimes such as fraud, forgery, bribery, and extortion. Moreno and Guariglia were indicted after both pleaded guilty to crimes charged against them. The owners of the Wedtech Corporation, Mariotta and Neuberger, were indicted on charges of forgery, extortion, and other crimes.

Attorney General Meese was investigated and charged with fraud regarding the Wedtech stock shares and using his influence to help the firm win defense contracts. The charges were dropped, however, when investigators concluded that his involvement was innocent. Wallach was indicted on charges of conspiracy and fraud when Wedtech employee and key witness to the trial Guariglia testified. Several years after the trial, his conviction was overturned when it was discovered that Guariglia had given false testimony concerning his own gambling habits.

See also: Wedtech Scandal

FURTHER READING

The Associated Press. "Judge Declares Mistrial in Wedtech Case." *New York Times* (July 31, 1993): 25.

French, Howard. "Ex-Meese Aide's Wedtech Efforts Detailed." *New York Times* (June 24, 1988): B1.

Hevesi, Dennis. "The Trail of Influence: 21 Key Figures in the Wedtech Scandal." *New York Times* (May 31, 1987): 20.

Lubasch, Arnold. "Three Are Charged with Plotting to Influence Meese for Wedtech." *New York Times* (Dec. 23, 1987): A1.

Safire, William. "New Teapot Dome." *New York Times* (April 30, 1987): A31.

"The Week." *National Review* 43.11 (1991): 10–11.

MARY BETH SARVER

WASTE MANAGEMENT, INC. Waste Management, Inc. (WMI) is the largest waste disposal firm and indeed one of the largest corporations in the world. It is also one of the most serious corporate repeat violators of civil and criminal laws for both trade and environmental practices. As its name implies, WMI is in the business of picking up, transporting, processing, and disposing of various waste streams from 21 million customers in homes and businesses, including nearly 90 million tons of solid waste annually. WMI was formed in 1968 by a merger of waste-disposal companies operating in Florida and Chicago. Formed as WMI, it became WMX in 1992, then changed back to Waste Management in 1997 amid reorganization and controversy. Waste Management Inc. (WMI) also owns or has owned various subsidiary companies, one of the more significant being Chemical Waste Management. WMI and these subsidiaries have a substantial record of criminal fines, convictions, and civil penalties.

WMI's criminal record consists primarily of charges of monopolization, unfair trade practices, and fraud. From 1970 to 1991, WMI was convicted of ten criminal violations in five states and fined in excess of $5 million. In the same time period, Sherman Anti-Trust Act civil cases in twenty-three states cost WMI over $23 million, and twenty-two environmental suits in twelve states cost the corporation over $5 million. Administrative cases and eighty-one actions against WMI's subsidiary Chemical Waste Management ended up costing another $18 million. WMI accrued a total of $52 million in criminal and civil fines and penalties before 1991.

WMI became WMX in 1992. Although the name changed, legal trouble continued; with violations accumulating in alarming numbers and scope. In 1997, WMX sold some of its less profitable subsidiaries and changed its name back to Waste Management. In 1998, WMI wrote off a massive $3.54 billion in inflated earnings. From 1994 through 1997, approximately 47 percent of the earnings WMI publicly reported were fictitious as the company understated its annual expenses by hundreds of millions of dollars. Floundering financially, WMI was acquired by a much smaller firm, USA Waste, in 1998. This merger did nothing to stop WMI's troubles, though.

In 1998, a total of twenty-three California indictments named five individuals, WMI, and three related companies in a conspiracy to commit criminal fraud, stemming from WMI's plan ("Rail-Cycle") to haul waste from Orange and San Diego counties to a landfill to be built in the Mojave Desert. An out-of-court settlement for $5 million addressed the actions of WMI and WMI's employees, allegedly with WMI's approval: a campaign to drive Cadiz, a corporate opponent of the project, out of business allegedly used corporate espionage, stolen files, falsified documents and reports, and rumors.

In 1999, the waste disposal industry's ten highest-paid executives left WMI and its companies in the face of fallout from bad financial decisions, disappointing earnings, and accusations of securities fraud. Millions of dollars in compensation came to these ten executives from payouts and the exercise of stock options amid a flurry of mergers and acquisitions. In 2000, WMI faced only small penalties from the Securities and Exchange Commission (SEC) for misleading investors with these reports but then ended up having to pay $457 million to settle a class-action lawsuit by its shareholders for these same deceptions. In 2000, eight of the industry's ten-highest paid executives left.

WMI was also at the heart of another landmark scandal. In 2001, Arthur Andersen was the first of the "Big Five" accounting firms in a decade to be sued by the Securities and Exchange Commission for accounting violations. It gained this notoriety for its role in failing to expose WMI's inflated earnings. Arthur Andersen paid $20 million in professional malpractice fines and $7 million to the SEC in a resulting civil suit.

Even though most of Waste Management's legal scrapes have been over its business practices, violations of environmental laws from WMI's waste-handling and disposal activities have been substantial. Chemical Waste Management was fined $3.3 million in 1991 for violations at a facility in Sauget, Illinois, and the company was ordered to pay $11.6 million when it pleaded guilty to six felony violations of environmental laws for mishandling wastes at a Pennsylvania Superfund site. Many smaller violations and the penalties associated with them caught up with WMI and its subsidiaries, such as a 1998 fine of $125,000 by the Commonwealth of Virginia for improperly disposing of medical waste hauled from New York, and a 2003 fine of just under $240,000 to the Texas Commission on Environmental Quality the largest fine of any kind ever paid to that agency, for violations at a landfill in Austin, Texas. Grassroots environmental resistance against WMI and its companies has naturally been fierce.

WMI takes the position that environmental suits and the resulting fines are just an inevitable consequence of the nature and the volume of its business. In 2005, WMI touted energy production from waste incineration and recovering gases produced by landfill operations, extensive recycling, and the development of both new technologies and ecologically motivated land uses. Regardless of how its current character is interpreted, however, WMI's scale of operations remains impressive. In 2003, WMI operated 293 landfills in North America with revenue for 2002 reported at $11.1 billion; in 2005, it had consolidated to 283 landfills and a reported revenue of $13.1 billion. WMI is certainly a unique high-profile company in that it has been the nexus of much corporate wrongdoing—from Superfund sites to its fiasco with Arthur Andersen.

See also: Environmental White-Collar Crime; Hazardous Waste Disposal

FURTHER READING

Crooks, Harold. *Giants of Garbage.* Toronto: James Lorimer, 1993.
Oliveira, Andrew, Schenck, Christopher, Cole, Christopher D., and Janes, Nicole L. "Environmental Crimes." *American Criminal Law Review* 42 (2005): 347–426.
Waste Management, Inc. 2005 Annual Report. April 2006. http://www.wm.com.

SAMUEL V. S. SWINDELL

WEDTECH SCANDAL. It began during President Reagan's administration in the 1980s with a small firm known as the Wedtech Corporation. Owners John Mariotta and Fred Neuberger paid several U.S. officials to help Wedtech gain millions of dollars in U.S. military defense contracts without competing bids. This firm was participating in a government agency program through the Small Business Administration during the time of the scandal. The aftermath of the Wedtech scandal caused the government to reevaluate the objectives and requirements of the program.

Background. John Mariotta was born in Spanish Harlem and was of Puerto Rican descent. He founded and worked for several years in Welbilt, a small manufacturing firm in the South Bronx that specialized in making baby carriages. Mariotta wanted to move the firm in a new direction and knew he would need help. This idea required him to bring Fred Neuberger in as a partner and co-owner. Their partnership formed the Wedtech Corporation and shifted the company's focus to military defense contracts for the Department of Defense. This corporation was set up in one of the poorest areas of New York, and it offered many jobs for individuals who would otherwise be unemployed. President Reagan saw what Wedtech had done for the city and gave the highest praises to Mariotta and his work.

The Wedtech Corporation was able to win several contracts for defense through the Small Business Administration (SBA) minority set-aside program. This program is a federally run agency that backs small businesses owned by members of minority groups. The SBA helps small businesses get started by helping them win federal contracts without bids from competitors until they are strong enough to stand on their own.

The Scandal. When the owners of Wedtech, Mariotta and Neuberger, submitted their application to the SBA for assistance, they falsely reported how many shares each owned in the corporation. Qualification for the program required the minority executive to own a majority of the firm; therefore, Mariotta claimed that he held 75 percent of the business, when in reality they each owned half of the corporation. To keep the truth hidden, the owners committed their first criminal act—fraud.

Once admitted into the SBA program, the owners engaged in a series of illegal acts, including extortion, deceit, and bribery. Wedtech executives began paying lawyers, business and financial consultants, and U.S. officials to use their influence on each other and in Washington, DC, to aid Wedtech in winning government defense contracts without bids. This web of corruption linked twenty-one people to Wedtech's dealings and helped the firm win a total of $250 million in contracts.

The Investigation. In 1986, John Mariotta, CEO and chairman of the Board of Directors, was fired from his positions at Wedtech Corporation. Mariotta's termination was reported in *The Wall Street Journal*, and the article caught the attention of Steve Marica, the SBA's assistant inspector general. Marica knew the rules and regulations of the SBA's programs very well, and he realized, after reading about Mariotta's firing, that Wedtech would fall under the ownership of Neuberger, meaning that the majority of the firm would no longer be owned by a person of minority descent. At this point, Marica waited for the corporation to be withdrawn from the SBA's program; when it was not, he began investigating Wedtech's dealings.

Other authorities, including United States Attorney Rudolph Giuliani, were also investigating Wedtech. When Marica heard of this, he asked Giuliani whether he could become part of his investigation. Giuliani declined at first because he believed that members of the SBA could not be trusted. To lessen Giuliani's apprehensions, Marica arranged with him that information regarding Wedtech would be available only to those individuals whom Marica specified.

The investigations of Giuliani and other authorities found that the value of Wedtech's defense contracts were growing with each contract that was awarded. They also found that Wedtech's creditors were being lied to about its financial situation; that bank accounts of individuals holding shares of Wedtech stock were gaining more assets; and that individuals promising to help the firm gain contracts were receiving greater fees for their services. All of Wedtech's dealings caused the corporation to lose money; in order to get out of the hole it had fallen into, the firm sold Wedtech stock to anyone who was willing to buy it. The firm eventually filed for bankruptcy.

After the investigations uncovered the many dirty secrets of the Wedtech scandal, a number of individuals involved were charged and indicted for such crimes as fraud, theft, extortion, bribery, perjury, tax evasion, illegal lobbying, and forgery. Persons indicted for their involvement in the scandal included Wedtech owner John Mariotta; President Reagan's former political adviser Lyn Nofziger; Congressman Mario Biaggi and his son Richard; United States Representative Robert Garcia; the Bronx Borough's former president Stanley Simon; Biaggi's law-firm partner and former National Guard major general Bernard G. Elrich; former New York regional director of the Small Business Administration Peter Neglia; financial consultants W. Franklyn Chinn and R. Kent London; and Californian lawyer E. Robert Wallach. Four other individuals who pleaded guilty to the charges included co-owner Neuberger and three employees, Mario Moreno, Anthony Guariglia, and Lawrence Shorten. Attorney General Edwin Meese III was charged with fraud during the trials but was eventually cleared of that charge. He later resigned from his position.

During the trials, the government reevaluated its SBA program for minority-owned businesses. Marica proved that the agency could be trusted in investigations when legal cases concerning it arose. He improved the image of the program by building new training programs for both employees and managers. Marica also helped the SBA enhance its criminal investigation skills.

See also: Wallach, E. Robert

FURTHER READING

Barbanel, Josh. "He Denies Charges: Congressman Is Accused in Extortion of Stock Worth $3.6 Million." *New York Times* (June 4, 1987): A1.

Hevesi, Dennis. "The Trail of Influence: 21 Key Figures in the Wedtech Scandal." *New York Times* (May 31, 1987): 20.

Johnston, David. "Wedtech's Legacy: Tighter Rules on Minority Contracts." *New York Times* (Dec. 27, 1987): E4.

May, Clifford. "Wedtech Scandal Gets Messier and Messier." *New York Times* (June 7, 1987): E5.

Riccucci, Norma. "Execucrats, Politics, and Public Policy: What Are the Ingredients for Successful Performance in the Federal Government?" *Public Administration Review* 55 (1995): 219–30.

Small Business Administration. "Dictionary of Government." May 2005. Available at http://www.explore-government.com. Accessed May 25, 2005.

Starr, R. "Too Good to Be True: The Outlandish Story of Wedtech." *American Spectator* 23.9 (1990): 33–34.

MARY BETH SARVER

Index

Bold page numbers indicate main entry.

Contributors

SCOTT AKINS is an Assistant Professor of Sociology at Oregon State University. His research is in the areas of substance use and abuse and the intersection of race, disadvantage, and crime.

KEN W. BALUSEK holds a doctorate of jurisprudence and is currently a doctoral candidate at Sam Houston State University in Huntsville, Texas. His research interests include criminological theory and corrections.

E. ELAINE BARTGIS is an Assistant Professor of Criminal Justice at the University of Central Oklahoma.

PAUL J. BECKER is an associate professor of sociology in the Department of Sociology, Anthropology, and Social Work at the University of Dayton, where he also is affiliated with the Criminal Justice Studies Program. His research interests include state and corporate crime, white racial extremism, criminology and film, and hate crimes.

SARA E. BERG is a student in the M.S. Information Technology program at the Rochester Institute of Technology in Rochester, New York. She has spoken at national conferences on the effects of identity theft victimization, and her thesis will examine the high-tech crime victimization of college students.

WILLIAM K. BLACK is an economist, lawyer, and criminologist who served as a chief regulator during the U.S. savings and loan crisis. His work on the Lincoln Savings and Loan case helped bring Charles Keating to justice. He has held a number of academic appointments and has given congressional testimony on many occasions, including the Keating Five scandal. He has written extensively on fraud in financial institutions, insider control frauds, and other topics in economics, law, and white-collar crime.

ASHLEY G. BLACKBURN is an Assistant Professor of Criminal Justice at the University of North Texas in Denton, Texas. Her research interests include corrections/prisoner's rights, controlled substances, and comparative criminal justice systems.

ANDREA BOGGIO is a researcher at the Institute of Bioethics of the University of Geneva, Switzerland. He holds a doctoral degree from Stanford Law School and has written in the areas of ethics, human rights, dispute resolution, and victim compensation.

REBECCA M. BRATSPIES is an Associate Professor of Law at CUNY School of Law. She has lectured and published widely on the topics of environmental liability, international fisheries, and genetically modified food crops.

HANK J. BRIGHTMAN is a professor at Saint Peter's College, located in Jersey City, New Jersey.

KATHERINE M. BROWN is a doctoral candidate in Criminal Justice at Sam Houston State University, Huntsville, Texas. Her research interests include: white-collar crime, child abduction murder investigation, crime scene investigation, forensic evidence, and other solvability factors affecting murder investigations.

RONALD BURNS is an Associate Professor of Criminal Justice at Texas Christian University and Director of the Criminal Justice Program. His research interests include white-collar crime and police use of force. He recently co-authored *Environmental Crime: A Sourcebook* and co-edited *Policing and Violence*.

STEPHEN A. CARLTON is president of Security Analysts in Minneapolis. He specializes in educating employees about protecting the confidentiality of sensitive information.

STEPHANIE E. CARMICHAEL is currently a doctoral candidate at the University of Florida in the Department of Criminology, Law and Society. She is currently a University of Florida Alumni Fellowship recipient. Her areas of interest are criminological theory and white-collar crime.

DR. WOJCIECH CEBULAK is Associate Professor of Criminal Justice at Minot State University, North Dakota. He has published extensively and presented papers on a variety of Criminal Justice topics, including white-collar crime, criminal law and procedure, comparative criminology, policing, and Eastern European transformations.

KELLY ANN CHEESEMAN is an Assistant Professor at Old Dominion University in Norfolk, Virginia. Kelly has published articles in *Corrections Management Quarterly*, *Southwestern Journal of Criminal Justice*, *Criminal Law Bulletin*, and *Deviant Behavior*. Her current research interests include correctional institutions, prison deviance, and the death penalty.

CHRISTIAN DESILETS is a research attorney with the National White Collar Crime Center. He provides legislative research support for state and local law enforcement officers involved in high-tech and white collar crime investigations as well as for academicians in related fields and interested members of the general public.

ADAM DULIN is a doctoral candidate in Criminal Justice at Sam Houston State University in Huntsville, Texas. He is also a research analyst for the Institute for the Study of Violent Groups (ISVG) and International Terrorism Editor for the publication *Crime and Justice International*.

SHIYLOH L. DUNCAN is a doctoral candidate in Criminology at Florida State University. Her research interests include juvenile justice program evaluation, women's correctional issues, female white collar criminals, and drug issues.

O. OKO ELECHI is an Assistant Professor of Criminal Justice at the University of Wisconsin—Parkside. He has written extensively on white-collar crime issues, particularly in the areas of corruption and governmental crime in Nigeria.

NUBIA EVERTSSON is a Ph.D. student in criminology at Stockholm University. She has written on political corruption, in particular about police corruption and corruption at the local level in Colombia, for about 10 years. She has worked as a consultant for the United Nations, the World Bank and USAID in anti-corruption projects in Colombia.

AMANDA L. FARRELL is a Master of Arts student at the College of Criminal Justice at Sam Houston State University in Huntsville, Texas. She is currently researching females who commit violent crimes.

JOSHUA FECTEAU completed research for this chapter while attending Stonehill College in North Easton, Massachusetts. Mr. Fecteau graduated magna cum laude in 2005 with a degree in Mathematics.

DAVID O. FRIEDRICHS is Professor of Sociology and Criminal Justice at the University of Scranton (Pennsylvania). He is the author of *Trusted Criminals: White Collar Crime in Contemporary Society*, second edition (2004), *Law in Our Lives: An Introduction*, – second edition (2005), is the editor of *State Crime—Volumes I and II* (1998), and has published some one hundred journal articles, book chapters, and essays in professional publications. He served as President of the White Collar Crime Research Consortium from 2002 to 2004.

JANE FLORENCE GAUTHIER is Assistant Professor of Criminal Justice at University of Nevada, Las Vegas. Her current research focuses on gender and crime and community and crime issues.

GILBERT GEIS is Professor Emeritus, Department of Criminology, Law and Society, University of California, Irvine. He is a former president of the American Society of Criminology and recipient of the Society's Edwin H. Sutherland Award for outstanding research.

PETER GRABOSKY is a Professor in the Regulatory Institutions Network, Research School of Social Sciences at The Australian National University in Canberra. He has written extensively on criminal justice, public policy, and regulation, and is past president of The Australian and New Zealand Society of Criminology.

GEORGEN GUERRERO is an Assistant Professor of Criminal Justice at Stephen F. Austin University in Nacogdoches, Texas. His research interests include adult and juvenile correctional populations, ethical behavior in criminal justice, deviant behaviors in society, and criminological theory.

SANDRA H. HAANTZ is a Research Assistant with the National White Collar Crime Center (NW3C). She provides support through applied research to state and local law enforcement, academicians, and the general public concerning high-tech and white-collar crime.

GREGORY HOOKS is Professor and Chair of the Department of Sociology at Washington State University. He has examined environmental justice issues, especially the disproportionate exposure to unexploded ordnance experienced by Native Americans. He has also examined the local economic impact of prisons in rural areas.

ERIC L. JENSEN, Ph.D., is Professor of Sociology at the University of Idaho. He was a Fulbright Lecturer/Researcher at the School of Law, University of Aarhus in Denmark, during the spring semester of 2002. He is coeditor with Jørgen Jepsen of *Juvenile Law Violators, Human Rights, and the Development* of *New Juvenile Justice Systems.*

DAVID KAUZLARICH is an Associate Professor of Sociology and Criminal Justice Studies at Southern Illinois University, Edwardsville. His research interests include state crime, peace studies, and criminological theory.

RONALD C. KRAMER is Professor of Sociology and Director of the Criminal Justice Program at Western Michigan University. His publications include *Crimes of the American Nuclear State* and *State-Corporate Crime: Wrongdoing at the Intersection of Government and Politics,* as well as articles on corporate violence, international law, and imperial wars.

JILETTA L. KUBENA is a doctoral candidate at Sam Houston State University in Huntsville, Texas. She has published on the topics of corporate criminality and the media and capital punishment.

LYNN LANGTON is a doctoral candidate in the Department of Criminology, Law and Society at the University of Florida. Her current research interests revolve around private security, employee theft, and criminological theory and white-collar/corporate crime.

JAMES TIMOTHY LINEHAN worked for over fifteen years in State and Federal Courts in Houston, Texas. He taught Political Science and Organized Crime classes at the University of Houston. His main focus of research is on the politics of organized crime.

MICHAEL J. LYNCH is a Professor of Criminology at the University of South Florida. His recent research has focused on: environmental crime, law and justice; corporate crime; and state crime. His recent books include *Primer in Radical Criminology* (2006) and *Environmental Crime: A Sourcebook.*

DANIEL MABREY is a doctoral candidate at Sam Houston State University in Huntsville, Texas. He is also the Director of the Institute for the Study of Violent Groups, which is a federally-funded terrorism research center. His research interests include terrorism, the role of intelligence in policing, and quantitative methods.

ADRIAN M. MASCARI is a Research Assistant with the National White Collar Crime Center. He provides support through applied research to state and local law enforcement, academicians, and the general public concerning high-tech and white-collar crime.

RICK A. MATTHEWS is an Associate Professor of Sociology and Criminal Justice at Carthage College. He has published in the areas of state crime, state-corporate crime, and juvenile delinquency. He is currently conducting research on corporate involvement in the Holocaust.

DANIELLE McGURRIN is an Assistant Professor of Criminology at Stonehill College, North Easton, Massachusetts. Her research and teaching interests include corporate-state crime; race, class, and gender in the criminal justice system, and prison education.

SHARON ANNE MELZER has a Masters in Public Administration (MPA) from Pennsylvania State University's School of Public Affairs; an M.S. in Criminology from Florida State University; and a B.A. in History and a B.A. in Administration of Justice from the Pennsylvania State

University. She has worked for the Pennsylvania Commission on Sentencing and Pennsylvania Commission on Crime and Delinquency. Her research interests include organized crime, white-collar crime, and transnational crime.

ROBERT G. MORRIS is presently a doctoral candidate in the College of Criminal Justice at Sam Houston State University in Huntsville, Texas. His current research interests include the development of scholarship toward understanding the crime of identity theft, research design, and criminological theory.

CLAYTON MOSHER is an associate professor in the Department of Sociology at Washington State University, Vancouver. His research focuses on criminal justice system policies with specific interests in racial profiling and inequality in criminal justice system processing. He also serves as associate editor for the journal *Social Problems*.

MARK MOTIVANS, Ph.D., is a statistician with the Bureau of Justice Statistics in Washington, DC.

CHRISTINE ABEL NIX is a doctoral candidate in Criminal Justice at Sam Houston State University, Huntsville, Texas.

BERNADETTE JONES PALOMBO is Professor of Criminal Justice at Louisiana State University in Shreveport. Her research interests include white collar crime/deviance in the criminal justice system and in the funeral industry. She is also involved in evaluating juvenile prevention/intervention programs and defense of indigent offenders in Caddo Parish, Louisiana. She is primary author of the July 1994 report presented to the Louisiana Governor's Task Force on Indigent Defense entitled "Provision of the Right to Counsel in Caddo Parish, Louisiana."

HENRY N. PONTELL is professor of criminology, law and society, and of sociology at the University of California, Irvine. His past research has concentrated on crime in the health care industry and financial fraud. In 2001 he received the Donald R. Cressey Award for lifetime achievement in the field of white-collar crime and the Albert J. Reiss, Jr. Distinguished Scholarship Award for the book *Big Money Crime: Fraud and Politics in the Savings and Loan Crisis*.

DONALD J. REBOVICH is associate professor and director of the Economic Crime Investigation Program at Utica College in Utica, New York. He has also served as research director for the National White Collar Crime Center (NW3C) and the American Prosecutors Research Institute He is the author of *Dangerous Ground: The World of Hazardous Waste Crime*.

GARY E. REED is an assistant professor of justice studies at Lewis-Clark State College. His research interests include the dynamics of decision making and corporate crime, police and society, and environmental crime.

STEPHEN M. ROSOFF is an associate professor of sociology and Director of the Graduate Criminology Program at the University of Houston—Clear Lake. He has written extensively on white-collar crime issues, particularly in the areas of medical fraud and computer crime.

DEBRA E. ROSS is an assistant professor and Director of the Criminal Justice Graduate program at Grand Valley State University in Grand Rapids, Michigan. Her current research is in the area of hazardous waste regulation and compliance, white-collar curriculum across the discipline, identity theft, and research methods.

JEFFREY IAN ROSS, Ph.D., is an Associate Professor in the Division of Criminology, Criminal Justice and Social Policy Fellow with the Center for Comparative and International Law, University of Baltimore.

DAWN L. ROTHE is an assistant professor of criminology at the University of Northern Iowa. Her research interests focus on state transnational crime, international law and institutions of social control, and criminological theory. She is coauthor of *Symbolic Gestures and the Generation of Social Control*."

MARY BETH SARVER is a doctoral candidate at Sam Houston State University. She recently conducted a study on law enforcement training in Texas and has worked with the U.S. Marshals Executive Development Training Program.

ROBERT A. SARVER III is a doctoral candidate at Sam Houston State University. He recently participated in an evaluation of the Drug Abuse Resistance Education (D.A.R.E.) program conducted by the Houston Police Department and is currently studying jury representativeness in Texas.

ANDREA SCHOEPFER is a doctoral candidate in Criminology at the University of Florida. Her interests lie in criminological theory, and white-collar and corporate crime.

REBECCA SELF is an assistant professor of international communication at Franklin College, Lugano, Switzerland. Her primary research interest is the global deregulation of media industries.

TARA O'CONNOR SHELLEY is an assistant professor at Colorado State University, Department of Sociology. She has worked for the Police Executive Research Forum (PERF) and the Justice Research and Statistics Association (JRSA). Her current research interests include environmental crime, white-collar crime, social threat and social control, and police practices. She has recently published in the *Journal of Drug Issues*, *Policing: An International Journal of Police Strategies and Management*, and *Policing and Program Evaluation*.

RASHI K. SHUKLA is an Assistant Professor of Criminal Justice at the University of Central Oklahoma. Her research interests include drug policy, white collar crime, and women in policing.

KATHLEEN M. SIMON is an associate professor of Political Science and Criminal Justice at Appalachian State University in Boone, North Carolina. Her research interests include judicial behavior in criminal procedure decisions, sentencing for corporate crimes, and administrative rules review across the states.

CHAD L. SMITH is Assistant Professor of Sociology at Texas State University—San Marcos. His research interests include environmental sociology, social inequality, and political sociology, specifically the historical relationship between housing inequality and environmental inequality in urban settings. His recent publications include articles in *American Sociological Review* and *Organization and Environment*.

STEVEN STACK is a Professor with appointments in the Department of Psychiatry & Neuroscience, and Criminal Justice at Wayne State University. His research interests include public opinion about white-collar crime, death penalty issues, tests of criminological theory, and the relationship between suicidal and criminal behavior patterns.

DANIEL M. STEWART is a doctoral candidate in criminal justice at Sam Houston State University. His research interests include policing, homeland security, and criminological theory.

PAUL B. STRETESKY is an Associate Professor of Sociology at Colorado State University—Fort Collins. His research on environmental crime and justice has appeared in journals in several different disciplines. He has recently completed a two-year grant provided by the U.S. Environmental Protection Agency on self-policing environmental compliance policies.

SAMUEL V. S. SWINDELL is a doctoral candidate at the College of Criminal Justice of Sam Houston State University. He was an active criminal litigator and member of the Virginia State Bar. He was accepted to the *New York Law School Law Review* in the writing competition and wrote regulatory entries for the *Virginia Environmental Law Digest*. His research interests include criminal justice policy and environmental law.

ELIZABETH SZOCKYJ is an associate professor of criminal justice at Buffalo State, State University College of New York, Buffalo, New York. She has published in the area of white-collar crime and is the author of *The Law and Insider Trading: In Search of a Level Playing Field* (Hein Publishing, 1994).

ROBERT H. TILLMAN is Professor of Sociology at St. John's University in New York City. He is the author and co-author of a number of recent books on white-collar crime, including *Pump and Dump: The Rancid Rules of the New Economy* (Rutgers University Press, 2005).

STEVE TOMBS is a Professor of Sociology at Liverpool John Moores University and Chair of the human rights charity the Centre for Corporate Accountability (www.corporateaccountability. org/). He has written extensively on the incidence, nature, and regulation of corporate crime. His recent publications have focused upon the political economy of criminological knowledge.

JONATHAN E. TURNER, CFE, CII, is a Managing Director with the fraud consulting firm of Wilson & Turner Incorporated. He is the author of over 36 articles and book chapters on fraud and investigation and is a frequent speaker and expert witness on fraud topics internationally.

GUDRUN VANDE WALLE is an assistant professor of Financial and Economic Crime and Sociology of Law at the Ghent University—Department of Penal Law and Criminology, Belgium. She is also member of the research unit Social Analysis of Security Research. Her research interests include combining the study of victims of corporate crime with the study of conflict resolution between victims and the responsible companies.

COURTNEY A. WAID is a doctoral candidate in the College of Criminology and Criminal Justice at Florida State University. Her research interests include the effectiveness of inmate treatment programs, specifically those that show promise for female offenders, and what works in the reform of juvenile justice practices.

APRIL D. WALL is a Research Assistant with the National White Collar Crime Center (NW3C). She provides support through applied research to state and local law enforcement, academicians, and the general public concerning high-tech and white-collar crime.

KELLY WELCH is an assistant professor in the Department of Sociology at Villanova University. Her research interests include criminological theory, race and crime, social justice, victimology, and the sociology of punishment.

DAVE WHYTE is a lecturer in Criminology at the University of Stirling, where he researches crimes of the powerful and the regulation of corporations. He has published on the role of criminal law in preventing safety crimes, the regulation of private military industry and transnational corporate crime.

SUSAN WILL is an assistant professor of sociology at John Jay College of Criminal Justice, City University of New York. Her research interests include financial crimes, environmental sociology, indigenous rights, and how elites use law.

FRANKLIN T. WILSON is an Assistant Professor at Middle Tennessee State University.

JUDITH WISE is an assistant professor of Law at Willamette University College of Law.

BRIAN WOLF is Assistant Professor of Sociology at Colorado State University—Pueblo. He recently earned his Ph.D. at the University of Oregon. His dissertation examined the environmental crimes committed by a sampling of manufacturing corporations over a six-year period. Apart from his interest in white-collar crime, he has also published works on social movements and complex organizations.

ROBERT WORLEY is an associate professor of Criminal Justice at the University of Texas—Permian Basin, located in Odessa, Texas.

JOHN PAUL WRIGHT is an Associate Professor and Senior Research Fellow for the Center for Criminal Justice Research at the University of Cincinnati in Cincinnati, Ohio. He has published widely on white-collar and corporate criminality.

WARREN WYLUPSKI is a doctoral candidate at the University of New Mexico, where he is studying Organizational Crime, Police Management, and Organizational Learning. He works in the private sector as a Corporate Finance Manager and consults in the area of Organizational Effectiveness. He has written and presented extensively on police status and is the author of a forthcoming book chapter in *Digital Crime and Forensic Science in Cyberspace*.

PETER CLEARY YEAGER is a professor of sociology at Boston University in Boston, Massachusetts. He has published widely in the areas of corporate lawbreaking, business ethics, and environmental law, advised the U.S. government on the development of a national research program on integrity in scientific research, and spent a fellowship year in Harvard University's Program in Ethics and the Professions.

About the Editors

JURG GERBER is Professor of Criminal Justice at Sam Houston State University. He has co-edited two books on drug policy and has published on white-collar crime, comparative criminology, and criminal justice education.

ERIC L. JENSEN is Professor of Sociology at the University of Idaho, where he specializes in drug policy, applied research methods, juvenile justice, and comparative criminology. He has co-edited three books and numerous articles on drug policy and has also published articles on juvenile justice, juvenile delinquency, and white-collar crime.